AFFECT, CONDITIONING, AND COGNITION:
Essays on the Determinants of Behavior

Richard L. Solomon

AFFECT, CONDITIONING, AND COGNITION:
Essays on the Determinants of Behavior

Edited by

F. ROBERT BRUSH
PURDUE UNIVERSITY
J. BRUCE OVERMIER
UNIVERSITY OF MINNESOTA

LAWRENCE ERLBAUM ASSOCIATES, PUBLISHERS
1985   Hillsdale, New Jersey   London

Lawrence Erlbaum Associates, Inc., Publishers
365 Broadway
Hillsdale, New Jersey 07642

Library of Congress Cataloging in Publication Data
Main entry under title:

Affect, conditioning, and cognition.

  Papers in honor of Richard L. Solomon.
  Bibliography: p.
  Includes index.
    1. Conditioned response—Congresses.   2. Affect
(Psychology)—Congresses.   3. Cognition—Congresses.
4. Solomon, Richard L.—Congresses.   I. Brush,
F. Robert.   II. Overmier, J. Bruce.   III. Solomon,
Richard L.
BF319.A43   1985   150   85-15862
ISBN 0-89859-586-X

Printed in the United States of America

Contents

PART III: INTEGRATION OF INFORMATION

PART VI: EXTENSIONS TO HUMAN AND CULTURAL ISSUES

Preface

Richard L. Solomon began his career as a psychology professor in September, 1947. He received his undergraduate and graduate training at Brown University and taught at Harvard University (Department of Social Relations) and at the University of Pennsylvania, where he is now James M. Skinner University Professor of Science. His career has been a distinguished one punctuated with awards for both teaching and research, including a Guggenheim Fellowship, the American Psychological Association's Distinguished Scientific Contribution Award, appointment to the National Academy of Sciences, the Warren Medal for Research from the Society of Experimental Psychologists, and the Society of Sigma Xi's Monie A. Ferst Award for distinguished teaching.

In May, 1983, his students and associates met to honor him in his thirty fifth academic year. His students, associates, coauthors, and even his former teachers assembled in Philadelphia from all over the United States for two days of scientific and social exchange; a few who could not attend sent their salutations. His pre- and postdoctoral students from past years presented the 22 papers which are published in this volume. Although the title of this book may sound ambitious, it reflects the breadth of Solomon's impact through his teaching and research. The diversity of the papers also reflects the enormous range of his thinking.

The first section contains a chapter that provides a bit of history in a retrospective appreciation of the several foci of Solomon's research career. It is laced with anecdotes which give some personal flavor as well. This chapter sets the stage for those that follow and reduces their diversity by providing a degree of historical understanding. Appendices provide a chronological list of Solomon's publications and of his students, with titles of their dissertations.

The second section on the role of properties of fear contains chapters that address various issues associated with the role of conditioned fear. Issues associated with genetic and ontogenetic determinants of fear, memory for fearful events, the discrimination of fearful from nonfearful situations, and the utility of aversion therapy are addressed. These reflect the two-process theorizing of R. L. Solomon.

The third section contains papers that address cognitive, information-processing issues in the context of Pavlovian conditioning of appetitive and aversive events, reasoning, and timing. We are especially grateful to be able to publish posthumously in this section a paper by Abe Black.

The next section contains papers which continue the exploration of the phenomenon of learned helplessness first discovered in Solomon's laboratory at the University of Pennsylvania. The phenomenon is extended to include effects on the immune system, endogenous opiates, tumor rejection, and depressed and nondepressed humans, as well as a reanalysis of the causes of learned helplessness.

The fifth section contains papers that address various issues associated with the Solomon and Corbit opponent-process theory of motivation and affect. As a group, these papers extend the opponent-process theory to various adjunctive behaviors ranging from schedule-induced drinking and aggression, morphine tolerance and binge-type eating behavior.

The last section, on applications to human and cultural issues, contains chapters on such diverse subjects as cross-cultural analyses of aggressive behavior in children, the analysis of resistance to change in industrial organizations, the concept of liberty in formulating research issues in developmental psychology, and the status of free will in modern American psychology.

As students of Richard L. Solomon, we, as a group, offer this volume to him in appreciation for all he has done, and with respect and love for the teacher and the man he is. We are grateful for the opportunity to honor him in this way.

A RETROSPECTIVE
APPRECIATION OF
RICHARD L. SOLOMON

1 Perspectives on the Psychology of Richard L. Solomon

Leon J. Kamin (et altera, et altera)[1]
Princeton University

And God gave Solomon wisdom and understanding exceeding much, and largeness of heart, even as the sand that is on the sea shore. And Solomon's wisdom excelled the wisdom of all the children of the east country, and all the wisdom of Egypt. For he was wiser than all men . . . and his fame was in all nations round about. And he spake three thousand proverbs: and his songs were a thousand and five . . . he spake also of beasts, and of fowl, and of creeping things, and of fishes. And there came of all people to hear the wisdom of Solomon, from all kings of the earth, which had heard of his wisdom. (I Kings 4:29–34)

The title of this chapter is open to at least two interpretations. It might mean the psychology produced by R. L. Solomon, his work. Then again, it might mean the psychology of Solomon, what makes him tick. Each of the contributors comments to some degree on each of those two aspects of the psychology of R. L. Solomon.

We begin with a couple of biographical tid-bits, perhaps not known to all of you. Dick Solomon was brought up in Brookline, MA, the son of a chartered public accountant, and destined to become a CPA himself. We owe a lot to a high school teacher named Tyler B. Kipner, who detected in Dick what he

---

[1]One part of the formal program honoring Dick Solomon dealt with his research career and its impact on the discipline. I agreed to lead such a session, but indicated that, although I agreed to get the fence painted, I would get it done in Tom Sawyer's fashion. Happily, a number of Dick's students volunteered to speak briefly about different aspects of his work. What is presented in this chapter is not a literal transcript of that session, but samples and elaborates on their remarks in the hope that some part of the mixture of intellectual awe and deep affection with which his students regard Dick might be shared.

believed to be college material and induced Dick to think of going to a liberal arts college.

We also owe a lot to the captain of the football team of Brookline High School, because when the time came for Dick to select a college, he didn't know where to go. He was greatly influenced by the fact that the football captain had gone to Brown—and by the fact that Brown was 45 miles from Brookline. So Dick went off to Brown as an undergraduate; there he studied economics and psychology and came under the influence of J. McV. Hunt.

Finally, we also owe a lot to the rampant anti-Semitism of the 1930's and early 1940's. Dick, in applying to graduate school in 1942, thought he would like to work with Kurt Lewin at Massachusetts Institute of Technology (MIT), but he received a letter from the Department of Economics and Social Science telling him that it simply wasn't politic to award a fellowship to a Jew at that time. So Dick went to Brown as a graduate student with a fellowship from Walter Hunter, who dashed to the rescue with $32.50 a month! We owe the fact that Dick isn't a social psychologist to Walter Hunter.

Although Dick is best known as an experimental psychologist, his transition from social psychology was not immediate (viz. Lemann & Solomon, 1952). There are a few very early papers that I don't think should be allowed to sink from sight.[2] I thought it would be a clever idea to go back to the very first paper that Dick published to see whether one could detect retrospectively within it that boldness of spirit and largeness of conception that has characterized his work in later years.

Dick's first publication in the 1942 *American Journal of Psychology,* titled "The Stability and Some Correlates of Group Status in a Summer Camp Group of Young Boys," was coauthored with J. McV. Hunt (Hunt & Solomon, 1942). I thought that surely I would see the seeds of Solomon's future greatness in this early work, but I was dead wrong. I've read the paper very sympathetically, and I must say, there's not a hell of a lot in it. It took 23 boys in the midget unit of Camp Indian Acres, in Fryeburg, Maine, and asked them who their favorite fellow campers were. They were asked this repeatedly, so that changes in the sociometric pattern over time could be plotted. I suppose you can see in this the beginnings of Dick's commitment to parametric analysis.

More seriously, there is something in that paper that I think is predictive of the broad scope of Dick's later work. When Hunt and Solomon discuss the significance of the tendency for the sociometric pattern to stablilize, they write: "It is probable that this process of stabilization, like that found in so many other forms of behavior, operates under what may be called the principle of organismic

---

[2]A complete chronological bibliography of Richard Solomon's published papers appears at the end of this chapter as Appendix A. A complete chronological list of students who completed the Ph.D. under Richard L. Solomon's direction and the titles of those dissertations appears as Appendix B.

economy. Freud's 'pleasure principle' and Thorndike's 'law of effect' can be considered as statements of the same principle." Dick is known for interpreting his data in broad contexts, and this quote indicates he must have learned part of that from Joe Hunt.

There's another early paper that illuminates the psychology of R. L. Solomon. It's about the relation of infantile experience to hoarding behavior in rats (Hunt, Schlosberg, Solomon, & Stellar, 1947). The authors start out with the following:

> In his original paper, Hunt noted that the evidence for the stress currently placed upon infantile experience as a determinant of adult behavior derives from approaches which observe first the effect in the adult and then look backward for the causes. In the psychoanalysis, the method consists of noting the characteristics of an adult and then looking backward for the cause through his free associations into a childhood already past. In comparative study of cultures, the method consists of noting certain common behavioral characteristics of the adults in a society, and then examining their method of rearing children for the causes. Hunt sought to provide a predictive, experimental test of the hypothesis that infantile experience can endure and can effect (sic) adult behavior. Using rats as subjects, because of their relatively brief span of life, he found that animals submitted to feeding-frustration in infancy hoarded more than two and one-half times as much as their freely fed litter-mate controls. (p. 291)

And they concluded this very interesting paper with: "These observations and those deriving from psychoanalysis and the comparative study of cultures, coupled with our own on rats, argue that we may be dealing with a phenomenon which can appear generally in mammals."

There is, I think, an absolutely unmistakable style here: Psychoanalysis, culture, and "generally in mammals" lead, in later years, to love, hate, fear, guilt, passion, imprinting, drug addiction, thrill seeking. . .

I also call your attention to an early paper by Dick on an extension of control group design (Solomon, 1949). In that paper he wrestles at great length with the history and purposes of control group designs and with whether control procedures might interact with the very things we're trying to control for. These same issues were addressed anew in a developmental context (Lessac & Solomon, 1969; Solomon & Lessac, 1968), and it is no accident that clear thinking about the yoked control procedure (Church, 1964) and the proper control procedures for Pavlovian conditioning (Rescorla, 1967) should have originated in the minds of students trained by Dick Solomon.

I'll conclude now with a couple of quotations, and, I'm afraid, a few more anecdotes. I've always understood Dick to be tremendously concerned with the interactions between affect, cognition, and behavior. I want to read to you a quotation from Solomon, Turner, and Lessac's (1968) paper on delay of punishment and resistance to temptation in dogs. The authors present what they call "a complicated theory of conscience." They write:

The authors assume that the dogs, even with long delays of punishment, quickly 'know' which food results in punishment administered by the experimenter. This is a type of cognitive learning that can span long temporal delays. The dogs know what they are not supposed to eat! However, when the experimenter is missing, and the dogs are faced with an uncertainty or a change in the controlling stimulus situation, the authors' argument is that cognition is not enough. The hungry dogs cannot be certain any longer that eating the taboo horsemeat will result in punishment, because the experimenter is gone. It is under these conditions of changed social stimulation that the authors believe the conditioned emotional reactions of the dogs "take over". If emotional conditioned responses take mediational control of behavior under conditions of cognitive uncertainty, the temporal characteristics of Pavlovian emotional conditioning will manifest themselves. This is why delay of punishment is a powerful determiner of subsequent resistance to temptation and the emotional concomitants of taboo violations. (p. 237)

And for still another view of Dick's combination of broadness and sagacity, I recommend to you his marvelous review of several chapters in the 1952 American Journal of Psychology of Stevens' *Handbook of Experimental Psychology*. Here is Dick, writing about George Miller's chapter on speech and language. Remember, the year is 1952.

The chapter on Speech and Language is new to experimental psychology. Miller's contribution is different and exciting. He gives a great deal of attention to the analysis of verbal productions, including statistical analyses and analysis in terms of information theory. Phonetics and phonemics are discussed. There are sections on "talking and thinking," which, while not as developed as some areas of experimental psychology, will probably become increasingly important. This chapter is worth studying. (p. 128)

That, if you remember the temper of the times, is a rather impressive tribute to Dick's broadness and openness. But what has always intrigued me about Dick's commitment to broadness was that at the same time there was his absolute demand for carefulness and precision in experimental work, his worrying control groups to death, his attempt to take everything apart—and still not end up with something small, trivial, and sterile. Thus, after the experiment was complete, one could go on to talk about really interesting things. That made it possible for Dick to write the following in his review of Kenneth Spence's chapter on theories of learning:

The only noticeable omission is psychoanalytic theory, which having considerably influenced experimentation in the last ten years, deserves inclusion as one way, inexact as it may be, of looking at the problems in this area. It is true, however, that this omission will not worry many psychologists whose main interests lie in conditioning and learning. (p. 126)

Who but Dick could have said that to Kenneth Spence in 1952? I think it is exactly because omissions of that sort worried Dick that all of us owe so very much to him.

Many of Dick's students recall him as an enthusiast of every new idea they had—saying "That's great!" or "That's superb!" to every half-baked idea they brought to him. Well, I'm afraid such recall is selective; one must listen very carefully to what he said. There were often little hookers at the end of "That's marvelous" or "That's great." This is illustrated in one of my favorite quotations from that same review, this time dealing with Wolf Brogden's chapter on animal learning:

> One of the most remarkable catalogues the reviewer has ever encountered. It stands as a masterpiece of descriptive behaviorism; pure, objective, and just about as unsullied by conjecture, interpretation, or theory as is pointing to a fly on the wall. (p. 125)

The lesson from all of this is, no matter what Dick is teaching, studying, or doing in the laboratory, in the end it always comes down to love, and hate, and hope, and fear, and attachment, and addiction, and things like that. Dick never forgets for a moment what psychology is all about.

SOLOMON AND THE "NEW LOOK" IN PERCEPTION[3]

At Harvard, Dick reacted somewhat against the *New Look* in perception which emphasized the role of vague socio-cultural variables (e.g., Bruner & Goodman, 1947). He felt the observed effects of these variables could be explained by simpler processes. In 1949, he published a well known experiment (Lambert, Solomon, & Watson, 1949) which showed the direct role of learning and reward in modulating perception. Nursery school children were asked to estimate the size of a poker chip by adjusting to "matching size" a camera diaphragm with a light behind it. The children made matches before any experimental manipulations and after them. The manipulation was turning a heavy crank 18 times to earn a reward. For the children in the experimental group, the reward was a poker chip which could be exchanged immediately for candy; for the children in the control group, the reward was the candy itself without any poker chip involved. Lambert, Solomon, and Watson showed that after their work was rewarded with the chip, children's judged size of the chip was larger than before and larger than that of the control group. Then, they showed that if you extinguished the cranking response (giving them no chip nor candy), the apparent size of the chip went back down to the baseline estimate and was the same as that of the control group. They called this the *cookie effect*. One of Dick's students, James Olds (1953) went on to show that increased amounts of work for longer periods of time—called wanting practice—resulted in increased effectiveness of the chip as a secondary reward. And, more recently, Mike Lewis (1964) working

---

in Dick's laboratory showed that work demands also increase the value of primary reinforcers. Reward and extinction were seen as a more parsimonious way to explain perceptual size changes than some of the socio-cultural variables emphasized by the New Look.

Later, Solomon with Davis Howes (1951; Howes & Solomon 1951) showed that at least one of the factors operating in many of the so-called *perceptual defense* experiments was simple familiarity or frequency. They showed a nice functional relationship between recognition and frequency of usage in the English language, even though the length of the words was controlled. Their data supported the idea that one more easily recognizes those words that are most familiar and that the notion of perceptual defense was unnecessary.

I want to reveal here for the first time a secret about Solomon. I was doing an experiment (Postman, Bruner, & Walk, 1951) in the perceptual defense tradition where we had a reversed letter at the beginning of a word; *plaster* was chosen as the word because the *P,* the *S,* and the *R* do not look the same when reversed. (We had hoped on the basis of these results to next investigate more dynamic incongruities, such as a business man in the middle of a lot of workers or a black in the middle of a lot of whites.) Dick was a pilot subject in getting this experiment set up. The average subject looked in the tachistoscope and said, "There is something wrong with that word," not sure what it was, and, after a while, the subject said, "Well, it is 'plaster,' but the *P* is reversed." Not Dick! He said, "There is a whole jumble of words in there. They're upside down and backwards and God knows what else." Most of the subjects were not nearly as interesting as he was.

SOLOMON AND AVOIDANCE LEARNING[4]

At Harvard, most people thought that the third floor of Emerson Hall was the top floor. However, there was a small, select group of cognoscenti who knew that there was a fourth floor, where a young assistant professor named Richard Solomon had built a shuttlebox and was experimenting with dogs. Dick had advertised for a graduate student to run dogs for pay, 80 cents an hour—not much under the minimum wage. That's how I got involved; I took on the job. I thought that my real interest was in the relation between psychology and politics.

My interest in avoidance behavior came about slowly. Dick talked casually about how his own interests evolved. Hobart Mowrer had been briefly at Harvard and had loaned Dick a rat shuttlebox. The Mowrer tradition clearly informed Dick's work. He was interested in the physiological underpinnings of avoidance, and Lyman Wynne, then at Harvard, pointed out that more was then known about the sympathetic nervous system of the dog than of any other beast. That fact drew Dick to work with dogs (e.g., Wynne & Solomon, 1955).

---

[4]Based on the remarks of Leon J. Kamin.

I suppose it's true that the problem of avoidance learning is not as central to learning theory today as it was in the 1950s. But I think that is so, in large measure, because of the definitive work of Dick and his students on the theoretical mysteries then surrounding avoidance behavior. Let me try to list, very briefly, a few of the problem areas that were tackled in Dick's laboratory.

It's easy to forget now, but a driving force for many of us at the time was that the study of avoidance behavior would tell us something about the conditions under which it might be necessary to impute cognitive processes to animals (Hilgard & Marquis, 1940). How can the absence of shock be a reinforcer unless there is an expectation of shock? Several of us, having learned from Dick how to tease confounded variables apart, tackled such problems as the roles of conditioned stimulus (CS-termination) and unconditioned stimulus (US-omission) as reinforcers (Kamin, 1956). We wondered—and that was exciting to us—would we be able to account for behavior that seems to demand analysis in terms of purpose, foresight, cognition, planning, and so forth, in a simpler and more mechanistic way?

Many of us, under Dick's guidance, went on to work in areas closely related to, or lineally descended from, the study of avoidance behavior. The avoidance paradigm served as the basis for the two-process theory that has influenced all of our work. And Dick involved us all in fundamental questions about the interaction of knowledge and affect (e.g., Solomon & Wynne, 1954). How, he asked, does the animal put his knowledge to use in regulating his affective life?

Dick's continuing interest in the physiology of learning, together with his commitment to two-process theory, made it possible for his students to branch out in many different, and fruitful, directions. We would watch the animals jump in a shuttlebox and ask, why are they jumping? We would answer, because they are afraid. Dick would ask, how do we know they're afraid? And we would answer, because they are jumping! He was unhappy with that circularity, encouraged us to break out, and taught us how to.

Abe Black reasoned that he could obtain, by studying heart rate, an independent, physiologically based measure of emotional arousal (Black, 1959). I took another route: Would it be possible to get an independent behavioral measure of fear? That question got me interested in the conditioned emotional response (CER). After a number of detours induced by interest in the CER itself, Abe and I eventually did a study in which we used the CER as a monitor of fear during the course of avoidance training (Kamin, Brimer, & Black, 1963). The CER itself turned out to be a pretty powerful tool for the analysis of Pavlovian conditioning, and it led me, as it did Bob Rescorla—who also started from avoidance behavior—to such Pavlovian phenomena as blocking and overshadowing.

Dick always managed to find more in our work than we knew was there. Who but Dick could look at the form of a dog's cardiac conditioned response and begin to talk about anticipation, love, fear, attachment, and so forth? The mere fact that Dick described our research as *traumatic avoidance learning* encouraged us all to believe that we were studying something more important than how dogs behave in shuttleboxes (Solomon, 1967). We were studying fear, anxiety, and negative affect in general. Morrie Baum's later use of massed extinction of avoidance behavior (*flooding*) as an animal model for psychotherapeutic procedures was in this tradition. The whole area of behavior modification has been influenced by Dick's seminal work on avoidance behavior.

SOLOMON AND PUNISHMENT[5]

The connection between avoidance training and punishment has seemed a natural one. But two-process theorists (e.g., Mowrer, 1960; Solomon & Brush, 1956) and operant conditioning theorists (e.g., Dinsmoor, 1954) converged on the definition of punishment as passive avoidance training. By definition, an avoidance training procedure is one in which an aversive stimulus follows all responses *except* some particular well-defined response; a punishment training procedure is one in which an aversive stimulus follows *only* some particular well-defined response. The task in an avoidance training procedure is to learn what to do; the task in a punishment training procedure is to learn what not to do. With such a close relationship between avoidance training and punishment, it was reasonable to believe that a common theory might account for both.

Dick's research at Harvard University on traumatic-avoidance learning led him into research on punishment. He found traumatic-avoidance learning was highly resistant to extinction. Under normal extinction procedures, in which no further shock would occur regardless of the dog's behavior, many animals continued to respond indefinitely. Various special techniques were tested that might speed up the extinction process. One of them was the punishment-extinction procedure in which shock occurred only if the animal jumped across the barrier in the presence of the CS. This procedure had a paradoxical result: Many dogs continued to respond when each response was punished, and they usually increased their speed of response (Solomon, Kamin, & Wynne, 1953)! It was clear to Dick that the failure to stop responding was not due to a lack of knowledge of the relevant contingencies. Prior to executing the jump, the dog often made vocalizations that indicated that it "knew" the punishment was about to occur, but it did not inhibit the response. This was one piece of "evidence" that he used to conclude that one cannot predict behavior of an animal on the basis of what the animal "knows." To understand behavior, it is essential to have a theory of learning and motivation as well as a theory of cognition.

Another punishment experiment in progress in the middle 1950's was known in the laboratory as the "superego" experiment (Black, Solomon, & Whiting, 1954). The major qualitative observation was as follows: Young dogs without much experience with people were allowed to eat a small amount of ordinary chow or a larger amount of preferred meat. When it was clear that the dogs would eat the preferred food first, punishment training began. The experimenter

---

[5]Based on remarks by Russell M. Church.

would rap the dogs on the nose with a rolled up newspaper either just before or just after they started to eat the meat. In either case, after a very few of these punishments, the dogs ate the chow, but not the meat—it was "taboo." Then the situation continued as before, except there was no experimenter present. The dogs would eat the chow and leave the meat, and this continued day after day, even under a level of food intake that was insufficient to sustain the animals. Of course, the animals eventually broke the taboo and ate the meat. The major observation was that the post-ingestional behavior of the dogs was a function of the timing of the punishment: Only those previously punished just after starting to eat the meat displayed a guilt reaction when they broke the taboo—they tucked their tails and hid in the corner! This is probably an important observation, but it was never published and probably cannot yet be properly appreciated, because we do not have a context in which to understand it.

As editor of the *Psychological Review,* Dick sought to promote the understanding of punishment among psychologists. To this end, he invited a review of the empirical and theoretical literature on punishment (Church, 1963). He also used the occasion of his presidential address to the Eastern Psychological Association in 1963 to make a major contribution to our thinking about punishment. In it, he developed three major points: one empirical, one theoretical, and one political. The empirical point was that the effects of various parameters determining the effectiveness of punishment on behavior were well known, and he listed a dozen. The theoretical point was that active and passive avoidance learning are similar processes and that two-process theory is a good organizational scheme for these results. The political point was that there were some unscientific, persisting legends that punishment was ineffective and necessarily had serious side effects, and that many textbooks did not properly represent what was known about the effects of punishment on behavior. The talk was published (Solomon, 1964) and had an enormous impact. It was clear, convincing, forceful, and timely. It contributed to a decade of good parametric research that made it clear and generally accepted that behavior could be controlled as well by aversive as by appetitive stimuli and that a reasonable theoretical understanding of punishment could be achieved.

SOLOMON AND TWO-PROCESS THEORY[6]

A major concern of Dick's was the interaction between Pavlovian conditioning and instrumental training. This interest began while he was a graduate student with Harold Schlosberg, who was one of the earliest psychologists to work on the problem. While at Harvard, Dick and his students began to develop ways of independently manipulating the fear thought to underlie avoidance behavior (Black, Carlson, & Solomon, 1962; Brush, Brush, & Solomon, 1955; Westcott & Huttenlocher, 1961). When Dick moved to the University of Pennsylvania in

---

[6]Based on remarks by Robert A. Rescorla.

the early 1960's, this continued to be a major focus of his research (e.g., Baum, 1969; Church, LoLordo, Overmier, Solomon, & Turner, 1966; Katcher, Solomon, Turner, LoLordo, Overmier, & Rescorla, 1969). He had become the foremost authority on Pavlovian/instrumental interactions and was invited to present a paper on this topic at a symposium in honor of Schlosberg. Having conceived a structure, he wished to publish an expanded version of the symposium paper and invited my participation.

I remember two things in particular about our interactions as we were writing the paper. First, Dick was always trying to get me to see the larger context in which things should be placed. He insisted that this broader view show up both in the content and the style of our writing. Second, every time the drafts came back from the secretary he somehow had placed me as first author. When I approached him about this mistake, he quickly closed off the discussion by saying, "I'm at a point in my career where I don't need to be first author on any more papers, but you are just starting and it can have a much bigger effect on your career." This example is only one of the ways Dick placed his students first.

The paper itself (Rescorla & Solomon, 1967) had three main parts: an historical review of how the distinction between Pavlovian and instrumental training evolved, a logical analysis of what it would take to defend the position that two learning processes exist, and a description of a framework within which one could categorize different types of Pavlovian/instrumental interactions. It was this latter portion which was to have the greatest impact on research in the field.

The attractiveness of this structure and the explicitness with which it assigned Pavlovian emotional conditioning a primary motivational role in instrumental learning contributed to a reorientation in the field of animal learning. It helped change the focus of research from the study of instrumental conditioning, which in many ways has stagnated, to the study of Pavlovian conditioning. The next 15 years were to see dramatic changes in our understanding of Pavlovian conditioning.

This paper pointed psychologists to the importance of that kind of learning by emphasizing the way it controls emotional and motivational processes and the way they, in turn, control behavior.

SOLOMON AND TRANSFER OF CONTROL[7]

In 1962, Solomon and Turner published a pivotal paper titled "Discriminative classical conditioning in dogs paralyzed by curare can later control discriminative avoidance responses in the normal state" (Solomon and Turner, 1962). It was an important paper then, and it continues to shape thinking today.

This paper has special significance on four grounds: (a) scholarly analytic, (b)

---

[7]Based on remarks by J. Bruce Overmier.

empirical, (c) theoretical, and (d) paradigmatic. Let me comment briefly on each one of these.

Analytically, it recounted the historically pervasive invocation of peripheral motor responses as mediators of acts and of thinking. The paper then reviewed the history of attempts to circumvent this class of explanation. Finally, it set out a way we could eliminate the learning of peripheral motor responses, and, thus, it provided a basis for challenging theories of learning that rely on mediation by peripheral-motor responses.

Empirically, it went on to show that stimuli, separately established as defensive Pavlovian CSs while the animal was paralyzed, could later evoke at full strength a previously trained instrumental avoidance response which had been trained elsewhere with another stimulus. Clearly, occurrence of the response during the Pavlovian phase of the experiment was not necessary to later control of the avoidance behavior by the CS. This was contrary to predictions derived from theories relying on motor mediation. (Note how Dick squeezed complete abstracts into the titles of his papers. This guards against people who aren't going to like your paper, because potential readers have to read the title to make the decision whether or not to read the paper itself.)

On the theoretical level, it was a key paper in the development of mediational theories of learning and acceptance of two-process theories. It demonstrated the operational separability and independence of S-S contiguity learning and S-R reinforcement learning. Pavlovian conditioning was carried out under curare in order to block any Rs from entering S-R associations. Because motor responses could not occur, explanation of the later transfer of control of the response to the CS on the basis of motor responses was precluded.

In addition, it demonstrated the power of the transfer paradigm, transfer from Pavlovian procedures to the instrumental response, as being a very powerful technique for evaluating the tenets of mediational theories of learning in general, as well as two-process theories in particular. It also showed that instrumental acts could be used to index the degree of Pavlovian conditioning. This is in contrast to the CER (Estes & Skinner, 1941) and secondary punishment paradigms (Mowrer & Solomon, 1954), which do not permit full assessment of the specific control of responses by the CS.

In the twenty years since the publication of this paper, many have continued to use variants of the transfer paradigm to assess important questions. For example, what is the role of safety in the reinforcement of avoidance responses (Moscovitch & LoLordo, 1968; Rescorla, 1968). Some have used it to provide new perspectives on the properties of inhibitory stimuli—Rescorla & LoLordo's (1965) paper is an important one of that sort (see also Hendersen, 1973). Others from Solomon's laboratory have used it to determine the features of Pavlovian conditioned states. For example, LoLordo asked questions about the similarity of differently generated fears in the control of responses (LoLordo, 1967). Still others have used it to ask whether the Pavlovian conditioned or mediating state, whatever it is, has stimulus properties as well as motivational-activational properties (Overmier & Lawry, 1979), and whether these stimulus properties are specific in guiding the choice of responses (Overmier, Bull, & Trapold, 1971). The transfer of control design has even been used to test Dick's new opponent-process theory of motivation (Overmier, Payne, Brackbill, Linder, & Lawry, 1980). Examples could go on and on.

The empirical and theoretical extensions of this seminal paper continue to be felt throughout psychology today. It is notable for the insights it has given us both into behavior and into ways of asking important psychological questions.

SOLOMON AND LEARNED HELPLESSNESS[8]

The original conception of the learned helplessness phenomenon that was bandied around in the laboratory was one of having "learned" not to respond, that is, it was an associative interference model. Dick resisted that idea, and, in keeping with his focus on motivational and affective processes, he eventually led us to think of the primary deficits underlying the phenomenon of learned helplessness as being a reduction in emotion and a loss of incentive to response (Overmier & Seligman, 1967). Dick has always been concerned with motivational-emotional concepts—the "guts" rather than the intellect. This sort of emphasis became central in the animal research on learned helplessness (Maier & Seligman, 1976). Dick did not want to give the central role to "knowledge."

In one chapter on learned helplessness (Maier, Seligman, & Solomon, 1969), Dick took responsibility for the first half, and Marty Seligman and I for the second half. In the middle of the paper, the conceptual focus shifted radically from conditioning and fears to expectations and cognitions, as we sought to address the mechanisms underlying learned helplessness. These ideas were unpopular at the time and received a great deal of criticism (Bracewell & Black, 1974; Levis, 1976). Dick's personal support and encouragement were especially vital in enabling us to persist. And persist we have, as several chapters in this volume attest!

Dick also provided a model for how scholarship should be conducted. First, Dick has persisted in pursuing the same set of problems for many years. For example, the seeds of opponent process theory are very clear in my old Proseminar notes from the early 1960's wherein he spoke of love as an addiction. This has shown some of the rest of us that one doesn't have to shift one's focus of interest with every new fad.

Second, Dick had continually related his laboratory work to phenomena occuring in "real life." This has made some of us less afraid to think that what we do in the laboratory has something to do with the real world.

---

[8]Based on remarks by Steven F. Maier.

Finally, and perhaps most important for learned helplessness research, Dick's approach has been multidisciplinary and multileveled in the analysis of psychological phenomena. Several of the chapters in this volume on learned helplessness are in this multidisciplinary and multileveled analytic tradition.

SOLOMON AND OPPONENT PROCESS THEORY[9]

Opponent process theory has been Dick's major theoretical and research interest for the past thirteen years. As a first year graduate student in 1970, I was initially totally absorbed studying a thousand or so pages of learning material that he had assigned to us in Proseminar. Of course, none of it was on opponent process theory because in 1970 there was nothing published on opponent process theory yet. I didn't spend too much time on the last two lectures, which had been on his fun new theory about addiction, because I couldn't imagine that it was going to be on the test. But, much to my dismay, one of the required questions involved applying opponent process theory to love and attachment relationships. I didn't do too well on that question, but I learned all about the theory afterwards. Ironically, eleven years later, I published a paper which applied opponent process theory to love, attachment, and separation responses in monkeys (Mineka, Suomi, and Delizio, 1981).

Dick's most influential paper on the opponent process theory was published in 1974 with John Corbit (Solomon & Corbit, 1974). It is a general theory of affective dynamics. It reflects Dick's broad and varied interests in psychology and has had a substantial impact on several areas of psychology. I thought I'd mention a few of them.

The theory uses the phenomena of drug addiction as a model for affective dynamics, and as a result, it has had a large impact on drug addiction research, both at a basic scientific level and also at an applied level (Seaman, this volume; Solomon & Corbit, 1973; Solomon, 1977a, 1977b). A second area in which opponent process theory has been very influential is in imprinting and attachment research (Hoffman & Solomon, 1974; Mineka et al., 1981; Starr 1978). And this work has used a variety of species, from baby ducklings, to guinea pigs, to rhesus, monkeys, and humans. The theory has also been used and influenced research on feeding and adjunctive behavior (Cantor, this volume; Cohen, this volume; Solomon, 1977; Rosselini, this volume). Because the theory specified one possible mechanism for habituation to hedonic events, it has also influenced research on a number of basic problems in classical conditioning (Maier, Rappaport, & Wheatley, 1976; Overmier et al, 1980; Schull, 1979). Opponent process theory has also suggested new research approaches to some clinical and social psychological problems, such as depression, boredom, altruism, even

---

[9]Based on remarks by Susan Mineka.

commitment to regular blood donation. Finally, opponent process theory is now presented and discussed in virtually every major introductory psychology textbook.

One of the reasons opponent process theory is so interesting is precisely because it unites such a broad and seemingly diverse array of topics within a unitary framework. The vitality of this theory was captured very nicely in Dick's *American Psychologist* paper a few years ago which he subtitled "the costs of pleasure and the benefits of pain" (1980). There are few theories in psychology today which encompass such a diverse array of very interesting topics.

THE PAST IS PROLOGUE

Although we have reviewed the segments of Dick's research which are most closely associated with him, there are portions we've omitted. These range from work on sensory processes in man, rats, even insects (Graham, Riggs, Mueller, & Solomon, 1949; Stellar, Hunt, Schlosberg, & Solomon, 1952, Dethier, Solomon, & Turner, 1965, respectively) to verbal learning (e.g., Solomon & Postman, 1952). Three things stand out about this body of research: (a) its dynamic range of problems and the multilevel attack on each—Dick is a general psychologist, (b) its innovativeness in each area addressed—Dick is not bound by the past and seeks new perspectives, and (c) its power to open exciting areas to others—Dick is a teacher.

The balance of this volume is composed of chapters which are extensions of lines of research initiated in the laboratories of Richard L. Solomon. The diversity of the chapters reflects the breadth of his conception of the psychological enterprise and his effectiveness as a teacher. These chapters are presented as a tribute to him. All of us agree that he is the most remarkable teacher we could possibly have had.

REFERENCES

Baum, M. (1969). Dissociation of respondent and operant processes in avoidance learning. *Journal of Comparative and Physiological Psychology, 67,* 83–88.

Baum, M. (1970). Extinction of avoidance responding through response prevention (flooding). *Psychological Bulletin, 74,* 276–284.

Black, A. H. (1959). Heart rate changes during avoidance learning in dogs. *Canadian Journal of Psychology, 13,* 229–242.

Black, A. H., Carlson, N. J., & Solomon, R. L. (1962). Exploratory studies of the conditioning of autonomic responses in curarized dogs. *Psychological Monographs, 76,* 548.

Black, A. H., Solomon, R. L., & Whiting, J. W. M. (1954, April). Resistance to temptation as a function of antecedent dependency relationships in puppies. Paper presented at the Eastern Psychological Association meeting, New York. In *American Psychologist, 9,* 579.

Bracewell, R. J., & Black, A. H. (1974). The effects of restraint and noncontingent pre-shock on subsequent escape learning in the rat. *Learning and Motivation, 5,* 53–69.

Bruner, J. S., & Goodman, C. C. (1947). Value and need as organizing factors in perception. *Journal of Abnormal and Social Psychology, 42,* 33–44.

Brush, F. R., Brush, E. S., & Solomon, R. L. (1955). Traumatic avoidance learning: The effects of CS-US interval with a delayed-conditioning procedure. *Journal of Comparative and Physiological Psychology, 48,* 285–293.

Church, R. H. (1963). The varied effects of punishment on behavior. *Psychological Review, 70,* 369–402.

Church, R. M. (1964). Systematic effect of random error in the yoked control design. *Psychological Bulletin, 62,* 122–131.

Church, R. M., LoLordo, V., Overmier, J. B., Solomon, R. L., & Turner, L. H. (1966). Cardiac responses to shock in curarized dogs: The effects of shock intensity and duration prior, experience with shock, and the presence of a warning signal. *Journal of Comparative and Physiological Psychology, 62,* 1–7.

Dethier, V. G., Solomon, R. L., & Turner, L. H. (1965) Sensory input and central excitation and inhibition in the blowfly. *Journal of Comparative and Physiological Psychology, 60,* 303–313.

Dinsmoor, J. A. (1954). Punishment: I. The avoidance hypothesis. *Psychological Review, 61,* 34–46.

Estes, W. K., & Skinner, B. F. (1941). Some quantitative properties of anxiety. *Journal of Experimental Psychology, 29,* 390–400.

Graham, C. H., Riggs, L. A., Mueller, C. G., & Solomon, R. L. (1949). Precision of steroscope settings as influenced by distance of target from a fiducial line. *Journal of Psychology, 27,* 203–207.

Hendersen, R. W. (1973). Conditioned and unconditioned fear inhibition in rats. *Journal of Comparative and Physiological Psychology, 84,* 554–561.

Hilgard, E. R., & Marquis, D. G. (1940). *Conditioning and Learning.* New York: Appleton-Century-Crofts.

Hoffman, H. S., & Solomon, R. L. (1974). An opponent-process theory of motivation: III. Some affective dynamics in imprinting. *Learning and Motivation, 5,* 149–164.

Hunt, J. McV., Schlosberg, H., Solomon, R. L., & Stellar, E. (1947). Studies of the effect of infantile experience on adult behavior in rats. I. Effects of infantile feeding frustration on adult hoarding. *Journal of Comparative and Physiological Psychology, 40,* 291–304.

Hunt, J. McV., & Solomon, R. L. (1942). The stability and some correlates of group status in a summer-camp group of young boys. *American Journal of Psychology, 55,* 33–45.

Kamin, L. J. (1956). The effects of termination of the CS and avoidance of the US on avoidance learning. *Journal of Comparative and Physiological Psychology, 49,* 420–424.

Kamin, L. J., Brimer, C., & Black, A. H. (1963). Conditioned suppression as a monitor of fear of the CS in the course of avoidance training. *Journal of Comparative and Physiological Psychology, 56,* 497–501.

Katcher, A. H., Solomon, R. L., Turner, L. H., LoLordo, V., Overmier, J. B., & Rescorla, R. A. (1969). Heart rate and blood pressure responses to signaled and unsignaled shocks: Effects of cardiac sympathectomy. *Journal of Comparative and Physiological Psychology, 68,* 163–167.

Lambert, W. W., Solomon, R. L., & Watson, P. D. (1949). Reinforcement and extinction as factors in size estimation. *Journal of Experimental Psychology, 39,* 637–641.

Lemann, T. B., & Solomon, R. L. (1952). Group characteristics as revealed in sociometric patterns and personality ratings. *Sociometry, 15,* 7–90.

Lessac, M. S., & Solomon, R. L. (1969). Effects of early isolation on the later adaptive behavior of beagles: A methodological demonstration. *Developmental Psychology, 1,* 14–25.

Levis, D. J. (1976). Learned helplessness: A reply and an alternative S-R interpretation. *Journal of Experimental Psychology: General, 105,* 47–65.

Lewis, M. (1964). Some nondecremental effects of effort. *Journal of Comparative and Phyiological Psychology, 57,* 367–372.

LoLordo, V. M. (1967). Similarity of conditioned fear responses based upon different aversive events. *Journal of Comparative and Physiological Psychology, 64,* 154–158.

Maier, S. F., Rappaport, P., & Wheatley, K. L. (1976). Conditioned inhibition and the UCS-CS interval. *Animal Learning and Behavior, 4,* 217–220.

Maier, S. F., & Seligman, M. E. P. (1976). Learned helplessness: Theory and evidence. *Journal of Experimental Psychology: General, 105,* 3–46.

Maier, S., Seligman, M. E. P., & Solomon, R. L. (1969). Pavlovian fear conditioning and learned helplessness: Effects on escape and avoidance behavior of (a) the CS-US contingency and (b) the independence of the US and voluntary responding. In B. A. Campbell & R. M. Church (Eds.), *Punishment and Aversive Behavior.* New York: Appleton-Century Crofts.

Mineka, S., Suomi, S. J., & Delizio, R. (1981). Multiple separations in adolescent monkeys: An opponent-process interpretation. *Journal of Experimental Psychology: General, 110,* 56–85.

Moscovitch, A., & LoLordo, V. M. (1968). The role of safety in the Pavlovian backward fear conditioning procedure. *Journal of Comparative and Physiological Psychology, 65,* 55–60.

Mowrer, O. H. (1960). *Learning theory and behavior.* New York: Wiley.

Mowrer, O. H., & Solomon, L. N. (1954). Contiguity vs. drive-reduction in conditioned fear: The proximity and abruptness of drive reduction. *American Journal of Psychology, 67,* 15–25.

Olds, J. (1953). The influence of practice on the strength of secondary approach drives. *Journal of Experimental Psychology, 46,* 232–236.

Overmier, J. B., Bull, J. A., & Trapold, M. A. (1971). Discriminative cue properties of different fears and their role in response selection in dogs. *Journal of Comparative and Physiological Psychology, 76,* 476–482.

Overmier, J. B., & Lawry, J. A. (1979). Pavlovian conditioning and the mediation of behavior. *The Psychology of Learning and Motivation* (ed. G. Bower), *13,* 1–55.

Overmier, J. B., Payne, R. J., Brackbill, R. M., Linder, B., & Lawry, J. A. (1980). In B. Zernicki & K. Zielinski (Eds.), *Instrumental Conditioning and Brain Research* (p. 384–402). The Hague: Martinus Nijhoff.

Overmier, J. B., & Seligman, M. E. P. (1967). Effects of inescapable shock upon subsequent escape and avoidance responding. *Journal of Comparative and Physiological Psychology, 63,* 28–33.

Postman, L., Bruner, J. S., & Walk, R. D. (1951). The perception of error. *British Journal of Psychology, 42,* 1–10.

Rescorla, R. A. (1967). Pavlovian conditioning and its proper control procedures. *Psychological Review, 74,* 71–80.

Rescorla, R. A. (1968). Pavlovian conditioned fear in Sidman avoidance learning. *Journal of Comparative and Physiological Psychology, 65,* 55–60.

Rescorla, R. A., & LoLordo, V. M. (1965). Inhibition of avoidance behavior. *Journal of Comparative and Physiological Psychology, 59,* 406–412.

Rescorla, R. A., & Solomon, R. L. (1967). Two-process learning theory: Relationships between Pavlovian conditioning and instrumental learning. *Psychological Review, 74,* 151–182.

Schull, J. (1979). A conditioned opponent theory of Pavlovian conditioning and habituation. In G. H. Bower (Ed.), *The Psychology of Learning and Motivation: Vol. 13.* (p. 57–90).

Solomon, R. L. (1949). An extension of control group design. *Psychological Bulletin, 46,* 137–150.

Solomon, R. L. (1952). Book review of Stevens' *Handbook. American Journal of Psychology, 65,* 117–135 (124–128).

Solomon, R. L. (1964). Punishment. *American Psychologist, 19,* 239–252.

Solomon, R. L. (1967). Aversive control in relation to the development of behavior disorders. In *Comparative psychopathology,* (pp. 228–239) New York: Grune & Stratton.

Solomon, R. L. (1977a) An opponent-process theory of acavired motivation: The affective dynamics of addiction. In. J. Maser & M. E. P. Seligman (Eds.), *Psychopathology: Experimental Models,* (pp. 66–103). San Francisco: W. H. Freeman.

Solomon, R. L. (1977b). An opponent-process theory of motivation: V. Affective Dynamics of eating. In L. Barker, M. Best, & M. Domjan (Eds.), *Learning mechanisms in food selection* (pp. 255–269). Waco, TX: Baylor University Press.

Solomon, R. L. (1980). The opponent-process theory of acquired motivation: The costs of pleasure and the benefits of pain. *American Psychologist, 35,* 691–712.

Solomon, R. L., & Brush, E. (1956). Experimentally derived conceptions of anxiety. In M. R. Jones (Ed.), *Nebraska Symposium on Motivation, Vol IV,* (pp. 212–305). Lincoln: University of Nebraska Press.

Solomon, R. L., & Corbit, J. D. (1973). An opponent-process theory of motivation: II. Cigarette addiction. *Journal of Abnormal Psychology, 81,* 158–171.

Solomon, R. L., & Corbit, J. D. (1974). An opponent-process theory of motivation: I. The temporal dynamics of affect. *Psychological Review, 81,* 119–145.

Solomon, R. L., & Howes, D. H. (1951). Word frequency, personal values, and visual duration thresholds. *Psychological Review, 58,* 256–270.

Solomon, R. L., Kamin, L. J., & Wynne, L. C. (1953). Traumatic avoidance learning: The outcomes of several extinction procedures with dogs. *Journal of Abnormal and Social Psychology, 48,* 291–302.

Solomon, R. L., & Lessac, M. S. (1968). A control group design for experimental studies of developmental processes. *Psychological Bulletin, 70,* 145–150.

Solomon, R. L., & Postman, L. (1952). Frequency of usage as a determinant of recognition thresholds for words. *Journal of Experimental Psychology, 43,* 195–201.

Solomon, R. L., & Turner, L. H. (1962). Discriminative classical conditioning in dogs paralyzed by curare can later control discriminative avoidances responses in the normal state. *Psychological Review, 69,* 202–219.

Solomon, R. L., Turner, L. H., & Lessac, M. S. (1968). Some effects of delay of punishment on resistance to temptation in dogs. *Journal of Personality and Social Psychology, 8,* 233–238.

Solomon, R. L., & Wynne, L. C. (1954). Traumatic avoidance learning: The principles of anxiety conservation and partial irreversibility. *Psychological Review, 61,* 353–385.

Starr, M. D. (1978). An opponent-process theory of motivation: VI. Time and intensity variables in the development of separation-induced distress calling in ducklings. *Journal of Experimental Psychology: Animal Behavior Processes, 4,* 338–355.

Stellar, E., Hunt, J. McV., Schlosberg, H., & Solomon, R. L. (1952). The effect of illumination on hoarding behavior. *Journal of Comparative and Physiological Psychology, 45,* 504–507.

Wescott, M. R., & Huttenlocher, J. (1961). Cardiac conditioning: The effects and implications of controlled and uncontrolled respiration. *Journal of Experimental Psychology, 61,* 353–359.

Wynne, L. C., & Solomon, R. L. (1955). Traumatic avoidance learning: Acquisition and extinction in dogs deprived of normal autonomic function. *Genetic Psychology Monographs, 52,* 241–284.

APPENDIX A
PUBLICATIONS OF RICHARD SOLOMON

Hunt, J. McV., & Solomon, R. L. (1942). The stability and some correlates of group status in summer-camp group of young boys. *American Journal of Psychology, 55,* 33–45.

Schlosberg, H., & Solomon, R. L. (1943). Latency of response in a choice discrimination. *Journal of Experimental Psychology, 33,* 22–39.

Solomon, R. L. (1943). Latency of response as a measure of learning a "single door" discrimination. *American Journal of Psychology, 56,* 422–432.

Solomon, R. L. (1943). Effort and extinction rate: A confirmation. *Journal of Comparative and Physiological Psychology, 41,* 93–101.

Hunt, J. McV., Schlosberg, H., Solomon, R. L., & Stellar, E. (1947). Studies of the effect of infantile experience on adult behavior in rats. I. Effects of infantile feeding frustration on adult hoarding. *Journal of Comparative and Physiological Psychology, 40,* 291–304.

Solomon, R. L. (1948). The influence of work on behavior. *Psychological Bulletin,* 1948, *45,* 1–40.

Graham, C. H., Riggs, L. A., Mueller, C. G., & Solomon, R. L. (1949). Precision of steroscope settings as influenced by distance of target from a fiducial line. *Journal of Psychology, 27,* 203–207.

Lambert, W. W., Solomon, R. L., & Watson, P. D. (1949). Reinforcement and extinction as factors in size estimation. *Journal of Experimental Psychology, 39,* 637–641.

Solomon, R. L. (1949). The role of effort in the performance of a distance discrimination. *Journal of Experimental Psychology, 39,* 73–83.

Solomon, R. L. (1949). A note on the alternation of guesses. *Journal of Experimental Psychology, 39,* 322–326.

Solomon, R. L. (1949). An extension of control group design. *Psychological Bulletin, 46,* 137–150.

Howes, D. H., & Solomon, R. L. (1950). A note on McGinnies' ''Emotionality and Perceptual Defense.'' *Psychological Review, 57,* 229–234.

Postman, L., & Solomon, R. L. (1950). Perceptual sensitivity to completed tasks and incompleted tasks. *Journal of Personality, 18,* 347–357.

Howes, D. H., & Solomon, R. L. (1951). Visual duration threshold as a function of work-probability. *Journal of Experimental Psychology, 41,* 401–410.

Solomon, R. L. (1951). Book review of Steven's *''Handbook.'' American Journal of Psychology, 65,* 117–135.

Solomon, R. L., & Howes, D. H. (1951). Work frequency, personal values, and visual duration thresholds. *Psychological Review, 58,* 256–270.

Lambert, W. W., & Solomon, R. L. (1952). Extinction of a running responses as a function of distance of block point from the goal. *Journal of Comparative and Physiological Psychology, 45,* 269–279.

Lemann, T. B., & Solomon, R. L. (1952). Group characteristics as revealed in sociometric patterns and personality ratings. *Sociometry, 15,* 7–90.

Solomon, R. L., & Postman, L. (1952). Frenquency of usage as a determinant of recognition thresholds for words. *Journal of Experimental Psychology, 43,* 195–201.

Stellar, E., Hunt, J. McV., Schlosberg, H., & Solomon, R. L. (1952). The effect of illumination on hoarding behavior. *Journal of Comparative and Physiological Psychology, 45,* 504–507.

Solomon, R. L., Kamin, L. J., & Wynne, L. C. (1953). Traumatic avoidance learning: The outcomes of several extinction procedures with dogs. *Journal of Abnormal and Social Psychology, 48,* 291–302.

Solomon, R. L., & Wynne, L. C. (1953). Traumatic avoidance learning: Acquisition in normal dogs. *Psychological Monographs, 67,* (Whole No. 354).

Solomon, R. L., & Coles, M. R. (1954). A case of failure of generalization of imitation across drives and across situations. *Journal of Abnormal and Social Psychology, 49,* 7–13.

Solomon, R. L., & Wynne, L. C. (1954). Traumatic avoidance learning: The principles of anxiety conservation and partial irreversibility. *Psychological Review, 61,* 353–385.

Brush, F. R., Brush, E. S., & Solomon, R. L. (1955). Traumatic avoidance learning: The effects of CS-US interval with a delayed-conditioning procedure. *Journal of Comparative and Physiological Psychology, 48,* 285–293.

Goldstein, R., & Solomon, R. L. (1955). A serial position effect in ''incidental learning.'' *Journal of General Psychology, 53,* 293–298.

Wynne, L. C., & Solomon, R. L. (1955). Traumatic avoidance learning: Acquisition and extinction in dogs deprived of normal autonomic function. *Genetic Psychology Monographs, 52,* 241–284.

Black, A. H., & Solomon, R. L. (1956). A method for continuously measuring the position of a rat in a runway. *American Journal of Psychology, 69,* 296–299.

Church, R. M., Brush, F. R., & Solomon, R. L. (1956). Traumatic avoidance learning: The effect of CS-US interval with a delayed-conditioning procedure in a free responding situation. *Journal of Comparative and Physiological Psychology, 49,* 301–308.

Church, R. M., & Solomon, R. L. (1956). Traumatic avoidance learning: The effects of delay of shock termination. *Psychological Reports, 2,* 357–368.

Solomon, R. L. (1956). The externalization of hunger and frustration drive. *Journal of Comparative and Physiological Psychology, 49,* 145–148.

Solomon, R. L., & Brush, E. S. (1956). Experimentally derived conceptions of anxiety and aversion. In M. R. Jones (Ed.), *Nebraska Symposium on Motivation. Vol. 4.* Lincoln: University of Nebraska Press.

Solomon, R. L., & Turner, L. H. (1960). Discriminative classical conditioning under curare can later control discriminative avoidance responses in the normal state. *Science, 132,* 1499–1500.

Solomon, R. L., & Turner, L. H. (1961). A note on the "goalless gradient." *Psychological Reports, 10,* 203–208.

Black, A. H., Carlson, N. J., & Solomon, R. L. (1962). Exploratory studies of the conditioning of autonomic responses in curarized dogs. *Psychological Monographs, 76,* (Whole No. 548).

Solomon, R. L., & Turner, L. H. (1962). Discriminative classical conditioning in dogs paralyzed by curare can later control discriminative avoidance responses in the normal state. *Psychological Review, 69,* 202–219.

Turner, L. H., & Solomon, R. L. (1962). Human traumatic avoidance learning. *Psychological Monographs, 76,* (Whole No. 559).

Solomon, R. L. (1964). Punishment. *American Psychologist, 19,* 239–254.

Dethier, V. G., Solomon, R. L., & Turner, L. H. (1965). Sensory input and central excitation and inhibition in the blowfly. *Journal of Comparative and Physiological Psychology, 60,* 303–313.

Church, R. M., LoLordo, V., Overmier, J. B., Solomon, R. L., & Turner, L. H. (1966). Cardiac responses to shock in curarized dogs: The effects of shock intensity and duration prior, experience with shock, and the presence of a warning signal. *Journal of Comparative and Physiological Psychology, 62,* 1–7.

Rescorla, R. A., & Solomon, R. L. (1967). Two-process learning theory: relationships between Pavlovian conditioning and instrumental learning. *Psychological Review, 74,* 151–182.

Solomon, R. L. (1967). Aversive control in relation to the development of behavior disorders. In J. Zubin & H. F. Hunt (Eds.), *Comparative Psychopathology: Animal and Human.* New York: Grune & Stratton.

Dethier, V. G., Solomon, R. L., & Turner, L. H. (1968). Central inhibition in the blowfly. *Journal of Comparative and Physiological Psychology, 66,* 144–150.

Solomon, R. L., & Lessac, M. S. (1968). A control group design for experimental studies of developmental processes. *Psychological Bulletin, 70,* 145–150.

Solomon, R. L., Turner, L. H., & Lessac, M. S. (1968). Some effects of delay of punishment on resistance to temptation in dogs. *Journal of Personality and Social Psychology, 8,* 233–238.

Katcher, A. H., Solomon, R. L., Turner, L. H., LoLordo, V., Overmier, J. B., & Rescorla, R. A. (1969). Heart rate and blood pressure responses to signaled and unsignaled shocks: Effects of cardiac sympathectomy. *Journal of Comparative and Physiological Psychology, 68,* 163–174.

Lessac, M. S., & Solomon, R. L. (1969). Effects of early isolation on the later adaptive behavior of beagles: a methodological demonstration. *Developmental Psychology, 1,* 14–25.

Maier, S., Seligman, M. E. P., & Solomon, R. L. (1969). Pavlovian fear conditioning and learned helplessness: Effects on escape and avoidance behavior of (a) The CS-US contingency and (b) The independence of the US and voluntary responding. In B. A. Campbell & R. M. Church (Eds.), *Punishment.* New York: Appleton-Century Crofts.

Seligman, M. E. P., Maier, S., & Solomon, R. L. (1970). Unpredictable and uncontrollable aversive events. In F. R. Brush (Ed.), *Aversive conditioning and learning.* New York: Academic.

Solomon, R. L., & Corbit, J. D. (1973). An opponent-process theory of motivation: II. Cigarette addiction. *Journal of Abnormal Psychology, 81,* 158–171.

Solomon, R. L., & Corbit, J. D. (1974). An opponent-process theory of motivation: I. The temporal dynamics of affect. *Psychological Review, 81,* 119–145.

Hoffman, H. S., & Solomon, R. L. (1974). An opponent-process theory of motivation: III. Some affective dynamics in inprinting. *Learning and Motivation, 5,* 149–164.

Turner, L. H., Solomon, R. L., Stellar, E., & Wampler, S. M. (1975). Humoral factors controlling food intake in dogs. *Acta Neurobiologiae Experimentalis (Warsz), 35,* 491–498.

Solomon, R. L. (1977). An opponent-process theory of motivation: IV. The affective dynamics of drug addiction. In J. Maser & M. E. P. Seligman (Eds.), *Psychopathology: Experimental Models.* San Francisco: W. H. Freeman Co.

Solomon, R. L. (1977). An opponent-process theory of motivation: V. Affective dynamics of eating. In L. M. Barker, M. R. Best, & M. Domjan (Eds.), *Learning Mechanisms in Food Selection.* Waco, TX: Baylor University Press.

Solomon, R. L. (1980). Recent experiments testing an opponent-process theory of acquired motivation. *Acta Neurobiologiae Experimentalis (Warsz), 40,* 271–290.

Solomon, R. L. (1980). The opponent-process theory of acquired motivation: The costs of pleasure and the benefits of pain. *American Psychologist, 35,* 691–712.

Solomon, R. L. (1980). Recent experiments testing an opponent-process theory of acquired motivation. In B. Zernicki & K. Zielinski (Eds.), *Instrumental Conditioning and Brain Research.* The Hague: Martinus Nijhoff.

Solomon, R. L. (1981). Prologue. In N. E. Spear & R. R. Miller (Eds.), Information processing in animals: Memory mechanisms. Hillsdale, NJ: Lawrence Erlbaum Associates.

Solomon, R. L. (1982). The opponent-process in acquired motivation. In D. W. Pfaff (Ed.), *The Physiological Mechanisms of Motivation.* New York: Springer-Verlag.

APPENDIX B
STUDENTS OF RICHARD L. SOLOMON AND THEIR
DISSERTATION TITLES

Harvard University

1950   *William W. Lambert*
The acquisition and extinction of instrumental response sequences in the behavior of children and rats.

1951   *Barbara Norfleet Cohn*
The role of frequency and consequence in bringing about cognitive organization.

1951   *Richard D. Walk*
The role of concept formation in discrimination learning.

1952   *James Olds* (Dec.)
The acquisition of motives.

1952   *Edgar H. Schein*
The effect of reward on imitation: An experimental analysis of behavior in small groups.

1953   *Ann Leigh Minturn*
Latent learning and discrimination reversal.

1954   *Leon J. Kamin*
The effects of the interval between signal and shock on avoidance learning.

1955   *Elaine Smulekoff Glazier*
The effects of lesions of the amygdaloid complex on traumatic avoidance learning in dogs.

1955 *Arnold E. Horowitz* (Dec.)
The effects of variation in linguistic structure on the learning of miniature linguistic systems.

1956 *Abraham H. Black* (Dec.)
The extinction of avoidance responses under curare.

1956 *F. Robert Brush*
Acquisition and extinction of avoidance learning as a function of shock intensity.

1956 *Russell M. Church*
Factors affecting learning by imitation in the rat.

1956 *Elinor Sacks Brush Prockop*
Duration of the conditioned stimulus as a factor in traumatic avoidance learning.

1958 *Malcolm R. Westcott*
Augmentation of anxiety responses with the passage of time.

1958 *Lyman C. Wynne*
The effects of deprivation of normal peripheral autonomic function in traumatic avoidance learning.

University of Pennsylvania

1965 *Russell C. Leaf*
Interaction of Pavlovian and instrumental effects of aversive CS termination.

1965 *Michael Lessac*
The effects of early isolation and restriction on the later behavior of beagle puppies.

1965 *J. Bruce Overmier*
UCS duration as a determinant of the efficacy of Pavlovian fear conditioning.

1966 *Judith L. Crooks*
The effect of overtraining on learning set formation in children.

1966 *Vincent M. LoLordo*
Summation of fear of different aversive events.

1966 *Robert A. Rescorla*
Inhibition of delay in Pavlovian fear conditioning.

1967 *Martin E. P. Seligman*
The disruptive effects of unpredictable shock.

1968 *Steven F. Maier*
Failure to escape traumatic electric shock: Incompatible skeletalmotor responses or learned helplessness?

1970 *David Adkins*
External inhibition and disinhibition of conditioned fear reactions.

1970 *Morrie Baum*
Perseveration of fear measured by changes in rate of avoidance responding in dogs.

1970 *Margaret Nelson*
Classical conditioning in the blowfly, *phormia regina meigen:* Associative and excitatory factors.

1972 *Alan B. Moscovitch*
Pavlovian cessation conditioning.

1973 *Robert W. Hendersen*
Compounds of conditioned fear stimuli.

1974   *Susan Mineka*
The effects of irrelevant flooding on the extinction of avoidance responses.

1976   *Mark D. Starr*
Imprinting: Factors affecting the development of separation-induced distress reactions in newly-hatched ducklings.

1979   *Lauren B. Alloy*
Instrumental to Pavlovian transfer: Learning about response-reinforcer contingencies affects subsequent learning about stimulus-reinforcer contingenciesw

1980   *Stephen F. Seaman*
Dose size and inter-dose interval effects on morphine tolerance in the rat.

THE ROLE AND PROPERTIES OF FEAR AND AVERSION

2 Genetic Determinants of Avoidance Learning: Mediation by Emotionality?

F. Robert Brush
Purdue University

Although instrumental avoidance learning has been the subject of numerous investigations and extensive theoretical discussion (e.g., Bolles, 1971; Herrnstein, 1969; Rescorla & Solomon, 1967; Seligman, 1970; Solomon, 1964, 1980; Solomon & Wynne, 1954), in recent years attention has focused on phenomena associated with avoidance behavior, such as learned helplessness (e.g., Alloy & Seligman, 1979; Maier & Jackson, 1979; Maier & Seligman, 1976) and Pavlovian-instrumental interactions (e.g., Overmier & Lawry, 1979). This trend has certainly advanced our understanding of the role of Pavlovian processes in avoidance behavior, but it has left unanswered fundamental questions about the psychobiological mechanisms that underlie the avoidance learning process. One approach to this issue is the analysis of the genetic contributions to individual differences in avoidance learning, that is, the determination of what predisposes an individual animal to learn to avoid.

INDIVIDUAL DIFFERENCES IN AVOIDANCE LEARNING

Even under optimal training conditions, learning of a shuttlebox or lever-press avoidance response by rats of most genetic strains is highly variable: Some will fail to learn, whereas other will learn rapidly and well. Manipulation of the training procedures can improve average performance (e.g., Berger & Brush, 1975), but the problem of some animals failing to learn persists for both tasks to varying degrees and depends largely on the strain or genetic origin of the rats (Anisman & Waller, 1972; Broadhurst & Levine, 1963; Fulker, Wilcock, & Broadhurst, 1972; Gray & Lalljee, 1974; Joffe, 1964; Katzev & Mills, 1974;

Levine & Broadhurst, 1963; Levine & Wetzel, 1963; Wilcock & Fulker, 1973). With respect to shuttlebox avoidance learning, for example, 28% of male Long-Evans rats failed to meet a learning criterion of three avoidances responses within 40 trials of training (Brush, 1966), and 39% failed to make 10 consecutive avoidance responses within 125 trials of combined escape/avoidance training (Singh, Sakellaris, & Brush, Experiment 1, 1971).

A genetic contribution to variation in probability and/or rate of avoidance learning is indicated by the following: (a) Significant differences exist between animals of different strains or genetic lines trained on the same task (see above references), (b) significant variance is found between animals of the same strain obtained from different commercial breeders, (Nakamura & Anderson, 1962; Ray & Barrett, 1975), presumably because of genetic drift that can occur in closed colonies; and (c) additional training does not improve the performance of those rats within a strain that fail to learn, suggesting that learners and nonlearners are of different genotypes (Brush, 1966). The presence within a strain of greater between-litter than within-litter variance is a microenvironmental effect, which may itself reflect genetic differences. Between-litter differences may be attributable to differences in maternal behavior, which themselves may be under genetic control. In general, one must not exclude the possibility that environmental variation can also influence avoidance learning either independently of genetic differences or in interaction with them. For example, differences between strains can be the result of different (genetically determined) responses to a common environment, and differences between colonies can also be due to different husbandry. Failure to learn can also be the result of variation in the ontogeny of learning and may depend critically on events that occur early in the course of training, for example, the learned helplessness phenomenon.

APPROACHES TO THE GENETIC ANALYSIS OF LEARNING

Biometrical genetic analysis of quantitative behavioral characteristics rests on the fundamental equation that relates phenotypic (P) variance to genetic (G) and environmental (E) components of variance or their interaction (I):

$$V_P = V_G + V_E + V_I \tag{1}$$

Because only V_P is directly observable, genetic manipulations are required to permit estimation of V_G and V_E. (Mather & Jinks, 1977, advocate elimination of V_I by appropriate scale transformations). There are two basic approaches to the genetic analysis of any behavioral phenotype such as avoidance learning. On the one hand, one may compare preexisting (usually inbred) strains for variation in the desired phenotype (e.g., Harrington, 1979; Sutterer, DeVito, & Rykaszewski, 1981). If significant phenotypic variance is found among the strains, phenotypic correlations can be determined (e.g., Fulker et al, 1972), and analyses to reveal the genetic and environmental contributions are possible using modern biometrical genetic analytic methods, including the diallel analysis (Royce, Yeudall, & Poley, 1971), the triple test cross (Hewitt & Fulker, 1983), or a combination of these techniques (Hewitt, Fulker & Broadhurst, 1981). On the other hand, one may selectively breed for the desired phenotypes, and if selection is successful, analyses of phenotypic correlations (e.g., Broadhurst & Bignami, 1965) and biometrical genetic analyses (Falconer, 1981; Hewitt et al, 1981; Mather & Jinks, 1977) are also applicable to the specifically selected lines.

GENETIC SELECTION FOR AVOIDANCE LEARNING

In 1966, I began to selectively breed Long-Evans rats for both good and poor avoidance learning in the shuttlebox. All animals were trained in automatic shuttleboxes in which the warning signal (WS) was light and white noise in the compartment occupied by the rat; the shock was 0.25 mA; the WS-shock interval was 5 sec; the maximum trial duration was 35 sec; and the intertrial interval (ITI) was 2 min during the initial 10 pretest trials (WS alone), and 1 min during the immediately following 60 trials of avoidance training. Animals were selected for breeding if they met both of two criteria: (a) few short latency responses to the WS during the pretest trials, and (b) either good or poor performance during the 60 trials of avoidance training (see Brush, Froehlich & Sakellaris, 1979, for details). In general, the animals making the most avoidance responses in the high avoidance line (SHA) and those making the fewest avoidance responses in the low avoidance line (SLA) were selected for breeding in sufficient numbers to ensure continuation of each line.[1] Selection pressure remained relatively constant in the SLA line, whereas it increased over generations of selection in the SHA line. This is illustrated in Figure 2.1 which presents the median number of avoidance responses made by the selected breeders in each line as a function of generations of initial selection. At the outset, two replicate lines, each based on full-sib matings, were established in each selected line. However, the 5th and 6th generations showed markedly reduced fertility, so the two replicate lines within each selected line were crossed to permit non-sib mating, which was the mating system used in subsequent selection. Selection continued for 21 generations in the low line and 25 generations in the high line. After this point the breeding program was shifted to free mating within each line, with avoidance of full- and half-sib mating. Free mating continued for 2.5 years after which selective breeding within each line was resumed for three generations. Both lines had become badly infected with M-Pulmonis, which probably caused the fertility problems,

---

[1]In Brush et al. (1979), these selected lines were designated SHA and SLA, the *S* standing for Syracuse University, from which that publication originated.

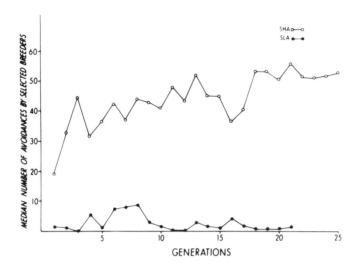

FIG. 2.1.   Median number of avoidance responses by selected breeders as a
function of generations of original selection.

so they were rendered gnotobiotic by Caesarean delivery of two litters of each
line, which were fostered to germ-free dams, after which selective breeding
continued for seven additional generations.

The outcome of this selection experiment is illustrated in Figures 2.2 and 2.3,
which plot median number of avoidance responses as a function of generation
during initial selection (Figure 2.2) and after Caesarean derivation (Figure 2.3).
The effect of selection was rapid, reached asymptote by the 12th generation, and
did not differ within line as a function of sex. The decrement in performance by
the SHA animals in Figure 2.2 at generations 15 and 16 is an artifact of apparatus: There was an inadvertent decrease in the intensity of the auditory component
of the WS. The difference in avoidance performance between the lines decreased
during the 2.5 years of free mating. However, subsequent selection was again
effective in reestablishing the separation of performances of the two lines. Realized heritability (Falconer, 1960) was estimated to be 0.16 (Brush et al., 1979),
which is comparable to values reported by others selecting for related behaviors
(e.g., DeFries, Gervais, & Thomas, 1978). Clearly, avoidance learning is a
heritable form of behavior.

PHENOTYPIC CORRELATES

An important issue concerning genetically selected animals such as these is the
characterization of the selected phenotype in terms of its phenotypic correlates
(Wahlsten, 1972, 1978; Broadhurst, 1975). It should be noted that the correlated
characters of any behavioral phenotype, including avoidance learning, may be

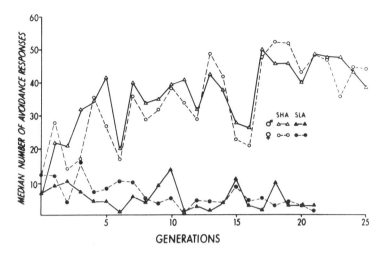

FIG. 2.2.   Median number of avoidance responses as a function of generations of original selection for males and females of the SHA and SLA lines.

behavioral, physiological, morphological, or some combination of these. The goal of phenotypic correlational analysis is to distinguish between potentially important and trivial correlates of the phenotype (Wilcock, 1969). For example, a genotype that reduced the number of retinal receptors might be expected to interfere with visual discrimination learning, but the cause of the learning deficit would not be surprising to anyone, would be described as trivial, and would be

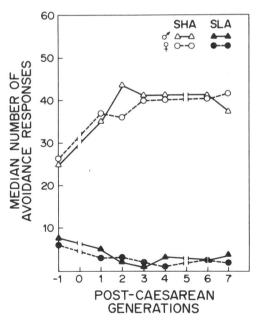

attributable to an interference with performance, not learning capacity, per se. Conversely, a genotype that increased the sensitivity of the adrenal response to stress might be expected to interfere with avoidance learning under some testing conditions, would be described as important, and might be attributable to an interference with fundamental learning processes.

At a behavioral level, for example, animals of the Roman High Avoidance (RHA) line (Bignami, 1965), which were selectively bred for good shuttlebox avoidance behavior, are more active in the open field and make more intertrial responses (ITRs) in the shuttlebox than do the Roman Low Avoidance (RLA) animals, which were selectively bred for poor avoidance performance (Broadhurst & Bignami, 1965; Fleming & Broadhurst, 1975; Holland & Gupta, 1966; Satinder, 1971, 1972). Thus, it is possible that Bignami's breeding program, although based on differences in avoidance behavior, in fact selected for differences in activity or locomotion, which could appear as the differences in avoidance performance. This is a likely possibility, because in testing the Roman lines for selective breeding, there was no assessment of initial responsiveness to the WS and all ITRs were punished. Thus, selection for differences in activity level would not have been detected. Furthermore, Satinder (1976, 1977, 1981) reported that animals of the Roman lines differ in sensory sensitivity and arousal. In addition, Durcan (1983), Driscoll & Battig (1982), and Driscoll, Dedek, Martin & Zivkovic (1983) have noted that RLA animals of some sublines are markedly inferior to RHA animals in escape responding. These results suggest that the Roman lines may differ in overall activity and/or sensitivity to electric shock. If this is true, the utility of these lines for genetic analysis of avoidance learning, per se, may be limited because of the correlated phenotypic differences.

Phenotypic Correlates: Behavior.   During the course of selective breeding, animals of the SHA and SLA lines were tested in the shuttlebox using the standard procedure of 10 pretest trials followed by 60 trials of avoidance training. Although selection was successful in producing profound differences in frequency of avoidance responding, the two lines do not differ in the latency of their escape or avoidance responses (Brush et al., 1985). During initial selection, the lines also did not differ in the frequency of ITRs, either during the pretest or during acquisition. After Caesarean derivation, however, animals of the SHA line made more ITRs during both pretest and acquisition than animals of the SLA line. However, the difference between the lines in ITRs during acquisition can only account for a difference of two avoidance responses on a chance basis. Presumably, the development of a line difference in ITRs following Caesarean derivation is attributable to the limited sampling of the gene pool at that time. Furthermore, the clear absence of differential ITRs during the 20+ generations of initial selection eliminates this variable as a causal correlate of the phenotypic difference in avoidance learning.

Although the two lines do not differ in the latency of their escape or avoidance responses in the shuttlebox, it seemed possible that they might differ in sensitivity to electric shock which need not be reflected in difference in response speed. For example, one could suppose that the SLA animals are more sensitive to electric shock, experience greater pain and, therefore, acquire greater fear of the WS than SHA animals. The poor avoidance behavior of the SLA animals could then be attributed to their intense fear of the WS, resulting in incompatible freezing responses. However, when they do respond, their latencies need not differ from those of the SHA animals. We tested this hypothesis in collaboration with Jim Ison by using shock to the tail as the prepulse in his reflex inhibition paradigm (Brush et al., 1985; Hoffman & Ison, 1980). In this paradigm, a suprathreshold stimulus of any sensory modality presented briefly before a startle-inducing stimulus profoundly inhibits the magnitude of the elicited startle reflex. The results of a titration experiment using this paradigm were overwhelmingly negative. That is, the absolute sensory sensitivity to electric shock was the same for animals of the two lines. The sensitivity of the method was confirmed by finding a reliable sex difference: As expected, females were more sensitive to shock than males. The startle-inducing stimulus in this experiment was a loud (120 dB) click, and there was no difference between the lines in the magnitude of induced startle, suggesting that neither line suffers from a gross auditory deficiency.

Absolute sensitivity, as measured by a detection threshold, is not the same as absolute aversiveness, as measured by an escape response threshold. Therefore, in collaboration with Lou Pellegrino, we measured the aversion threshold in SHA and SLA animals using escape from unsignalled shock in a titration procedure in the shuttlebox. Animals were trained to asymptote using 0.25 mA shock, and, as before, no difference in escape latency was found between the two lines. Escape threshold was determined for each animal over the course of several days of testing. Shock intensity was lowered progressively in blocks of 10 trials until the animal failed to escape on 50% or more trials in a block. Shock was then increased until the escape response returned, and it was subsequently lowered for another threshold determination. The average aversion thresholds determined in this way were not different for animals of the two lines.

In the absence of deficient auditory functioning or a difference in sensitivity or reactivity to electric shock, one might suppose that the poor avoidance learning of SLA animals is due to a visual deficit, because the compound WS also contained a visual component, or to a more general learning deficit. This idea was tested in collaboration with Dave Phillips in experiments utilizing his 4-choice visual-pattern oddity discrimination task based on food reward (Brush et al., 1985; Phillips, 1968, 1970). This task involved presentation, on a horizontal array of four doors, of visual patterns (black figures on a white ground), three of which were the same, and reinforcement of choice of the odd pattern. Table 2.1 presents the distributions, means, and medians of the numbers of trials required

TABLE 2.1
Distributions, Means, and Medians of Trials to
Criterion on Original Discrimination Problem

SHA	SLA
100	600
75	800
50	225
50	250
50	300
150	775
75	375
75	200
50	350
Mean 75	431
Median 75	350

From Brush et al., 1985. © 1985 by the American Pychological Association. Reprinted by permission of the publisher.

by males of each line to reach the acquisition criterion in this task. The lines were obviously different on this measure. Analysis of the acquisition data indicated that the animals of both lines initially hugged the walls of the apparatus and obtained reinforcements only by choosing the odd (correct) pattern when it was on the doors nearest the walls of the apparatus, thereby obtaining only 50% of their reinforcements. However, the SHA animals rapidly learned to track the reinforced cue when it was on the middle doors, whereas the SLA animals persisted in hugging the walls and choosing the doors nearest the walls. Subsequent training on a series of nine four-choice oddity discrimination problems that used similar stimuli in a learning set paradigm showed that the animals of the two lines did not differ from each other in their ability to solve visual discrimination tasks. The persistent wall hugging behavior (thigmotaxis) exhibited by the SLA animals relative to the SHA animals during the original training suggests that the animals of the SLA line are more emotional or emotionally reactive to mild stressors than those of the SHA line, because thigmotaxis in rats is usually interpreted in those terms (Munn, 1950). The absence of a difference in subsequent performance in the learning set problems indicates that the two lines do not differ in their capacity to form visual discriminations or in their generalized learning ability.

Because of the suggested line difference in emotionality in this experiment, males and females of each line were tested in an open-field situation similar to that described by Broadhurst (1960). Three daily test sessions of 2 min each were conducted, and frequencies of ambulation, rearing, and defecation were recorded. Table 2.2 presents the summary data for each measure from three replications involving a total of 98 animals distributed roughly equally between sexes and lines (Brush et al., 1985). There was no significant difference between the lines in ambulation or rearing, although females were significantly more

TABLE 2.2
Mean (± S.E.) Ambulation Score and Frequency of Rearing
and Defecation per Day During Three Days of Open-Field Testing

Ambulation

	Male	Female	
SHA	35.1 ± 1.9	41.7 ± 1.7	38.5 ± 1.3
SLA	36.7 ± 2.0	42.1 ± 2.0	39.4 ± 1.4
	35.9 ± 1.3	41.9 ± 1.3	

Rearing

	Male	Female	
SHA	10.0 ± 0.6	10.7 ± 0.6	10.3 ± 0.4
SLA	9.2 ± 0.5	10.8 ± 0.8	10.0 ± 0.5
	9.6 ± 0.4	10.7 ± 0.5	

Defecation

	Male	Female	
SHA	1.5 ± 0.2	1.7 ± 0.6	1.6 ± 0.1
SLA	2.6 ± 0.3	2.5 ± 0.3	2.5 ± 0.2
	2.1 ± 0.2	2.1 ± 0.2	

From Brush et al., 1985. © 1985 by the American Pychological Association. Reprinted by permission of the publisher.

active than males within each line. In contrast, frequency of defecation was significantly greater in SLA than SHA animals, and this effect was comparable in both sexes. These data lend support to the hypothesis that SLA animals are more emotional or emotionally reactive than their SHA counterparts.

To test this hypothesis further, males and females of the two lines were given defensive Pavlovian conditioning using a standard conditioned suppression paradigm (Estes & Skinner, 1941; Kamin, 1965). Baseline operant lever pressing was established, using a 1.5-min VI schedule of food reward, and CS-US pairings (2-min light paired with a 0.5-sec shock) were superimposed on that baseline. Conditioning began, using a shock intensity of 0.21 mA, which was increased progressively over varying numbers of sessions to 0.29, 0.43, and 0.64 mA. This was followed by four extinction sessions during which shock was omitted. The results are illustrated in Figure 2.4, which plots the conventional suppression ratio as a function of days of conditioning or extinction. It is appar-

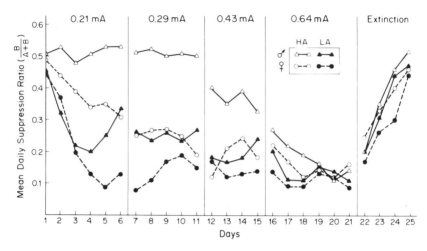

FIG. 2.4.   Mean daily suppression ratio as a function of days of conditioning and shock intensity in males and female rats of the SHA and SLA lines.

ent that SLA animals of both sexes show conditioned suppression at lower shock intensities than do SHA animals. In general, females show more conditioned suppression than males at a given shock intensity. All animals, however, show comparable suppression at the highest shock intensity, and all extinguish at the same rate. Baseline responding was more suppressed in SLA than SHA animals at low shock intensities; baseline actually accelerated in SHA animals, particularly at the higher shock intensities. These findings, together with the open-field data, provide convincing support for the hypothesis that SLA animals are more emotional or emotionally reactive than SHA animals, because they exhibit appropriately different behaviors in two situations which index that dimension. These data suggest that SLA animals avoid poorly because of their hyperemotional response to the WS, which results in freezing behavior that is incompatible with the active responding required to avoid the shocks. Alternatively, the hyperemotionality of the SLA animals may result in reduced reinforcement from avoidance of shock, because of relatively little fear reduction during the intertrial interval (McAllister, McAllister & Douglass, 1971). By whatever mechanism, it is possible, but certainly not demonstrated by these experiments, that this behavioral correlate may be causally involved in mediating the phenotypic difference in avoiding learning.

Phenotypic Correlates: Physiology.   Hormones of the pituitary-adrenal system are known to influence avoidance behavior and to mediate emotional reactions to stressful stimuli. It seemed likely, therefore, that the difference in emotional reactivity that accompanies the phenotypic difference in avoidance learning of the SHA and SLA lines might be mediated by corresponding differences in the physiology of the pituitary-adrenal system of these animals. Initially, we measured basal plasma concentration of corticosterone in males and females from the two lines. Table 2.3 presents these data from four consecutive contemporaneous generations during initial (pre-Caesarean) selection. There were no generational differences, so the data were pooled. As expected, females of each line had higher resting concentrations of corticosterone than males. In addition, however, SHA animals had higher basal concentrations than SLA animals. This result was surprising, because we expected to find higher basal concentrations in SLA rather than SHA animals.

Basal hormone levels, however, can be independent of the levels induced by stress. Therefore, we measured the plasma concentration of corticosterone following an open-field test. As illustrated in Table 2.3, the stress of open-field testing resulted not only in significant sex and line differences but also in a significant sex x line interaction: For males, SHA animals have a higher stress-induced concentration of corticosterone than SLA animals, whereas the reverse is true for females. These findings are not easily interpreted in terms of our emotionality hypothesis, but the presence of significant line and sex effects suggests that there may be significant differences in the physiology of pituitary-adrenal systems in animals of these two genetic lines.

Phenotypic Correlates: Morphology.   Given the above indications of physiological differences between the two lines, we wondered whether the lines might differ in pituitary-adrenal morphology, which might integrate the complex dynamic differences suggested by the plasma corticosterone data. Our initial approach to this question was to compare adrenal weight between animals of the two lines. The two lines differed in absolute weight of their adrenal glands: Those from SLA animals were approximately 6 mg heavier than those from SHA

TABLE 2.3
Mean ($\pm$ S.E.) Plasma Corticosterone Concentration
(μg/100ml)

	Basal	
	Male	Female
SHA	12.2 $\pm$ 1.5	20.6 $\pm$ 3.4
SLA	4.2 $\pm$ 1.0	13.6 $\pm$ 2.2

	After Open-Field Test	
	Male	Female
SHA	45.8 $\pm$ 1.4	76.3 $\pm$ 3.4
SLA	38.4 $\pm$ 2.5	103.8 $\pm$ 6.3

animals. However, the lines also differed in body weight: SHA animals averaged approximately 20 g heavier than SLA animals at 90–100 days of age. Therefore, Table 2.4 presents the adrenal-weight data in terms of gland-weight to body-weight ratios. It is apparent that the ratios for SLA animals are significantly greater than those for SHA animals. The expected six difference is also significant. A comparable analysis of anterior pituitary gland weights indicated that SLA animals have larger (heavier) glands than SHA animals. However, this difference is eliminated when the gland weights are adjusted for differences in body weight. The sex difference in anterior pituitary weight (females have the larger glands) survives the adjustment for body weight.

These findings suggest that the anterior pituitary glands of animals of the two lines are not differentially active despite the marked difference in adrenal morphology. Thus, one is led to suspect that the adrenal glands of these animals may be differentially responsive to a given ACTH stimulus, an easily tested hypothesis. Alternatively, differential size of the adrenal medulla might account for the differential adrenal weight, which could be tested by appropriate morphometric analysis.

TABLE 2.4
Mean (± S.E.) Adrenal-Gland Weight/Body-Weight/Body Ratio (mg/g × 1000)

	Male	Female
SHA	43.2 ± 1.3	81.9 ± 2.0
SLA	60.5 ± 1.7	124.3 ± 2.8

Phenotypic Correlates: Summary.   The phenotypic differences in avoidance learning between the SHA and SLA lines is not attributable to (a) a difference in escape or avoidance latency, (b) a difference in ITRs or overall activity level, (c) a difference in sensory sensitivity or reactivity to electric shock, (d) an auditory or visual deficit, or (e) a general learning deficit. Of the above five factors, the first four would probably be classified by most psychologists as trivial correlates of the phenotypic difference had they not been eliminated by these experiments. The last, would probably be of considerable interest to most psychologists, but it, too, must be eliminated as a potentially important phenotypic correlate. The one factor that does survive as a possible causal correlate is differential emotionality or emotional reactivity. This correlate is supported by line differences in (a) persistence of thigmotaxis, (b) open-field defecation, (c) acquisition of CER suppression, and (d) morphology of the adrenal gland. Measures of pituitary-adrenal physiology, however, reveal line differences that are difficult to interpret in terms of the emotionality correlate.

As with all phenotypic correlates, the causal status of the emotionality factor can only be assessed by appropriate genetic manipulations. First, estimates of V_G and V_E can be obtained from segregating and non-segregating generations derived from reciprocal F_1, F_2, and back-cross generations. In addition, depending on the obtained estimates of V_G and V_E, it may be possible to estimate the number of segregating genetic units that differentiate the two lines (Bruell, 1962). Finally, by determining the correlation between avoidance learning and indices of the emotionality correlate in the segregating F_2, B_1, and B_2 generations, one may establish the genetic status of those measures of emotionality. A strong correlation between avoidance learning and any or all such measures would indicate that the segregating genetic units control both avoidance learning and those measures of emotionality. It is unlikely that all indices of the emotionality correlate would segregate with the avoidance genetic units, but this would only serve to clarify our definition and understanding of the concept of emotionality.

If any index of emotionality segregates with the genetic units that control avoidance learning, their role in avoidance learning would be established, and a greater understanding of a complex learning phenomenon would be achieved. We intend to continue using this genetic model of avoidance learning in order to reach that goal.

REFERENCES

Alloy, L. B., & Seligman, M. E. P. (1979). On the cognitive component of learned helplessness and depression. In G. H. Bower (Ed.), *The psychology of learning and motivation, Vol. 13* (pp. 219–276). New York: Academic Press.

Anisman, H., & Waller, T. G. (1972). Facilitative and disruptive effects of prior exposure to shock on subsequent avoidance performance. *Journal of Comparative and Physiological Psychology, 78*, 113–122.

Berger, D. F., & Brush, F. R. (1975). Rapid acquisition of discrete-trial lever-press avoidance: Effects of signal-shock interval. *Journal of the Experimental Analysis of Behavior, 24*, 227–239.

Bignami, G. (1965). Selection for high rates and low rates of avoidance conditioning in the rat. *Animal Behavior, 13*, 221–227.

Bolles, R. C. (1971). Species-specific defense reactions. In F. R. Brush (Ed.), *Aversive conditioning and learning* (pp. 183–233). New York: Academic.

Broadhurst, P. L. (1960). Experiments in psychogenetics: Application of biometrical genetics to the inheritance of behavior. In H. J. Eysenck (Ed.), *Experiments in personality. Vol. 1: Psychogenetics and psychopharmacology* (pp. 1–102). London: Routledge & Kegan Paul.

Broadhurst, P. L. (1975). The Maudsley reactive and nonreactive strains of rats: A survey. *Behavior Genetics, 5*, 299–319.

Broadhurst, P. L., & Bignami, G. (1965). Correlative effects of psychogenetic selection: A study of the Roman high and low avoidance strains of rats. *Behavior Research and Therapy, 2*, 273–280.

Broadhurst, P. L., & Levine, S. (1963). Behavioral consistency in strains of rats selectively bred for emotional elimination. *British Journal of Psychology, 54*, 121–125.

Bruell, J. H. (1962). Dominance and segregation in the inheritance of quantitative behavior in mice. In E. L. Bliss (Ed.), *Roots of behavior* (pp. 48–67). New York: Harper.

Brush, F. R. (1966). On the differences between animals that learn and do not learn to avoid electric shock. *Psychonomic Science, 5*, 123–124.

Brush, F. R., Baron, S., Froehlich, J. C., Ison, J. R., Pellegrino, L. J., Phillips, D. S., Sakellaris, P. C., & Williams, V. N. (1985). Genetic differences in avoidance learning by Rattus norvegicus: Escape/avoidance responding, sensitivity to electric shock, discrimination learning and open-field behavior. *Journal of Comparative Psychology, 99,* 60–73.

Brush, F. R., Froehlich, J. C., & Sakellaris, P. C. (1979). Genetic selection for avoidance behavior in the rat. *Behavior Genetics, 9,* 309–316.

DeFries, J. C., Gervais, M. C., & Thomas, E. A. (1978). Response to 30 generations of selection for open-field activity in laboratory mice. *Behavior Genetics, 8,* 3–14.

Driscoll, P., & Battig, K. (1982). Behavioral, emotional and neurochemical profiles of rats selected for extreme differences in active, two-way avoidance performance. In I. Lieblich (Ed.), *Genetics of the brain* (pp. 96–123). Amsterdam: Elsevier.

Driscoll, P., Dedek, J., Martin, J. R., & Zivkovic, B. (1983). Two-way avoidance and acute shock stress induced alterations of regional noradrenergic, dopaminergic and serotonergic activity in Roman high- and low-avoidance rats. *Life Sciences, 33,* 1719–1725.

Durcan, M. J. (1983, July). *Differences in the behavioural responses to apomorphine in the Roman high and low avoiding strains of rats.* Paper presented at the meeting of the Behavior Genetics Association, London.

Estes, W. K., & Skinner, B. F. (1941). Some quantitative properties of anxiety. *Journal of Experimental Psychology, 29,* 390–400.

Falconer, D. S. (1981). *Introduction to quantitative genetics,* New York: Ronald Press.

Fleming, J. C., & Broadhurst, P. L. (1975). The effects of nicotine on two-way avoidance conditioning in bi-directionally selected strains of rats. *Psychopharmacologia (Berlin), 42,* 147–152.

Fulker, D. W., Wilcock, J., & Broadhurst, P. L. (1972). Studies on genotype-environment interaction. I. Methodology and preliminary multivariate analysis of a diallel cross of eight strains of rat *Behavior Genetics, 2,* 261–287.

Gray, J. A., & Lalljee, B. (1974). Sex differences in emotional behavior in the rat: Correlation between open-field defecation and active avoidance. *Animal Behavior, 22,* 856–861.

Harrington, G. H. (1979). Strain differences in shuttle avoidance conditioning in the rat. *Bulletin of the Psychonomic Society, 13,* 161–162.

Herrnstein, R. J. (1969). Method and theory in the study of avoidance. *Psychological Review, 76,* 49–69.

Hewitt, J. K., & Fulker, D. W. (1983). Using the triple test cross to investigate the genetics of behavior in wild populations. II. Escape-avoidance conditioning in *Rattus norvegicus. Behavior Genetics, 13,* 1–15.

Hewitt, J. K., Fulker, D. W., & Broadhurst, P. L. (1981). Genetics of escape-avoidance conditioning in laboratory and wild populations of rats: A biometrical approach. *Behavior Genetics, 11,* 533–544.

Hoffman, H. S., & Ison, J. R. (1980). Reflex modification in the domain of startle: I. Some empirical findings and their implications of how the nervous system processes sensory input. *Psycholoigcal Review, 87,* 175–189.

Holland, H. C., & Gupta, B. D. (1966). Some correlated measures of activity and reactivity in two strains of rats selectively bred for diferences in the acquisition of a conditioned avoidance response. *Animal Behavior, 14,* 574–580.

Joffe, J. (1964). Avoidance learning and failure to learn in two strains of rats selectively bred for emotionality. *Psychonomic Science, 1,* 185–186.

Kamin, L. J. (1965). Temporal and intensity characteristics of the conditioned stimulus. In W. F. Prokasy (Ed.), *Classical conditioning: A symposium* (pp. 118–147). New York: Appleton.

Katzev, R. D., & Mills, S. K. (1974). Stain differences in avoidance conditioning as a function of the classical CS-US contingency. *Journal of Comparative and Physiological Psychology, 87,* 423–428.

Levine, S., & Broadhurst, P. L. (1963). Genetic and ontogenetic determinants of adult behavior in the rat. *Journal of Comparative and Physiological Psychology, 56,* 423–428.

Levine, S., & Wetzel, A. (1963). Infantile experiences, strain differences and avoidance conditioning. *Journal of Comparative and Physiological Psychology, 54,* 879–881.

Maier, S. F., & Jackson, R. L. (1979). Learned helplessness: All of us were right (and wrong): Inescapable shock has multiple effects. In G. H. Bower (Ed.), *The psychology of learning and motivation, Vol. 13,* (pp. 155–218). New York: Academic Press.

Maier, S. F., & Seligman, M. E. P. (1976). Learned Helplessness: Theory and evidence. *Journal of Experimental Psychology: General, 105,* 3–46.

Mather, K., & Jinks, J. L. (1977). *Introduction to biometrical genetics.* London: Chapman & Hall.

McAllister, W. R., McAllister, D. E., & Douglass, W. K. (1971). The inverse relationship between shock intensity and shuttle-box avoidance learning in rats. *Journal of Comparative and Physiological Psychology, 74,* 426–433.

Munn, N. L. (1950). *Handbook of psychological research on the rat.* Boston: Houghton Mifflin.

Nakamura, C. Y., & Anderson, N. H. (1962). Avoidance behavior differences within and between strains of rats. *Journal of Comparative and Physiological Psychology, 55,* 740–747.

Overmier, J. B., & Lawry, J. A. (1979). Pavlovian conditioning and the mediation of behavior. In G. H. Bower (Ed.), *The psychology of learning and motivation. Vol. 13,* (pp. 1–55). New York: Academic Press.

Phillips, D. S. (1968). Olfactory cues in visual discrimination problems *Physiology and Behavior, 3,* 683–685.

Phillips, D. S. (1970). Effects of olfactory bulb ablation on visual discrimination. *Physiology and Behavior, 5,* 13–15.

Ray, O. S., & Barrett, R. J. (1975). Behavioral, pharmacological and biochemical analysis of genetic differences in rats. *Behavioral Biology, 15,* 391–418.

Rescorla, R. A., & Solomon, R. L. (1967). Two-process learning theory: Relationships between Pavlovian conditioning and instrumental learning. *Psychological Review, 74,* 151–182.

Royce, J. R., Yeudall, L. T., & Poley, W. (1971). Diallel analysis of avoidance conditioning in inbred strains of mice. *Journal of Comparative and Physiological Psychology, 76,* 353–358.

Satinder, K. P. (1971). Genotype dependent effects of d-amphetamine sulphate and caffeine on escape-avoidance behavior of rats. *Journal of Comparative and Physiological Psychology, 76,* 359–364.

Satinder, K. P. (1972). Effects of intertrial crossing punishment of d-amphetamine sulphate on avoidance and activity in four selectively bred rat strains. *Psychonomic Science, 29,* 291–293.

Satinder, K. P. (1976). Sensory responsiveness and avoidance learning in rats. *Journal of Comparative and Physiological Psychology, 90,* 946–957.

Satinder, K. P. (1977). Arousal explains difference in avoidance learning of genetically selected rat strains. *Journal of Comparative and Physiological Psychology, 91,* 1326–1336.

Satinder, K. P. (1981). Ontogeny and interdependence of genetically selected behaviors in rats: Avoidance response and open field. *Journal of Comparative and Physiological Psychology, 95,* 175–187.

Seligman, M. E. P. (1970). On the generality of the laws of learning. *Psychological Review, 77,* 406–418.

Singh, P. J., Sakellaris, P. C., & Brush, F. R. (1971). Retention of active and passive avoidance responses tested in extinction. *Learning and Motivation, 2,* 305–323.

Solomon, R. L. (1964). Punishment. *American Psychologist, 19,* 239–253.

Solomon, R. L. (1980). The opponent-process theory of acquired motivation: The costs of pleasure and the benefits of pain. *American Psychologist, 35,* 691–712.

Solomon, R. L., & Wynne, L. C. (1954). Traumatic avoidance learning: The principles of anxiety conservation and partial irreversibility. *Psychological Review, 62,* 353–385.

Sutterer, J. R., DeVito, W. J., & Rykaszewski, I. (1981). Developmental aspects of 2-way shuttlebox avoidance in the sponaneously hypertensive and normotensive rat. *Developmental Psychobiology, 14,* 405–414.

Wahlsten, D. (1972). Genetic experiments with animal learning: A critical review. *Behavioral Biology, 7,* 143–182.

Wahlsten, D. (1978). Behavioral genetics and animal learning. In H. Anisman & G. Bignami

(Eds.), *Psychopharmacology of aversively motivated behavior* (pp. 63–118). New York: Plenum Press.

Wilcock, J. (1969). Gene action and behavior: An evaluation of major gene pleiotropism. *Psychological Bulletin, 72,* 1–29.

Wilcock, J., & Fulker, D. W. (1973). Avoidance learning in rats: Genetic evidence for two distinct behavioral processes in the shuttlebox. *Journal of Comparative and Physiological Psychology, 82,* 247–253.

3 Fearful Memories: The Motivational Significance of Forgetting

Robert W. Hendersen
University of Illinois at Urbana-Champaign

There is a tradition in the study of memory that, like a great many others, can be traced to Ebbinghaus (1885). The tradition is that the materials used in memory experiments are exceedingly boring. Ebbinghaus himself, of course, used non-sense syllables. A century later, the nonsense syllable has all but disappeared, but the materials that have replaced it are barely more thrilling. If subjects in a contemporary memory experiment are lucky, they will be asked to study, and subsequently to remember, what is euphemistically called "meaningful prose," and a fairly written informed-consent form should remind potential subjects that "meaningful" does not mean "interesting."

Do the rules that govern memory for trivial events also apply to memory for important events? Or has the way we think about memory been distorted by a research tradition that has focused almost exclusively on phenomena that involve memory for trivial, affect-free materials? In this chapter I address this question in two ways. First, I identify some assumptions that pervade the study of memory processes, and I argue that these assumptions have never been properly tested; they are accepted more for reasons of historical accident and experimental convenience than because substantive evidence demands their acceptance. Then, I review some findings that suggest memory for important events follows rules whose interpretation requires knowledge of the motivational significance of the memories. Such knowledge cannot be obtained through studies of memory for trivial, affect-free events.

Assumptions Implicit in Most Memory Research

The primary contemporary manifestation of the Ebbinghaus tradition is the wide-spread belief that psychological representations both can and should be reduced to a lowest-common-denominator form. This belief has been bolstered by the popularity of computer metaphors for describing psychological phenomena. The binary voltage levels which represent information in a silicon chip are indistinguishable at the level where most processing occurs; stunningly complex accretions of information are, at core, reducible to strings of ones and zeroes. If we accept the assumption that information stored in biological memories has been reduced, like that in computer memories, to such a lowest-common-denominator, then Ebbinghaus's assumption that we can learn most of what we need to know about memory and forgetting by studying the most trivial of materials is appropriate, because all memorial information is fundamentally the same. It is this assumption I wish to challenge.

Suppose history were different. Suppose (wildly!) that Ebbinghaus had taken the opposite approach, arguing thus: "If we wish to understand fundamental properties of memory, we must start by studying memory for very important events. Some memories are particularly consequential and meaningful, determining action and affect. To understand fundamental properties of memory and forgetting, we should focus on how subjects remember events of considerable importance."

There are several ways the issue can be approached. One is to study how people remember events that have weak affective content, in the hope that memory for weak affect may involve some of the same processes as does memory for strong affect; ethical considerations make it difficult or impossible to manipulate strong affect directly in a well-controlled memory experiment with human subjects. A second approach (and the one taken here) is to study an animal model of memory for important events. Using animals does not eliminate the ethical constraints, but it enables the experimenter to arrange conditions so that there can be reasonable certainty that no lasting psychological harm will be done to the animal subjects. Animals can be exposed to events carefully designed to be indistinguishable from genuine threats and completely safe to the subjects. These events can be presented against the background of life circumstances so benign (with food, water, warmth, shelter all provided) that they are likely to be particularly salient. During the retention interval that separates the initial experience of the important events from a subsequent test of memory for those events, conditions can be stringently controlled, ensuring that (a) no animal receives components of the earlier experience that could function as reminders during the retention interval, and (b) no animal experiences new events contradictory to the earlier experience. None of these conditions can be arranged ethically and conveniently in studies of human long-term memory.

Is It Bad to Forget?

Related to the assumption that the fundamental features of memory systems can be revealed by studying memory for trivial items is the assumption that forgetting is a bad thing. In studies of long-term recall, for example, any response that does not reproduce the study item is scored as an error or "failure to recall," and errors and failures are obviously to be avoided. We are accordingly biased to view any instance of forgetting as an organismic flaw to be eliminated in an ideal memory system. Forgetting is often ascribed to such system inadequacies as limitations in capacity, inefficiency of retrieval mechanisms, weakness of initial encoding, overlap of stored representations, and a variety of other mechanisms that could be avoided in a system that was sufficiently large and powerful. The implication is that forgetting is an unfortunate and undesireable design flaw which evolution has not yet succeeded in eliminating.

Precisely the opposite may be the case. That is, forgetting may serve important functions that are not apparent to us primarily because forgetting is usually studied under circumstances where its motivational consequences are obscure. It simply does not matter very much if a college sophomore forgets a couple of items on a list he or she has been asked to memorize. Contrast this instance with an animal experiencing an event that recruits a full affective reaction—that is, an event perceived as important. In the course of its experience, the animal will learn something about the predictive contingencies associated with the aversive event, as well as learning something about the nature of the event itself. Now suppose the animal leaves the circumstances where it sustained its unpleasant experience, only to return some weeks or months later. In a laboratory setting, the duration of the retention interval is a reasonably simple independent variable, and the experimenter can hold everything else pristinely constant. Outside the laboratory, things are not so orderly. The longer an animal is away from a situation where it experienced an important event (i.e., the longer the retention interval), the greater the likelihood that some aspects of the situation will have changed. The real world, in contrast to the laboratory, is inherently unstable, and the longer the time interval between successive contacts with a particular situation, the more likely that the situation will change. Forgetting processes that help map an animal's behavior to the instabilities inherent in a changing world could thus contribute to survival.

How are such forgetting processes to be identified? Even if we believe that forgetting may have evolved because of selective pressures exerted by instabilities, over time, of real-world contingencies, our ignorance of what those instabilities are is far too profound to yield any useful speculations about what features of an animal's memorial representation are likely to change systematically over time. Thus, there is a rationale for looking for systematic patterns in forgetting about important events, but the rationale is not specific enough to suggest just what patterns should occur. To find out, we must study the phenomena directly.

Retention of Conditioned Fear

How do we go about asking an animal what it knows about an earlier, important experience? Perhaps the simplest way to proceed is to expose an animal to simple, excitatory conditioning and to measure the strength of the conditioned response after a substantial retention interval has passed. This simple approach has been used several times to assess retention of fear conditioning, and the typical result is that there is little or no obvious forgetting that occurs over a long-term retention interval (Gleitman & Holmes, 1967; Hendersen, 1978; Hoffman, Fleshler, & Jensen, 1963). Michael Blacconiere and I have done an experiment that reveals how extraordinarily well rats retain the intensity of fear acquired in a simple fear conditioning treatment, even when a 60 day retention interval separates the conditioning treatment from the memory test. Separate groups of rats were exposed to repeated pairings of a tone/light conditioned stimulus (CS) with a shock unconditioned stimulus (UCS). The intensity of the shock varied among groups. Half the animals were given a retention test the day following the conditioning treatment, while the other half were tested after 60 days. The test consisted of placing the water-deprived animals in a chamber equipped with a drinking tube. A drinkometer device detected licks at the tube. As soon as each animal had made exactly 100 licks, the CS from the previous conditioning treatment was presented, and we measured the extent to which this CS disrupted drinking. The results, which are shown in Figure 3.1, were clear: The amount of drinking during the CS was determined by the intensity of the shock used in initial conditioning, and neither this relationship nor the degree of disruption were affected by interposing a 60 day retention interval. Not only did the animals remember to be afraid, they remembered just how afraid to be.

Such excellent retention of excitatory fear conditioning contrasts sharply with what happens to inhibitory fear conditioning. When an animal is exposed to a

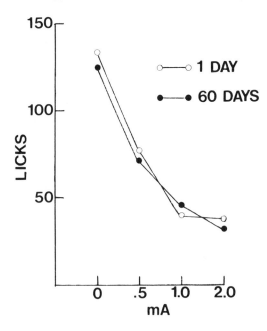

FIG. 3.1. Retention of conditioned fear as a function of the intensity of the shock used in conditioning.

fear conditioning treatment, it learns not only about those aspects of the situation that predict aversive consequences, but it also learns about aspects of the situation that predict a period of safety from painful UCSs (Rescorla, 1969). Such safety-predicting cues can actively inhibit fear. Unlike excitatory fear conditioning, inhibitory fear conditioning is lost over a long-term retention interval (Hendersen, 1978; Thomas, 1979). That is, under the same conditions where animals remember learned fears remarkably well, they seem to forget what aspects of the situation cue safety. The selective forgetting of inhibition of fear thus yields a shift in the pattern of reactions an animal shows when returned to the fear-inducing situation: It remains wary of the cues that previously signalled danger, but cues that previously signalled safety no longer attenuate fear. In a sense, forgetting has caused the animal to become more warily conservative.

A second type of forgetting seen after fear conditioning induces another kind of increased wariness. Using transfer-of-control measures to assess the nature of the learned fears, Hendersen, Patterson, and Jackson (1980) found that a signal that predicted the occurrence of one aversive stimulus (airblast) would modulate the rate of a coping behavior that had been trained using a second, different aversive stimulus (shock). Furthermore, the extent of this modulation varied over a long-term retention interval. In particular, a learned fear activated more coping behavior following a long-term retention interval than it did shortly after the fear conditioning experience. Empirically, this result is an *incubation effect*—the phenomenon of a fear CS apparently growing stronger over time. However, other measures of fear indicate that fear intensity remains relatively constant over a long-term retention interval. To resolve this disparity, we proposed that animals who have forgotten specific features of the aversive stimulus that a fear CS signals may engage in a broader range of coping behaviors when that CS is presented. Thus, loss, over time, of specific information about the nature of the UCS (i.e., forgetting) expands the range of activating effects of the learned fear signal, producing the apparent incubation effect.

Asking an Animal If It Knows What It Is Avoiding

That forgetting can expand the effects of a fear CS is illustrated by a retention experiment employing a strategy that JoAnn Graham and I developed for assessing the specificity of fear in an avoidance task. We began by training rats to avoid radiant heat; the avoidance response was jumping onto a ledge in a one-way avoidance apparatus. Once the animals had met a learning criterion, we tested them by administering a series of extinction trials in controlled thermal environments. The advantage of this procedure is that it permits the experimenters to manipulate the value of the avoided heat stimulus by manipulating the thermal context; heat is aversive in a warm environment, but the same radiant heat stimulus will function as a positive reinforcer if the animal is cold enough. We used a strategy adapted from Irwin (1971; see also Seligman & Johnston,

1973) to assess whether the animals knew that the aversive event they were avoiding was heat. Once the animals had met an acquisition criterion learning to avoid heat in a warm environment, we gave each animal a series of extinction trials. The procedure on the test day included an episode, administered prior to the extinction test, in which the rats were given a series of free exposures to radiant heat while they were in a cold chamber; this was to ensure that the animals had had some experience with the value of heat in a cold context. Half the animals received the extinction trials in a warm room where heat would be aversive, and half received extinction trials in a cold room where heat would be desired. No heat was presented during the extinction trials; this was to ensure that performance was determined by what the rats had learned about radiant heat during the acquisition phase of the experiment, rather than by new learning about heat during the test phase. The speed with which the animals reached an extinction criterion was determined by the thermal context in which the extinction test was administered, with animals tested in the cold environment meeting the extinction criterion in significantly fewer trials than did animals tested in the warm room. Thus, a manipulation designed to change the value of the avoided stimulus affected the persistence of the avoidance behavior in a direction appropriate to the shift in thermal context and, hence, the changed value.

This context-appropriate shift in behavior only occurred in animals that, as part of the test procedure, had been given some direct experience with radiant heat while they were in a cold environment. Animals that had not received such heat experience while they were in the cold did not show the shift in avoidance persistence with the thermal context manipulation in the extinction test. Rats reared in a relatively homogeneous thermal environment apparently need to have experience with radiant heat in both warm and cold environments before they modulate their heat-directed coping behavior in a way that maps it appropriately to thermal context. Although the added procedural requirement makes experiments of this type rather complicated, it also has an important theoretical consequence. It makes implausible the hypothesis that the shift in behavior with thermal context is a simple case of generalization decrement, and it bolsters the hypothesis that the perceived value of radiant heat in the two different contexts determines how persistent the avoidance behavior is.

Recent experiments in my lab have revealed that this effect, the modulation of heat-avoidance by the thermal context at the time of the test, disappears when a long-term (90 day) retention interval separates the initial heat avoidance training from the extinction test. That is, the heat-avoidance behavior persists just as long in the cold environment as it does in the warm one, if sufficient time has passed between the initial training and the retention test. This effect is shown in Figure 3.2. Informally, it is as though the animal has forgotten, over the long-term retention interval, the specific features of the aversive stimulus (radiant heat) originally used to motivate the avoidance behavior, so the behavior is no longer sensitive to shifts in context that specifically affect the value of heat. The memo-

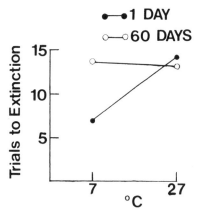

FIG. 3.2. The effect of thermal context on the extinction of heat avoidance at two retention intervals.

ry that remains is clearly sufficient to motivate the avoidance behavior, so it appears that the animal remembers that the situation threatens something bad, even if the rat fails to recall precisely what that bad something is. Empirically, the effect shown in Figure 3.2 is an increased generalization, as a function of retention interval, of avoidance behavior to the cold thermal context. The mechanism that appears to generate this effect is a change, over time, in the specificity of the memorial representation of the threatened stimulus (heat) that the avoidance response prevents.

Does Forgetting Induce Conservatism?

The longer an animal is away from a situation that it has learned has dangerous features, the more likely the features of that situation are to have changed. It makes a certain amount of sense, then, for forgetting to cause an animal to grow increasingly wary as a retention interval passes. Both types of forgetting of fear identified above—loss of inhibition of fear and loss of specificity of the object of avoidance behavior—result in coping behavior generalizing to a wider variety of settings after a long-term retention interval. Thus, it is tempting to hypothesize that forgetting processes affecting learned fears serve to make animals increasingly wary and conservative, the longer the interval that passes between successive exposures to the threatening situation. The conservatism hypothesis is an appealing simple way to characterize the forgetting of fear, but it is probably wrong.

Evidence that disconfirms the conservatism hypothesis comes from experiments designed to assess how forgetting affects the malleability of learned fears. The basic procedure is the one I mentioned earlier, describing the experiment in which Blacconiere and I demonstrated that the intensity of learned fear is well retained over a long interval. The method we used to assess fear, presenting the

CS on a baseline of licking behavior, was selected because of the particular advantages this technique has for retention experiments. Most recent studies of conditioned fear use a conditioned emotional response (CER) technique adapted from the Estes and Skinner (1941) procedure. This involves pretraining animals to perform on an operant baseline, with ingestive reinforcers. The fear CS is then presented while the animals is performing on this operant baseline, and the degree of suppression provides a sensitive measure of the fear state. The standard CER procedure poses some theoretical difficulties when it is employed in a retention experiment focusing on conditioned fear, because it is difficult to guarantee that groups tested after varying retention intervals are precisely equivalent in their baseline performance. Unless arduous and costly control procedures are used to insure that baselines are equivalent, differences among retention groups can be attributed to differences in baseline performance (including forgetting of the baseline contingencies) rather than to forgetting of the fear measured on that baseline. The lick baseline produces more between-animal variability than does the standard CER procedure, but this is more than compensated for by the fact that the lick baseline does not require extensive pretraining. Thus, it is possible to equate differing retention groups by assessing fear conditioning by presenting CSs while animal are performing on a lick baseline that can be established on the day of the test.

In our experiments, fear conditioning takes place in a chamber different from the one where the lick test is conducted. Variable duration CSs (mean duration of 30 sec) are paired with half-second shocks. We use a variable-duration CS to discourage the development of inhibition-of-delay, which would complicate the interpretation of a retention experiment because inhibition-of-delay appears to be lost over a long-term retention interval (Hammond & Maser, 1970).

Using this procedure, we conditioned several groups of rats with a shock UCS of medium intensity (.8 mA). Half of the animals were tested by presenting them with the CS on the lick baseline 24 hrs following the fear conditioning treatment, while the other half of the animals were given the same test 60 days after conditioning. On the day of the test, each group received one additional treatment, prior to the test of the CS's effect. This extra treatment consisted of a return to the same chamber where the initial fear conditioning treatment had been administered and the delivery of two unsignalled shocks. For half the animals, the two intervening shocks were lower in intensity (.3 mA) than the shocks used in the initial conditioning treatment, while, for the other half, the two shocks were stronger in intensity (2.2 mA).

This procedure is a degraded version of a general strategy developed by Rescorla (1974). Rescorla manipulated the representation of the UCS by giving rats, subsequent to a conditioning treatment, a series of 12 unsignalled shocks of greater intensity than the shocks used in conditioning. Our experiment differed from Rescorla's in that we chose to give our animals only two intervening shocks rather than 12. We made this choice because preliminary work had indicated that the smaller number of intervening shocks produced little, if any, US-inflation effect in animals tested the day after conditioning.

The purpose of this experimental strategy was to determine if conditioned fears, which we had already determined are retained in an intensity-specific fashion, remain intensity-specific when shocks of a different intensity are presented just prior to the test of the CS. The results are shown in Figure 3.3.

The intervening shocks had a much bigger effect on old fears than on fresh ones. That is, exposing rats to two free shocks that differ in intensity from the shocks used in initial conditioning has a far greater effect when the extra shocks and the CS test are administered 60 days after the conditioning treatment. Learned fears appear to grow increasingly malleable over time. Furthermore, this increased malleability is reflected not only in the capacity of intervening strong shocks to increase the intensity of the learned fear, but also in the capacity of intervening weak shock to decrease the intensity of the fear. Thus, the animals do not simply become more conservative over time. Instead, they grow increasingly susceptible to the influence of extra events that occur just prior to the final test. Keep in mind that in the absence of intervening events, the rats retain fear intensity extremely well. It follows that some sort of intensity-specific memory must persist until the day of the test, even in the long-term retention groups. What appears to change over time is the degree to which this intensity-specific memory remains specific after the animal has been exposed to new information. Far from becoming more conservative over time, the animals become increasingly willing to abandon their older representations of shock intensity in favor of representations based on more recent, albeit incomplete, information.

Reconstructive Memory in Animals

These results suggest that old memories of fear may have a strongly reconstructive character, reflecting not only the residual effects of an initial conditioning experience, but also modifications of that fearful memory brought about by

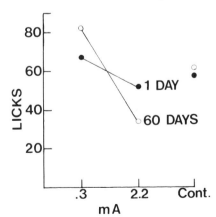

FIG. 3.3. The effects of intervening shocks on the retention of conditioned fear at two retention intervals.

subsequent exposure to partial features of the earlier conditioning experience. The extent to which the memorial representation is modified by the subsequent experiences depends on whether a substantial time interval has passed since the initial conditioning experience. If the time interval has been long enough, a very degraded, partial component of the conditioning procedure (in this case, only two shocks, and no CS whatsoever) suffices to alter the memorial representation that determines the intensity of expressed fear. In basic form, this is an interference paradigm. Note, however, that the degree of interference produced by the intervening shocks depends on the retention interval; in this case, forgetting seems to potentiate interference, rather than the other way around.

In studies of human memory for the trivial, it is possible to find several phenomena that are analogous to the forgetting patterns I have described above. If memory for important events is indeed more fundamental than memory for trivia, then the patterns of forgetting observed in studies of memory for trivial materials may be but pale shadows of patterns seen in motivationally significant forgetting.

If this is the case, continued study of memory for the trivial will necessarily provide only a limited and incomplete understanding of fundamental memory processes. Only more detailed attention to the emotional and motivational consequences of forgetting will suffice to provide a full understanding of the nature of memory and forgetting.

REFERENCES

Ebbinghaus, H. (1885). *Memory,* New York: Teacher's College, Columbia University, 1913. (Reprint edition, New York: Dover, 1964).

Estes, W. K., & Skinner, B. F. (1941). Some quantitative properties of anxiety. *Journal of Experimental Psychology, 29,* 390–400.

Gleitman, H., & Holmes, P. A. (1967). Retention of incompletely learned CER in rats. *Psychonomic Science, 7,* 19–20.

Hammond, L. J., & Maser, J. (1970). Forgetting and conditioned suppression: Role of a temporal discrimination. *Journal of the Experimental Analysis of Behavior, 13,* 333–338.

Hendersen, R. W. (1978). Forgetting of conditioned fear inhibition. *Learning and Motivation, 8,* 16–30.

Hendersen, R. W., & Graham, J. (1979). Avoidance of heat by rats: Effects of thermal context on rapidity of extinction. *Learning and Motivation, 10,* 351–363.

Hendersen, R. W., Patterson, J. M., & Jackson, R. L. (1980). Acquisition and retention of control of instrumental behavior by a cue signaling airblast: How specific are conditioned anticipations? *Learning and Motivation, 11,* 407–426.

Hoffman, H. S., Fleshler, M., & Jensen, P. (1963). Stimulus aspects of aversive controls: The retention of conditioned suppression. *Journal of the Experimental Analysis of Behavior, 6,* 575–583.

Irwin, F. W. (1971). *Intentional behavior and motivation: A cognitive theory,* Philadelphia: Lippincott.

Rescorla, R. A. (1969). Pavlovian conditioned inhibition. *Psychological Bulletin, 72,* 77–94.

Rescorla, R. A. (1974). Effect of inflation of the unconditioned stimulus value following conditioning. *Journal of Comparative and Physiological Psychology, 86,* 101–106.

Seligman, M. E. P., & Johnston, J. C. (1973). A cognitive theory of avoidance learning. In F. J. McGuigan & D. B. Lumsden (Eds.), *Contemporary approaches to conditioning and learning* (pp. 69–110). Washington: V. H. Winston.

Thomas, D. (1979). Retention of conditioned inhibition in a bar-press suppression paradigm. *Learning and Motivation, 10,* 161–177.

4 The Frightful Complexity of the Origins of Fears

Susan Mineka
University of Wisconsin-Madison

Historically there have been thought to be two major classes of fears in higher animals—those that are innate or instinctive and those that are learned (see Marks, 1969, for a review). In addition, there has been some recognition that genetic/constitutional differences play a role in both of these classes of fears (e.g., see Brush, this volume). Within the fields of learning and clinical psychology, considerable attention has been directed toward understanding how the fears that are *not* innate do in fact develop, and what factors are responsible for their maintenance over time. In addition, there has been considerable interest in the extent to which similar mechanisms apply to the development and maintenance of more extreme or pathological forms of fear or anxiety such as occur in full-blown phobias, obsessive-compulsive disorders, and generalized anxiety states. Consensus has certainly never been reached on this issue of whether the origins of "normal" fears and anxieties differ in a qualitative way, or simply in a quantitative way, from the origins of their more extreme pathological counterparts. One of the goals of this chapter is to further an understanding of the frightful complexity of the origins of *all* fears. Once this complexity is acknowledged and better understood, then the differences between the origins of normal fears and their pathological counterparts may well become more one of degree than of kind.

One popular and influential view of the origins of fear and anxiety disorders stems from the behaviorist learning theory tradition started by Pavlov (1927) and Watson and Rayner (1920). The general view espoused by most learning theorists has been that fears and anxiety-based disorders can all be viewed either as instances of classically conditioned fear or anxiety responses, or as instances of avoidance responses motivated by classically conditioned fear and reinforced by anxiety reduction (e.g., Eysenck & Rachman, 1965; Mowrer, 1939; Wolpe, 1958). Over the years, a great deal of attention has been directed toward documenting the similarities between classically conditioned fear or avoidance responses as studied in the laboratory, and anxiety disorders as they present clinically. Recently, there has been increasing dissatisfaction with these models for several very good reasons (see Mineka, 1985, for a complete review). First, these models have been overly simplistic in conceptualizing these disorders as originating out of simple instances of classical conditioning or avoidance learning occurring more or less in a vacuum. Indeed, it has become increasingly evident that there are a wide range of experiential variables that can occur *prior to, during, or following* a traumatic event to strongly affect the level of fear that is experienced, or that gets conditioned, or that is maintained over time. Consequently, in order to understand the full complexities of what goes into the development and maintenance of a person's fear or phobia, one must examine a multitude of factors or experiences that may have occurred prior to, during, or after a particular traumatic experience that that person may have undergone. Some of the research described below illustrates each of these kinds of variables as they affect the origins and maintenance of fear.

A second major source of dissatisfaction with conditioning models of fear and anxiety disorders comes from increasing evidence that, in many cases, people with these disorders have no known traumatic conditioning history. Indeed, many have speculated that vicarious or observational learning accounts for the origins of a greater proportion of human fears and anxiety disorders than does direct classical conditioning (e.g., Bandura, 1969; Murray & Foote, 1979; Rachman, 1978). Unfortunately, the bulk of the evidence supporting this argument has been fairly unconvincing. Some of the research described below does, however, provide convincing evidence that intense and long-lasting learning of phobic-like fears can indeed occur through observational learning alone in a very short period of time.

EFFECTS OF A PRIOR HISTORY OF CONTROL OVER APPETITIVE EVENTS ON FEAR AND EXPLORATORY BEHAVIOR

The idea that a history of control over one's environment can affect an organism's sense of mastery and ability to cope with threatening situations has received increasing support in recent years (see Gunnar, 1980; Mineka & Hendersen, 1985; Seligman, 1975, for reviews). However, most of the studies supporting this proposition have been correlational in nature, or have only involved short-term manipulations of control. The results of a recent experiment done at the Wisconsin Primate Laboratory involving long-term direct manipulations of control provide what is probably the strongest evidence to date that a history of control over positive reinforcements early in life can reduce the amount the fear later experienced in the presence of innately fear provoking stimuli.

In this experiment, done in collaboration with Megan Gunnar of the University of Minnesota, it was demonstrated that, compared to monkeys reared in an uncontrollable environment or to monkeys reared in a standard laboratory environment, monkeys reared in an environment where they had control over access to their food, water, and treats later showed both less fear when faced with a fear-provoking mechanical toy monster and more bold exploratory behavior in a novel playroom situation (Mineka, Gunnar, & Champoux, 1985, submitted for publication). Two groups of 4 infant monkeys each (Masters) were reared from approximately 6 or 8 weeks of age until 9–10 months of age in quad cages where they had access to six manipulanda (bars, keys, chains) that delivered their food (Similac), water, sugar pellets, and various treats (raisins, Froot Loops, chocolate chips). The manipulanda were introduced gradually over a period of weeks and response requirements were increased from CRF to FRIO. Availability of reinforcements was signalled by visual discriminative stimuli, and the subjects averaged 50–60 sugar pellets or treats each day, as well as 50 limited duration drinks of Similac before weaning. Two other groups of monkeys were yoked to these first two Master groups. These Yoked groups lived in identical environments to the Master groups except that their manipulanda were inoperative. Instead, they received reinforcers identical to those received by Master group subjects whenever Master subjects successfully operated their manipulanda. The experiment was run in two replications in two successive years. In the second replication, there was also a No Stimulation Control group that did not have access to the variety of reinforcers received by the Master and Yoked groups. This group was included to assess whether any differences between the Master and Yoked groups were a function of the beneficial effects of having early experience with control and/or the deleterious effects of having early experience with uncontrollable stimulation.

Until the monkeys were 6–7 months of age they were left undisturbed except for daily observations of their social behavior every morning. At 6–7 months of age, they were all subjected to 3 biweekly fear tests. During these fear tests, they were exposed to an electrically operated mechanical toy monster which had flailing arms and legs, flashing eyes, and made a loud noise. The monster was placed directly in front of their home cage and was turned on and off over a period of 30 minutes during which the monkeys' behaviors were scored. When normal infant monkeys reared with their peers are frightened, their general tendency is to cling tightly to one another and to retreat to the back of their cage as far away from the fear-evoking stimulus as possible. Thus, greater amounts of clinging behavior are taken as indicative of more fear, and greater amounts of time spent in the front of the cage near the monster are indicative of greater boldness and lower levels of fear. While the monster was turned on, all groups spent most of their time clinging to one another. However, in both replications, the Master group exhibited significantly less clinging behavior when the monster was turned off than did the Yoked and Control groups. This was true on all 3 tests in Replication 1 and for 1 of the 3 in Replication 2. In addition, on 2 of the 3 fear tests in each replication, the Master group spent significantly more time in the front of the cage than did the Yoked or Control groups. Thus, there was evidence in both replications that the Master groups were significantly less disturbed by the fear provoking monster than were the Yoked and Control groups.

Two weeks after giving the tests for fear when the subjects were 8–9 months old, playroom tests were conducted to assess the monkeys' responses to a novel open-field situation. Each group was placed in a transport cage in the middle of a relatively large and spacious primate playroom containing 12 different objects to touch or play with. The time to emerge from the transport cage was recorded; any subjects who had not emerged in 10 minutes were taken out by the experimenter. The playroom tests lasted 30 minutes, during which the subject's behavior was carefully observed and scored.

As seen in Figure 4.1, there were highly significant effects for both replications on the emergence test into the playroom. On Test 1, no monkey spontaneously left the transport cage, but by the second and third tests, the Master subjects were virtually all emerging, whereas few of the Yoked or Control subjects did so. Unfortunately, because of inadequate pilot testing, the observational scoring techniques during the playroom tests themselves in Replication 1 were not sensitive to what the experimenters and an independent observer were certain were differences between the groups: The Master group seemed to touch more different objects, they left the floor more, and they climbed more often to the highest points in the room. In Replication 2, more sensitive scoring tech-

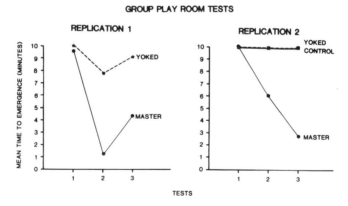

GROUP PLAY ROOM TESTS

FIG. 4.1.   Mean number of minutes to emerge from the transport cage on each of the three playroom tests for the Master and Yoked groups of Replication 1, and for the Master, Yoked, and Control groups of Replication 2. (From Mineka et al., 1985.)

niques were used; here significant differences were found which largely paralleled those perceived by the Experimenters for Replication 1. These differences will be focused on in the present discussion. As seen in Figure 4.2, in Replication 2, the three groups did not differ on the number of times objects were touched on the first test, but by the second test, the Master group touched objects more times than the Yoked group, and by the third test, the Master group touched objects more times than both the Yoked and Control groups, which did not differ from each other. Also, the Master group touched a greater number of different objects than the Yoked group on all 3 tests, and more than the Control group on 2 of the 3 tests. Not surprisingly, given these differences, there also were differences between groups in the amount of locomotion and contact clinging behavior exhibited. These latter differences are shown in Figure 4.3. The Master group showed significantly less time clinging to one another than the Control group and marginally less than the Yoked group. The Master group also showed more locomotion than the Yoked group on all 3 tests and more than the Control group on the last 2 tests. Thus, in both replications, there was evidence that Master groups were more eager to enter the novel playroom situation, and once there, they showed far more exploratory behavior and less clinging behavior. One might ask the extent to which these differences were simply a manifestation of differences between groups or between individuals within the groups as well. In other words, were the master animals only bold and exploratory when with their peers, or had their experience with control altered their behavior when alone as well? In order to assess this in Replication 2, tests of individual activity in the playroom were conducted at the end of the experiment, while the monkeys were

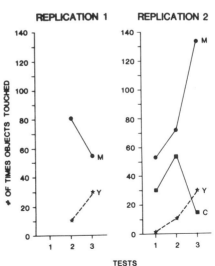

GROUP PLAY ROOM TESTS

FIG. 4.2. Mean number of times different objects were touched during the three playroom tests for the Master and Yoked groups of Replication 1 (Numbers are approximate as scored off videotapes) and for the Master, Yoked, and Control groups of Replication 2. (Redrawn from Mineka et al., 1985.)

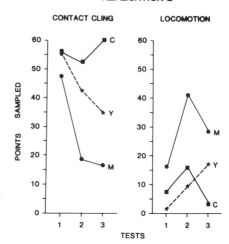

FIG. 4.3. Mean number of points sampled, during which contact cling and locomotion occurred during the three playroom tests of Replication 2, for the Master, Yoked, and Control groups. (From Mineka et al., 1985.)

undergoing a series of four 4 day separations from each other. Each subject was given a 15 minute test in the playroom on the third day of 2 of their 4 separations. Again, Master subjects exhibited more exploratory behavior than both Yoked and Control subjects.

It appears that a prior history of control over appetitive events in one's environment can reduce one's emotionality in fear-provoking situations. In a sense, it is somewhat amazing that the observed effects were as strong as they were. These infants' experience with control was of a somewhat different sort and occurred in a very different context than they would experience in nature, and yet it had big effects. This observation would seem to suggest that infants are very sensitive to the experience of controlling their environment and will profit from that experience even when it occurs in somewhat unnatural circumstances. One speculation that arises from these results, although not yet directly tested, is that one might expect that such early experience with control could serve to reduce susceptibility to, or immunize the organism against, the development of phobic or other anxiety-based disorders later in life (cf. Mineka, 1985; Seligman, 1975).

EFFECTS OF CONTROL OVER, OR FEEDBACK ABOUT, SHOCK TERMINATION DURING CONDITIONING ON LEVELS OF FEAR

As suggested earlier, experiential variables that occur during a conditioning experience, as well as before it, may also be important in determining the level of fear that is experienced or conditioned. One example of such a variable is, again, control, but in this case control over the termination of the aversive event. For some years, it has been known that less fear is conditioned to neutral stimuli paired with escapable as opposed to inescapable shock. Mowrer and Viek (1948) first reported this finding of fear *from a sense of helplessness,* and it has since been replicated in a number of laboratories (e.g., Desiderato & Newman, 1971). Generally, these results have been interpreted in terms of the increased aversiveness or stressfulness of uncontrollable shocks (e.g., Seligman, Maier, & Solomon, 1971). Recently, however, Mineka, Cook, & Miller (1984a) have suggested that another explanation of such results is more viable. This explanation stems from a theory proposed by Averill (1973), who argued that the beneficial effects of having control over the offset of aversive events stem primarily from the added predictability inherent in having a controlling response, that is, organisms with control ipso facto also know when the event will terminate and have a salient predictor of the shock-free interval that follows. In two experiments using an unsignalled escape paradigm and multivariate fear-assessment techniques, as well as in two experiments using a signalled escape paradigm and freezing as an index of fear, Mineka et al. (1984a) found strong support for this idea that control per se is not necessary to produce the lower level of fear characteristic of subjects with control. They found that simply mimicking the response of the master subjects with control by presenting an exteroceptive feedback signal to yoked subjects without control whenever the master subject makes a response is sufficient to produce the lower level of fear in the yoked subjects.

For example, in Mineka et al.'s (1984a) third experiment, three groups of rats all received 50 fear conditioning trials with a 20 sec tone CS. Twenty-four hours later, fear of the tone was assessed in a different context by observing the number of freezing responses made during and after the presentation of the tone as compared to before the tone. During the conditioning phase, the Master group (M-NFB) could terminate the shock after one second by pressing down a ledge on one side of the conditioning chamber. Each subject in the Yoked-No Feedback group (Y-NFB) received an identical amount of shock to its Master but had no control over shock termination (i.e., the ledge mechanism was inoperative). Finally, each subject in the Yoked-Feedback group (Y-FB) also received an identical amount of shock to its Master and a 3 second lights-off feedback stimulus when its Master made an escape response. As seen in Figure 4.4, the Yoked-No feedback group showed higher levels of freezing in the presence of the tone on the fear test than did the Master and Yoked-Feedback groups, which did not differ from each other. In a fourth experiment, the Master group also received a feedback stimulus every time they made their escape response. The results of that experiment showed that feedback added to control did not further reduce the level of fear below that seen in subjects with only control. Thus, it seemed likely that feedback and control were producing their effects through the same rather than a different mechanism; if there were different mechanisms of action for these two factors, one would have expected there to be additive effects of feedback and control, but there were not.

Mineka et al. (1984a) considered a number of different possible explanations

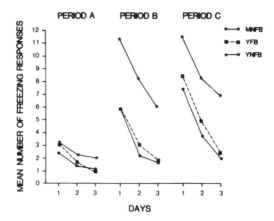

FIG. 4.4. Mean number of freezing responses per day for each of the three groups (Master-No Feedback, Yoked-No Feedback, and Yoked-Feedback) across the 4 test trials of each day, summed separately for Period A (before the CS), Period B (during the CS), and Period C (after the CS). (From Mineka et al., 1984a. By permission of the Americal Psychological Association.)

of their results and concluded, that at the present time, no one explanation could definitively account for all of their results. It seems likely, however, that an adequate explanation will have to incorporate the notion that the escape response and/or the feedback stimulus acquire fear inhibitory properties. Using the Rescorla-Wagner model (1972) one might predict that their inhibitory strength would compete with background contextual stimuli for inhibitory strength, and in turn allow the background cues to compete more successfully with the CS for excitatory strength, accounting for the lower level of fear of the CS in the Master and Yoked-Feedback groups. Alternatively, as the escape response and the feedback stimulus acquire fear inhibitory properties in the Master and Yoked-Feedback groups, a process of counterconditioning may occur that reduces fear of the CS. Because there is no powerful inhibitor of fear for the Yoked-No Feedback group the possibility of such counterconditioning does not exist for this group and so fear of the CS remains higher. Further work will have to be done to tease apart these two alternatives, as well as the several other possibilities discussed in detail by Mineka et al. (1984a).

In spite of the uncertainty as to the mechanism that accounts for these results, they are useful in highlighting the importance of two issues. First, they raise some doubt as to the validity of the conclusions of the multitude of experiments conducted over the past 15 years examining the effects of controllable versus uncontrollable shock on a host of dependent variables (see Maier & Seligman, 1976; Mineka & Hendersen, 1985; Overmier, Patterson, & Wielkiewicz, 1980; for reviews). Nearly all of these experiments have assumed that the use of a yoked control design is sufficient to draw conclusions about the effects of control per se. However, the present results suggest that at least some effects that have been attributed to *control* may in fact more correctly be attributable to the fear-inhibitory properties that accrue to the stimulus attributes of the escape response. In other words, the present results suggest that such experiments should include groups comparable to the Yoked-Feedback groups described above before concluding that their effects are a function of control rather than the added feedback or predictability that stems from having control.

A second issue highlighted by these results is the importance of examining the dynamics of fear-conditioning in more complex contexts than has been done in the past. The great majority of conclusions about the dynamics of Pavlovian conditioning have been derived from the traditional paradigm in which the subject has no control over the US and no feedback about the offset of the US. However, many of the everyday events where Pavlovian conditioning occurs are situations in which subjects have some control over the US and/or some feedback that the US has terminated and will not occur again for awhile. The present results highlight the fact that such factors can play an important role in how much fear-conditioning occurs to the neutral stimuli paired with such USs.

EFFECTS OF CONTROL AND FEEDBACK DURING AND FOLLOWING CONDITIONING ON FEAR MAINTENANCE

A now well-known finding in the literature on avoidance learning is that fear of the CS diminishes as an avoidance response becomes well-learned (e.g., Kamin, Brimer, & Black, 1963; Mineka & Gino, 1980; Starr & Mineka, 1977). It was originally thought that this diminution in fear over the course of avoidance-learning was simply a function of the fact that each successful avoidance trial is a Pavlovian fear extinction trial (i.e., a CS followed by no US). However, several experiments have now shown that this account of the diminution in fear that occurs over the course of avoidance learning is not correct. Instead, as described above for escape learning, it appears to be the control and its correlated feedback, or the added predictability inherent in having an avoidance response available, that is responsible for the reduction in fear that occurs over the course of avoidance learning (Cook, Mineka, & Trumble, in preparation; Starr & Mineka, 1977).

For example, in their first experiment, Starr and Mineka (1977) trained three groups of Master rats to criteria of 3, 9, or 27 consecutive avoidance responses as had Kamin et al. (1963). They found the usual reduced level of fear in the Master-27 group as compared to that in the Master-3 and Master-9 groups using the traditional conditioned emotional response (CER) technique to measure the level of fear. They also had three Yoked groups that received the same number and pattern of CS-US pairings and CS alone trials as the Master groups but without an effective avoidance response available. Thus, the Master and Yoked groups were equated for the number of Pavlovian excitatory and extinction trials, but they differed in whether or not they had control over CS and US termination. Of particular interest was the finding that the Yoked-27 group did not show an attenuation of fear in comparison to the Yoked-3 and Yoked-9 groups and was significantly more afraid of the CS than the Master-27 group. In other words, some aspect of the control available to the Master-27 group seemed to be responsible for the attenuation of fear that they experienced. In a second experiment, Starr and Mineka (1977) provided preliminary evidence that it was the feedback or predictive properties of the avoidance response that were responsible for this effect rather than control per se. In that experiment, yoked animals given a feedback signal when the master animal made its escape or avoidance response did not differ from the masters (trained to 36 consecutive avoidance responses) in levels of fear of the CS, although yoked animals without the feedback signal were significantly more afraid than the other two groups.

More recently, Cook et al. (in preparation) further explored the same issue with a different fixed trials design for overtraining the avoidance response (50 vs 200 trials) and a different measure of fear (levels of freezing during and after the CS as compared to before the CS). Again, as shown in Figure 4.5, they found less fear of the CS in the Master-200 group that had received 200 training trials than in Master-50 group that had received only 50 trials, but the same attenuation did not occur in a Yoked-200 group as compared to a Yoked-50 group. However, they also found that the Yoked-200-FB group that received a feedback signal when the Master group made its response did not differ from the Master-200 group. Thus, again, it seems that control per se is not necessary to produce the attenuation of fear seen in well-trained avoidance responders. Instead, some

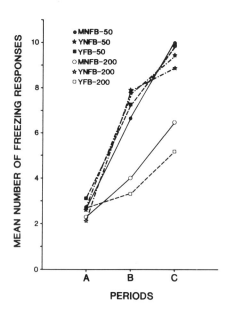

FIG. 4.5.   Mean number of freezing responses for each of the 6 groups (Master-200, Yoked-No Feedback-200, Yoked-Feedback-200, Master-50, Yoked-No Feedback-50, and Yoked-Feedback-50), summed across the 4 test trials of each day, and averaged across the 3 test days, separately for Period A (before the CS), Period B (during the CS), and Period C (after the CS).

aspect of the added response feedback or predictability about the impending shock-free intervals is the important aspect of the avoidance response that is responsible for fear attenuation over the course of avoidance learning.

As discussed above regarding the Mineka et al. (1984a) escape learning experiments, one important issue highlighted by these experiments is the importance of studying the dynamics of Pavlovian conditioning in more complex paradigms than those in which it has traditionally been studied. These results clearly illustrate that the presence of an avoidance and/or an escape response affects the dynamics of both fear conditioning in the presence of only excitatory trials (Mineka et al., 1984a), and the reduction in fear that occurs over the course of avoidance learning as more and more Pavlovian extinction trials become intermixed with fewer and fewer Pavlovian excitatory trials (Cook et al., in preparation). Furthermore, they also illustrate that it is probably the feedback or safety-signal properties of the response rather than the controlling aspect of the response per se that are responsible for reducing the level of fear that is conditioned (Mineka et al., 1984a) or causing the reduction in fear over the course of avoidance training (Cook et al., in preparation; Starr & Mineka, 1977).

Other variables that occur following conditioning have also been shown to affect the level of fear that is maintained over time. For example, Rescorla (1974) showed that if, at some point in time following conditioning, an animal is exposed to a higher intensity traumatic US (with no CS) than was involved in the original conditioning, the fear of CR becomes inflated in the direction that would be expected if the higher intensity US had been involved in the conditioning in the first place. Furthermore, Hendersen (this volume) showed that the greater the time interval following the original conditioning experience until the higher intensity US occurs, the greater the inflation effect. It is as if the organism has a memorial representation of the original US that can be altered through later experience with other USs, and that the malleability of the memory increases with time. Thus, a person who had had a conditioning experience and acquired a fear of nonphobic intensity might be expected to show an increase in that fear, perhaps to phobic intensity, if a noncontingent traumatic experience occurred at a later point in time.

In addition, Hendersen's work on the forgetting of fear also suggests important reasons why many fears and phobias show increasing generalization of situations and places in which they occur over time. First, conditioned inhibitors of fear are quite easily forgotten, but conditioned excitors are not. Second, although fears per se are not forgotten simply through the passage of time, Hendersen showed the *objects* of the fear are forgotten with time. As a consequence of this forgetting the animal comes to respond in a more conservative fashion by behaving fearfully in situations in which it would not have right after the conditioning experience when it remembered the specific object of which it was afraid. The forgetting of fear inhibition, combined with the forgetting of the specific object of a fear, may together play an important role in explaining the increasing generalization of situations and places in which fears and phobias occur over time. (See Mineka, 1985, for a more extensive discussion of such points.)

OBSERVATIONAL CONDITIONING OF FEAR— CONDITIONING WITH NO OVERT TRAUMATIC US

We have now seen that conditioning models of fear and anxiety disorders need not be overly simplistic if they incorporate a number of the kinds of experiential variables discussed above occurring prior to, during, and following stressful events that strongly affect the level of fear that is experienced, or that is conditioned, or that is maintained over time. We now turn to the second kind of criticism mentioned at the outset of the chapter that has been directed at conditioning models of fear acquisition. That is, many people with fears and anxiety disorders appear to have no known traumatic conditioning history that could account for the origins of their fears. Consequently, there have been an increasing number of proposals in recent years that vicarious or observational conditioning may play a more prominent role in the origins of many fears and anxiety disorders than does direct conditioning. Unfortunately, however, there has been a dearth of evidence to support such proposals. Only about a dozen studies have demonstrated observational conditioning of autonomic responses in human subjects. The conclusions that can be drawn from these studies are extremely limited for several reasons. First, they have only involved autonomic indices of fear which do not always correlate highly with other indices of fear (Hodgson & Rachman, 1974; Lang, 1968, 1971; Mineka, 1979). Thus, the extent to which observational conditioning of the other fear response systems (e.g., behavioral avoidance and the cognitive/subjective fear systems) can occur is unknown. Second, because of ethical constraints that do not allow induction of long-lasting fears in human subjects, these experiments have nearly all taken place in a single laboratory session, with extinction taking place quite rapidly, and without any tests for the context specificity of the fears. Yet many human fears, and certainly human phobias, are characterized by their persistence and lack of context specificity. Recently, these problems inherent in the human observational conditioning literature were circumvented by demonstrating rapid, strong, and persistent observational conditioning of snake fear in rhesus monkeys. The fear is manifest in two of Lang's three-response systems of fear (1968, 1971); it is not context specific; and it shows no signs of diminution at 3 month follow-up.

By way of background, there has been a long-standing controversy as to whether a fear of snakes in primates is innate or learned (see Mineka, Keir, & Price, 1980, for a review). Recent evidence strongly suggests that it is learned, at least in rhesus and squirrel monkeys. Joslin, Fletcher, and Emlen (1964), Mineka, Keir, and Price (1980) and Murray and King (1973) all found that only wild-reared monkeys (rhesus and squirrel) demonstrate a fear of snakes, whereas their lab-reared counterparts do not. Although the failure of the lab-reared monkeys to exhibit the fear could be an abberation from normal development, these investigators all suggested that the more likely explanation of this pattern of findings was that the lab-reared monkeys simply lacked the necessary learning experience that the wild-reared monkeys had had to acquire the fear. Furthermore, given that it was unlikely that the 80–90% of wild-reared monkeys who exhibited a fear of snakes had all had direct traumatic conditioning experiences, these investigators all suggested that the fear most likely had been acquired through observational learning.

Only recently, however, has there been strong evidence for the plausibility of such an argument. Mineka, Davidson, Cook, and Keir (1984b) first examined this issue in the context of whether adolescent rhesus monkeys could acquire a fear of snakes if they observed their wild-reared parents behave fearfully in the presence of a live boa constrictor and a toy snake. Six adolescent/young-adult rhesus monkeys and their wild-reared parents with whom they had lived all their lives in the Wisconsin Primate Laboratory's nuclear family environment (Harlow, 1971) were first pretested for their fear of snakes using previously validated procedures. The wild-reared adults all showed a strong fear of snakes as measured by three indices: (a) a marked avoidance during a 5 minute choice test of compartments in the Sackett Self-Selection Circus (1970) that had the live, toy, or model snakes just outside them, plus a concomitant preference for a compartment that had a neutral object (wood block) outside of it; (b) while in a Wisconsin General Testing Apparatus (WGTA) apparatus, a refusal to reach for a food treat that was on the far side of an open Plexiglas box containing either a live boa constrictor or a toy or model snake; and (c) manifestation of several different fear or disturbance behaviors in the presence of the live, toy, or model snake in the WGTA (e.g., withdrawal to the back of the cage, clutching the cage, eye aversion, fear grimaces, threat faces, piloerection, etc.). By contrast, only one of the 6 adolescent/young-adult lab-reared monkeys showed even minimal signs of fear in the presence of the live and toy snakes prior to conditioning (see Figures 4.6 and 4.7).

Following these pretests, the adolescent/young-adult *observers* received 6 discriminative observational conditioning sessions with one of their parents serving as a *model* for the exhibition of fear of snakes. During each of these 6 sessions, the parental models had fifteen 40-second trials in the WGTA, during which their offspring could observe them reach or not reach for food in the presence of the live and toy snakes as well as neutral objects (Six trials per session were with the live or toy snakes, and nine trials per session were with neutral objects). During these sessions, the observers were in a transport cage with two Plexiglas sides within a few feet of their parental models so that they could observe both the food-reach latency and the disturbance behaviors exhibited by the models. Then the observers were tested for their fear of the snake in

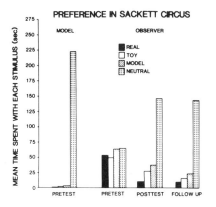

FIG. 4.6. Mean amount of time spent with the 4 different objects in the Sackett Circus for the 5 parental models in the pretest, and for the 5 adolescent/young-adult observers who learned in a pretest, a posttest after learning, and a 3 month follow-up test. (Redrawn from Mineka, 1984b.)

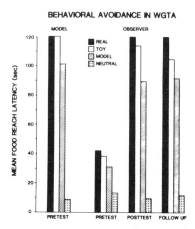

FIG. 4.7. Mean food-reach latency in the WGTA in the presence of the 6 different objects for the 5 parental models in the pretest and for the 5 adolescent/young-adult observers who learned in a pretest, in a posttest after learning, and in a 3 month follow-up test. (Redrawn from Mineka, 1984b).

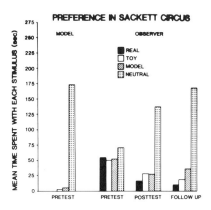

FIG 4.8. Mean amount of time spent with the 4 different objects in the Sackett Circus for the 2 models in the pretest and for the 10 unrelated observers in the pretest, the posttest and the 3 month follow-up test. (From Cook et al., in press.)

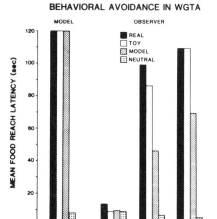

FIG. 4.9. Mean food reach latency in the WGTA in the presence of the 6 different objects for the 2 models in the pretest and for the 10 unrelated observers in the pretest, posttest, and 3-month follow-up test. (From Cook et al., in press.)

the Sackett Self-Selection Circus after the second, the fourth, and the sixth conditioning sessions. Five out of the six monkeys showed marked signs of avoidance of the real and toy snakes on these three tests. Thus, they exhibited significant signs of behavioral avoidance in a different context than where they had observed their parents behave fearfully after only 8 minutes (twelve 40-second trials) of watching their parents behave fearfully in the presence of the snake objects (see Figure 4.6). Following the sixth conditioning session, they were also tested by themselves for their fear of the snake objects in the WGTA itself. Here, too, 5 out of 6 exhibited highly significant behavioral avoidance, refusing to reach for the food treat in the presence of the snake (see Figure 4.7), as well as showing a significant number of fear/disturbance behaviors in the presence of the snake. In fact, it is clear from Figures 4.6–4.7 that after a total of only 24 minutes of observing their parents behave fearfully in the presence of the snake object, these adolescent/young-adult observers were showing a level of fear that was nearly as strong as that of their wild-reared parents (See Figures 4.6–4.7). Furthermore, as also seen in these figures, when the observer monkeys were tested 3 months later for retention of their observationally learned fear, there were no significant signs of diminution of acquired fear in either the Sackett Circus or the WGTA.

More recently, the question of whether such observational learning only occurs in the context of a parent-child relationship has been examined. In this experiment (Cook, Mineka, Wolkenstein, & Laitsch, in press) the models and observers were unrelated monkeys which knew each other only slightly by virtue of having lived in the same room together (but in separate cages) for a period of at least several months in the recent past. The two models were wild-reared monkeys like those described above, who had lived in the wild for at least two years prior to being brought to the Primate Laboratory over 20 years ago. They both showed an intense fear of snakes during pretests in both the WGTA and the Sackett Circus. The 10 observers were lab-reared monkeys (with an age range of 4–8 years) who did not exhibit a fear of snakes in the WGTA or Sackett Circus pretests. The discriminative observational conditioning procedure was identical to that described above for the parent-child pairs. The results, as illustrated in Figures 4.8 and 4.9, were strikingly parallel to those described for the previous experiment except that 3 out of the 10 (instead of 1 out of 6) did not show very pronounced levels of conditioning. Thus, it does indeed seem that such observational conditioning can occur among unrelated monkeys who have had very little contact with each other.

An interesting question raised by the fact that 4 of the 16 subjects in these two experiments did not show very significant conditioning is, what is the source of the differences between the four who did not learn and the twelve who did learn? For example, were the four who did not learn simply bolder and less emotional monkeys who would show weaker conditioning in any fear conditioning paradigm? Or alternatively, were the observational conditioning experiences of the four subjects who did not learn somehow different from those of the twelve subjects who did learn? The latter possibility must be especially carefully considered because the experimenter does not have control over the fearful models' behavior during the observational conditioning sessions. As a result, the observational conditioning experience varies across sessions and across subjects in a way that it does not in traditional classical conditioning paradigms where the experimenter controls UCS presentation.

One way to begin to answer this question about the source of the individual differences in learning is to examine the relationship between the models' level of fear exhibited during conditioning and the observers' level of fear in the posttest. Because the models' behavior during the observational conditioning sessions (food-reach latency and levels of behavioral disturbance) had been recorded, it was possible to correlate the level of fear that they exhibited with that of the observers in the posttest. In the first experiment described above, there was a very high correlation ($r = .986$) between the total amount of disturbance behaviors exhibited by the parental models to the three snake stimuli during conditioning and by the adolescent/young-adult observers in the WGTA posttest. In the second experiment, the same correlation between the total amount of disturbance behaviors shown by the models during conditioning and by the observers on the posttest was also very high ($r = .95$). These high correlations in both experiments suggest that there may be very close modeling by an observer of the degree of fear or disturbance that a particular stimulus elicits in the model. This is especially likely, given that the correlations were comparably high both in the first experiment, where the models and observers were closely related and had lived together for the entire lives of the observers and in the second experiment, where the models and observers were only minimally acquainted. In sum, at least a partial answer to the question of the source of the marked individual differences in observational learning seems to lie in the differences in the observational conditioning experiences that the different observers receive. In fact, not surprisingly given the very high correlations noted above, the four observers who did not learn in the two experiments all had models that for some reason showed the lowest average levels of fear exhibited by any of the models in any of the conditioning sessions.

SUMMARY AND CONCLUSIONS

In conclusion, the research reviewed above suggests that the origins of fears and anxiety disorders are considerably more complex than has often been assumed by behavioral learning theorists in the past. It is highly unlikely that most fears or anxiety disorders can be thought to originate from a single or even a few trials of classical fear conditioning or avoidance learning occurring in a vacuum, as has often been proposed in the past. Instead, a multitude of experiential variables may occur prior to, during, or following a stressful experience and interact to affect the level of fear that is experienced, conditioned, or maintained over time. For example, early experience with control and mastery can reduce the level of fear that is experienced in several different fear-provoking situations later in an infant monkey's life (Mineka, Gunnar, & Champoux, submitted for publication). In addition, control of, or feedback about US offset during conditioning reduces the level of fear that is conditioned to a neutral stimulus, thereby showing that the dynamics of fear conditioning are powerfully influenced by the controllability and predictability of the US (Mineka et al., 1984a). Following conditioning, animals that are allowed to avoid the US (another form of control), and/or receive feedback about CS and US offset, show more rapid attenuation of fear than do animals that cannot avoid the US but receive equivalent amounts of nonreinforced CS exposure (Cook, Mineka, & Trumble, in preparation; Starr & Mineka, 1977). Also, a host of other factors occurring following conditioning, such as inflation and forgetting of US specificity (Hendersen, this volume; Rescorla, 1974) can result in increases in fear or in the places in which fear is exhibited. Finally, very intense and persistent fears can be learned through observational learning experiences alone, in the absence of any overt traumatic US (Cook et al., submitted; Mineka et al., 1984b). Thus, it is only with an acknowledgement of this kind of complexity and interaction of a wide range of experiential variables affecting conditioning that conditioning models will continue to prosper and maintain their usefulness in the future.

ACKNOWLEDGMENT

The research reported in this chapter was supported in part by grants to S. Mineka from the University of Wisconsin Graduate School and from the National Science Foundation (BNS-7823612 and BNS-8216141). Some of the research was also supported by grant BNS-8119041 from the National Science Foundation to S. Mineka and M. Gunnar. During preparation of this chapter the author was supported by a Faculty Development Award from the University of Wisconsin, and by a NIMH Clinical Internship stipend at Michael Reese Hospital, Chicago, Illinois. The author would like to thank J. B. Overmier for his helpful editorial comments on an earlier version of this chapter.

REFERENCES

Averill, J. (1973). Personal control over aversive stimuli and its relationship to stress. *Psychological Bulletin, 80,* 286–303.

Bandura, A. (1969). *Principles of behavior modification.* New York: Holt, Rinehart, & Winston.

Cook, M., Mineka, S., & Trumble, D. (1985). *The role of control and feedback in the attenuation of fear over the course of avoidance learning.* Unpublished manuscript.

Cook, M., Mineka, S., Wolkenstein, B., & Laitsch, K. (1985). *Observational conditioning of snake fear in unrelated rhesus monkeys. Journal of Abnormal Psychology,* in press.

Desiderato, O., & Newman, A. (1971). Conditioned suppression produced in rats by tones paired with escapable or inescapable shock. *Journal of Comparative and Physiological Psychology, 77,* 427–431.

Eysenck, H. J., & Rachman, S. (1965). *Causes and cures of neurosis.* London: Routledge & Kegal Paul.

Gunnar, M. R. (1980). Contingent stimulation: A review of its role in early development. In S. Levine & H. Ursin (Eds.), *Coping and health.* New York: Plenum.

Harlow, M. K. (1971). Nuclear family apparatus. *Behavior Research Methods and Instrumentation, 3,* 301–304.

Hodgson, R., & Rachman, S. (1974). Desynchrony in measures of fear. *Behaviour Research and Therapy, 10,* 111–117.

Joslin, J., Fletcher, H., & Emlen, J. (1964). A comparison of the responses to snakes of lab- and wild-reared rhesus monkeys. *Animal Behavior, 12,* 348–352.

Kamin, L. J., Brimer, C. J., & Black, A. H. (1963). Conditioned suppression as a monitor of fear of the CS in the course of avoidance training. *Journal of Comparative and Physiological Psychology, 56,* 497–501.

Lang, P. J. (1971). The application of psychophysiological methods to the study of psychotherapy and behavior modification. In A. E. Bergin & S. L. Garfield (Eds.), *Handbook of psychotherapy and behavior change.* New York: Wiley.

Lang, P. J. (1968). Fear reduction and fear behavior: Problems in treating a construct. In J. M. Shlein (Ed.), *Research in psychotherapy: Vol. III.* (pp. 90–103). Washington, D.C.: American Psychological Association.

Maier, S. F., & Seligman, M. E. P. (1976). Learned helplessness: Theory and evidence. *Journal of Experimental Psychology: General, 105,* 3–45.

Marks, I. M. (1969). *Fears and phobias.* New York: Academic Press.

Mineka, S. (1979). The role of fear in theories of avoidance learning, flooding, and extinction. *Psychological Bulletin, 86,* 985–1010.

Mineka, S. (1985). Animal models of anxiety based disorders: Their usefulness and limitations. In J. Maser & A. H. Tuma (Eds.), *Anxiety and anxiety disorders.* Hillsdale, NJ: Lawrence Erlbaum, Associates, Inc.

Mineka, S., Cook, M., & Miller, S. (1984a). Fear conditioned with escapable and inescapable shock: The effects of a feedback stimulus. *Journal of Experimental Psychology: Animal Behavior Processes, 10,* 307–323.

Mineka, S., Davidson, M., Cook, M., & Keir, R. (1984b). Observational conditioning of snake fear in rhesus monkeys. *Journal of Abnormal Psychology, 93,* 355–372.

Mineka, S., & Gino, A. (1980). Dissociation between CER and extended avoidance performance. *Learning and Motivation, 11,* 476–502.

Mineka, S., Gunnar, M., & Champoux, M. (1985). Control and early socioemotional development. Studies of infant rhesus monkeys reared in controllable vs. uncontrollable environments. Submitted to *Child Development.*

Mineka, S., & Hendersen, R. (1985). Controllability and predictability in acquired motivation. *Annual Review of Psychology, 36,* 495–529.

Mineka, S., Keir, R., & Price, V. (1980). Fear of snakes in wild- and lab-reared rhesus monkeys. *Animal Learning and Behavior, 8,* 653–663.

Mowrer, O. H. (1939). A stimulus-response analysis of anxiety and its role as a reinforcing agent. *Psychological Review, 46,* 553–565.

Mowrer, O. H., & Viek, P. (1948). An experimental analogue of fear from a sense of helplessness. *Journal of Abnormal Social Psychology, 83,* 193–200.

Murray, E., & Foote, F. (1979). The origins of fear of snakes. *Behaviour Research and Therapy, 17,* 489–493.

Murray, S., & King, J. (1973). Snake avoidance in feral and laboratory reared squirrel monkeys. *Behaviour, 47,* 281–289.

Overmier, J., Patterson, J., & Wielkiewicz, R. (1980). Environmental contingencies as sources of stress in animals. In S. Levine & H. Ursin (Ed.), *Coping and health* (pp. 1–38). New York: Plenum.

Pavlov, I. P. (1927). *Conditioned reflexes.* London: Oxford University Press.

Rachman, S. (1978). *Fear and courage.* San Francisco: Freeman.

Rescorla, R. A. (1974). Effect of inflation of the unconditioned stimulus value following conditioning. *Journal of Comparative and Physiological Psychology, 86,* 101–106.

Rescorla, R. A., & Wagner, A. R. (1972). A theory of Pavlovian conditioning: Variations in the effectiveness of reinforcement and nonreinforcement. In A. Black & W. F. Prokasy (Eds.), *Classical conditioning II* (pp. 64–99). New York: Appleton-Century-Crofts.

Sackett, G. (1970). Unlearned response, differential rearing experiences, and the development of social attachments by rhesus monkeys. In L. A. Rosenblum (Ed.), *Primate behavior, Vol. 1.* New York: Academic.

Seligman, M. E. P. (1975). *Helplessness: On depression, development, and death.* San Francisco: Freeman.

Seligman, M. E. P., Maier, S. F., & Solomon, R. L. (1971). Unpredictable and uncontrollable aversive events. In F. R. Brush (Ed.), *Aversive conditioning and learning.* New York: Academic.

Starr, M. D., & Mineka, S. (1977). Determinants of fear over the course of avoidance learning. *Learning and Motivation, 8,* 332–350.

Watson, J. B., & Rayner, R. (1920). Conditioned emotional reactions. *Journal of Experimental Psychology, 3,* 1–14.

Wolpe, J. (1958). *Psychotherapy by Reciprocal Inhibition.* Stanford, CA: Stanford University Press.

5

Development of a New Clinical Procedure for Conditioning Aversions to Cigarette Smoking with Perceptually Induced Nausea

Russell C. Leaf
Rutgers University

Stacy Lamon
University of Vermont

Betsy Haughton
University of Tennesee

INTRODUCTION

Clinically useful conditioned taste aversions may be most easily established when nausea is used as an unconditioned response (Garb and Stunkard, 1974; Lazarus, 1968; Logue, Logue, & Strauss, 1983; Logue, Ophir & Strauss, 1981; Wilson & Davison, 1969). The argument for pairing taste cues with nausea is simple (Seligman, 1970). Intragastric distress seems to provide biologically appropriate aversive consequences that selectively condition to taste cues (Lamon, Wilson, & Leaf, 1977; Milgram, Krames, & Alloway, 1977; Seligman & Hager, 1972). When taste cues are followed by nausea, aversions develop after very few trials and long interstimulus delays (Revusky & Garcia, 1970).

Clinical methods for establishing nausea-based conditioned aversions have most often used drugs to induce nausea. Nausea has been induced by apomorphine, disulfiram, metronidazole, and emetine (Baker & Cannon, 1979; Elkins, 1975; Lemere, Voegtlin, Broz, O'Hollaren, & Tupper, 1942; Mottin, 1973; Wilson, 1978). Conditioning of nausea-based aversions to cigarette smoking has been reported (Raymond, 1964), and many studies have induced aversions to alcoholic beverages (Rachman & Teasdale, 1969). Despite their persuasive rationale, and even though these procedures have produced intended clinical results, the actions of the drugs used to induce nausea have been incon-

75

sistent, and side effects and toxic sequelae have been frequent, so improved methods have seemed necessary (Boland, Mellor, & Revusky, 1978; Mellor and White, 1978; Pohl, Revusky, and Mellor, 1980).

A wide variety of perceptual experiences induce nausea (Money, 1970; Sartre, 1938; Sontag, 1966; Tyler & Bard, 1949). Motion sickness induced by illusions probably involves the same physiological mechanisms as nausea induced by drugs (Money & Cheung, 1983). Among the possible candidates for clinical use, several illusions initiate nausea more rapidly than any available drug. In clinical settings, visual illusions seem potentially more controllable and safer than drugs or actual motion. When nausea is induced by illusions, clients can control it by closing their eyes, and therefore prevent or terminate untoward effects. We use an illusion that initiates nausea in one or a few minutes and can be terminated in seconds (Dichgans & Brandt, 1973, 1974).

A CLINICAL PILOT STUDY

Our first effort to develop a clinical procedure was a pilot study in which we tried to develop aversions to cigarette smoking. In this study, we sought to pair smoking with the maximum amount of nausea that our clients could tolerate. The clients gave prior informed consent for their treatment procedures, but the development of aversions probably did not depend on any additional voluntary responses. In these cases, the clients had all failed to stop smoking after previous treatment with a variety of self-control procedures. Aversive conditioning was attempted as a "last resort."

Case 1 was a 26-year-old male, employed as an engineer, who smoked approximately 30 cigarettes per day. He had smoked for 12 years. He said he was motivated to quit smoking because his wife was pregnant, and he felt his smoking would effect her and their child's health. He had attempted to quit smoking for four years without success, by a variety of methods.

Case 2 was a 29-year-old male, also employed as an engineer, who smoked approximately 20 cigarettes per day. He had smoked for 14 years. During his earliest years as a smoker, he lived in India and may not have smoked on a daily basis. Since immigrating to the United States, however, he did smoke daily. He reported that he had attempted to quit by several methods for several years, without success, and said that his principal motive was to improve his health.

Case 3 was a 24-year-old female, employed as a secretary, who smoked approximately 30 cigarettes per day. She had smoked for 8 years. She was the wife of a graduate student in clinical psychology who was carrying out research on behavioral self-control procedures. She had tried these (e.g., monitoring, time out, token reinforcement, imagery, etc.) without success. She said she was motivated both by scientific curiosity and by a desire to improve her health.

Case 4 was a 23-year-old female college graduate, employed as a secretary, who smoked approximately 20 cigarettes per day. She had smoked for 7 years.

She had attempted to quit for two years, by resolutions and self-control, without success. Her expressed motives were a desire for self-improvement and a concern for health.

Case 5 was a 24-year-old female college graduate, beginning a career as an actress and singer, who smoked approximately 30 cigarettes per day. She had attempted to quit for two years, by a variety of methods, without success. She said she wanted to improve her voice for both singing and acting roles.

The apparatus for inducing nausea is shown in the left panel of Figure 5.1. It consists of a motor-driven, tent-like cylinder that contains a small stool.

The cylinder is 1.6 m in diameter and 1.8 m in height. It is made of 50 alternating black and white canvas strips, each of which is 10 cm wide, subtending 7.2° of the visual field. They are sewn together and connected to circular tubes at the top and bottom. Each of the circular tubes is made from flexible plastic pipes, and the top tube is cross-braced with light wood strips and attached rigidly to a pulley. The bottom tube hangs free, and the bottom of the tent-like structure can be lifted for entry. Four vertical wood strips are attached to hold the top and bottom tubes in rigid alignment after the client has entered the structure.

The pulley wheel attached to the cylinder is driven by a belt attached to a $\frac{1}{12}$ horsepower electric motor. The motor is controlled by a variable current motor controller that permits us to vary the rotational speed of the cylinder from 0 to 16 rpm.

Each client was read a series of standard instructions describing the procedures that were about to take place. The client then signed an informed consent statement that was approved by the Rutgers University Committee for the Protection of Human Subjects in Research. Each client was given four treatment trials per day for three consecutive days, except as noted below.

Before each conditioning trial, the client was asked to smoke three cigarettes of his or her usual brand at his or her normal rate of smoking. After these cigarettes had been smoked, the client was seated on the stool located in the center of the cylinder, and was asked to maintain a constant visual focus on the area of the cylinder directly in front of him or her. The cylinder was gradually accelerated, over a 10-sec period, from 0 to 16 clockwise revolutions per minute. The client notified the therapist when he or she seemed to be spinning in the direction opposite to that of the cylinder. A buzzer was then activated at 10-sec intervals for the duration of the session. At each sound of the buzzer, the client performed a head tilting sequence (Figure 5.1, upper right panel). The start and stop pattern, range, and timing of this head turning sequence are critical factors that determine whether or not the illusion is nauseogenic (Guedry & Benson, 1978; Lackner & Teixeira, 1977; Smith, 1982; Teixeira & Lackner, 1979; Wood, 1895). This sequence, which took about 3 sec consisted of first tilting the head to the right at a 45° angle, then immediately returning the head to the upright position, pausing briefly, then tilting the head to the left at a 45° angle, and then immediately returning to the upright position. The client repeated the head movement sequence in response to each activation of the buzzer, until he or

FIG. 5.1.   The apparatus for producing illusion-induced nausea is shown in the left panel, the range and pattern of inducing head movements in the upper right panel, and vomiting in the lower right panel.

she felt clearly nauseous. With these clients, any level from minimal queasiness to vomiting could be induced within a few minutes. We encouraged them to continue looking until high levels of nausea occurred on each trial, even if this would sometimes induce vomiting. When the client did not wish to tolerate further nausea, the client simply closed his or her eyes and informed the therapist that the apparatus should be stopped. No client was permitted to endure the procedure for more than 20 min during any single trial. The trials within each treatment session followed each other as rapidly as possible, with intervals between them only long enough for each client to recover from the acute effects of the preceding trial.

OUTCOME

Our clients had no difficulty in assessing the level of nausea or in choosing when to terminate the inducing, unconditioned, stimulation. Even in those cases when they voluntarily allowed nausea to escalate to levels where vomiting occurred, the vomiting was reported as less distressing than vomiting they had previously experienced after drugs (e.g. alcohol) or illness.

Despite their initial ability to tolerate and control the treatment, all of these clients eventually experienced untoward reactions. On the third day of treatment, during the treatment session, each of them reported a variety of negative emotional reactions, including feelings of panic, sadness, and anger. In addition, all five clients complained of some persisting anxiety and depression, lasting for about 1 hr after the final session. All clients were aware that they could terminate treatment at any time, and they were reminded of this frequently during treatment. Client 1 did so after 11 trials, and client 3 did so after 10 trials; and it is likely that the other clients might also have terminated treatment, because of their negative emotional reactions, if the day on which these feelings appeared had not already been scheduled as the final treatment day.

All five clients stopped smoking, except for the smoking required during the treatment trials, after the first treatment day. Each client was contacted frequently, and questioned about whether he or she was smoking, for six months after treatment. Approximately three months after treatment, Client 1 said that he had taken two or three inhalations of a cigarette and was neither pleased nor repulsed by the taste. He said, "It tasted like hot air." Clients 2, 3 and 5 remained abstinent during the six month follow-up period. Client 4 began smoking moderately five days after the end of treatment, and gradually increased her rate of smoking. One month after treatment she was smoking at her pre-treatment level. She said she continued to enjoy smoking cigarettes. This client, interestingly enough, had experienced the least nausea during the treatment period.

Clients 1, 2, 3, and 5 reported that the smell of cigarettes neither bothered them nor seemed pleasant to them. All four of these clients reported that when placed in situations in which they were exposed to cigarette smoking, (e.g., busses, offices, waiting rooms, etc.) they found the smoke to be neither pleasant nor unpleasant, and they said that it did not result in any desire to smoke. Each said that he or she had simply lost the desire to smoke, without acquiring an aversion to smoke *per se*.

We expected our treatment to produce distaste for cigarette smoke. As noted above, clients 1, 2, 3, and 5, all of whom quit smoking, simply reported that they had "lost the desire" to smoke cigarettes. Their reports, which stressed affective neutrality, do not seem consistent with theoretically based predictions that aversions to cigarette smoke should develop (Solomon, 1962). We are puzzled by these findings. Further research is obviously necessary to clarify the relationships between nausea, taste, and aversion (Hallam & Rachman, 1972; Rachman & Seligman, 1976).

Although all motion sickness procedures sometimes produce such reactions (Money, 1970), we did not expect the anxiety and depression that we observed. We had never seen such reactions in earlier studies with illusion-induced nausea (Lamon, Wilson, & Leaf, 1977). The fact that these effects occurred in all five clients, even though the reactions were transient, poses obvious problems for future use of procedures that seek to induce maximal levels of nausea. The absence of these reactions in our previous work, in contrast to their invariable appearance here, may have been at least partly due to the fact that we had previously used a more spaced and less intense treatment procedure. Anxiety and depression might, therefore, be avoided by using more widely spaced and less traumatic conditioning trials (Solomon and Corbit, 1973).

Our clients, with the intense and massed conditioning procedure used here, also vomited more often than our experimental subjects (Lamon, Wilson, and Leaf, 1977). We thought that more intense aversions would be produced if the treatment produced more vomiting, and we encouraged these clients to endure high levels of nausea, even when it induced vomiting (Merbaum, Avimier, and Goldberg, 1979). On further reflection, after observing and talking with these clients, we realized that there was no good reason to assume a simple, single, relationship between aversion intensity and vomiting. Although vomiting is aversive, vomiting terminates nausea and it is therefore an escape response. Vomiting is not necessary to condition powerful, motion-sickness based taste aversions in other species (Fox and Daunton, 1982; Ordy and Brizzee, 1980; Roy and Brizzee, 1979), and it may be undesirable, as well as unnecessary, with humans. The transient emotional reactions we saw may have been due, at least in part, to vomiting. Relatively mild nausea, without vomiting, might have avoided the untoward emotional reactions and, nevertheless, produced strong aversions.

AVERSIONS CONDITIONED WITH MINIMAL QUEASINESS

Our second experiment was designed to test the hypothesis that intense nausea and vomiting were not necessary for the development of powerful taste aversions. This was an analog study of aversions to novel beverages, in which we compared aversions that were developed with moderate nausea to those developed with minimal queasiness.

The principal purpose of this study was to find the lowest level of illusion-induced motion sickness that would produce any measurable degree of taste aversion. Because our interest was focused primarily on weak treatments, we limited the most severe sickness to moderate levels which had never produced intense anxiety or depression. We wished to confirm that moderate levels were generally safe and to explore the least stressful conditions under which the effectiveness of illusion-based conditioning procedures could be maintained.

The subjects were 24 male and 24 female undergraduate students. They were all informed in advance about the procedures of the experiment; they signed informed consent forms approved by the Rutgers Committee for the Protection of Human Subjects in Research, and were debriefed after completion of the experiment.

The Apparatus was the same equipment used in the pilot study, and the general procedure was similar to our previous analog studies (Lamon, Wilson & Leaf, 1977). Subjects were asked to participate in an experiment studying the effects of perceived motion on taste. They were given five experimental sessions, which were alternately taste test and conditioning sessions. Taste and conditioning sessions were carried out in different, procedure-specific rooms.

In the taste sessions (the 1st, 3rd, and 5th) they filled out questionnaires rating the sensory qualities of four beverages (fruit punch, lemon-lime, grape, and orange-flavored drinks made from tap water and powdered mix). Consumption measures were obtained unobtrusively.

Conditioning sessions (the 2nd and 4th) consisted of two trials, spaced 30 min apart. Six male and six female subjects were randomly assigned to each of four treatment groups. One group, the Nausea Conditioning group, was exposed to moderate levels of nausea, using procedures identical to those of the conditioning group in Experiment 1 of our previous studies (Lamon, Wilson and Leaf, 1977). Subjects of this group drank the beverage he or she had consumed most, during the first taste test, immediately prior to and during exposure to the sickness-inducing illusion described above. The other three groups were never allowed to become more than minimally queasy. On each trial, they were instructed to report the point at which they first felt queasy, and the apparatus was then stopped. Among these, only the Queasy Conditioning subjects actually received pairings of their most highly consumed beverage (the *target* beverage) with motion sickness; the other two groups received either immediate or delayed pseudoconditioning trials with unflavored tap water. The Nausea Conditioning subjects, and those of the Queasy Conditioning and Immediate Pseudoconditioning groups were all given conditioning sessions immediately after their first two taste sessions, on the 1st, 3rd and 5th days of the experimental period; while the Delayed Pseudoconditioning subjects were given conditioning sessions 24 hr after their first two taste sessions, on the 2nd and 4th days of the experimental period.

OUTCOME

Because our purpose was to develop a minimally stressful procedure for later clinical application, we chose to transform our data into a form which would be useful for comparing results from a wide range of both clinical and experimental situations. The data for each subject for each beverage for each session were converted into *suppression ratios,* using the formula (later taste session amount − 1st taste session amount)/(later taste session amount + 1st taste session amount). These values can range from −1.00 when a treatment completely suppresses consumption, to 0.00 when it has no effect, to +1.00 when it induces consumption that had been completely absent. Unlike raw data measures, these values have the same range for and give equal weight to the data of each subject, so they provide a basis for judging the effectiveness of treatment in every individual case, a feature which is not only useful in experimental but also in clinical situations.

The effect of the treatments was significant ($p < 0.05$): the Queasy Condition-

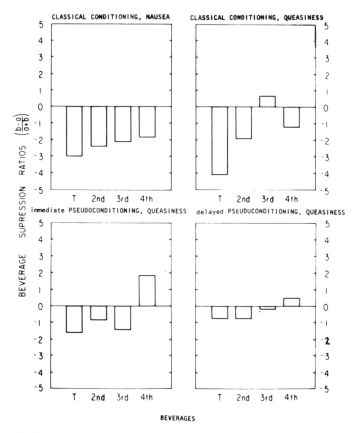

FIG. 5.2.   Suppression ratios for the most highly consumed beverage (the *target* beverage used during conditioning in the Nausea and Queasy Conditioning groups), labeled *T,* and for the less preferred beverages, labeled *2, 3,* and *4* respectively, for each treatment group.

ing group differed significantly from both Pseudoconditioning groups; the Nausea Conditioning group differed significantly only from the Delayed Pseudoconditioning group. The target beverage differed significantly from all other beverages; and beverages 2 and 3 did not differ significantly from each other, but both differed significantly from beverage 4. The final taste-test suppression ratios for each beverage for each group are shown in Figure 5.2. It is clear that the Nausea and Queasy groups clearly suppressed their drinking of the target beverages. Some generalization of conditioning from target to other beverages or some direct effect of the treatments on immediately prior taste test drinking of all beverages, was apparent in all three groups given immediate treatments. The subjects of the Queasy group were, perhaps, slightly less likely to suppress drinking of non-target beverages than were those of the Nausea group. Neither pseudoconditioning group showed clear effects of conditioning, although the subjects of the Immediate group showed a slight conditioned suppression. The weak effects in the Immediate Pseudoconditioning group and on non-target beverages in the Nausea and Queasy groups are consistent with previous findings that our conditioning procedure can be effective after delays of 1 hr. between beverage tasting (during the taste test) and nausea (Gloster, 1980).

It seems clear that minimal queasiness, without side-effects, can produce powerful conditioned taste aversions in humans. Our findings here support the theoretical arguments that intragastric distress has a highly selective, perhaps biologically primitive effect relative to prior taste cues. None of the treatments used here was especially distressing, and no untoward side-effects or terminations from the study occurred; yet the aversions conditioned in the Queasy subjects were quite powerful, and some aspects of our data suggest that even the Immediate Psuedoconditioning subjects may have had weak aversions established because the time interval between their taste session and queasiness induction may have fallen within the range for effective conditioning. Motion-illusion-induced queasiness may provide the most selective, least noxious, and safest method for establishing such aversions.

A CONTROLLED CLINICAL TRIAL

The evidence that queasiness, alone, can produce human taste aversions strengthens both theoretically and empirically based arguments for using a minimal treatment in a controlled clinical trial. The major problem we faced in designing such a trial was not the experimental treatment, which could, ethically and practically, have used motion sickness levels as low as we used with our Queasy or as high as with our Nausea Conditioning groups, but with the control treatment. We know that a variety of treatments can produce substantial, possibly placebo-induced reductions in smoking (Cottraux, Harf, Boissel, Schbath, Bouvard, & Gillet, 1983). We, therefore, tried to include a feature in our experimental design which, we hoped, would maximize placebo effects in *both* experimental and control conditions, so that the baseline conditions for our trial would meet two requirements for any future clinical use—first, that it provide some genuine specific effect beyond the maximal, non-specific, placebo effect that could be obtained without conditioning; and second, that the ratio of risks and costs (i.e., side-effects and distress) to benefits (i.e., effectiveness) be as favorable as possible.

Because placebo effects seem to depend on contact between those who provide treatments and those who receive them (Bailly, Franklin, Leroy, de Bory, & Lavoisier, 1784), we sought to maximize relevant contact by including a *booster session* feature in our experimental design. We offered to give booster sessions, identical to their initial treatment sessions, to all subjects, upon request. These booster sessions were, of course, less stressful for the control subjects than the experimental ones. We assumed that, if our conditioning procedure was effective, it should result in fewer requests for booster sessions than our control treatment, and that this alone might provide a measure of the differential effectiveness of the two treatment conditions. If conditioning were ineffective, on the other hand, its relatively greater stressfulness might still lead to a reduction in requests for booster sessions, and a consequently smaller placebo effect might make the conditioning treatment *less* effective than the control. The booster session feature, thus, provided baseline conditions which were relevant for actual future clinical use.

The subjects were 12 female and 8 male students. All had been smoking for at least two years, had previously tried and failed to stop smoking, knew that they might receive either an experimental or a placebo treatment, volunteered, and signed the informed consent forms required by the Rutgers Committee for the Protection of Human Subjects in Research.

The apparatus was the same as that used in the previous studies. Four male and six female subjects were randomly assigned to each of two treatment groups. Subjects in the Conditioning group were treated like those in the Pilot Study, above, except that they were given three trials per day for only two days, and they were instructed to report during each trial the first time they definitely felt queasy, and the trial was terminated. Subjects in the Sham group were treated like those of the Conditioning group except that the conditioning procedure to which they were exposed was designed to be ineffective, so subjects of the Sham group were matched with those of the Conditioning group, and the durations of their trials were yoked to the durations of Conditioning group subjects. The rationale for treatment given to both groups, was identical; subjects were told that novel perceptual stimulation during smoking produced conditioned aversions, and that the illusion of self-motion that they all experienced might help them stop smoking. The Sham subjects were not instructed to report about queasiness during the trial but they did rate symptoms of motion sickness after each trial. The critical feature of the Sham procedure that caused it to be ineffective, its only difference from the Conditioning procedure aside from reporting about queasiness, was that it required tilting the head forward 45°, rather than from side to side (Lamon, Wilson and Leaf, 1977).

After each conditioning session, each subject and the experimenter (either the second or third author) filled out a three item symptom rating scale on which each item could be scored either 0 = *none*, 1 = *some, not much*, 2 = *rather much*, or 3 = *very much*. Two symptom items were common to both the subject and experimenter scales: nausea and sweating. In addition, the subject scale called for ratings of dizziness which, because of its subjective character, presumably could not be rated by the experimenter; and the experimenter scale called for ratings of pallor which, because the subject could not see his or her image, could not be rated by the subject.

After completion of the treatment sessions, clients were given a number so that they could call the experimenters for booster session treatment, if needed. In addition, they were contacted monthly to obtain self-report data on their smoking levels, to offer booster sessions if they reported they were smoking, and to maintain their morale while they remained abstinent.

The Conditioning and Sham groups differed dramatically in the extent to which they experienced symptoms of motion sickness during the treatment period. The total amounts of self reported symptoms (the sum of the ratings of 0, 1, 2, or 3 combined for all six trials), were significantly greater among the Conditioning than the Sham subjects for nausea (means = 3.90 and 0.50, $p < 0.001$), dizziness (means = 2.10 and 0.40, $p < 0.01$), and sweating (means = 2.70 and 0.50, $p < 0.02$). The total amounts of experimenter reported symptoms were significantly greater when the conditioning subjects were rated for nausea (means = 4.40 and 2.30, $p < 0.05$), and pallor (means = 3.60 and 0.30, $p < 0.001$) but not for sweating (means = 1.10 and 0.10). The apparent over-reporting of nausea and under-reporting of sweating by experimenters, relative to subjects, suggests that valid detection of these symptoms may be difficult for external observers, because of their large subjective component. All the subject self-ratings and the most objective experimenter rating (pallor) agree in indicating that the Conditioning subjects experienced low intensities of motion sickness, on the average, and that the Sham subjects experienced almost none.

The Conditioning and Sham groups did not differ significantly in the numbers who underwent booster sessions (4 Sham and 5 Conditioning) or in numbers of sessions administered (1 session per subject for all 5 Conditioning subjects and 2 Sham subjects, and 2 sessions per subject for the other Sham subjects), partly because the subjects who relapsed would not accept further offers of treatment.

All subjects stopped smoking after either treatment, at least for a few days. Figure 5.3 shows suppression rations, changes in smoking levels, and cigarettes smoked for six months after treatment. As this figure indicates, the Conditioning group smoked somewhat (but non-significantly) more than the Sham group before treatment and much less at the end of the follow-up period; the Sham group

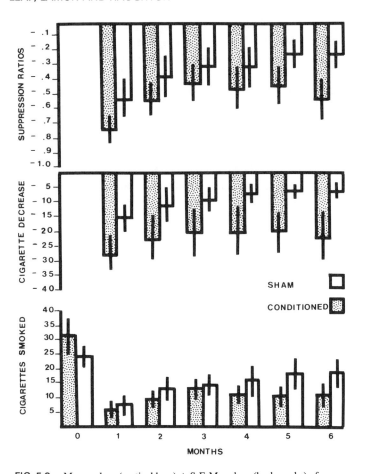

FIG. 5.3.   Mean values (vertical bars) ± S.E.M. values (hash marks) of suppression ratios, changes in numbers of cigarettes smoked, and cigarettes smoked for each month after treatment, for Conditioning and Sham treatment groups.

initially stopped smoking, but relapsed during the follow-up period so that their final smoking levels were not much below their initial levels. At the termination of the study, one sham and four conditioning subjects were completely abstinent. Analyses of variance showed significant treatment relapse with time; smoking was significantly more suppressed during the first month than all later months, and none of the later months differed significantly from each other. As has been found in other studies (Shiffman, 1982), subjects reported that situational emotional distress precipitated most relapses; by the end of the follow-up period, one of the Conditioning subjects and six of the Sham subjects had relapsed completely, to pre-treatment smoking levels. These analyses also showed that the trend toward greater suppression in the Conditioning than the Sham group did not reach conventional levels of statistical significance. This latter result is not a test of the difference between the two treatments, however, because we used a control treatment that was not only initially 100% successful, but had some apparent effectiveness even at the end of our follow-up period. The two treatment groups therefore should not have differed during the early part of our follow-up period and might not have differed statistically for the follow-up period as a whole, even if the Conditioning treatment was much more effective, over time, than its Sham control. The critical test of differential effectiveness is based not on the whole duration of follow-up, but on the final smoking levels. When the appropriate statistical test, which must be non-parametric because of the numerical restrictions on suppression ratios, is computed, the six month suppression ratios for the Conditioning subjects are significantly more negative than those of the Sham subjects (Mann-Whitney $U = 81$, $p < 0.05$).

The findings of this study indicate that illusion-induced queasiness, of minimal intensity, is sufficient to establish lasting, clinically useful, taste aversions. They support the hypothesis that nausea has a special, biologically predisposed, value for conditioning such aversions, but we must remain cautious, and await clarification of several issues, before we can treat the *preparedness* hypothesis as either a definitive explanation of our results or a definitive theoretical basis for designing treatments for smoking. Although self-report is a highly reliable and valid outcome criterion (Colletti, Supnick, & Abueg, 1982) it would be desirable to obtain physical evidence of smoking reduction. It would also be helpful to know how credible each of the two treatments seemed, and whether their credibility was as similar as their rationales (Hynd, Stratton, & Severson, 1978). It would also be prudent to make further efforts to maximize the effectiveness of our placebo inducing procedures (Colletti & Brownell, 1982), and it would be useful for comparative purposes to know if our methods are as effective and less distressing than the presently most widely used nausea-based technique, the rapid-smoking treatment method (Danaher & Lichtenstein, 1978; Hall, Sachs, & Hall, 1979; Lichtenstein & Glasgow, 1977; Lichtenstein & Rodrigues, 1977; Linberg, Horan, Hodgson, & Buskirk, 1982; Poole, Dunn, Sanson-Fisher, & German, 1982; Poole, Sanson-Fisher, & German, 1981; Poole, Sanson-Fisher, German, & Harker, 1980). It is important to know whether or not conditioning based on illusion-induced nausea would add to the effects of a good multiple-component or sequential treatment program (Colletti, Supnick, & Rizzo, 1982; Elliot & Denney, 1978; Foxx & Axelroth, 1983; Lando & McGovern, 1982), and it is necessary for public policy formation to know how this treatment, which cannot easily be self-administered, compares in effectiveness, cost and relapse rate to the best self-help and non-professionally administered procedures (Glasgow, Schafer, & O'Neill, 1981; Jeffery, Danaher, Killen, Farquhar, & Kinnier, 1982; Orleans and Shipley, 1982).

The diseases caused by smoking may be the most important public health consequences of recreational drug use. Although smokers persist in believing that their habit has beneficial effects, they seem to be incorrect (Costa & Mc-Crae, 1981), and, despite widespread denial that it may have deleterious personal consequences (Weinstein, 1980), smoking continues to have an enormous personal, as well as social, cost (AMA, 1978; Boss, Sparrow, Rose, & Weiss, 1981; DHEW, 1977; Lall, Stinghi, Gurnani, & Garg, 1980; United States Surgeon General, 1979). Understanding how to treat it most effectively remains one of the most pressing problems, both theoretically and practically, for researchers interested in either behavior modification or in social influence (Condiotte & Lichtenstein, 1981).

Further research defining the nature and power of involuntary conditioning processes will help us weigh the use of methods that emphasize the control of "voluntary" behavior by reflexive processes (Leaf, 1964; Solomon and Turner, 1962; Turner and Solomon, 1962). It is necessary to understand both their nature and their power in order to decide whether these methods should continue to be used at current rates, be prohibited or used less frequently, or be used more widely. The methods described here may eventually provide a practical, inexpensive, and rationally based conditioning treatment for smoking; they are simpler and more consistent than previous conditioning methods (Danaher & Lichtenstein, 1978; Franks, Fried & Asheim, 1966). Practicality and a good theoretical rationale are, unfortunately, no guarantee of either the clinical effectiveness or suitability of new treatment methods. The data we have reported here suggest that our methods may prove effective and ethically responsible, but definitive conclusions will require additional controlled outcome studies.

REFERENCES

American Medical Association-Education and Research Foundation. (1978). Committee for Research on Tobacco and Health *Tobacco and Health*. Chicago, Illinois: American Medical Association Education and Research Foundation.

Bailly, J. S., Franklin, B., Leroy, C., de Bory, G., & Lavoisier, A.-L (1784, September). Expose des experiences qui ont ete faites pour l'examen du magnetisme animal. Lu a l'Academie des Sciences. Imprime Royale.

Baker, T. B., & Cannon, D. S. (1979). Taste aversion therapy with alcoholics: Techniques and evidence of a conditioned response. *Behaviour Research and Therapy, 17,* 239–242.

Boland, F. J., Mellor, C. S., & Revusky, S. (1978). Chemical aversion treatment of alcoholism: Lithium as the aversive agent. *Behaviour Research and Therapy, 16,* 401–409.

Boss, E. R., Sparrow, D., Rose, C. L., & Weiss, S. T. (1981). Longitudinal effects of age and smoking cessation on pulmonary function. *American Review of Respiratory Disease. 123(4, Part 1).* 378–381.

Colletti, G., & Brownell, K. D. (1982). The physical and emotional benefits of social support applications to obesity, smoking, and alcoholism. In M. Hersen, R. M. Eisler, & P. M. Miller (Eds.), *Progress in behavior modification, Vol. 13,* New York: Academic Press.

Colletti, G., Supnick, J. A., & Abueg, F. R. (1982). Assessment of the relationship between self-reported smoking rate and ecolyzer measurement. *Addictive Behaviors, 7,* 183–186.

Colletti, G., Supnick, J. A., & Rizzo, A. A. (1982). Long-term follow-up (3–4 years) of treatment for smoking reduction. *Addictive Behaviors, 7,* 429–433.

Condiotte, M. M., & Lichtenstein, E. (1981). Self-efficacy and relapse in smoking cessation programs. *Journal of Consulting and Clinical Psychology, 49(5)*, 648–658.

Costa, P. T., Jr., & McCrae, R. (1981). Stress, smoking motives, and psychological well-being: The illusory benefits of smoking. *Advances in Behaviour Research and Therapy, 3*, 125–150.

Cottraux, J. A., Harf, R., Boissel, J.-P., Schbath, J., Bouvard, M., & Gillet, J. (1983). Smoking cessation with behavior therapy or acupuncture—A controlled study. *Behaviour Research and Therapy, 21(4)*. 417–424.

Danaher, B. G., & Lichtenstein, E. (1978). *Become an ex-smoker*. Englewood Cliffs, NJ: Prentice-Hall.

Department of Health, Education and Welfare. (1977). *Proceedings of the 3rd world conference on smoking and health. II: Health consequences, education, cessation activities, and social action* (DHEW Publication No. [NIH] 77-413) Washington, DC: U.S. Government Printing Office.

Dichgans, J., & Brandt, T. (1973). Optokinetic motion sickness and pseudo-coriolis effects induced by moving visual stimuli. *Acta Oto-Laryngologica, 76*, 339–348.

Dichgans, J., & Brandt, T. (1974). The psychophysics of visually induced perception of self-motion and tilt. In F. O. Schmitt, & F. G. Worden, (Eds.), *The neurosciences: Third study program* (pp. 123–129). Cambridge, MA: MIT Press.

Elkins, R. L. (1975). Aversion therapy for alcoholism: Chemical, electrical or verbal imaginary? *Internation Journal of the Addictions, 10*, 157–159.

Elliot, C. H., & Denney, D. R. (1978). A multiple-component treatment approach to smoking reduction. *Journal of Consulting and Clinical Psychology, 46(6)*, 1330–1339.

Fox, R. A., & Daunton, N. G. (1982). Conditioned feeding suppression in rats produced by cross-coupled and simple motion. *Aviation, Space, and Environmental Medicine, 53*, 218–220.

Foxx, R. M., & Axelroth, E. (1983). Nicotine fading, self-monitoring and cigarette fading to produce cigarette abstinence or controlled smoking. *Behaviour Research and Therapy, 21(1)*, 17–27.

Franks, C. M., Fried, R., & Asheim. (1966). An improved apparatus for the aversive conditioning of cigarette smokers. *Behaviour Research and Therapy, 4* 301–308.

Garb, J. L., & Stunkard, A. J. (1974). Taste aversions in man. *American Journal of Psychiatry, 131*, 1204–1207.

Glasgow, R. E., Schafer, L., & O'Neill, H. K. (1981). Self-help books and amount of therapist contact in smoking cessation programs. *Journal of Consulting and Clinical Psychology, 49(5)*, 659–667.

Gloster, J. L. (1980). *The effects of consumption versus non-consumption of a flavored beverage and immediate versus delayed conditioning on pseudo-coriolis induced taste aversions.* Unpublished Ph.D. thesis, Rutgers University, New Brunswick, NJ.

Guedry, F. E., Jr., & Benson, A. J. (1978). Coriolis cross-coupling effects: Disorienting and nauseogenic or not? *Aviation, Space, and Environmental Medicine, 49*, 29–35.

Hall, R. G., Sachs, D. P. L., & Hall, S. M. (1979). Medical risk and therapeutic effectiveness of rapid smoking. *Behavior Therapy, 10*, 249–259.

Hallam, R., & Rachman, S. (1972). Theoretical problems of aversion therapy. *Behaviour Research and Therapy, 10*, 341–353.

Hynd, G. W., Stratton, T. T., & Severson, H. H. (1978). Smoking treatment strategies, expectancy outcomes, and credibility in attention-placebo control conditions. *Journal of Clinical Psychology, 34(1)*, 182–186.

Jeffery, R. W., Danaher, B. G., Killen, J., Farquhar, J. W., & Kinnier, R. (1982). Self-administered programs for health behavior change: Smoking cessation and weight reduction by mail. *Addictive Behaviors, 7*, 57–63.

Lackner, J. R., & Teixeira, R. A. (1977). Optokinetic motion sickness: Continuous head movements attenuate the visual induction of apparent self-rotation and symptoms of motion sickness. *Aviation, Space, and Environmental Medicine, 48*, 248–253.

Lall, K. B., Stinghi, S., Gurnani, M., & Garg, O. P. (1980). Somatotype, physical growth, and sexual maturation in young male smokers. *Journal of Epidemiological Community Health, 34(4),* 295–298.

Lamon, S., Wilson, G. T., & Leaf, R. C. (1977). Human classical aversion conditioning: Nausea versus electric shock in the reduction of target beverage consumption, *Behaviour Research and Therapy, 15,* 313–320.

Lando, H. A., & McGovern, P. G. (1982). Three year data on a behavioral treatment for smoking: A follow-up note. *Addictive Behaviors, 7,* 177–181.

Lazarus, A. A. (1968). Aversion therapy and sensory modalities: Clinical impressions. *Perceptual and Motor Skills. 27,* 178.

Leaf, R. C. (1964). Avoidance response evocation as a function of prior disriminative fear conditioning. *Journal of Comparative and Physiological Psychology, 58,* 446–450.

Lemere, F., Voegtlin, W. L., Broz, W. R., O'Hollaren, P., & Tupper, W. E. (1942). The conditioned reflex treatment of chronic alcoholism. viii. A review of six years' experience with this treatment of 1,526 patients. *Journal of the American Medical Association, 120(4),* 269–271.

Lichtenstein, E., & Glasgow, R. E. (1977). Rapid smoking: Side effects and safeguards. *Journal of Consulting and Clinical Psychology, 45(5),* 815–821.

Lichtenstein, E., & Rodrigues, M. R. (1977). Long-term effects of rapid smoking treatment for dependent cigarette smokers. *Addictive Behavior, 2(2–3),* 109–112.

Linberg, S. E., Horan, J. J., Hodgson, J. E., & Buskirk, E. R. (1982). Some physiological consequences of the rapid smoking treatment for cigarette addiction. *Archives of Environmental Health, 37(2),* 88–92.

Logue, A. W., Logue, K. R., & Strauss, K. E. (1983). The acquisition of taste aversions in humans with eating and drinking disorders. *Behaviour Research and Therapy, 21(3),* 275–289.

Logue, A. W., Ophir, I., & Strauss, K. E. (1981). The acquisition of taste aversion in humans. *Behaviour Research and Therapy, 19,* 319–333.

Mellor, C. S., & White, H. P. (1978). Taste aversions to alcoholic beverages conditioned by motion sickness. *American Journal of Psychiatry, 135,* 125–126.

Merbaum, M., Avimier, R., & Goldberg, J. (1979). The relationship between aversion, group training and vomiting in the reduction of smoking behavior. *Addictive Behaviors, 4,* 279–285.

Milgram, N. W., Krames, L., & Alloway, T. M. (Eds.). (1977). *Food aversion learning.* New York: Plenum Press.

Money, K. E. (1970). Motion sickness. *Physiological Reviews, 50,* 1–39.

Money, K. E., & Cheung, B. S. (1983). Another function of the inner ear: Facilitation of the emetic response to poisons. *Aviation Space, and Environmental Medicine, 54(3),* 208–211.

Mottin, J. L. (1973). Drug-induced attenuation of alcohol consumption: A review and evaluation of claimed, potential or current therapies. *Quarterly Journal for the Study of Alcohol, 34,* 444–472.

Ordy, J. M., & Brizzee, K. R. (1980). Motion sickness in the squirrel monkey. *Aviation, Space, and Environmental Medicine, 51,* 215–223.

Orleans, C. S., & Shipley, R. H. (1982). Worksite smoking cessation iniatives: Review and recommendations. *Addictive Behaviors, 7,* 1–16.

Pohl, R. W., Revusky, S., & Mellor, C. S. (1980). Drugs employed in the treatment of alcoholism: Rat data suggest they are unnecessary. *Behaviour Research and Therapy, 18,* 71–78.

Poole, A. D., Dunn, J., Sanson-Fisher, R. W., & German, G. A. (1982). The rapid-smoking technique: Subject characteristics and treatment outcome. *Behaviour Research and Therapy, 20(1),* 1–7.

Poole, A. D., Sanson-Fisher, R. W., & German, G. A. (1981). The rapid-smoking technique: Therapeutic effectiveness. *Behavior Research Therapy, 19(5),* 389–397.

Poole, A. D., Sanson-Fisher, R. W., German, G. A., & Harker, J. (1980). The rapid-smoking technique: Some physiological effects. *Behaviour Research and Therapy, 18(6),* 581–586.

Rachman, S., & Seligman, M. E. P. (1976). Unprepared phobias: "Be prepared." *Behaviour Research and Therapy, 14,* 333–338.

Rachman, S., & Teasdale, J. (1969). *Aversion therapy and behaviour disorders: An analysis.* London: Routledge and Kegan Paul.

Raymond, M. (1964). The treatment of addiction by aversion conditioning with apomorphine. *Behaviour Research and Therapy, 1,* 287–291.

Revusky, S., & Garcia, J. (1970). Learned association over long delays. In G. H. Bower, (Ed.). *The psychology of learning and motivation: Advances in research and therapy,* New York: Academic Press.

Roy, M. A., & Brizzee, K. R. (1979). Motion sickness-induced food aversions in the squirrel monkey. *Physiology and Behavior, 23,* 39–41.

Sartre, J. P. (1938). *La nausee.* Paris: Gallimard.

Seligman, M. E. P. (1970). On the generality of the laws of learning. *Psychological Review, 77,* 406–418.

Seligman, M. E. P., & Hager, J. L. (Eds.). (1972). *Biological boundaries of learning.* New York: Appleton-Century-Crofts.

Shiffman, S. (1982). Relapse following smoking cessation: A situational analysis. *Journal of Consulting and Clinical Psychology, 50(1),* 71–86.

Smith, D. E. A. (1982). A statistical examination of three approaches for predicting motion sickness. *Aviation, Space, and Environmental Medicine, 53,* 162–165.

Solomon, R. L. (1962). Punishment. *American Psychologist, 19,* 239–253.

Solomon, R. L., & Corbit, J. D. (1973). An opponent process theory of motivation: II. Cigarette addiction. *Psychological Bulletin, 81,* 158–171.

Solomon, R. L., & Turner, L. H. (1962). Discriminative classical conditioning under curare can later control discriminative avoidance responses. *Psychological Review, 69,* 202–219.

Sontag, S. (1966). The anthropologist as hero. In *Against interpretation, and other essays* (pp. 69–81). New York: Farrar, Straus and Giroux.

Teixeira, R. A., & Lackner, K. A. (1979). Optokinetic motion sickness: Attenuation of visually-induced apparent self-rotation by passive head movements. *Aviation, Space, and Environmental Medicine, 50,* 264–266.

Turner, L. H., & Solomon, R. L. (1962). Human traumatic avoidance learning: Theory and experiments on the operant-respondent distinction. *Psychological Monographs, 70,* (Whole No. 559), 1–32.

Tyler, D. B., & Bard, P. (1949). Motion sickness. *Physiological Reviews, 29,* 311–369.

U.S. Surgeon General. (1979). *Smoking and health: A report of the surgeon general,* (DHEW Publication No. [PHS] 79-50066). Washington, DC: U.S. Government Printing Office.

Weinstein, N. D. (1980). Unrealistic optimism about future life events. *Journal of Personality and Social Psychology, 39(5),* 806–820.

Wilson, G. T. (1978). Alcoholism and aversion therapy: Issues, ethics and evidence. In G. A. Marlatt & P. E. Nathan (Ed.). *Behavioral approaches to alcoholism* (pp. 90–113). New Brunswick, NJ: Rutgers Center of Alcohol Studies.

Wilson, G. T., & Davison, G. C. (1969). Aversion techniques in behavior therapy: Some theoretical and meta-theoretical considerations. *Journal of Consulting and Clinical Psychology, 33,* 327–329.

Wood, R. W. (1895). The 'haunted swing' illusion. *Psychological Review, 2,* 277–278.

INTEGRATION OF INFORMATION

6 Reasoning in the Rat Reconsidered

Abraham H. Black
Andrew Dalrymple
McMaster University

This paper is concerned with animal problem solving, in particular with problems that have been characterized as requiring an animal to reason. The problems which fall into this class differ markedly—for example, delayed responding, detour, multiple choice, and Maier's three table reasoning tasks (Munn, 1950). We shall focus on a subset of these tasks which are presumed to involve reasoning, here defined as the combination of representations of events that have not been experienced in temporal contiguity (Maier, 1932a,b; Deutsch, 1956a).

The main purposes of this paper are threefold. The first is to analyze the structure of this set of reasoning tasks. The second is to provide an account of the psychological processes that might be occurring during the solution of the problem. The third is to employ this account to predict the conditions that will lead to successful problem solving. We attempt to evaluate these predictions with data that were obtained in previous research as well as with some recent data of our own.

BACKGROUND

Early research on problem solving was concerned with the specification of the mental and behavioral processes that were employed in the attempt to reach a solution. For certain problems, reasoning was proposed to be the primary solution process (Maier, 1932a,b; Munn, 1950). To evaluate this proposal, one has to formulate an operational characterization of reasoning.

Three features are common to many of the definitions of reasoning that were given in the early research on animal problem solving. One is the notion that animals form central representations of events in the environment. The second is that these representations are related to each other—usually in terms of standard dimensions such as space, time and similarity. (A particular set of related representations is what Tolman (1948) called a *cognitive map*.) The third and crucial feature is the operations carried out by the animal on these representations and on their relationships. Maier, for example, suggested the one basic operation in reasoning is the combination of representations of events that had not been experienced together. Integrations produced by reasoning "require the ability to bring together spontaneously two elements of past experience without having them previously associated by contiguity" (Maier, 1932a, p. 46).

More recently, Deutsch has defined reasoning in a similar manner: "We talk of reasoning when the animal has to combine two sets of information in some way in order to find a solution. All the information which the animal must utilize in order to solve the problem is never presented together. The animal is then set a goal which it can only reach without error by 'putting together the various pieces of knowledge'." (Deutsch, 1956, p. 115). Tolman (1932, p. 175) considered the process of combining experiences to be one type of *inference,* and contrasted solution by inference with solution on the basis of directly perceived stimuli or simple memory. The specification of operations that are carried out on a set of related representations is fundamental.

Researchers who argued that animals employed reasoning in problem solving directed their efforts to finding or constructing problems that could be solved only by reasoning—a task arduous enough in itself without the impediments added by imprecision of the operational definitions of reasoning. Their opponents, of course, attempted to demonstrate that these problems could be solved in other ways; the other ways usually took the form of solution by means of S-R mechanisms—that is, the classical conditioning and the operant reinforcement of particular responses. To facilitate description of the issues that developed in this controversy, we describe two problems that are representative of the tasks in which we are interested. These tasks usually involved three sequential stages. We call these *component-modification problems.*

A first example is provided by Maier's three table reasoning problem (Maier, 1932a). The apparatus consisted of three small distinctive elevated tables (A, B and C) which were connected by three open elevated runways that met at a point equidistant from the tables. The tables had walls so that the rats could not see from one table to another. There were three phases to the experiment. In Phase 1, the rats were allowed to explore the tables and runways. In Phase 2, the rats were placed directly on one table (A) and fed there. Then, in Phase 3, the rats were placed on another table and required to choose between Tables A and C. The question was, "Do the rats return to A?"

A second example is provided by Tolman and Gleitman (1949). The apparatus was a T-maze with very distinctive enclosed goal boxes (A and B). Again, there were three phases to the experiment. In Phase 1, the rats were trained to go to *both* goal boxes of the T-maze to obtain food. Reinforcements were distributed equally to the two sides. In Phase 2, the rats were placed directly into one goal box (B) and shocked there and into the other goal box (A) and fed there. In Phase 3, the rats were placed in the start-box of the T-maze. The question was "Do rats run to goal box A or not?"

The rats were capable of solving these problems, but successful performance was not sufficient to convince everyone that reasoning was involved. Skeptics argued that it was necessary to provide a plausible account of the reasoning process and to demonstrate the implausibility of a solution based on S-R associations.

The account of *solution by reasoning* usually took the following form. In Phase 1, representations of the experimental apparatus, the surrounding environment, and their relationships were established. In Phase 2, an additional set of representations was established by exposing the animal to another set of events. In Phase 3, the animal was replaced in the Phase 1 situation and was required to make a choice between the event manipulated in Phase 2 and some other event. The assumption is made that the rat cannot perceive those events directly when it is making the choice in Phase 3. A correct choice in Phase 3 was assumed to indicate that the animal had combined the Phase 1 experience with Phase 2 experiences and employed the memory of this integrated information to guide its choice. In short, *correct choice could have occurred only if the rat could reason.*

Two control procedures were usually employed to rule out solution by S-R association: (To simplify the exposition we will limit the discussion of possible S-R solutions to the Tolman and Gleitman (1949) experiment.)

1. *Direct reinforcement of stimuli or stimulus generalization:* One obvious S-R mechanism arises when the subject can perceive stimuli in Phase 3 that have been associated with shock in Phase 2, resulting in avoidance of these aversive stimuli. In an effort to rule out this possibility, Tolman and Gleitman employed enclosed goal boxes and placed them in different rooms when the rats were shocked in Phase 2. This ensured that those stimuli in the presence of which shock was administered could not be perceived in Phase 3, nor generalized to the choice point stimuli. (Others have used a between-groups comparison to control for conditioning of extramaze stimuli [see Gaffan & Gowling, 1984].)

2. *Direct reinforcement of responses:* To ensure that there was not direct conditioning of stimuli or of responses in an S-R chain leading to shock in the goal box in Phase 2, Tolman and Gleitman placed the rat directly into the goal box in Phase 2.

While taking these precautions did make it more difficult to interpret these results on animal problem solving in terms of S-R associations, they did not settle the controversy. This failure to resolve the issue occurred in part because the results of additional experiments were not uniformly supportive of the reasoning position, and in part because S-R theoreticians developed the r_g-s_g mechanism to account for some of the features of the reasoning data (Moltz, 1957; Spence, 1956).

Our purpose in this paper, however, is not to provide an extensive analysis of this controversy, nor to revive arguments as to whether reasoning is necessarily involved in animal problem solving (e.g., Deutsch, 1956; Gonzalez & Diamond, 1960). Rather, our purpose is to present what we think is a more suitable account of component-modification problem solving, and to employ this account to explain the reported successes and failures to solve such problems.

AN ALTERNATIVE FORMULATION OF THE SOLUTION PROCESSES

Those aspects of the reasoning process assumed to be essential for problem-solving are the operations that are performed on central representations and on their relationships. Most specifications of these operations for component-modification problems state simply that animals put together isolated bits of information from the first two phases. This specification seems vague and incomplete. The experiences may be isolated in the sense that they are separated in time and so cannot be associated directly by contiguity, but the experiences are not isolated in the sense that they contain no common elements; in every case in which successful problem solving was observed, there was a common subset of events to which the animal was exposed in the first two phases. In the Maier experiment, the table which was empty in Phase 1 becomes associated with food in Phase 2. In the Tolman and Gleitman experiment, the goal-box which was associated with food in Phase 1 becomes associated with shock in Phase 2. Following this line of argument, one could suggest further that in Phase 2 the motivational significance of the subset of elements that is being experienced for a second time is modified. For this reason, the term *component-modification* seems appropriate for labeling the class of problems in which we are interested.

This characterization of the processes involved in the solution of component-modification problems is analogous to that employed by Rescorla in accounting for the results of research on the effects of changing the value of the US in classical conditioning and on sensory preconditioning (Holland & Rescorla, 1975a; Rescorla, 1973, 1974; Rescorla & Heth, 1975; Rizley & Rescorla, 1972). The experiments on US modification in classical conditioning are analogous to experiments in which reinforcements were presented in Phase 1, and the sensory preconditioning experiments are analogous to experiments in which the animal is exposed to the apparatus without being reinforced in Phase 1.

The essential features of our characterization are as follows:

1. In Phase 1, a set of organized associational relationships among all the components (a cognitive map) is established.

2. In Phase 2, the motivational significance of a Phase 1 component is changed.

3. It is assumed that the components which are common to Phases 1 and 2 will be treated by the rat as being the same.

4. In Phase 3, the animal is reintroduced to the Phase 1 situation. Given points 1, 2 and 3 above, the organized associational relationships (cognitive map) that were established in Phase 1 are unchanged, except for the motivational significance of one component. (The animal is not permitted to perceive the events whose motivational significance was modified in Pahse 2). The modified component's effect on behavior is mediated through the already existing relationships among the other components of the cognitive map.

To distinguish this account from other cognitive and S-R accounts of problem solving, we call it a *cognitive map-redintegrative* process or *CMR* process for short. One can consider the CMR process as the simplest member of a class of cognitive hypotheses about the processes involved in the solution of component-modification problems.

We do not assume that *only* the CMR process occurs in component-modification experiments. Our position is that animals can learn a variety of different things during Phase 1 and, as a consequence, may attempt to solve the problem in different ways. It may be that an animal forms a cognitive map of the environment under certain circumstances, S-R associations under others, and perhaps both under still others. What *is* learned in Phase 1 determines success or failure in Phase 3. If an animal learns about the location of reinforcement in Phase 1, the problem could be solved by a CMR process. If it learns to make a particular turning response in Phase 1, the CMR process cannot be employed, and some other method of solving the problem would be attempted. We assume that what is learned in Phase 1 is controlled by the experimental conditions. For convenience, we call the basis of the performance in Phase 1 a *strategy*. The term strategy captures, we hope, the idea that only part of what has been learned may be functional at a given time. We call the process employed during all phases of a component modification problem, a *problem solving method*. For some problems, solutions occur when only one particular method is employed; for other problems, a solution occurs when any one of several different methods are employed.

In summary, we propose that different methods can be employed in a given problem solving situation, that the experimental conditions determine the selection of strategy and method, that only certain methods lead to the solution of a given problem, and that the CMR process results in the solution of component modification problems.

EVIDENCE ON CMR PROCESSES

Is there any evidence which indicates that simple S-R mechanisms cannot account for component modification problem solving? Such evidence would be consistent with the view that CMR or other cognitive problem solving methods are involved.

We must first identify operational procedures for ruling out S-R interpretations of the data. The first requirement is that there should be no direct reinforcement of choice point responses and/or stimuli, and the second requirement is that stimuli which are reinforced in Phase 2 not be present in Phase 3. The operational procedure that is usually employed to meet these requirements in Phase 2 is to place the animal directly in a section of the apparatus which is isolated from the rest of the apparatus. We shall consider separately (a) the direct placement and (b) the isolation of the section of the apparatus into which the animal is placed.

When direct placement is *not* employed (i.e., the animal is permitted to run from a start box to a goal box in Phase 2 and is then reinforced or punished when it reaches the goal box), successful performance could have resulted from the CMR process or from the direct reinforcement of responses and/or stimuli. Data suggests that it is the latter, because the direct placement procedure failed in a number of experiments, whereas the procedure permitting the animal to run through the apparatus in Phase 2 resulted in successful problem-solving (Holman, 1975; Honzik & Tolman, 1936, exp. 10; Morrison & Collyer, 1974; Tolman, 1933).

The simplest way to isolate the section of the apparatus into which an animal is placed is to employ what might be called a *between-room design*. The goal is in one room, and the rest of the apparatus in another room; the walls of the rooms are constructed to prevent visual, auditory, olfactory, or other stimuli from being transmitted from room to room. When these conditions are not met, we might say that we have a ''within-room design.'' In the latter case, cues associated with the goal box can be perceived in the rest of the apparatus. The results of problems that employ within-room designs are necessarily ambiguous, because the animal could navigate to the correct location in the maze using CMR processes or could do so in terms of directly perceived stimuli.

The closest approximation to the design which meets both requirements is provided by the experiments of Tolman and Gleitman (1949) and Gleitman and Herman (1962). In these experiments, the goal boxes were completely enclosed, which, in a sense, is equivalent to the use of a room (albeit a small one) for each goal box. Also, the goal box enclosures were moved to a new room during Phase 2 so that olfactory, auditory, and other stimuli from the original room would not be available. In both experiments, solution of the problem did occur, which indicates that S-R explanations will not account for the solution of some component-modification problems and which suggests that CMR or some similar process does occur.

In the within-room situation, animals can solve the problem by using the CMR process or some other alternatives. We may ask therefore whether there is any evidence from within-room situations indicating that S-R alternatives have *not* been employed. The standard S-R approach to the analysis of the Maier three table problem predicts that successful solution occurs because distant cues are associated with the correct table in Phase 2, and the animal approaches these positively reinforced cues in Phase 3. If this hypothesis is correct, exploration of the apparatus in Phase 1 should be unnecessary, because the necessary learning occurs during Phase 2. Experiments employing the three table reasoning problems (Maier, 1929, exps. E, F; Stahl & Ellen, 1974, exp. 4) and a T-maze paradigm (Seward, 1949) provide a test of this hypothesis. In these experiments one group of rats was allowed to explore the apparatus during Phase 1 while another was not. Only the group with the opportunity for preliminary exploration solved the problem; the other group performed at chance level. These data indicate that under some circumstances, an available simple S-R method is *not* employed to solve these component-modification problems.

Although not overwhelming, the evidence does suggest that CMR processes are employed to solve the component-modification problems. Given that they are used, what predictions about the conditions that lead to success or to failure in component-modification problem-solving follow from the analysis of CMR processes? Do these conditions actually result in success and failure as predicted? Finally, what conditions will lead an animal to employ CMR processes in component-modification problem solving? The answer to the second of these questions will determine to a considerable extent the utility of our analysis.

DETERMINERS OF SUCCESS AND FAILURE IN PROBLEM SOLVING

The analysis of the CMR process suggest several conditions which must be met if the problem is to be solved. Three of these are discussed, and the relevant data are presented.

The Identity Requirement

The animal will fail to solve the problem if the component modified in Phase 2 is not perceived to be identical to the corresponding Phase 1 component. Experiments have shown that differences between the Phase 1 and Phase 2 components result in a decrement in problem-solving performance. Denny and Davis (1951), for example, employed different apparatuses in Phase 1 and Phase 2 (a T-maze in Phase 1 and straight runway in Phase 2) and found no effects of Phase 2 treatment. Also, other experiments contained control groups in which the Phase 2 goal box differed markedly from the Phase 1 goal box. (These groups controlled for the effects of the operation that was employed to change the motivational significance of the goal box.) A marked difference in the properties of the goal box resulted in a decrement or failure of problem-solving (Barch, Ratner, & Morgan, 1965; Brown & Halas, 1957c; Dyal, 1962, 1963, 1964; Gonzalez & Diamond, 1960; Gonzalez & Shepp, 1965, exps. 1 and 2; Honzik & Tolman, 1936, exp. 6; Miller, 1935, exps. 1 and 3; Seward, Jones, & Summers, 1960; Thomas, 1958).

These results tempt one to propose that perceived equivalence of the corresponding Phase 2 and Phase 1 components can be assured simply by making the Phase 2 component physically identical to the Phase 1 component. There are, however, two difficulties: First, the Phase 2 and Phase 1 components need to be identical in terms of *distinctive features,* which are defined as those which differentiate that component from other parts of the apparatus. These may be extra- or intra-apparatus cues or both. An experiment by Gonzalez and Diamond (1960) illustrates the importance of such distinctive features. They employed a straight runway. For one group of rats the goal box was identical to the runway and start-box; for a second group, the goal box was different from the runway and start-box. The group for which the goal box was different from the rest of the runway showed a more profound effect of the Phase 2 treatment than the group in which the goal box was the same as the rest of the apparatus. Hughes, Davis, and Grice (1960) obtained similar results. Apparently, the less distinctive the features of the manipulated component, the smaller is the effect of the Phase 2 treatment. Data from Bugelski, Coyer, and Rogers (1952), Seward (1949, exp. 3A), Stein (1957), and Swift and Wike (1958) support this prediction. In the extreme case, when the component modified in Phase 2 has no distinctive features, one might expect no effect of the Phase 2 treatment.

The second difficulty in making the Phase 1 and Phase 2 components physically identical arises from the effort to rule out S-R interpretations by avoiding the reinforcement of stimuli in Phase 2 that could be perceived in Phase 3. Honzik and Tolman (1936), and Denny and Ratner (1959), for example, have shown that the presence of extra maze cues that can be perceived from the choice point potentiates the effect of the Phase 2 treatment. In a within-room design, the attempt in Phase 2 to prevent the reinforcement of stimuli that might be perceived in Phase 3 often leads the experimenter to carry out Phase 2 in a new situation, and this *mutatus mutandus* decreases the likelihood that the Phase 2 component will be treated as identical to the Phase 1 component because they occur in different extramaze contexts. If a discrimination is formed, the identity requirement is not met, and the animal cannot solve the problem. For example, Honzik and Tolman (1936, exp. 6) employed a T-maze with two open roof goal boxes which were identical in terms of within-apparatus cues. The only distinctive cues, therefore, were extra-apparatus cues. When the goal box was placed in a different location in Phase 2, solution of the problem in Phase 3 did *not* take place. Presumably, the different extra-maze cues contributed to the failure to treat as identical the Phase 2 and Phase 1 goal boxes. It is important to note that when successful performance has been obtained when the location of an open goal box is changed in Phase 2 (Croake, 1971, exps. 1 and 2; Miller, 1935, exp. 1), distinctive within-apparatus cues were present, and the Phase 2 and Phase 1 goal boxes were identical in terms of these within-apparatus cues. Failures to demonstrate problem solving may occur when within-apparatus cues are few in number and not sufficiently distinctive (Minturn, 1954; Koppman & Grice, 1963; Seward, 1949, exp. 3B).

In summary, meeting the identity requirement by ensuring that the component modified in the Phase 2 event has sufficiently distinctive features so that it *is discriminated* from the rest of the experimental situation and, at the same time, *is not discriminated* as different from the corresponding component in Phase 1 is necessary for solution in the component modification problem.

Requirement to Establish Organized Representations

Failure to solve the problem could occur because the relationships among representations (cognitive map) were not properly established in Phase 1. As a consequence, the representations of the component, the motivational significance of which is changed in Phase 2, cannot influence other components of the cognitive map, because no organized set of relationships was established to act as mediators. A simple test of this notion is to omit the Phase 1. As was noted earlier, Maier (1929, exps. E and F; 1932), Seward (1949), and Stahl and Ellen (1974, exp. 4) omitted Phase 1 and found that rats failed to solve the component-modification problem.

Requirement to Employ Organized Representations

Failure to solve the problem can occur if the behavior of the animal is not guided in Phase 3 by a set of organized representations that were established in Phase 1. Suppose that an animal is employing an S-R response strategy to obtain food in a T-maze in Phase 1 of the experiment. Suppose further than an attempt is made to manipulate its cognitive map of the situation in Phase 2 (for example, shock is administered in the food location). One might expect the animal to fail to solve the problem in Phase 3, because the representations that were changed in Phase 2 were not being employed to guide behavior in Phases 1 and 3.

This analysis suggests that one crucial factor which determines whether success or failure will occur in CMR problem-solving is the strategy that is used in Phase 1. If a cognitive strategy is used, the problem will be solved. If some other strategy (e.g., S-R) is employed, then the problem will not be solved. This generalization holds true only for those situations in which some element of the cognitive map is manipulated in Phase 2 of the experiment. (Other types of Phase 2 manipulation will be discussed later.) Thus, it is important to determine the factors which lead an animal to employ a cognitive strategy in Phase 1. If one could specify these factors, one could predict when successful solutions should occur. The available data provide some hints about these factors. First, exploration facilitates the formation of cognitive maps. When an animal is exploring an environment in the absence of rewards, reinforcement of particular responses does not occur.

Those experiments in which rewards are administered in Phase 1 are more difficult to interpret. Tolman (1948, p. 205) suggests that one factor which seems to interfere with the formation of cognitive maps in Phase 1 of these experiments is overtraining. Hicks (1964), Mackintosh (1964), and Means (1969) reported data which suggest that rats: (a) learn the location of a food reinforcement after brief periods of training in a T-maze and (b) learn to perform a particular turning response to obtain reinforcement after longer periods of training. Overtraining could, therefore, result in the animal employing an S-R response strategy in Phase 1, rather than a cognitive strategy, which would interfere with problem solving. Data from a number of experiments support this hypothesis (Dyal, 1963; Tolman, 1933, p. 71; Garcia, Kovner, & Green, 1970, p. 314; Holman, 1975; Morrison & Collyer, 1974). On the other hand, when relatively few reinforced trials are given in Phase 1, problem solution occurred (Honzik & Tolman, 1936; Seward & Levy, 1949; Tolman & Gleitman, 1949).

However, retrospective analyses of experiments such as these are not satisfactory, because crucial information is often not available, and the experiments differ in many dimensions. Therefore, we carried out an experiment on overtraining to determine whether our analysis was correct.

TWO EXPERIMENTS

The major purpose of the first experiment was to determine the effects of overtraining in Phase 1 on the solving of component-modification problems. In addition, we repeated the procedure employed by Hicks (1974) and Mackintosh (1964) to find out whether overtraining results in a switch from cognitive (place learning) strategy to a response strategy.

The subjects in the experiment were 20 naive male hooded rats. They were maintained at 80% normal body weight during the experiment. The apparatus was an open elevated T-maze with distinctive enclosed goal boxes. (One was large, black and dark, and the other small, white and illuminated.) A 87 cm × 97 cm wall separated the goal boxes from the rest of the T-maze so that the goal boxes were not visible from any point on the T-maze. (This apparatus approximated that required for a between-room design.) Translucent guillotine doors were placed at a distance of 6.5 cm from the choice point on the two arms of the T-maze. When the rat passed through the correct door, it was closed, and, simultaneously, the door to the goal-box was opened. A correction procedure was employed. The experimental room provided light and noise sources located on one wall of the room behind the goal box. The reinforcement was wet mash placed in a small food cup. Shock was delivered through the grid floor of the goal-boxes.

The rats were first permitted to explore the maze for three days. Phase 1 of training followed on Day 4. The animals were trained to turn to the non-preferred goal box until they met a criterion of 9 out of 10 correct choices employing a correction procedure. The intertrial interval was approximately one minute. As soon as the rats reached criterion, a probe trial was carried out to determine whether the animals had adopted a strategy of approaching a particular location or making a particular turn. On the probe trial, the start arm of the T-maze was rotated 180 degrees. If the rat went to the goal box that had been reinforced during acquisition, it would have to make a turn opposite to the one that it had made during acquisition. If the rat had made the turn that had been reinforced during acquisition, it would have to go to the goal box opposite the one entered during acquisition. No reinforcement was given on this probe trial.

For 10 rats, a single reacquisition trial was given on Day 5, and then Phase 2 of the experiment was carried out. The other 10 rats received a further 150 acquisition trials, 10 trials a day. Then, on Day 20, they received a single reacquisition trial and Phase 2 followed.

In Phase 2, the rats were placed in the previously reinforced goal box and shocked. A .6-mA shock was administered intermittently for 40 seconds over a 3 minute period. The rats were then given a 3 minute rest in a restraining cage in another room. Phase 3 followed, in which the rats were given a test trial identical to an acquisition trial, except that no reinforcement was given.

The results of this experiment replicated those of Hicks (1964) and Mackintosh (1964). On the test probe at the end of Phase 1, 10 out of 10 animals selected the previously reinforced goal box after the brief training period, whereas only 4 out of 10 selected it after overtraining, Fischer's exact test, $p < .01$. (One tailed tests were employed in this and subsequent comparisons unless otherwise noted.) Brief training led to place learning, whereas longer training resulted in more response learning.

The more interesting question is, of course, whether overtraining led to a deterioration of performance on the component modification test in Phase 3. Again the answer is yes; 7 out of 10 rats which received brief training solved the problem successfully, but only 1 out of 10 solved it after overtraining, Fischer's exact test, $p < .01$.

Although these results are consistent with the hypothesis that we proposed earlier, other interpretations can be suggested. Overtrained animals received more reinforcements. Therefore, one could argue that the strength of the approach habit in Phase 1 is much greater in overtrained animals. Consequently, overtrained rats should be more persistent in making the original response in the face of punishment than animals which had received brief training in Phase 1. The data on the number of place and response strategy rats that solved the problem support this notion. Seven out of 14 rats that exhibited a place strategy on the probe trial solved the problem in Phase 3. Only 1 out of 6 rats that exhibited response strategy on the probe trial solved the problem, Fischer's exact test, $p < .01$. Although the results are in the correct direction, they are not as pronounced as the results when the outcomes are classified in terms of degree of overtraining. This suggests that overtraining involved more than the difference between place and response strategies, perhaps something associated with the additional reinforcements in the overtraining procedure.

To determine the role of stragegy-induction by a means other than overtraining, a further experiment was carried out. To do this, rats that were trained using a correction procedure were compared with rats trained using a non-correction procedure. Previous research (Kalish, 1946; Tolman, Ritchie & Kalish, 1947) as well as our own pilot work, has shown that the correction procedure favors a place strategy, whereas the non-correction procedure favors a response strategy. Correction procedures are similar to exploration in that the animal can wander about the apparatus, and reinforcement of particular responses is less likely to result than in the non-correction procedure. On the other hand, in the non-correction procedure, the correct turn always precedes reinforcement and is more likely, therefore, to result in the reinforcement of a specific response.

The apparatus was similar to that of the previous experiment. For the correction group (n = 14) the procedure was identical to that employed for the group given the short training period in the first experiment. For the non-correction group (n = 15) the procedure was identical with the following exception. If the rat moved 25 cm beyond the door on the incorrect arm of the T-maze, the door closed to prevent retracing and the rat was removed from the apparatus.

There was no significant difference between the correction and non-correction procedures in number of trials to reach criterion in Phase 1 (correction med. = 2, non-correction med. = 3), Mann-Whitney U = 93, p > .05, 2-tailed test. Therefore, differences in number of reinforcements cannot be a basis for any differences in subsequent procedures. However, 14 out of 14 rats trained with the correction procedure approached the rewarded goal-box on the probe trial at the end of Phase 1, whereas only 8 out of 15 rats trained with the non-correction procedure did so, Chi square = 6.25, $p < .01$. In short, the correction procedure resulted in place learning, whereas the non-correction procedure resulted in both place and response learning. Seventeen out of the 22 rats using the place strategy solved the Phase 3 problem successfully; only 2 out of 7 rats using the response strategy did so, Chi square = 3.63, p < .05.

The data that we have described are consistent with the view that the particular strategy and problem solving method which an animal employs is determined by the experimental procedure. Furthermore, they are consistent with our hypothesis that whatever is manipulated in Phase 2 of a component-modification task must be related to the strategy that is adopted in Phase 1. If an animal adopts a cognitive strategy in Phase 1, and a component of that cognitive map is manipulated in Phase 2, success will occur. If, on the other hand, the animal adopts an S-R response strategy in Phase 1, and a component of a cognitive map is manipulated in Phase 2, success will not occur. This may be summarized in terms of a congruence principle as follows: If, and only if, one manipulates in Phase 2 some component of the strategy that was employed in Phase 1, successful *reasoning* will occur. This congruence principle suggests then that a response strategy in Phase 1 and the reinforcement or punishment of a particular response in Phase 2 will lead to successful reasoning in Phase 3. However, response strategies seem to be very difficult to change, even by direct contingent extinction or reinforcement procedures (Black, O'Keefe, & Nadel, 1977; DeCastro, 1974).

We have categorized Phase 1 strategies using the terms *place* and *response*. But, there is no guarantee that this traditional categorization of strategies provides an exhaustive list nor, for that matter, the most appropriate one. Animals employ a wide variety of strategies. The type of experimental design we have discussed in this paper may provide a technique for finding out more about the nature of Phase 1 strategies as well as for exploring the variables that result in successful problem-solving.

CONCLUSION

We have presented an analysis of the psychological processes that may be involved in the solution of component-modification problems. S-R mechanisms did not seem adequate to account for the solution of some of these problems. The CMR process which we suggested may be employed to solve such problems involved four main stages: (a) the formation of a cognitive map, (b) a change in the motivational significance of one component of the map, (c) the treatment of two inputs as identical, and finally (d) mediation through already existing relations among components of the map so that behavior is affected even though the modified component cannot be perceived directly. This CMR process can be conceived of as one of a set of cognitive hypotheses which would account for the solution of component-modification problems.

Our analysis suggested some variables that might be important in determining whether a component-modification problem will be solved. For example, variables which would reduce the likelihood that the identity requirement would be met (such as employing an open goal box in different locations in Phases 1 and 2) resulted in failure to solve the problem. In addition, variables which increased the likelihood that a strategy that did not involve the use of cognitive maps would be employed in Phase 1 also resulted in a failure to solve the problem. For example, the use of a non-correction procedure decreased the likelihood that a cognitive map strategy would be employed in Phase 1, and also decreased the likelihood that the problem would be solved. We are not suggesting that the variables which we have discussed in this paper are more important in some absolute sense than others. Other variables, such as the interval between Phase 2 and Phase 3 (Dyal, 1964; Seward, Datel & Levy, 1952; Thomas, 1958; Young, Mangum, & Capaldi, 1960) and the magnitude and number of reinforcements in Phase 2 (Davenport & Mueller, 1968; Porter, Madison, & Swatek, 1971; Senkowski, Porter, & Madison, 1968; Trapold & Bell, 1964) influence performance on component-modification problems as well. Rather, the conclusion which we wish to make here is simply that our account of the solution process is useful in the sense that it draws attention to important variables that might not have been considered otherwise.

The analysis of component-modification problem-solving presented in this paper involves the assumption that animals can learn different methods to solve the problem. In some cases, only a small subset of methods result in solution of the problem; in others, a much larger subset results in solution. But whatever the size of the subset, it is important to realize that mulitple problem-solving methods are possible—both cognitive and S-R—and that experimental conditions determine which method will be employed. For this reason, a purely cognitive or purely S-R theory of component-modification problem-solving is inadequate.

There is a further point that must be discussed in dealing with the CMR process. Because most of the problems we have discussed involved spatial situations, the cognitive maps are likely to emphasize spatial relationships. But it is perfectly clear that cognitive maps can and do involve other types of relationships—for example, temporal, sequential relationships. It is necessary to explore these other types of maps, not only to make the picture more complete, but, more importantly, because different maps may be commutative with respect to the sequence in which information was acquired. That is, a rat may be allowed to explore a situation only by moving from location A to location B in a between-room design. But, if it is then shocked in A and then replaced in A, it will run to B; similarly if it is shocked in B and then replaced in B, it will run to A, even though it has never done so previously. Temporal maps, on the other hand, may not have this property, in the sense that the animal can use information only in the sequence in which it was acquired—that is, only in the forward direction with respect to time. Also, some of the differences between classical conditioning analogues (e.g., US modification and sensory preconditioning experiments) and component-modification problems may be related to the fact that the former are primarily temporal and sequential, whereas the latter are spatial. It is important, therefore, to provide more data on component-modification in which the organized representations established in Phase 1 are temporal and sequential as well as spatial in nature.

Finally, we should point out that we have focused on only one type of problem-solving task that has been used in animal research on reasoning. A number of other tasks (e.g., Menzel, 1976), and, presumably, therefore, a number of other solution processes should be studied. We think that the analysis of such tasks—in particular tasks which approximate the animal's natural habitat more closely—will reveal additional problem-solving methods that involve operations on central representations more complex than those that we have discussed in this paper.

ACKNOWLEDGMENT

The preparation of this paper and the research was supported in part by National Research Council of Canada (# A0042 to A. H. Black). We would like to thank H. M. Jenkins, L. E. Roberts, and R. M. Church for their comments on the paper. Parts of this paper were presented at a meeting of the Canadian Psychological Association, June, 1976. A. Dalrymple is now at Ministry of Community and Social Services, Orillia, Ontario, L3V-6L2.

This is A. H. Black's last paper and is published posthumously with the kind permission of his wife Janet and the cooperation of his coauthor, Andy Dalrymple. The editors of this volume have shortened considerably the original manuscript and accept responsibility for errors of omission, comission, or distortion that may have been introduced.

REFERENCES

Barch, A. M., Ratner, S. C., & Morgan, F. (1965). Latent reacquisition and extinction. *Psychonomic Science, 3*, 495–496.

Black, A. H., O'Keefe, J., & Nadel, L. (1977). Hippocampal function in avoidance learning and punishment. *Psychological Bulletin*, 1977, 1107–1129.

Brown, W. L., & Halas, E. S. (1957). Latent extinction in a multiple-T maze within heterogeneous and homogeneous environments. *Journal of Genetic Psychology, 90*, 259–266.

Bugelski, R., Coyer, A., & Rogers, W. A. (1952). A criticism of pre-acquisition and pre-extinction of expectancies. *Journal of Experimental Psychology, 44*, 27–30.

Croake, J. W. (1971). Unrewarded exploration and maze learning. *Psychological Reports, 29*, 1335–1340.

Davenport, G. D., & Mueller, J. H. (1968). Resistance to extinction as a function of non-response incentive shift. *Psychonomic Science, 10*, 243–244.

DeCastro, J. M. (1974). A selective spatial discrimination deficit after fornicotomy in the rat. *Behavioural Biology, 12*, 373–382.

Denny, M. R., & Davis, R. H. (1951). A test of latent learning for a non-goal significance *Journal of Comparative and Physiological Physiology, 44*, 590–595.

Denny, M. R., & Ratner, S. C. (1959). Distal cues and latent extinction. *The Psychological Record, 9*, 33–35.

Deutsch, J. A. (1956). A theory of insight, reasoning and latent learning. *British Journal of Psychology, 47*, 115–125.

Dyal, J. A. (1962). Latent extinction as a function of number and duration of pre-extinction exposures. *Journal of Experimental Psychology, 63*, 98–104.

Dyal, J. A. (1963). Latent extinction as a function of number of training trials. *Psychological Record, 13*, 407–414.

Dyal, J. A. (1964). Latent extinction as a function of placement-test interval and irrelevant drive. *Journal of Experimental Psychology, 68*, 486–491.

Gaffan, D., & Gowling, E. A. (1984). Recall of the goal box in latent learning and latent discrimination. *Quarterly Journal of Experimental Psychology, 36B*, 39–51.

Garcia, J., Kovner, R., & Green, K. F. (1970). Cue properties vs palatability of flavors in avoidance learning. *Psychonomic Science, 20*, 313–314.

Gleitman, H., & Herman, M. (1962). Replication report: Latent learning in a T-maze after shock in one end-box. *Journal of Experimental Psychology, 64*, 646.

Gonzalez, R. C., & Diamond, L. (1960). A test of Spence's theory of incentive-motivation. *American Journal of Psychology, 73*, 396–403.

Gonzalez, R. C., & Shepp, B. (1965). The effects of end-box placement on subsequent performance in the runway with competing responses controlled. *American Journal of Psychology, 78*, 441–447.

Hicks, L. H. (1964). Effects of overtraining on acquisition and reversal of place and response learning. *Psychological Reports, 15*, 459–462.

Holland, P. C., & Rescorla, R. A. (1975). The effect of two ways of devaluing the unconditioned stimulus after first-and second-order appetitive conditioning. *Journal of Experimental Psychology: Animal Behavior Processes, 1,* 355–363.

Holman, E. W. (1975). Some conditions for the dissociation of consummatory and instrumental behavior in rats. *Learning and Motivation, 6,* 358–366.

Honzik, C. H., & Tolman, E. C. (1936). The perception of spatial relations by the rat: A type of response not easily explained by conditioning. *Journal of Comparative Psychology, 22,* 287–318.

Hughes, D., Davis, J. D., & Grice, G. R. (1960). Goal box and alley similarity as a factor in latent extinction. *Journal of Comparative and Physiological Psychology, 53,* 612–614.

Kalish, D. (1946). The non-correction method and the delayed response problem of Blodgett and McCutchan. *Journal of Comparative Psychology, 39,* 91–108.

Koppman, J. W., & Grice, R. G. (1963). Goal-box and alley similarity in latent extinction. *Journal of Experimental Psychology, 66,* 611–612.

Mackintosh, N. J. (1964). Overtraining, transfer to proprioceptive control and position reversal. *Quarterly Journal of Experimental Psychology, 16,* 32–36.

Maier, N. R. F. (1929). Reasoning in white rats. *Comparative Psychology Monograph, 6,* 1–93.

Maier, N. R. F. (1932a). The effect of cerebral destruction on reasoning and learning in rats. *The Journal of Comparative Neurology, 54,* 45–75.

Maier, N. R. F. (1932b). Cortical destruction of the posterior part of the brain and its effect on reasoning in rats. *The Journal of Comparative Neurology, 56,* 179–214.

Means, L. W. (1969). *Cue utilization and perservation in the hippocampectomized rat.* Unpublished doctoral dissertation, Claremont Graduate School, Claremont, CA.

Menzel, E. (1976, June). *Cognitive mapping in Chimpanzees,* presented at the Conference on Cognitive Aspects of Animal Behaviour, Dalhousie University, Halifax.

Miller, N. E. (1935). A reply to "Sign-gestalt or conditioned reflex?" *Psychological Review, 42,* 280–292.

Minturn, L. (1954). A test for sign-gestalt expectancies under conditions of negative motivation. *Journal of Experimental Psychology, 48,* 98–100.

Moltz, H. (1957). Latent extinction and the fractional anticipatory response mechanism. *Psychological Review, 64,* 229–241.

Morrison, G. R., & Collyer, R. (1974). Taste-mediated conditioned aversion to an exteroceptive stimulus following LiCl poisoning. *Journal of Comparative and Physiological Psychology, 86,* 51–55.

Munn, N. L. (1950). *Handbook of psychological research on the rat.* New York: Houghton Mifflin.

Porter, J. J., Madison, H. L., & Swatek, A. J. (1971). Incentive and frustration effect of direct goal placement. *Psychonomic Science, 22,* 314–316.

Rescorla, R. A. (1973). Effect of US habituation following conditioning. *Journal of Comparative and Physiological Psychology, 82,* 137–143.

Rescorla, R. A. (1974). Effect of inflation of the unconditioned stimulus value following conditioning. *Journal of Comparative and Physiological Psychology, 86,* 101–106.

Rescorla, R. A., & Heth, C. D. (1975). Reinstatement of fear to an extinguished conditioned stimulus. *Journal of Experimental Psychology: Animal Behavior Processes, 104,* 88–96.

Rizley, R. C., & Rescorla, R. A. (1972). Associations in second-order conditioning and sensory preconditioning. *Journal of Comparative and Physiological Psychology, 81,* 1–11.

Senkowski, P. C., Porter, J. P., & Madison, H. L. (1968). Goal gradient effect of incentive motivation (K) manipulated through prior goal box placements. *Psychonomic Science, 11,* 29–30.

Seward, J. P. (1949). An experimental analysis of latent learning. *Journal of Experimental Psychology, 39,* 177–186.

Seward, J. P., & Levy, N. (1949). Sign learning as a factor in extinction. *Journal of Experimental Psychology, 39,* 660–668.

Seward, J. P., Datel, W. E., & Levy, N. (1952). Tests of two hypotheses of latent learning. *Journal of Experimental Psychology, 43,* 274–280.

Seward, J. P., Jones, R. B., & Summers, S. (1960). A further test of 'reasoning' in rats. *American Journal of Psychology, 73,* 290–293.

Spence, K. W. (1956). *Behavior theory and conditioning.* New Haven: Yale University Press.

Stahl, J. M., & Ellen, P. (1974). Factors in the reasoning performance of the rat. *Journal of Comparative and Physiological Psychology, 87,* 598–604.

Stein, L. (1957). The classical conditioning of the consummatory response as a determinant of instrumental performance. *Journal of Comparative and Physiological Psychology, 50,* 269–278.

Swift, C. F., & Wike, E. L. (1958). A test of Spence's theory of incentive motivation. *The Psychological Record, 8,* 21–25.

Thomas, A. R. (1958). Some variables affecting latent extinction. *Journal of Experimental Psychology, 56,* 203–212.

Tolman, E. C. (1932). *Purposive behaviour in animals and men.* New York: Century.

Tolman, E. C. (1933). Sign-gestalt or conditioned reflex? *Psychological Review, 40,* 69–76.

Tolman, E. C. (1948). Cognitive maps in rats and men. *Psychological Review, 55,* 189–208.

Tolman, E. C. & Gleitman, H. (1949). Studies in learning and motivation: I. Equal reinforcements in both end-boxes followed by shock in one end-box. *Journal of Experimental Psychology, 39,* 810–819.

Tolman, E. C., Ritchie, B. F., & Kalish, D. (1947). Studies in spatial learning. V. Response learning vs. place learning by the non-correction method. *Journal of Experimental Psychology, 37,* 285–292.

Trapold, M. A., & Bell, J. E. (1964). Effect of non-contingent exposure to shifts in reward magnitude on subsequent instrumental runway performance. *Psychological Reports, 15,* 679–684.

Young, R. K., Mangum, W. P., & Capaldi, E. J. (1960). Temporal factors associated with non-response extinction. *Journal of Comparative and Physiological Psychology, 53,* 435–438.

7 Pavlovian Conditioning Analogues to Gestalt Perceptual Principles

Robert A. Rescorla
University of Pennsylvania

INTRODUCTION

This chapter describes some recent research we have been doing on the role of Gestalt perceptual principles in Pavlovian conditioning. The work has been motivated by a simple proposition, often stated by the Gestalt psychologists, but generally only given lip service by students of learning, that variables which affect the way we perceive the world should also importantly affect the way we learn about it. Kohler (1947) stated the general position in a passage in which he characterized Pavlovian conditioning as a special case of association, " . . . the association of two processes is only the aftereffect of their (perceptual) organization." He went on to add, "At this point, animal psychology has the opportunity to test the value of two assumptions at the same time: First, is it true that conditioning involves the associating of two sensory facts? And secondly: Does conditioning depend upon factors of organization?" (Kohler, 1947, p. 163). The discussion which follows suggests an affirmative answer to both of Kohler's questions. I will argue that conditioning does often involve the association of sensory information and that it is importantly influenced by organizational factors.

This chapter is organized in terms of two types of learning which have been distinguished by subsequent Gestalt psychologists, such as Asch (1969). The first is the formation of associations between perceptually distinct events. The discussion of that form of learning will illustrate the value of thinking about Gestalt grouping principles as a heuristic. The second is the learning which constitutes the representation of the events themselves. We will see the value of giving a Gestalt flavor to the integration of the events which become associated.

ASSOCIATIVE LEARNING

Consider first associations between events, what we normally study in Pavlovian conditioning experiments. In recent years, our attitude toward Pavlovian conditioning has changed considerably. It has become less common to describe conditioning as the transfer of control over a response from one stimulus to another. Instead, many favor a description in terms of the organism using one stimulus as a source of information about the occurrence of another (e.g., Mackintosh, 1975; Rescorla, 1972; Wagner, 1978). Although it is only a·heuristic, a useful way to characterize the animal in a Pavlovian experiment is as a detector of causal structure. The animal is like a scientist, trying to determine the cause of the reinforcer; conditioning of a stimulus occurs to the degree that it is a potential cause. If one adopts this view, then it is natural to anticipate that perceptual variables which influence perceived causality might also influence Pavlovian conditioning. To emphasize this point, I will describe experiments exploring the impact on conditioning of three commonly described Gestalt grouping principles: proximity, similarity, and closure (Wertheimer, 1923).

1. Proximity

The first fact any student learns about Pavlovian conditioning is that the contiguity between the conditioned stimulus (CS) and unconditioned stimulus (US) is of critical importance. Those CSs and USs which are close in time become associated, whereas those separated in time do not. Contiguity, of course, corresponds to the Gestalt principle of proximity. Stimuli which are spatially or temporally proximal are typically perceived as going together. But Gestalt Psychology has emphasized an important difference between the two concepts. The Gestalt term *proximity* implies a relativity which is absent from standard discussions of contiguity. Thus, in determinations of perceptual grouping, it is not the absolute distances among elements, but rather the relative distances in the array, which are of importance. The likelihood that two events will be grouped perceptually depends not only on their distance from each other but also on the distance of each from other elements in the display. This is illustrated for spatial displays in Figure 7.1. The upper and lower half of that figure arrange the same absolute distance between each O and the next X. The upper array is commonly perceived in terms of two O-X pairs, since each X is closest to the O on its left; but that perception is destroyed in the lower array by the simple expedient of adding extra Xs. Those additional Xs change the relative distances in the array such that the original Xs are no longer uniquely close to the antecedent Os. By giving each X another event with which it can be perceptually grouped, we have reduced the strength of the O-X grouping. It is the relative proximity rather than the absolute contiguity which determines perceptual grouping.

There are two important findings which suggest that relative proximity is also important in Pavlovian conditioning. The first is well illustrated by several recent

FIG. 7.1. Grouping by relative proximity. Two spatial arrays which share O-X intervals but differ in degree of O-X perceptual grouping.

autoshaping experiments conducted by Gibbon and his collaborators (e.g., Gibbon & Balsam, 1981). In an autoshaping experiment, pigeons are shown an illuminated response key (an illuminated circular disk), followed in a Pavlovian fashion by the availability of grain. They rapidly learn the association between the events and display that knowledge by pecking the key when it is illuminated. Notice that the procedure is purely Pavlovian; the keylight CS and the food US are paired whatever the bird's behavior. Gibbon and his collaborators have extensively studied the variables which affect the simple acquisition of this pecking. One of the most striking findings is that the rate of acquisition of pecking depends not simply on the absolute CS-US interval but on that interval relative to the interval between trials. With a particular CS-US interval, learning can be excellent when trials are spaced but poor when they are massed. Moreover, across a surprisingly broad range, acquisition is well-predicted by the *ratio* of the CS-US interval to the intertrial interval. Even though the absolute values vary widely, similar ratios produce similar acquisition performance. It is not simply the absolute contiguity but rather the relative proximity of CS to US that governs acquisition rate.

A second relevant finding was a phenomenon reported several years ago by Rescorla (1967). Using a fear conditioning preparation, Rescorla found that a CS-US contiguity capable of producing considerable conditioning is rendered dramatically less effective if additional USs occur between CS-US trials, in the absence of the CS. In fact, if USs occur at the same rate during the CS and in its absence, one often observes little conditioning, despite the occurrence of a fair number of CS-US contiguities. Rescorla used that finding to argue that it is the information which the CS gives about the likelihood of the US occurrence which determines conditioning. But in the present context, one could view that finding as one of relative proximity. Indeed if one simply identifies the O as a CS and the X as a US, the procedure is a temporal analog of the spatial display in Figure 7.1. In conditioning, as in Figure 7.1, the tendency to group the CS (O) and the US (X) together depends upon the distance of those events relative to the other USs (X) in the setting. When the other USs are added, they undermine the perceptual organization of CS and US.

These sorts of data have encouraged more global descriptions of the animal's performance in Pavlovian conditioning. For instance, Rescorla (1967) suggested that it is the contingency between CS and US which matters for the development of an association. The animal appears to examine not simply the likelihood of the US during the CS but to compare that likelihood to the one which obtains in the absence of the CS. More recently, Gibbon and Balsam (1981) and Jenkins, Barnes, and Barrera (1981) have suggested somewhat different accounts in which the animal compares the rate during the CS with the overall rate in the session as a whole and generates performance based on the discrepancy between the two.

In contrast to those global descriptions, Rescorla & Wagner (1972) offered a more molecular account. Their account leans heavily on a finding reported by Kamin (1969). Kamin found that USs which are expected on the basis of one CS are relatively less effective in conditioning a second, concurrently present CS. In the present instance, one can think of the US as conditioning two stimuli, the explicit CS and the situational cues. When extra USs are given, they especially establish conditioning of the situational cues, allowing them to block conditioning of the explicit CS. In effect, the organism learns to expect the US all the time in the situation, and is therefore not surprised to receive it during the CS. Since he learns best when he is surprised, he learns little about the CS-US relation. When those intertrial USs are absent, less background conditioning occurs, and, therefore, there is less blocking of the conditioning to the CS. According to this account, the failure of conditioning to the CS is mediated by the success of conditioning to the background. Although it has not gone unchallenged, this account has enjoyed substantial success in dealing with phenomena such as those described here (Gibbon & Balsam, 1981; Rescorla, Durlach, & Grau, 1985).

Moreover, some recent data collected in our laboratory indicate that this molecular account has the power to make novel predictions. For instance, according to this account, intertrial USs matter only because they condition the background; if they failed to do so, their occurrence would produce no damage. In addition, the account suggests one way to prevent those USs from conditioning the background—signal them with yet another CS. Under those circumstances, the other CS would become a good signal of the "intertrial" USs and prevent them from conditioning the background; as a result, the background would no longer block the conditioning of the original CS.

Figure 7.2 shows some relevant data recently collected in our laboratory by Durlach (1983). Durlach's autoshaping experiment contained three groups of pigeons, all receiving a keylight followed by food on 25% of its occurrences. Group 25 experienced only these events. Their treatment is a temporal analog to the spatial arrangement shown in the top array of Figure 7.1, and they rapidly learned to associate the keylight CS with food. Group Unsignaled received additional foods in the intertrial interval so as to make the keylight noninformative (analogous to the bottom array in Figure 7.1). These animals showed little evidence of acquisition. The difference between the performances of these two groups shows the powerful depressive effect of the extra USs. However, in

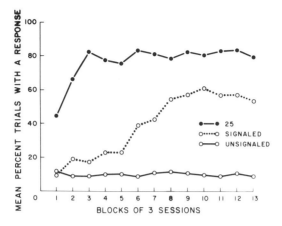

FIG. 7.2.   Acquisition of autoshaped keypecking in birds receiving 25% of the CSs followed by USs when that was their only treatment or was accompanied by signaled or unsignaled intertrial USs (From Durlach, 1983. Reprinted by permission of the American Psychological Association.)

the present context, interest centers on Group Signaled, which also received those additional USs, but each US was signaled by a tone. It is clear that signaling those USs produced a substantial reduction in their ability to interfere with conditioning of the keylight CS. When the additional USs were signaled, moderate levels of conditioning did develop to the original CS. That result is clearly in agreement with the prediction from a molecular account in terms of blocking from background stimuli. A manipulation which reduces the background conditioning attributable to the intertrial USs also reduces their negative impact on conditioning of the CS. Notice in particluar that this signaling operation leaves the keylight CS uncorrelated with the US; yet conditioning of that keylight results. Consequently, this molecular account not only allows one to describe many of the data supporting a global view, it also correctly predicts data at variance with that view (see also, Rescorla, 1972).

   Although this chapter primarily focuses on perceptual analogies in conditioning, Durlach's experiment reveals an instance in which the analogy works the other way. Figure 7.3 shows two arrays, one identical to that at the bottom of Figure 7.1 and a similar one in which each "extra" X is immediately preceded by a filled square. That filled square is a spatial counterpart to Durlach's temporal signal of the extra USs. For many observers it has an analogous affect. Like Durlach's signal, the square restores some, but not all, of the O-X preceptual grouping.

   These data indicate that one Gestalt principle, relative proximity, has a useful analogy in Pavlovian conditioning. In this particular case, we may be able to provide a more molecular analysis which gives some insight into the mechanism. The other cases we examine are less well analyzed.

FIG. 7.3. Spatial analogy to Durlach's experiment. The poor O-X grouping evident above the line is improved in the array below the line by attaching a filled square to each X not preceded by an O.

2. Similarity

A second interesting Gestalt grouping principle is similarity. In spatial arrays, stimuli that are similar tend to be grouped perceptually. One may then ask whether similarity promotes Pavlovian conditioning; are similar events more associable?

This question turns out to be relatively tricky to answer if one wants to rule out a variety of other ways in which similarity might function, such as stimulus generalization. But a design used by Rescorla and Furrow (1977) provides informative results. In one experiment, they used the autoshaping preparation but employed a second-order conditioning procedure. In such a procedure one stimulus, S_1, is first paired with a US; then another stimulus, S_2, is paired with S_1. In this case, the association formed between S_2 and S_1 is the one of interest. This is indexed by the occurrence of pecking during S_2, as a result of its pairing with S_1. One reason for using a second-order procedure is that it allows us to pick S_2 and S_1 on the basis of the variable of interest, perceptual similarity. We can convert one stimulus (S_1) into a reinforcer by pairing it with food and then use it to establish an association to S_2.

In their experiment, Rescorla and Furrow exploited this advantage, picking as stimuli two colors, blue (B) and green (G), and two line orientations, horizontal (H) and vertical (V) grid patterns. Blue and horizontal were paired with food, to make them reinforcers. They were then used as reinforcers to establish second-order conditioning of green and vertical. For half the animals the second-order procedure paired similars: G with B and V with H; the other animals received the same stimuli but with dissimilars paired. Notice that the groups were matched on all individual stimulus occurrences. All animals received B and H paired with food as well as G and V paired with either B or H; they differed only in the pairing relations among the S_1 and S_2 stimuli. It is this feature that allows the experiment to rule out alternatives such as stimulus generalization and differential pseudoconditioning as responsible for any differential outcomes.

The primary issue is whether the rate of conditioning will depend on the similarity relations. The results, shown in Figure 7.4, suggest a positive answer. That figure shows the course of second-order conditioning of G and V when they

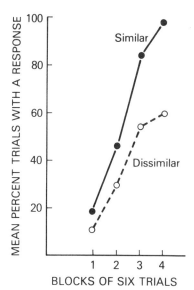

FIG. 7.4. Effect of similarity on second-order autoshaping. Acquisition is shown for a second-order CS followed by either a similar or a dissimilar reinforcer (After Rescorla & Furrow, 1977. Reprinted by permission of the American Psychological Association.)

were paired with similars or dissimilars. It is clear that conditioning proceeded more rapidly and to a higher level when similars were paired. The Gestalt principle of similarity does seem to affect conditioning; similars are more associable.

This finding is important because it means that a qualitative perceptual relation affects conditioning. To correctly anticipate the outcome of a conditioning experiment, one must know not only the identities of the events, but also the similarities among those events. This finding is comparable to the cue-to-consequence findings often described for flavor aversion preparation (e.g., Garcia, McGowan, & Green, 1972). But in the present context, it is of interest to note that the importance of qualitative relations was recognized quite clearly by the Gestalt psychologists, long before its current popularity. Kohler (1947, p. 153), for instance, complained that "in the classical law of association by contiguity, the nature of the things which become associated is tacitly ignored." He offered the possibility that stimulus similarity mattered and even reported some data on the point (Kohler, 1941). Asch (1969, p. 93) was more blunt: "There is no place for relations (such as similarity) in the psychologies of Ebbinghaus or Thorndike, of Guthrie or Hull, or of their successors. . . . This neglect of relations is, in my judgment, a blunder." Gestalt Psychology has always seen as important what Rescorla and Holland (1976) termed "intrinsic" stimulus relations.

Although the simple demonstration of similarity's impact is of interest, I want to make four further points about the character of that impact. First, the impact of similarity is widespread and applies to several different ways in which similarity can be instantiated. Shared stimulus modality, whole-part relations, and shared spatial contiguity are a few examples which have been explored (see Rescorla, 1980).

Second, like proximity, the Gestalt notion of similarity has a relative aspect. It is not the absolute physical properties of two stimuli which determine their perceived similarity, but rather those properties relative to the properties of other stimuli in the environment. Stimuli perceived as similar in one context may not be so viewed in another. It is then of interest to ask whether it is relative similarity which determines the course of conditioning. Further consideration of the Rescorla-Furrow experiment suggests that possibility. Notice that in that experiment there is a sense in which all four stimuli are highly similar to one another. The green, blue, horizontal striped, and vertical striped stimuli all had a common duration, occurred at a common locus, and are in the visual modality. Thus, the stimuli we have termed "dissimilars," such as green (G) and horizontal stripes (H), are actually quite similar in some absolute sense. However, when the "dissimilars" G and H are paired, another reinforcer, blue (B), is relatively more similar to G than is its paired H. This suggests that the poor performance observed when G and H were paired arose from the fact that the pairing occurred in a context which also contained another event, B, which was relatively more similar to G but which was unpaired with it. On those grounds, one would expect that the same G-H pairing could produce relatively better learning if those other stimuli were absent, so as to reduce the differences in relative similarity. That view is supported by the fact that other experiments in our laboratory regularly employ "dissimilars" such as G and H to produce substantial second-order conditioning when they are the only stimuli to which the organism is exposed.

A recent experiment in our laboratory provides further confirmation. Figure 7.5 shows the results of an unpublished experiment identical to that of Rescorla and Furrow except that during second-order conditioning, the similar and dissimilar treatments only contained one pairing (e.g., G-H or G-B). That variation effectively removes from the design the stimuli which induce the different contexts for similarity. Under those conditions, the similarity effect is markedly undermined. The "dissimilar" G-H association proceded as rapidly as did the "similar" G-B association. Those results suggest that relative similarity determines the course of conditioning, as would be expected on the basis of the Gestalt analogy.

Third, similarity promotes not just excitatory Pavlovian conditioning but also inhibitory conditioning. In recent years, we have come to recognize that animals can learn not only when stimuli go together but also when they go apart—they learn that one stimulus means another will not occur. That learning, termed conditioned inhibition, is also facilitated when the events are similar (Rescorla, 1980). This suggests that similarity may have a general facilitative effect on the learning of any logical relation between two events. This finding has the important implication that similarity cannot promote conditioning simply because a

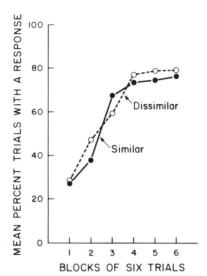

FIG. 7.5.   Failure of a similarity effect when the conditioning context is changed to remove relative similarity. Acquisition of second-order autoshaping when the green CS is followed by either a similar (blue) or a dissimilar (grid pattern) reinforcer.

particular type of association already exists between similars prior to the experiment. That, in turn, has implications for how this qualitative relation must be incorporated into theories of learning.

Finally, similarity does more that improve learning; it sometimes changes its nature. For instance, recent evidence suggests that when a CS is paired with a reinforcer which has multiple aspects, the organism selects among the reinforcer aspects which it will encode (Rescorla, 1980). One of the important determinants of encoding is the similarity of the various aspects to the signal; those reinforcer aspects which are similar are favored for encoding. An important instance of this selection occurs in the determination of whether conditioning will be S-S or S-R in nature. In some cases, the organism learns about the response features of the reinforcer, and in others it apparently learns about the stimulus features. Similarity of the CS to the stimulus aspects of the reinforcer is one important determinant of which form the learning will take. When a signal is similar to the stimulus features of the reinforcer, then that reinforcer is especially likely to be encoded in stimulus terms, and S-S learning is encouraged (Rescorla, 1980). Thus, the Gestalt principle of similarity changes not only the rate but also the nature of learning in Pavlovian conditioning. In this case it speaks to a question of lasting concern in Pavlovian conditioning.

Unlike the case of proximity, we do not have very good molecular accounts of how similarity has its effect. Rescorla and Gillan (1980) put forth some suggestions, but our understanding of this grouping principle remains at the heuristic level. Nevertheless, it is clear that similarity is a powerful determinant of Pavlovian conditioning, with important implications for theories of associative learning.

3. Closure

A third important perceptual grouping principle is that of closure or good continuation. Two elements in a perceptual display are better grouped if the space between them is filled than if it is left empty. Figure 7.6 shows an illustration of that phenomenon. In the upper array, each X is slightly closer to its preceding O, but that grouping is not particularly compelling; an X is almost as readily grouped with the subsequent O. The lower array is physically identical except that each O and the next X are connected by parallel lines; in that case the O-X grouping is quite striking, and the X-O grouping is more difficult to achieve.

This improvement in grouping with the addition of an intervening stimulus has an analogy in the detection of causal sequences. The cause of an event is rarely separated in time and space from that event unless there are some mediating events. So if A is to be the cause of a distant B, the relation is most easily perceived if there is another event, C, which intervenes, transmitting the causal relation.

This phenomenon also has an analogy in Pavlovian conditioning. Several authors (e.g., Bolles, Collier, Bouton, & Marlin, 1978; Kaplan & Hearst, 1982) have reported that if a CS bears a trace relation to a US, then conditioning can be improved if another CS fills the trace interval. An illustration of that finding is given by a recent autoshaping experiment in our laboratory, the results of which are shown in Figure 7.7. In that experiment, each pigeon received two 5-sec color keylight CSs, each followed, after a 5-sec trace, by food. But for one of the colors a 5-sec horizontal keylight pattern intervened between the color and food. The other color had the time unfilled by any explicit event. The middle panel of Figure 7.7 shows the acquisition of keypecking to those two color CSs and to the intervening pattern. The CS without a filler (open circles) showed little evidence of conditioning; 5-sec is a substantial gap in an autoshaping preparation. However, the CS (filled circles) whose trace was filled by a line pattern showed considerable improvement. Apparently, there is an analogy in Pavlovian conditioning to the grouping principle of closure. Of course, the line pattern filler,

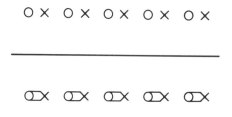

FIG. 7.6.   Effect of closure on perceptual grouping. The ambiguous organization shown above the line is decided in favor of O-X grouping by the addition of parallel lines in the bottom array.

FIG. 7.7.   Effect of closure on conditioning. The middle panel shows acquisition of autoshaping to two color CSs both having a 5-sec trace relation with the US. For one color, the trace interval was filled with another line pattern stimulus. The right hand panel shows test responding to the colors after their filler had either been extinguished or not; also shown is responding to the unfilled color (From Rescorla, 1982. Reprinted by permission of the American Psychological Association.)

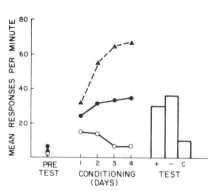

being the most proximal stimulus of all to the reinforcer, showed the greatest level of conditioning.

One may entertain two general interpretations of this finding. The first is that emphasized by its analogy to the Gestalt observation, that the filler somehow promotes the association of the color with food. The role of the filler is to improve the color-food relation; it serves a kind of catalytic function, assisting other events in becoming associated. However, a second interpretation, in terms of second-order Pavlovian conditioning, readily comes to mind. The high level of responding to the horizontal pattern which served as a filler suggests that it might be a powerful reinforcer capable of bestowing second-order conditioning upon the color. On that account, responding is superior in the color with the filled interval because it benefits not only from the ultimate food US but also from second-order conditioning by the horizontal pattern. That account seems less interesting, but it is the explanation most frequently given for analogous data in the instrumental learning situation (e.g., Spence, 1947).

Recently, Rescorla (1982) reported some experiments which help evaluate the contributions of these accounts. Those experiments depend on an important fact about second-order conditioning in the autoshaping preparation: responding to a second-order S_2 which has been paired with an S_1 can be manipulated by operating on S_1. For instance, if the response to S_1 is extinguished after S_2 and S_1 have been paired, then the response to S_2 is adversely affected (e.g., Rashotte, Griffin, & Sisk, 1977; Rescorla, 1979). This has been taken as evidence of the presence of an S_2-S_1 association. But in the present case, one can use that manipulation to assess the contribution of second-order conditioning to the gap filling phenomenon. To the degree that second-order conditioning is involved, then extinction of the filler should reduce the effect. But the right-hand side of Figure 7.7 shows results which suggest this is not the case. That panel displays responding to the former filled CS after intervening treatment in which the horizontal pattern alone was either repeatedly reinforced ($+$) or nonreinforced ($-$). Despite the substantial differences in responding to the filling pattern itself, there were no differences in responding to the filled CS. In both cases, the formerly filled stimulus continued to show greater responding than did the unfilled control (C) stimulus. Apparently, separate mainpulation of the filling stimulus following its use as a filler had no detectable effect on responding to the color CS. On the other hand, Rescorla (1982) found that manipulations which changed the value of the reinforcer had a major effect on responding to the color. Those results suggest that in this situation, the filler is not well associated with the CS but rather improves the CS-US association.

We have no real analysis of this catalytic effect. We are just now beginning to see clear demonstrations of its impact on conditioning. Presumably, we can now proceed to develop molecular explanations, as we did for the case of relative proximity. Obviously, the Gestalt analogy is not an explanation; rather it is a heuristic which provides data to challenge our theories. But, in this instance, that heuristic has suggested a different kind of function which a stimulus can play in conditioning settings—as a promoter of associations among other stimuli.

Our conclusion from this discussion is that three Gestalt principles of perceptual organization may importantly affect associations between events. That learning seems promoted by relative proximity, relative similarity, and closure.

EVENT LEARNING

There is another sort of learning that also occurs in Pavlovian experiments, but normally receives less attention—learning about the events among which we form associations. This distinction between learning about events and learning associations between events runs through Gestalt psychology, especially as recently stated by Asch (1969). But until recently it has been largely ignored within the Pavlovian literature.

One reason for neglecting this distinction is that it is very difficult to specify what we mean by a single event as distinct from multiple events. We can offer no general solution to that problem here. But we can note that one important component of this distinction might be distribution in time. Multiple events tend to be distributed sequentially in time, whereas the features of a single event occur with temporal and spatial simultaneity. Consequently, for the present discussion, within-event learning will refer to learning about simultaneously presented stimulus features. Our laboratory has recently engaged in extensive investigation of this sort of learning (see Rescorla, 1981a; Rescorla & Durlach, 1981). Here, I want just to note three points about within-event learning: that it occurs, that we know something about its rules, and that it interacts with between-event associative learning.

1. Existence of Within-Event Learning

The existence of such within-event learning can be illustrated in a variety of conditioning preparations. For instance, if a pigeon is given the simultaneous illumination of a response key by a color on its left half and a line pattern on its right half, the bird learns not only whatever relation that stimulus has to USs such as food but also that the color and pattern co-occurred. The occurrence of that latter learning can be demonstrated by inducing a response to one component and inspecting the bird's performance to the other. For instance, if after presentation of a red-horizontal stimulus, the bird is trained to peck at horizontal, it will also tend to peck at red. Moreover, that pecking depends on the bird's having previously been exposed to the red-horizontal compound (Rescorla, 1981b).

Similarly, if rodents are exposed to a compound stimulus consisting of a light and a tone, they will learn that those components cooccurred. To expose that learning, one need only pair one component with shock and measure the animal's fear during the other component (Rescorla, 1981a).

An especially powerful instance of such learning appears with flavor stimuli in rats. If a thirsty rat consumes a liquid with multiple flavor components (such as sweet and salt), it readily learns that those components cooccurred. Subsequent information that the salty taste is especially aversive or attractive transfers to the sweet taste. If, for instance, one induces an illness in the rat after consumption of salt, then sweet substances are rejected in a subsequent test. Alternatively, if one induces a specific hunger for salt, the willingness to consume a sweet substance is enhanced. With flavor stimuli, to which rodents are particularly sensitive, this learning is very rapid and powerful (Rescorla, 1981a).

A final example emerges from recent work with learning in bees by Bitterman and his collaborators (e.g., Couvillon & Bitterman, 1982). Using techniques like those described above, they have found that bees readily learn the flavors of colored objects.

These examples leave little question that learning about the multiple features of an event does occur over a wide variety of organisms, preparations, and stimuli.

2. Rules of This Learning

We have learned something about the rules of occurrence of this sort of learning (see Rescorla & Durlach, 1981). Some of those rules would be expected on the basis of our knowledge of other learning processes. For instance, this learning proceeds in an orderly fashion as a function of number of exposures to the event, growing in a negatively accelerated fashion. However, the initial growth is often extremely rapid, with the process well underway in one exposure. Moreover, discrimination and extinction can be readily demonstrated.

Some of these rules suggest the operation of Gestalt-like principles. For instance, in unpublished work we have found the organism to be particularly good at learning the co-occurrence of event features if those features are similar to each other. When given a two-component visual stimulus, a pigeon integrates that stimulus especially well if the components are both colors or line orientations as distinct from being composed of a color-pattern combination. Moreover, the elementary principle of figure/ground seems relevant. It is easier to integrate a color with a form if the color is contained in the form than if the form appears on a colored ground. This latter finding agrees with observations of figural learning in humans made by Asch (1969).

Some of the rules are surprising in the light of our knowledge of other learning processes. For instance, this sort of learning appears to occur most readily when the components are simultaneous, rather than successive (Rescorla, 1981a). And this learning appears to extinguish readily but be relatively difficult to retrain (Rescorla & Durlach, 1981).

On the basis of such observations, we have elsewhere suggested a way of viewing within-event learning which has more in common with Gestalt psychology than with traditional associationism (e.g., Rescorla and Durlach, 1981). According to that view, the organism does not analyze an event into its component features only to resynthesize it in terms of associations among the components. Rather it forms a more unitary representation of the event, decomposing the event only as its elements occur separately.

3. Interaction with Between-Event Learning

Finally, there is the important issue of how the representation of events interacts with the learning of the relations among them. Consider a case in which we ask the organism to associate two multifeatured events. The prior discussion indicates that it will learn about the cooccurrences within each event as well as forming associations between events. But what is the relation between those two kinds of learning?

One simple associative possibility is that the individual elements of each event become associated with the elements of the other—that multiple associations are formed all at one level. As implausible as some may find such an account, it has been the dominant approach within animal studies of associative learning. A possibility more in line with modern thinking in cognitive psychology and with Gestalt psychology is heirarchical in character—that the organism intergrates within each event and then associates those integrated representations with each other.

It turns out to be surprisingly difficult to develop differential predictions from those two possibilities, at least within the context of Pavlovian conditioning. However, one recent autoshaping experiment we have done provides some support for the heirarchical notion. In this experiment, we first paired two colors, red and yellow, each with food, in order to make them first-order stimuli capable of serving as reinforcers. However, in each case, the color occupied only half the standard response key. As a result it was possible to construct a red-yellow compound stimulus. We then used a second-order conditioning procedure in which that red-yellow compound was signaled by a black X projected on a white key. As the bird learned this signaling relation, it rapidly came to peck at X.

The question of interest is what the organism has associated with X. There are two quite different associative structures which might support this responding to

X. On the one hand, the bird might form separate associations between X and each component of the reinforcer, generating its responding on the basis of summation of those associations. Alternatively, the organism might associate X with a single representation of the reinforcing event (RY). Has the organism integrated the reinforcer or has it kept its parts separate?

One way to answer the question is to teach the bird to discriminate between the RY compound and its R and Y components. Consequently, we exposed half the birds to a discrimination of the form RY+,R−,Y− whereas the other half we taught a discrimination of the form RY−,R+,Y+. If the organism has formed an integrated representation of the RY reinforcer, then the former discrimination maintains the strength of that reinforcer while extinguishing that of its components; on the other hand the reverse discrimination extinguishes the integrated reinforcer. Consequently, an organism that knows it was RY serving as the reinforcer would respond more to X following the RY+,R−,Y− discrimination. On the other hand, if the organism has learned separate X-R and X-Y associations, then there is no reason to expect more responding after the RY+,R−,Y− discrimination than after the RY−,R+,Y+ discrimination; indeed one might expect to see more behavior after the reverse discrimination, which maintains the value of the individual R and Y elements.

Figure 7.8 shows the results of this experiment. To the left is shown the responding to X in the two groups at the end of second-order conditioning; it is substantial and about equal. Clearly, learning of some sort occurred. In the middle is shown the course of the configural discrimination in which the RY compound and its elements were differentially reinforced. It is clear that such a discrimination can be learned, which in itself suggests that the organism *can* easily treat a compound as different from its elements. However, the question of interest is whether it did so during the associative learning in which the compound was a reinforcer for X. The data at the right indicate that it did: responding to X is maximum when the RY compound, rather than its elements, was fol-

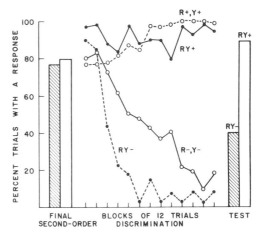

FIG. 7.8.   Heirarchical organization of between- and within-event learning. The left-hand panel shows performance in two groups both given second-order conditioning of a grid pattern (H) by a compound color (RY) reinforcer. In the middle panel, one group received an RY+,R−,Y− discrimination; the other received the converse. The right-hand panel shows responding to H as a function of this discrimination (From Rescorla, 1979. Reprinted by permission of the American Psychological Association.)

lowed by food. Responding to X was better predicted by the current state of the RY compound than by the state of the individual elements. The fact that there was residual responding to X in the animals receiving the $RY-,R+,Y+$ discrimination may suggest that the organism also forms associations between X and the individual R and Y elements. But, apparently, performance to X is dominated by its association with an integrated reinforcer. So the organism not only forms organized event representations; it uses them as the basis of its associative learning. A heirarchical structure is clearly indicated. It is worth commenting that this is one of very few empirical results which force the conclusion that such a heirarchical organization occurs.

CONCLUSION

This discussion suggests that it may be useful to consider the analogy between Gestalt principles of perception and the learning which occurs in Pavlovian conditioning. Our consideration of associative learning pointed to the involvement of three grouping principles: proximity, similarity, and closure. For the case of proximity, we saw the importance of a relativity like that emphasized by the Gestalt psychologists, and we were able to give some analysis of that relativity. In the case of similarity, we found evidence for the operation of a qualitative relation in associative learning, which may force a modification in current theories of associative learning. In the case of closure we found evidence for the operation of a somewhat different function of a stimulus, that of a catalyst promoting associations among other events. None of these grouping principles provides an explanation of learning phenomena any more than they provide one for perceptual phenomena. Rather, they are heuristics suggesting new variables and phenomena. But such heuristics have an important role to play, and it is clear that the grouping principles can be very powerful heuristics.

We have also followed the Gestalt suggestion that there is an organization within events. And we have seen evidence for a heirarchical structure in which the product of within-event organization enters into association.

These results seem to me to be of sufficient interest to justify Kohler's (1947) optimism about the potential of Pavlovian conditioning for elucidating the nature of associative and event learning. But they might also encourage a more positive attitude among students of conditioning for the usefulness of Gestalt perceptual ideas.

ACKNOWLEDGMENTS

This chapter represents the influence on my thinking of three of my former teachers, each a superb instructor and a powerful intellect. Hans Wallach first introduced me to perception and to the excitement of experimental analysis; S. E. Asch exposed me to the richness of Gestalt Psychology and allowed me to see glimpses of his brilliant mind; Dick Solomon taught me to appreciate Pavlovian conditioning and provided an atmosphere in which creative integration was encouraged and supported. I am deeply grateful to each.

The research described here has been generously supported by funds from the National Science Foundation.

REFERENCES

Asch, S. E. (1969). A reformulation of the problem of associations, *American Psychologist, 24*, 92–102.

Bolles, R. C., Collier, A. C., Bouton, M. E., & Marlin, N. A. (1978). Some tricks for ameliorating the trace-conditioning deficit. *Bulletin of the Psychonomic Society, 11*, 403–406.

Couvillon, P. A., & Bitterman, M. E. (1982). Compound conditioning in honeybees, *Journal of Comparative and Physiological Psychology, 96*, 192–199.

Durlach, P. J. (1983). Effect of signaling intertrial unconditioned stimuli in autoshaping, *Journal of Experimental Psychology: Animal Behavior Processes, 9*, 374–389.

Garcia, J., McGowan, B. K., & Green, K. F. (1972). Biological constraints on conditioning, in A. Black, & W. F. Prokasy (Eds.), *Classical conditioning II* (pp. 3–27). New York: Appleton-Century-Crofts.

Gibbon, J., & Balsam, P. (1981). Spreading association in time, in L. C. Locurto, H. S. Terrace, & J. Gibbon (Eds.), *Autoshaping and conditioning theory* (pp. 219–253). New York: Academic Press.

Jenkins, H. M., Barnes, R. A., & Barrera, F. J. (1981). Why autoshaping depends on trial spacing. In L. C. Locurto, H. S. Terrace, & J. Gibbon (Eds.), *Autoshaping and conditioning theory* (pp. 255–289). New York: Academic Press.

Kamin, L. J. (1969). Predictability, surprise, addention and conditioning. In B. A. Campbell & R. M. Church (Eds.), *Punishment and aversive behavior* (pp. 279–296). New York: Appleton-Century-Crofts.

Kaplan, P. S., & Hearst, E. (1982). Bridging temporal gaps between CS and US in autoshaping: Insertion of other stimuli before, during and after CS. *Journal of Experimental Psychology: Animal Behavior Processes, 8*, 187–203.

Kohler, W. (1941). On the nature of associations. *Proceedings of the American Philosophical Society, 84*, 489–502.

Kohler, W. (1947). *Gestalt psychology*. New York: Liverright.

Mackintosh, N. J. (1975). A theory of attention: Variations in the associability of stimuli with reinforcement. *Psychological Review, 82*, 276–298.

Rashotte, M. E., Griffin, R. W., & Sisk, C. L. (1977). Second-order conditioning of the pigeon's keypeck. *Animal Learning and Behavior, 5*, 25–38.

Rescorla, R. A. (1967). Pavlovian conditioning and its proper control procedures, *Psychological Review, 74*, 71–80.

Rescorla, R. A. (1972). Informational Variables in Pavlovian conditioning. In G. W. Bower & J. T. Spence (Eds.), *The psychology of learning and motivation* (pp. 1–46). New York: Academic Press.

Rescorla, R. A. (1979). Aspects of the reinforcer learned in second-order Pavlovian conditioning. *Journal of Experimental Psychology: Animal Behavior Processes, 5*, 79–95.

Rescorla, R. A. (1980). *Pavlovian second-order conditioning: Studies in associative learning*, Hillsdale, NJ: Lawrence Erlbaum Associates.

Rescorla, R. A. (1981a). Simultaneous associations. In P. Harzem & M. Zeiler (Eds.), *Advances in analysis of behavior (Vol. 2)*, (pp. 47–80). New York: Wiley.

Rescorla, R. A. (1981b). Within-signal learning in autoshaping. *Animal Learning and Behavior, 9,* 245–252.

Rescorla, R. A. (1982). Effect of a stimulus intervening between CS and US in autoshaping. *Journal of Experimental Psychology: Animal Behavior Processes, 8,* 131–141.

Rescorla, R. A., & Durlach, P. J. (1981). Within-event learning in Pavlovian conditioning. In R. R. Miller, & N. E. Spear (Eds.), *Information processing in animals: Memory mechanisms* (pp. 83–111). Hillsdale, NJ: Lawrence Erlbaum Associates.

Rescorla, R. A., Durlach, P. J., & Grau, J. W. (1985). Contextual learning in Pavlovian conditioning. In P. D. Balsam & A. Tomie (Eds.), *Context and learning.* Hillsdale, NJ: Lawrence Erlbaum Associates.

Rescorla, R. A., & Furrow, D. R. (1977). Stimulus similarity as a determinant of Pavlovian conditioning. *Journal of Experimental Psychology: Animal Behavior Processes, 3,* 203–215.

Rescorla, R. A., & Gillan, D. J. (1980). An analysis of the facilitative effect of similarity upon second-order conditioning. *Journal of Experimental Psychology: Animal Behavior Processes, 6,* 339–351.

Rescorla, R. A., & Holland, P. C. (1976). Some behavioral approaches to the study of learning, In E. Bennett & M. R. Rosensweig (Eds.), *Neural mechanisms of learning and memory* (pp. 165–192). Cambridge, MA: MIT Press.

Rescorla, R. A., & Wagner, A. R. (1972). A theory of Pavlovian conditioning: Variations in the effectiveness of reinforcement and nonreinforcement. In A. Black & W. F. Prokasy (Eds.), *Classical conditioning II* (pp. 64–99). New York: Appleton-Century-Crofts.

Spence, K. W. (1947). The role of secondary reinforcement in delayed reward learning, *Psychological Review, 54,* 1–8.

Wagner, A. R. (1978). Expectances and the priming of STM. In S. H. Hulse, H. Fowler, & W. K. Honig, (Eds.), *Cognitive processes in animal behavior.* Hillsdale, NJ: Lawrence Erlbaum Associates.

Wertheimer, M. (1955). Laws of organization in perceptual forms. In W. D. Ellis (Ed. and Trans.), *A source book of Gestalt psychology.* New York: The Humanities Press. (Original work published 1923)

8

The Effect of Context upon Responses to Conditioned Inhibitors

Vincent M. LoLordo
Jeffrey L. Fairless
Kelly J. Stanhope
Dalhousie University, Halifax, Nova Scotia

For the last decade the dominant account of the role of context in simple associative learning has been the model proposed by Rescorla and Wagner (1972; also see Wagner & Rescorla, 1972). The Rescorla-Wagner model treats context like any other conditional stimulus. Since context is always present, whenever a discrete conditional stimulus (CS) is presented on a conditioning trial, the model treats that trial as a presentation of the discrete CS plus context. The fundamental feature of the model is its assertion that the associative strengths of the various conditional stimuli, including contextual stimuli, which are present on a trial, interact to determine the outcome of that trial. More specifically, changes in the associative strengths of stimuli presented on a conditioning trial are a function of the discrepancy between the maximum associative strength supportable by the unconditioned stimulus (UCS) and the current sum of the associative strengths of all stimuli present on the trial. Consequently, when a contingency between a CS and a UCS is arranged in some context, the associative strength of the CS interacts with the associative strength of the context to determine the effect of a conditioning trial in changing both associative strengths.

The Wagner-Rescorla model's prediction of an interaction between learning about the CS and learning about context is exemplified by an experiment in which three groups of subjects receive positive, zero, and negative contingencies between an intermittently presented CS and an intermittently presented UCS. Suppose that all groups receive the same, moderate rate of UCS presentations during the CS, but group Mod-Hi is given a high rate of UCSs in the absence of CS; group Mod-Mod, a moderate rate of UCSs in the absence of CS; and group Mod-Lo, a low rate of UCSs in the absence of CS. The Rescorla-Wagner model predicts that the asymptotic associative strength of the CS should be inversely related to the frequency of UCSs in the absence of CS, with the CS becoming inhibitory in group Mod-Hi, neutral in group Mod-Mod, and excitatory in group Mod-Lo.

Despite the interaction between discrete CS and context in acquisition, the Rescorla-Wagner model, as commonly interpreted, asserts that once conditioning has occurred, performance of a conditioned response to a CS depends only on the associative strength of that CS, and is independent of the associative strength of the context in which it is presented. Thus, a CS which has become a conditioned inhibitor as a result of a treatment administered in one context will still be an inhibitor when it is presented in a new context.

In the last few years, many students of animal learning have turned their attention to the role of context in conditioning and learning, and several new theoretical accounts of this role have been proposed (Gibbon & Balsam, 1981; Jenkins, Barnes, & Barrera, 1981; Miller & Schachtman, 1985; Nadel & Willner, 1980; O'Keefe & Nadel, 1978). Several of these accounts (Gibbon, 1981; Gibbon & Balsam, 1981; Jenkins, Barnes, & Barrera, 1981; Miller & Schachtman, 1985) construe the relationship between discrete CSs and context in conditioning experiments very differently from the Wagner-Rescorla model. They assert that learning about the CS is independent of learning about the context in which it occurs. We shall refer to this claim as the assumption of independence of learning. The Scalar Expectancy Theory (SET) advocated by Gibbon and Balsam is the most fully developed model incorporating the assumption of independence of learning, and will be the example used in our discussions of this assumption. Applying the assumption of independence of learning to the hypothetical experiment described above, SET would claim that all three groups should learn to expect UCSs at a moderate rate during the CS, but should learn to expect UCSs at relatively high, moderate, and low rates, respectively, during experimental sessions (i.e., in the experimental context).

Since the acquisition of conditioned responses to a discrete CS is known to be affected by p(UCS) in its absence, SET must find a place for this interaction between cue and context. It places the interaction at the level of performance. Specifically, in an autoshaping situation, if the rate of food (the UCS) presentation in the presence of the key light CS is sufficiently greater than the rate of food presentation in the session, the pigeon will peck the key light. If the two rates are roughly equal, as would result from a zero-contingency treatment, the bird will not peck. SET has only recently, and tentatively, been applied to the case of negatively correlated CS and food (Balsam, 1984; Kaplan, 1984). However, SET seems to imply that if the rate of food is sufficiently less during the CS than for the session as a whole, the pigeon should withdraw from the CS (review in LoLordo & Fairless, 1985; Wasserman, Franklin, & Hearst, 1974).

Now, consider an experiment in which pigeons receive food at a moderate rate during a key light CS, but at a high rate in its absence. Both the Rescorla-Wagner model and SET correctly predict that the pigeons should come to withdraw from this CS (Hearst & Franklin, 1977). Suppose we now move the pigeons and the key light CS to a discriminably different context in which the pigeons have previously received food at a low rate, and follow each CS presentation by food in a retardation of acquisition test (LoLordo & Fairless, 1985; Rescorla, 1969). The Rescorla-Wagner model predicts that, since the CS should be inhibitory even in this new context, the pigeons should be slow to learn to peck it. In contrast, SET predicts that since the expectation of food during the CS should be considerably greater than the expectation of food in the test context, the pigeons should peck the CS at the beginning of the test. The present experiment tests these predictions.

Fourteen experimentally naive, male, White Carneaux pigeons were used as subjects. They were maintained at 80% of their free-feeding weights throughout the experiment.

Three three-key conditioning chambers with the center keys covered were used in this experiment. Inserts with alternating black and white 5-cm-wide stripes could be attached to the chamber walls whenever a context manipulation was required. Holes cut in these inserts accommodated the observation window, food aperture, house light, and the two side keys. These key openings were covered with black electrical tape until the final testing phase of the experiment.

During all experimental sessions, the conditioning chambers were illuminated by a light mounted behind a Plexiglass disc 4.0 cm in diameter located in the upper right corner of the intelligence panel.

In-line projectors mounted behind the keys could illuminate either key with one of two stimuli: either red light or white light. Centered on the white field was a small oval drawn with a 1-mm black line, the horizontal axis inscribed with a 0.8-cm long black line.

Two probability generators controlled the probability of food presentation (UCS) during CS-on and CS-off times. The minimum time between two UCSs was 1 sec, and food presentations were 3 sec in duration.

Each chamber was equipped with a tilting floor (Wasserman, Franklin, & Hearst, 1974), with the fulcrum perpendicular to the center of the food aperture. A microswitch mounted under the floor made it possible to record the time spent by the pigeon on the side of the chamber containing the CS. Moreover, it permitted measurement of the pigeon's locomotor activity.

During the initial phase of the experiment, hopper training, the striped inserts were not present, and the keys were covered. Subjects were placed in the chamber with the hopper up and heaped full of grain. Once the subject approached and ate for approximately 10 sec, the tray was lowered and immediately raised again. As training progressed, the interval between grain presentations was increased to a maximum of 1 min and the duration of grain presentations was decreased until it reached a value of 3 sec.

Each subject received at least one 20-min hopper-training session per day for 3 consecutive days. Subjects that did not eat consistently received an additional session on those days. On the fourth day, subjects experienced a 40-min session designed to further facilitate hopper approach and eating. Three-second presentations of grain occurred during this session at a rate of 1.19 reinforcements/min.

Aside from ensuring eating efficiency, this magazine training procedure should have resulted in strong excitatory conditioning of the unlined context prior to the presentations of the negatively contingent key light and food (cf. Balsam & Schwartz, 1981).

The subjects were randomly assigned to one of two groups (see Table 8.1 for the experimental design), and both groups received daily 40-min training sessions in the unlined chambers (context H) for 40 days. Twenty, 20-sec presentations of red key light occurred during each session, ten on the right key and ten on the left. Key-light presentations were scheduled in a semi-random manner with the restriction that no more than three consecutive CSs occurred on the same side of the chamber. Treatments of the two groups differed only with regard to the probability of food occurrence during key light presentations. For one group (Group p=0) food presentations could not occur while the CS was present. The second group (Group p>0) received UCSs in the presence of the CS at a rate of 0.57 per min. When no CS was present, both groups received food at a rate of 1.19 per minute. Thus, both groups experienced a negative contingency between the CS and food.

Approach-withdrawal scores were calculated according to the formula A/(A + B), where A is the total amount of trial time during which the pigeon stood on the side of the chamber containing the illuminated-key CS, and B is the total amount of trial time during which the subject was on the opposite side. Thus, approach-withdrawal ratios less than 0.5 indicate withdrawal, and ratios greater than 0.5 indicate approach. Figure 8.1 presents the average of these ratios as a function of 2-day blocks of the negative contingency treatment. Data from blocks 13 and 14 are not plotted since equipment failures prevented the collection of data on these days. In addition, during one session of block three the data for one bird in Group p>0 were lost. This subject was assigned a score for that block equal to its score on the one day for which data were available. The vertical dashed line between blocks 20 and 21 indicates the end of this initial negative contingency treatment.

TABLE 8.1
Experimental Design

GROUP	NEGATIVE CONTINGENCY TRAINING Context H Red Key	CONTEXT DISC. Context H/Context L Red Key Only in H	RESISTANCE TO REINFORCEMENT TEST Context L Red Key, Circle Key
p > 0	R(UCS/CS) = 0.57 R(UCS/$\overline{CS}$) = 1.19	In H: as in negative contingency training	R(UCS/CS) = 3.0
p = 0	R(UCS/CS) = 0 R(UCS/$\overline{CS}$) = 1.19	In L: R(UCS) = 0.16	R(UCS/$\overline{CS}$) = 0

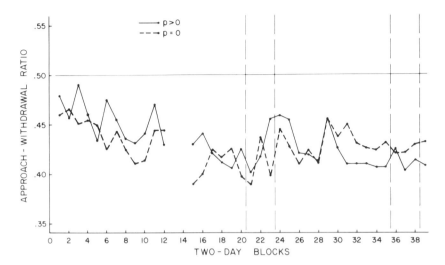

FIG. 8.1. Mean approach-withdrawal ratios for Groups p>0 and p=0 across two-day blocks of the negative contingency treatment. The pairs of vertical, dashed lines demarcate periods in which negative contingency sessions alternated randomly with sessions of exposure to a second, low food-rate context. No CSs were presented during the latter sessions.

The decreases in the approach-withdrawal ratios in Figure 8.1 indicate that both groups came to withdraw from the CS by the end of this phase. Performance of the two groups did not differ.

Following day 40 (Block 20) of the negative contingency treatment, the pigeons were subjected to the first context discrimination phase of the experiment. During this phase, which lasted 22 days, standard negative contingency sessions were alternated with low food-rate sessions. The black and white striped inserts (Context L) were in place during the low food-rate sessions, which also lasted 40 min. All keys were covered on low food-rate days. The rate of food delivery during these low food-rate sessions was 0.15 food presentations per min.

There were a total of six sessions of each type, one session per day. The two types of sessions were alternated semi-randomly with the constraint that no more than three sessions of one type could occur in succession. A pigeon's activity during the first 100 sec of each session (i.e., prior to the presentation of any food) was taken as a measure of discrimination between the two contexts. Birds in both groups were significantly more active in the context in which they were fed more frequently.

Introduction of the context discrimination procedure appeared to disrupt the withdrawal response in Group p>0 (see Figure 8.1). Consequently, all birds were given 24 additional sessions of the negative contingency treatment in the chambers without the striped inserts (Context H). At the completion of this second series of successive withdrawal training sessions, approach-withdrawal ratios appeared stable in both groups. A statistical analysis of the entire negative contingency phase (through block 35) indicated that the decrease in approach-withdrawal ratios depicted in Figure 8.1 was statistically reliable, and that neither the effect of group nor the groups by blocks interaction was significant. A post-hoc contrast indicated that the ratios for the last three training blocks (33–35) were reliably lower than those for the first three training blocks.

The second exposure to the context discrimination procedure was identical to the first. As before, withdrawal training alternated semi-randomly with exposure to the low food-rate setting, but in this case there was no apparent disruption of withdrawal (blocks 36–38, Fig. 8.1). Two successive withdrawal-training sessions concluded this phase of the experiment (block 39, Fig. 8.1). Approach-withdrawal ratios during this final training block did not differ reliably from those observed during the session immediately preceding context discrimination training (block 35). As in the first context discrimination phase, during the second one, the pigeons were more active in the high food-rate context than in the low one.

The resistance to reinforcement test took place in the striped (L) context. The side keys were uncovered and, after an initial, 100-sec activity measurement period, CS presentations were scheduled to occur according to a variable-time 115-sec schedule. The red key light stimulus (CS−) and the novel stimulus, an oval on a white field (CSN), were presented semi-randomly to either the left or right key, with the restriction that there were no more than three consecutive presentations of either stimulus. All CSs were reinforced, with food delivery occurring during the last three seconds of each 20-sec stimulus.

Subjects were tested in this manner until they reached a criterion of at least one peck on four consecutive presentations of each stimulus or until there had been 10 sessions.

Early in the resistance to reinforcement test, the birds appeared to be indifferent to the familiar CS, neither withdrawing from it, approaching it, nor pecking at it.

Table 8.2 presents the number of trials required by each bird to reach the acquisition criterion for both the withdrawal training (CS−) and novel (CSN) stimuli. The third column of Table 8.2 lists the stimulus for which this criterion was first achieved by each animal ("T" indicates a tie). Five of the seven birds in Group p>0, which experienced the low but non-zero rate of food delivery within CS presentations during withdrawal training, acquired key-pecking to the CS− before acquiring pecking to the novel cue. One bird (1956) did not learn to peck either stimulus, and another (1418) showed nearly equivalent acquisition to the cues. In Group p=0, three of the birds acquired the key-peck response to the novel stimulus before acquiring the response to the CS−, whereas one acquired the response to the CS− first. Bird 1846 showed equivalent acquisition to the two cues, and birds 3069 and 1437 failed to acquire the response to either CS.

TABLE 8.2
Trials to Criterion

	Bird	CS-	CS N	First Met Criterion In
	1358	45	90	CS-
	3009	31	37	CS-
	1384	27	42	CS-
Group	1365	65	84	CS-
p > 0	1402	16	24	CS-
	1956	90	90	T
	1418	27	26	CS N
	1947	28	18	CS N
	3019	26	7	CS N
	1871	90	36	CS N
Group	3069	90	90	T
p = 0	1846	23	23	T
	1437	90	90	T
	1415	32	40	CS-

Birds that did not acquire the response to a CS were assigned a trials to criterion score of 90.

Figure 8.2 depicts the mean number of trials required by each group to reach the acquisition criterion for each stimulus. An ANOVA performed on these data revealed no reliable effect for stimuli or groups. The group by stimulus interaction evident in Figure 8.2 was statistically reliable, and supports the conclusion that relative rates of acquisition to the two stimuli were a function of previous experience with the CS−.

SET asserts that conditioning of an expectation of food to a discrete CS proceeds independently of conditioning of an expectation of food to the context. Therefore, the pigeons in Group p>0 should have come to expect food during the red key light CS in the course of the negative contingency treatment. That these birds nonetheless learned to withdraw from the CS is consistent with the

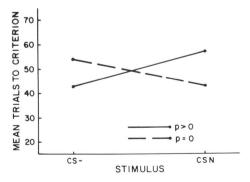

FIG. 8.2.   Mean trials to a criterion of four consecutive trials with at least one key peck in the resistance to reinforcement test. Both Group p>0 and Group p=0 received two stimuli, CS- and CSN.

performance rule central to SET, because the rate of food presentation during the CS was considerably lower than the rate during the session as a whole. This difference between the rates of food in CS and in session were even greater for Group $p=0$, and one might therefore expect the magnitude of withdrawal to have been relatively greater in this group.

The Rescorla-Wagner model also predicts the withdrawal from CS observed in both groups. In addition, it clearly predicts that the larger negative contingency between the CS and food in Group $p=0$ than in Group $p>0$ should result in a larger inhibitory CR in the former. However, equivalent withdrawal was observed in the two groups. This result may reflect equivalent magnitudes of conditioned inhibition. Alternatively, it may simply reflect an insensitivity of the approach-withdrawal index to different magnitudes of conditioned inhibition. Hearst and Franklin (1977) obtained data that support the latter possibility. They observed equivalent amounts of withdrawal from a key light CS in a group of pigeons that received food presentations at a rate of 0.5/min during the CS and 1.0/min in its absence and a group that never received food during CS but received it at a rate of 1.5/min in its absence. However, in a subsequent resistance to reinforcement test, Group 0.5–1.0 acquired an approach response to the CS more rapidly than Group 0–1.5.

The two theories under consideration predict different behavioral outcomes on the initial trials of the resistance to reinforcement treatment. Because the Rescorla-Wagner model asserts that the CS should remain inhibitory for both groups, it predicts that both should withdraw from the CS on these trials. However, manipulations designed to reduce the associative strength of a context in which inhibitory conditioning had been carried out have recently been shown to mask the ability of the inhibitor to evoke withdrawal in that context (Bottjer, 1982; Kaplan and Hearst, 1985). Our context shift manipulation, whereby pigeons were tested in a context in which they had been reinforced infrequently, seems to have had a similar effect, since the birds appeared indifferent to the stimuli on the first few trials. Perhaps the same manipulation was responsible for the relatively weak resistance to reinforcement effect observed in Group $p=0$ (e.g., as compared with Tomie & Kruse, 1980; Wasserman & Molina, 1975; Wessells, 1973).

A straightforward and strong version of SET's assertion of independence of learning about cue and context implies that pigeons in Group $p>0$ should approach and peck the familiar red key upon its first presentation in the low food-rate context. This immediate expression of a previously acquired expectation of food was not observed; the birds did not approach or peck the key on the first few trials. Because the birds' activity levels were reliably different in the two contexts, it cannot be claimed that they had failed to discriminate the contexts.

One could weaken the prediction made by SET somewhat by postulating some disruptive, short-lived effect of the context shift manipulation, which would allow behavioral evidence of an expectation of food conditioned to the CS to emerge only slowly. Our experiment, which entailed a resistance to reinforcement test rather than the unreinforced test trials used in other studies (Balsam,

1982; Durlach, 1982), was designed in anticipation of this possibility. In this case, SET predicts that pigeons in Group p>0 should begin pecking the CS− before pigeons in Group p=0. More importantly, in Group p>0, acquisition of pecking at CS− should proceed more rapidly than acquisition of pecking at the novel key light, an outcome inconsistent with the notion that the CS− had become inhibitory, in the traditional sense, during the negative contingency treatment. SET's predictions concerning possible acquisition differences between the two stimuli within Group p=0 are less straightforward, because the relative position of the CSs on the hypothetical expectancy continuum is difficult to specify a priori.

The reliable interaction of groups and stimuli illustrated in Figure 8.2 provides some support of SET's claim that acquisition of responding to CS− (re CSN) should be facilitated in Group p>0. Moreover, the interaction implies that this facilitative effect is as large as the retardation of pecking at CS−, re CSN, in Group p=0. However, we must emphasize that neither of these within-subjects effects is very large. They are no larger than the differential effect of the novel CS in the two groups. Moreover, a subsequent study using a between-groups design failed to replicate even this interaction; there were marked individual differences in acquisition within each group.

A number of conditioning phenomena are thought to depend critically on the interaction between a discrete cue and the context in which it is presented. These include the UCS pre-exposure effect, and the effects of zero and negative contingencies between a CS and a UCS. It is generally agreed that the occurrence of UCSs in the presence of context alone is important in producing these effects (Baker, 1977; Dweck & Wagner, 1970; Tomie, 1981). However, as we have indicated, there is as yet no consensus about the level at which the interaction between cue and context takes place. SET claims that the influence of expectancies evoked by context is purely behavioral. According to this view, the CS's acquisition of the capacity to evoke an expectancy of the UCS is merely masked, and not blocked, as a result of prior or concurrent presentations of unsignaled UCSs.

With regard to the UCS pre-exposure effect, SET claims that the attenuated acquisition of excitatory CRs characteristic of animals that have been pre-exposed to the UCS in the conditioning context cannot be taken as evidence for attenuated acquisition of CS-controlled expectancies of reinforcement. It maintains that the preexposed group and a non preexposed control acquire equivalent expectancies, but that the strong expectation of the UCS evoked by context in the preexposed animals prevents the developing CS-evoked expectation from being manifested in performance. By this account, an appropriate context manipulation following conditioning should reveal equivalent behavioral control by the CS in the two groups.

A study by Randich and Ross (1985) tested this prediction using the Conditioned Emotional Response (CER) procedure with rats. Two distinctly different experimental settings were employed. Two groups of rats were preexposed to shock in context 1, whereas two control groups were not. One experimental and one control group were then given CER training in this same setting, whereas the other pair received this training in the non preexposed context 2. UCS preexposure did attenuate the rate of conditioning, and this effect was context specific. That is, the experimental group preexposed and conditioned in the same setting (Group +C1) exhibited retarded acquisition of the CER relative to its control, whereas the group preexposed in context 1 but conditioned in context 2 (Group −C2) acquired conditioned suppression at the same fairly rapid rate as its control.

The critical test of SET's independence-of-learning assertion took place in a subsequent phase of the experiment. Subjects from both experimental groups were given non-reinforced presentations of the CS in context 2. Thus, if the attenuated performance of Group +C1 reflected context-based masking of a CS-controlled expectancy of shock as large as that acquired by Group −C2, then this expectancy should have been manifested in equivalent conditioned suppression by the two groups in a test context associated with a weak expectation of UCS. However, strong suppression was evident only in the animals that had been conditioned in the non-preexposed setting. The context shift manipulation did not result in unmasking of conditioned suppression in Group +C1, and this finding supports the context-blocking interpretation of the UCS preexposure effect.

Several other studies have been designed to permit unmasking of learned expectations. Durlach (1982) exposed pigeons to two contexts. In context 1, key light CS1 was followed by food 25% of the time. In context 2, key light CS2 was also reinforced 25% of the time, but enough intertrial UCSs were presented to eliminate the contingency between CS2 and food. After several sessions of this procedure, both CSs were presented in extinction in each context. Several comparisons seem relevant to the assumption of independence of learning. First, contradicting SET, the birds pecked less often at CS2 than at CS1 in context 1. SET predicts unmasking of the learning about CS2, and, thus, equal responding to the two CSs. On the other hand, the Rescorla-Wagner model predicts the observed superiority of responding to CS1. However, comparison of the amount of responding to CS2 in the two contexts revealed greater responding to that cue in context 1, the low reinforcement rate context. That difference is in accord with the prediction from SET, and contradicts the Rescorla-Wagner model.

In a conceptually similar experiment reviewed by Rescorla, Durlach and Grau (1985), Durlach did not observe any unmasking of an expectancy of food in response to a behaviorally neutral, zero-contingency key light. This finding contrasts with the context-based facilitation observed in the study just reviewed. A potentially important difference between the two studies is that, in the first study, stimulus generalization resulted in a low, but apparently stable, rate of pecking at the zero-contingency key prior to the context-shift. The between-groups design of the second study precluded the development of generalized responding, and virtually no key pecking was evident during either zero-contingency training or on the non-reinforced test trials in a context in which the birds had never been fed.

In an unpublished M.A. thesis, Fairless (1982) used a related procedure. Instead of attempting to unmask learning by moving the CS to another context in which the subject had experienced a relatively low reinforcement rate, he attempted to unmask learning by exposing the subject to a lowered (zero) reinforcement rate in the original conditioning context.

Two groups of pigeons, Groups ZC-EXT and ZC-HC, were exposed to twelve sessions in which there was a zero-contingency between a key light CS and food. A third group, Group UCS-EXT, received only the food presentations during this phase of the experiment. Next, Groups ZC-EXT and UCS-EXT received 10 daily context extinction sessions, while birds in Group ZC-HC remained in their home cages. Finally, all birds received a resistance-to-reinforcement test. In this test Groups ZC-EXT and UCS-EXT did not differ, and both acquired the key peck CR in fewer trials than Group ZC-HC (see Figure 8.3). SET erroneously predicts that the unmasking procedure should have revealed a greater expectation of food during the CS in Group ZC-EXT than in Group UCS-EXT (for which the CS was novel) at the start of the test, and, thus, should have resulted in faster acquisition by the former. It should be noted that in this study, as in the second Durlach study reviewed above, the pigeons in the zero-contingency groups were not pecking the key at all, before the test phase of the experiment.

Parallels to these findings of Durlach and Fairless are evident in an experiment by Lindblom and Jenkins (1981; see also Jenkins & Lambos, 1983, Exp. 2), which focused on the effectiveness of a zero-contingency treatment in eliminating excitatory conditioned responding to a key light CS. Introduction of the zero-contingency procedure, in which $p(UCS/CS)$ was unchanged, but $p(UCS/\overline{CS})$ was increased, did eliminate key pecking, as did the standard, CS-alone, extinction treatment administered to another group. However, when these groups were given additional sessions of standard extinction, there was a marked recovery of key pecking in the group that had previously experienced the zero-

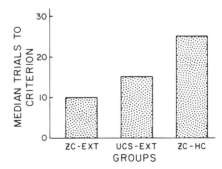

FIG. 8.3.   Median trials to a criterion of three consecutive trials with at least one key peck for Groups ZC-EXT, UCS-EXT, and ZC-HC.

contingency treatment. There was no spontaneous recovery in the group that simply received additional extinction sessions.

This outcome can be construed as supporting SET's assumption of independence of learning, if one is willing to assume that at the start of the first extinction session, the expectation of food evoked by the context was reduced more rapidly than the expectation evoked by the CS, which had been maintained throughout the zero-contingency treatment. Consequently, the expectation evoked by the CS would have been unmasked and manifested in key pecking, once the first few minutes had elapsed. However, two other results from the Lindblom and Jenkins experiment cannot readily be explained by SET and cast doubt on its explanation of the extinction-induced recovery of responding. First, prior exposure to a positive contingency between CS and food was necessary for the recovery of key pecking in extinction. That is, a group that had been exposed only to a zero-contingency treatment prior to extinction did not peck the key at any stage of the experiment, even though SET predicts that such a group should have pecked in extinction. Furthermore, a group that had experienced a positive contingency between CS and food, and then a lengthy negative contingency treatment in which the CS was never reinforced, also showed a marked recovery of key pecking early in extinction. Indeed, the recovery was as large as in the group which had received the zero-contingency in phase 2.

This finding is similar to the observation by Kaplan and Hearst (1985) that the approach-eliciting power of a key light CS that had initially signalled food survived a long period in which the CS was never reinforced, although reinforcers occurred in its absence. After the birds had learned to withdraw from the CS as a result of this negative contingency treatment, they received several sessions of non-reinforced exposure to the context. When the CS was again presented, it immediately evoked approach. These findings are not readily interpreted by either the Rescorla-Wagner model or SET. The Wagner-Rescorla model predicts no recovery of excitatory conditioned responding in this group, because non-reinforced exposure to the context should not alter the inhibitory associative strength that the CS had acquired as a result of the negative contingency treatment. SET predicts no recovery of excitatory conditioned responding in this group, or in the negative contingency group of Lindblom and Jenkins, because exposure to the non-reinforced CS during the negative contingency treatments should have led the birds to expect no food during the CS, thus eliminating any associative basis for recovery.

All the studies we have reviewed in one way or another attempt to unmask a CS-evoked expectation of reinforcement by presenting that CS in a context in which the rate of reinforcement has been low. None of these studies provides compelling evidence for SET's assumption of independence of learning. As we have noted, the experiments by Lindblom and Jenkins yielded some data compatible with that assumption, but other features of their data contradicted it or other assumptions of the theory.

Durlach's within-subjects experiment also produced results which are compatible with the assumption of independence of learning, but in that study there was a fair amount of pecking at the zero-contingency CS during the zero-contingency treatment, perhaps reflecting stimulus generalization of pecking at the other CS, upon which food was positively contingent. When the zero-contingency stimulus was subsequently presented in the low food-rate context 1, increased pecking occurred. This pecking may reflect this generalized excitation, rather than any associative learning specific to the zero-contingency treatment. If that is so, Durlach's data could be taken to support SET's performance rule, but not its assumption of independence of learning.

ACKNOWLEDGMENTS

This research was supported by Grant A-0283 from the Natural Sciences and Engineering Research Council of Canada. During the course of this research, J. L. F. was supported by NSERC and I. W. Killam Scholarships.

REFERENCES

Baker, A. G. (1977). Conditioned inhibition arising from a between-sessions negative correlation. *Journal of Experimental Psychology: Animal Behavior Processes, 3,* 144–155.

Balsam, P. D. (1982). Bringing the background to the foreground: The role of contextual cues in autoshaping. In M. Commons, R. Herrnstein, & A. Wagner (Eds.), *Quantitative analyses of behavior: Vol. III: Acquisition* (pp. 145–171). New York: Ballinger.

Balsam, P. D. (1984). Relative time in trace conditioning. In J. Gibbon and L. Allan (Eds.), *Timing and time perception* (pp. 211–227). New York: New York Academy of Sciences.

Balsam, P. D., & Schwartz, A. L. (1981). Rapid contextual conditioning in autoshaping. *Journal of Experimental Psychology: Animal Behavior Processes, 7,* 382–393.

Bottjer, S. W. (1982). Conditioned approach and withdrawal behavior in pigeons: Effects of a novel extraneous stimulus during acquisition and extinction. *Learning and Motivation, 13,* 44–67.

Durlach, P. (1982). Pavlovian learning and performance when CS and US are uncorrelated. In M. Commons, R. Herrnstein, and A. Wagner (Eds.), *Quantitative analyses of behavior: Vol. III: Acquisition* (pp. 173–193). New York: Ballinger.

Dweck, C. S., & Wagner, A. R. (1970). Situational cues and correlation between CS and US as determinants of the conditioned emotional response. *Psychonomic Science, 18,* 145–147.

Fairless, J. L. (1982). *Contingency effects in animal learning: A review and experiment.* Unpublished master's thesis, Dalhousie University, Halifax, Nova Scotia.

Gibbon, J. (1981). The contingency problem in autoshaping. In C. M. Locurto, H. S. Terrace, & J. Gibbon (Eds.). *Autoshaping and conditioning theory* (pp. 285–308). New York: Academic Press.

Gibbon, J., & Balsam, P. D. (1981). The spread of association in time. In C. M. Locurto, H. S. Terrace and J. Gibbon (Eds.), *Autoshaping and conditioning theory* (pp. 219–254). New York: Academic Press.

Hearst, E., & Franklin, S. R. (1977). Positive and negative relations between a signal and food: Approach-withdrawal behavior to the signal. *Journal of Experimental Psychology: Animal Behavior Processes, 3,* 37–52.

Jenkins, H. M., Barnes, R. A., & Barrera, F. J. (1981). Why autoshaping depends on trial spacing. In C. M. Locurto, H. S. Terrace, & J. Gibbon (Eds.), *Autoshaping and conditioning theory* (pp. 255–284). New York: Academic Press.

Jenkins, H. M., & Lambos, W. A. (1983). Test of two explanations of response elimination by noncontingent reinforcement. *Animal Learning and Behavior, 11*, 302–308.

Kaplan, P. S. (1984). Importance of relative temporal parameters in trace autoshaping: From excitation to inhibition. *Journal of Experimental Psychology: Animal Behavior Processes, 10*, 113–126.

Kaplan, P. S., & Hearst, E. (1985). Contextual control and excitatory vs. inhibitory learning: Studies of extinction, reinstatement, and interference. In P. Balsam and A. Tomie (Eds.), *Context and learning* (pp. 195–224). Hillsdale, NJ: Lawrence Erlbaum Associates.

Lindblom, L. L., & Jenkins, H. M. (1981). Responses eliminated by noncontingent or negatively contingent reinforcement recover in extinction. *Journal of Experimental Psychology: Animal Behavior Processes, 7*, 175–190.

LoLordo, V. M., & Fairless, J. L. (1985). Inhibition: The literature since 1969. In R. R. Miller and N. E. Spear (Eds.), *Information processing in animals: Inhibition and contingencies*. Hillsdale, NJ: Lawrence Erlbaum Associates.

Miller, R. R., and Schachtman, T. R. (1985). Conditioning context as an associative baseline: Implications for the content of associations and the epiphenomenal nature of conditioned inhibition. In R. R. Miller and N. E. Spear (Eds.), *Information processing in animals: Inhibition and contingencies*. Hillsdale, NJ: Lawrence Erlbaum Associates.

Nadel, L., & Willner, J. (1980). Context and conditioning: A place for space. *Physiological Psychology, 8*, 218–228.

O'Keefe, J., & Nadel, L. (1978). *The hippocampus as a cognitive map*. Oxford: Oxford University Press.

Randich, A., & Ross, R. T. (1985). The role of contextual stimuli in mediating the effects of pre- and post exposure to the unconditioned stimulus alone on acquisition and retention of conditioned suppression. In P. Balsam and A. Tomie (Eds.), *Context and learning* (pp. 105–132). Hillsdale, NJ: Lawrence Erlbaum Associates.

Rescorla, R. A. (1969). Pavlovian conditioned inhibition. *Psychological Bulletin, 72*, 77–94.

Rescorla, R. A., Durlach, P. J., & Grau, J. W. (1985). Contextual learning in Pavlovian conditioning. In P. Balsam and A. Tomie (Eds.), *Context and learning* (pp. 23–56). Hillsdale, NJ: Lawrence Erlbaum Associates.

Rescorla, R. A., & Wagner, A. R. (1972). A theory of Pavlovian conditioning: Variations in the effectiveness of reinforcement and nonreinforcement. In A. H. Black and W. F. Prokasy (Eds.), *Classical conditioning II: Theory and research* (pp. 64–99). New York: Appleton-Century-Croft.

Tomie, A. (1981). Effects of unpredictable food on the subsequent acquisition of autoshaping: Analysis of the context-blocking hypothesis. In C. M. Locurto, H. S. Terrace, and J. Gibbon (Eds.), *Autoshaping and conditioning theory* (pp. 181–215). New York: Academic Press.

Tomie, A., & Kruse, J. (1980). Retardation tests of inhibition following discriminative autoshaping. *Animal Learning and Behavior, 8*, 401–409.

Wagner, A. R., and Rescorla, R. A. (1972). Inhibition in Pavlovian conditioning: Application of a theory. In R. A. Boakes and M. S. Halliday (Eds.), *Inhibition and learning* (pp. 301–336). London: Academic Press.

Wasserman, E. A., Franklin, S. R., & Hearst, E. (1974). Pavlovian appetitive contingencies and approach vs. withdrawal to conditioned stimuli in pigeons. *Journal of Comparative and Physiological Psychology, 86*, 616–627.

Wasserman, E. A., & Molina, E. (1975). Explicitly unpaired key light and food presentations. Interference with subsequent auto-shaped key-pecking in pigeons. *Journal of Experimental Psychology: Animal Behavior Processes, 104*, 30–38.

Wessells, M. G. (1973). Autoshaping, errorless discrimination, and conditioned inhibition. *Science, 182*, 941–943.

9 An Empirical Legacy of Two-process Theory: Two-term versus Three-term Relations

Lynn J. Hammond
Temple University

Appetitive operant behavior may appear far afield from the topical focus of Richard L. Solomon's laboratory. While I was a postdoctoral student there, research was focused on aversive control, Pavlovian inhibition, classical to instrumental transfer, conditioned helplessness, and several other topics neatly tied together (at the time) by a version of two-process theory that stressed motivational influences of Pavlovian conditioning on Thorndikian conditioning (Rescorla & Solomon, 1967). The subtle but enormously influential stamp of Solomon's views on his students of that era can still be seen in their papers today.

One legacy of Solomon's two-process theory approach to the analysis of behavior that is apparent today is the effort by many to analyze complex instrumental or operant situations as an interaction between Pavlovian (S-S*) and Thorndikian (R-S*) relations,[1] whether one emphasizes transfer of hypothetical motivational processes to instrumental responding (e.g., Bolles, 1972), parallels between associative learning for the two kinds of relations (e.g., Mackintosh, 1974), or more descriptive approaches that focus upon the empirical manipulations associated with S-S* and R-S* relations (e.g., Jenkins, 1977). This paper is written in the context of the latter or more empirical, operational form of two-process analysis. Although, much of the conceptualization in this latter, more empirical, vein (e.g., Jenkins, 1977; Williams, 1981) has developed as an ob-

---

[1]The term "relation" is used in a very general, unspecified sense, much as Jenkins (1977, p. 47) has used the term.

vious theoretical consequence of the research on autoshaping, the work I will describe below does not deal with autoshaping at all, but deals instead with appetitive free operant behavior.

Another topic which was also developing in Solomon's laboratory when I was there was a concern about the adequacy of the contiguity between S and S* as the empirical basis for Pavlovian conditioning (Rescorla, 1967). Simultaneously, concerns about noncontiguity interpretations of operant avoidance were to be seen in the work of Herrnstein and Hineline (1966) at Harvard. If one is to analyze the interaction of S-S* and R-S* relations, the nature of the relation, contiguity or otherwise, ought to play a critical role in such analysis. Thus, two-process theory and theories such as contingency theory, which stress more than just the contiguity between the two events of conditioning, must be intertwined.

AN APPETITIVE PARALLEL TO TWO-PROCESS AVOIDANCE STUDIES

The history of the two-process approaches to avoidance is a chronicle of attempts to disentangle the effects of two possible relations, S-S* and R-S*. The impetus for doing so appears stronger in the case of avoidance than in the case of appetitive operant conditioning, possibly because two-process critics such as Sidman (1953) treated the problem in very empirical terms. It strikes this author that appetitive two-process theory approaches placed less emphasis upon the difference between S-S* and R-S* relations because of the stronger theoretical tradition that stressed separation between habit and incentive—especially the fractional anticipatory goal mechanism. Be that as it may, no fully parallel argument about the role of stimuli in the development and maintenance of instrumental conditioning exists for the appetitive case as it does for the aversive case.

In their attempts to explain avoidance, opponents of the two-process approach developed special techniques which they hypothesized would rid the avoidance situation of possible S-S* relations, and, thus, the actual avoidance behavior could then be explained solely in terms of R-S* relations without the invocation of conditioned fear stimuli (Herrnstein and Hineline, 1966: Sidman, 1953). In the course of these attempts, it was not unusual for investigators from the same camp to turn around and re-introduce explicit stimuli for the purpose of demonstrating how S-S* relations could influence avoidance behavior (e.g., Sidman, 1955), even though, according to their argument, such S-S* relations were not necessary to produce adequate avoidance behavior.

Our work on appetitive operant behavior has in some sense been guided by a latter day parallel to the research strategies of these investigators who minimized stimuli in avoidance. We, too, sought a paradigm that could support operant behavior and yet be as devoid as possible of S-S* relations. And, after that goal was accomplished, we, too, re-introduced stimuli to study their effect upon operant behavior, but, in our appetitive studies, we have focused on three-term or S, R, S* relations which, as we shall point out, are quite complex.

Paynter, working in our laboratory (unpublished) has shown that the appetitive analog to the "Herrnstein-Hineline" schedule, wherein each response shifts the organism to a higher density of variable time (VT) reinforcement, supports lever-pressing behavior of rats very effectively. However, there are two reasons why this schedule did not meet our needs for disentangling S-S* and R-S* relations. For one, as in the work on avoidance (Herrnstein & Hineline, 1966), the average delay between a response and the reinforcer (shock or reward) increases as the two values of low and high density reinforcement are made increasingly disparate. Thus, the operant control over behavior may be interpreted as a product of this difference in delay of reinforcement. Because time is a cue that enters into S-S* relations (witness the common temporal cue interpretation of Sidman avoidance), we sought a schedule which would minimize such S-S* relations to an even greater extent—although as the history of animal learning illustrates, such S-S* relations may never be eliminated entirely (e.g., responses have cue properties which could enter into S-S* relations). Second, the schedule we sought must also be one where S* consequences of not responding can be manipulated independently of those for responding; in other words we wanted the schedule to make it possible for one to experimentally evaluate a contingency theory of R-S* relations.

A TRULY CONSTANT PROBABILITY SCHEDULE

The schedule we selected to minimize S-S* relations and to manipulate R-S* contingency is one of a large class developed by Schoenfeld (Schoenfeld, Cummings, & Hearst, 1956) in the context of some very complex arguments about schedules of reinforcement (the T-tau system)— arguments we wish to circumvent here. Therefore, we will call this procedure a truly *constant probability schedule* of reinforcement. This schedule treats each brief period of time (in our case, 1 sec) independently of all other time periods and allocates reinforcement for responding or not responding at the end of that time period according to prearranged, independent probabilities. In this way, reinforcement can be made to occur as a consequence of the immediately proceding response or absence of response such that reinforcement is independent of any earlier responding and independent of the time since the last reinforcement. In other words, there are no programmed ratio or interval characteristics of this schedule.

To program this constant probability schedule, a random number table was used to determine two independent sets of random times, one set for reinforcement given for a response, R, and the other for reinforcement given for *no-R*. At the end of each second, reinforcement was allocated by one of these two sets of random times depending on whether the rat made at least one response in the preceding second. In this way, earned and unearned reinforcements were completely independent of each other (cf. Hammond, 1980). Each schedule was characterized by its two probability values (e.g., .20-.05), the first for *if-R* reinforcement the second for *if no-R* reinforcement. Furthermore, reinforcement did not "set up" and "wait" for a response on this schedule.

We have found that rats can be quickly trained to lever-press on such schedules (as would be expected from Schoenfeld's work), and that when the probability of reinforcement is equal for both R and no-R, response rates decline radically (Hammond, 1980). The aim of this earlier work was to study the applicability of one form of contingency theory to free operant appetitive behavior. But much simpler questions about R-S* relations can be asked using this procedure. For example, are rats sensitive to the probabilistic relationship between R and S* when S-S* relations are minimized? We turn now to that question.

THE EFFECT OF R-S* RELATIONS UPON RESPONDING

From the viewpoint of a parallel to the study of avoidance, our appetitive reinforcement schedule was selected to minimize the role of cues in operant behavior just as was the case for work on avoidance behavior by Sidman and by Herrnstein and Hineline. And just as they were able to demonstrate strong avoidance behavior under conditions of minimal signaling of reinforcement (especially with the Herrnstein-Hineline schedule), so also demonstrations of robust responding under truly constant probability schedules (e.g., Sidley & Schoenfeld, 1964) actually make the same point for appetitive operant behavior—that it can be sustained by R-S* relations alone.

Given that probabilistic relations between R and S* are adequate to maintain operant behavior, the question can then be asked as to how the parameters of this probabilistic R-S* relation influence operant performance. As is well known, traditional approaches to appetitive operant behavior have emphasized the discriminative characteristics of such schedules such as interval and ratio characteristics and it has been shown that these variables have a powerful influence upon operant behavior. The questions being asked here are quite different and, indeed, perhaps independent of these traditional schedule manipulations.

The parameters of the truly constant probability schedule are the liklihood of reinforcement given a response (if-R, S* probability) and the liklihood of reinforcement given no response (if-no-R, S* probability). Each individual schedule is described by two probability values, the first for R and the second for no-R reinforcement probability (e.g., .10-.05). The first point we wish to make about R-S* relations using this technique is that if there was no unearned reinforcement in the situation, then our rats were virtually unresponsive to changes in the probability of reinforcement given a response. This was shown in a series of unpublished experiments with Michael Weinberg. As long as the reinforcement probability for an R was above some threshold value, each rat appeared to respond at a fairly set rate, even when S* probability was eight times as great as that threshold value, and the rat was earning what would be considered a very rich or dense rate of reinforcement on traditional schedules.

As an example of this research, consider a case where Weinberg and I placed two groups of four rats each on multiple constant probability schedules of water reinforcement. There were two components, each 3.75 min long, one with a flashing light present and one with no light present during that component. There was no unearned reinforcement in this experiment, and, for one group, the control, the earned reinforcement probability was always 0.16 in both components. For the other or experimental group, the earned reinforcement probability was also 0.16 in the absence of light, but dropped four-fold to .04 in the light component. Figure 9.1 plots the mean proportion of responses in the light versus the total number of responses in a session for the two groups across relevant sessions in this experiment. A ratio of 0.50 indicates no difference in responding between components. The ratios are slightly smaller for the experimental group in the beginning of training, but as training on the multiple schedule continues, these differences seem to disappear. Continued training with the same animals in an additional experiment did not reveal any difference between components.

We do not dwell upon these negative findings; rather, we wish to point out their implications for an analysis in terms of R-S* relations. First of all we argue that even though rats appear insensitive to the probabilities of earned reinforcement when S-S* relations are minimized, this does not mean that these earned reinforcement probabilities exert no effect upon the organism. Weinberg (1982) has shown that rats will readily choose the higher of two, truly constant, proba-

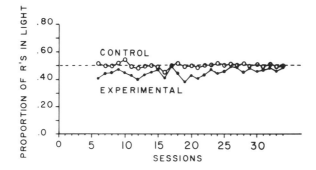

FIG. 9.1.   A daily measure of differential responding to the two components of a multiple schedule where a low probability of reinforcement (.04) for responding in the light was compared to a high probability of reinforcement (.16) in the absence of light in the experimental group. The control group received the high probability for responding in both light and its absence. A score of .50 indicates equal responding in both components.

bility schedules when neither schedule involves unearned reinforcement, and the schedules are presented concurrently in a free operant two-lever choice situation. Secondly, when we pool our data from published and unpublished studies of single, truly constant, probability schedules of reinforcement, it would appear that the probability of the earned reinforcement relative to the probability of unearned reinforcement governs operant performance in a rather complex way, and, thus, the probability of reinforcement given a response is important for predicting behavior even in single alternative response situations. Such considerations have usually been discussed under the topic of contingency theory, and, in the next section, we discuss that approach and our own suggested alternatives.

CONTINGENCY, NECESSITY AND SUFFICIENCY IN R-S* RELATIONS

Contingency theories of conditioning have stressed that more than R-S* contiguity is important in determining conditioning. When these theories have been explicit, they have specified that instances in which the response occurs by itself (molecular extinction), instances in which the reinforcement occurs by itself (unearned reinforcement), and instances in which neither occur (intertrial or response interval) are also very important in determining conditioning. These explicit theories, each of which can be represented by a mathematical formula which combines the frequency of each of the four categories of instances listed above, have been reviewed by Hammond and Paynter (1983). Our findings about the insensitivity of rats to the probabilities of earned reinforcement are very relevant to the evaluation of such different contingency theories, for all the formulas (as noted in Hammond & Paynter, 1983) predict differences in response rate under different earned reinforcement probabilities, when these formulas are applied to the specifics of our experimental situations. Thus, there seems to be some difficulty with these explicit contingency theories.

Unfortunately, some investigators see this theoretical issue as a simple choice between something (undefined) called contingency and the older traditional contiguity viewpoint. In this simplistic view, a telling criticism of contingency theory (in general) is an argument for R-S* contiguity. But explicit contingency theory argued for many additional empirical considerations—what we have shown is difficulty with one of these four empirical determinants of conditioning, as suggested by current contingency theories, namely the manipulation of the number of response-followed-by-non-reinforcement instances. The other empirical arguments of contingency theory are still quite valid—that one must take into account (a) the number of times that S* occurs without an R, if we are to specify the R-S* relation that produces the best conditioning and (b) the length of the intertrial interval in classical conditioning.

Another way of talking about how unreinforced responses and reinforcement presented alone define the R-S* relation that specifies conditioning other than mathematical contingency theory, has been suggested to me by my colleague

Walter Paynter. He argues for an analysis in terms of the logical relations between R and S*, based on the extent to which R is necessary for S* and the extent to which R is sufficient for S*. This argument is not to be confused with arguments about whether conditions are necessary or sufficient for conditioning to occur. Here, the object of the terms necessary or sufficient is S*, not conditioning. In logic, if one term, say R, is necessary for a second term to exist, say S*, then S* can never occur by itself. If R is sufficient for S*, then R should never occur alone. If the logical terms of necessary and sufficient are to be applied to the R-S* relation that determines conditioning, adaptions of the logical relation must be made. In logic, a single violation of the necessary or sufficient relation invalidates that relation. Thus, logically, if a single R occurs alone, then R is not sufficient for S*. To apply these logical concepts to the real world conditioning situation, the rationale must be changed, so that one could speak of necessary and sufficient conditions as though they were on a continuum rather than all-or-none, as is the case in a truth table analysis. One way of doing so is to speak of the degree to which the organism is sensitive to instances that are logically contrary to the necessity of R for S* and the sufficiency of R for S*.

Both our findings on the insensitivity of rats to variations in earned S* probability and the ubiquitious demonstrations of the ability of organisms to perform under conditions of extreme intermittency of S* illustrate how uninfluenced organisms are by information that their behavior is not sufficent for S* to occur. On the other hand, there are quite a few studies that have found that unearned reinforcement (S* without an R) produces lowered rates of responding (e.g., Hammond, 1980). So, one could summarize these two findings about R-S* relations by saying that organisms react rather strongly to the necessary relation between R and S* but very poorly, if at all, to the sufficient relation between R and S*.

This argument is related to contingency theories, because all such explicit theories, as reviewed by Hammond and Paynter (1983), are expressed as formulae whose indicies often vary as the sufficiency and the necessity of R for S* is varied in the manner described above. This is directly the case with the phi correlation coefficient, indirectly or accidently the result with most calculations of other contingency indices. Without going into great detail at this point, one can broadly conclude that operant contingency as indexed by these formulae is based on both the necessity and the sufficiency of R for S*. Since organisms react poorly to the sufficient relation between R and S*, explicit contingency theories are poorly descriptive of how organisms condition. But most research on contingency (e.g., Hammond, 1980) has inadvertently manipulated the necessary relation between R and S* (or CS and US) and, thus, has typically been very successful in showing that as the index of contingency varies, so does the degree of conditioning. Contingency indices also vary as the time between conditioning events varies (e.g., intertrial interval in classical conditioning) and some, such as that by Gibbon and Balsam (1981), have been successful in making predictions about that variable.

DO SUFFICIENCY AND NECESSITY OF R-S*
RELATIONS INTERACT?

Our comments about how the sufficiency of the relationship between R and S* has little or no influence upon rates of responding in operant conditioning apply primarily to situations where no unearned S* occurs. As we examine the data from varied experiments using the constant probability schedule, we can see instances where unearned reinforcement is present, and the rats are sensitive to the probability of earned reinforcement.

For example, a group of rats was trained to lever-press on a .08-.00 schedule of reinforcement, which produced a high level of responding. They were then placed on a .08-.08 schedule, where earned and unearned reinforcement equalled one another, and they declined to approximately one-quarter of their earlier level of responding. So far, these findings are the same as those reported before (Hammond, 1980). However, in this unpublished experiment with Paynter, a further phase was added in which these rats were now shifted to a .16-.08 schedule. Under this new .16-.08 schedule, they increased their response rate to almost but not quite as high a response rate as the rats had originally shown under the .08-.00 schedule. Notice that the only variable which changed from the second to the third and last phase was the probability of earned reinforcement (a manipulation of the sufficiency of the R-S* relation). In this sense, it can be argued that the necessity and sufficiency of R for S* interact to determine response rate.

Our experimentation is far too incomplete to describe this interaction with any confidence, but one loose speculation that goes farther in summarizing this complex interaction than any others which we can generate is surprising simple. Assume for the moment that our rats do not react to the quantitative difference between earned and unearned S* but react instead to the qualitative difference. If the earned S* probability is noticeably greater than the unearned S* probability, then the organism responds at some response rate characteristic of its performance with that manipulandum and that particular S* used in that experiment. As the unearned reinforcement probability gets perceptually similar to the earned reinforcement probability, then the rat's response rate drops down to its rate that it displays under so called zero contingencies (a rate which varies widely from rat to rat). If the unearned reinforcement probability is perceptually greater than the earned reinforcement probability, response rate may decline to zero. This is a very loose notion, but it serves to quickly summarize the unpublished data pattern for the reader and serves as a further guide or heuristic for our research on so-called contingency.

THREE TERM RELATIONS: S, R, AND S*

At the outset, we stressed that our goal (in common with the more empirical offshoot of two-process theory) was to disentangle S-S* and R-S* relations so that we could study them in isolation. Our analysis of R-S* relations in the appetitive operant has lead us to a close scrutiny of the relative value of earned and unearned reinforcement. But as we noted, our concern, like students of avoidance, is also with the the role stimuli play in the control of behavior that is otherwise maintained by R-S* relations.

What can happen when a stimulus is added to an operant baseline maintained by R-S* relations? For one, that stimulus can enter into relation with the S* of the situation independently of the Rs. In such a case, one would now have operant behavior governed by two different categories of two-term relations, S-S*, and R-S*. I believe such a notion is part of the legacy of empirical two-process theory. Rescorla and Solomon (1967) argued that the transfer of control experiments showing that S-S* relations or Pavlovian conditioning can modulate R-S* baselines of responding increased the liklihood that operant conditioning observed apart from the transfer design could also be at least partially a concatenation of S-S* and R-S* effects.

In somewhat similar fashion, portions of the autoshaping literature have also analyzed operant conditioning-like situations as a competition between S-S* and R-S* relations (i.e., omission manipulations of autoshaping), or as a concatenation of the two types of relations (i.e., the additivity theory of behavioral contrast, see Schwartz & Gamzu, 1977). At the same time, it is quite clear that in addition to a concatenation or competition between S-S* and R-S* relations, there can also be 3-term relations. The traditional operant discrimination phenomena illustrates how potent these 3-term relations can be in controlling operant behavior. Jenkins (1977) has already discussed the distinction between 2-term and 3-term relations.[2] However, in our consideration of such 3-term relations, we will focus on unearned versus earned reinforcement and the qualitative contingencies that are produced by such relations.

In the classic theory of operant discrimination Skinner (1938), two different 3-term relations were used to describe the gamut of S, R, and S* relations. These were the discriminative stimulus which signaled that a response would lead to reinforcement (S, R, S*) and an S-delta that could be the absence of the discriminative stimulus, which then signaled that a response would lead to no reinforcement (no-S, R, no-S*).

When earned and unearned reinforcement are also considered in the specification of 3-term relations, it can be seen that there are more than two, 3-term relations which may influence behavior. In fact, if we consider only one stimulus and one response, and deal with the presence or the absence of these three events (S, R, and S*), eight possible combinations, each representating a potentially

---

[2]Belatedly, it should be noted that Catania (1971) has also discussed the role of 2-term relations, 3-term relations, and contingency as they influence conditioning. Although there are some similarities, the scheme presented here is quite different than Catania's, and it would require extensive discussion to compare the two approaches. Perhaps the most salient difference is that the present scheme signals the consequences of responding independently of the consequences of not responding, whereas the Catania scheme appears to signal only the consequences of responding.

separate 3-term relation, can be envisioned, each of which may or may not influence behavior. We will present evidence that several of these newer 3-term relations, which involve unearned reinforcement, do indeed influence behavior very strongly. But before we do so, we wish to present an analysis that would enable one to calculate what the remaining 2-term relations would be if the programmed 3-term relations in a situation are ignored by the organism. This analysis then becomes a tool in exploring whether 2-term or 3-term relations are governing behavior in a situation where either could be doing so.

Let us first consider the hypothetical case where both S-S* and R-S* relations strongly influence behavior but do so independently of one another; that is, imagine a situation wherein the 2-term relations are manipulated orthogonally, and any 3-term relations that occur do so in some sense spuriously. This is not to be seen as an argument that there are no real 3-term relations, but is presented instead as a starting point or base for later consideration of the 3-term relations. There is more than one way to picture the orthogonal combination of the 2-term relations, but I have chosen to do so by considering each 2-term relation as the correlation (or lack thereof) between the two terms; then, somewhat arbitrarily, three points have been selected on the correlational continuum ($+1$, 0, -1) for examination of a limited but meaningful number of combinations of independent S-S* and R-S* correlations.[3]

This yields the 3×3 matrix shown in Table 9.1, where the columns represent S-S* correlations, the rows represent R-S* correlations, and the nine cells represent combinations of these correlations. In Table 9.1, cell 5 represents the complete absence of any relations at all (two zero correlations superimposed on one another), and, although some would argue that a kind of learning may occur here (e.g. learned irrelevance, Mackintosh, 1973, or learned helplessness, Maier, Seligman, and Solomon, 1969), in the present context this will be treated as the control condition for learning of any relations which involve the events S, R, and S*. Cells 2, 4, 6, and 8 represent cases in this scheme where, although all three events are present, only one 2-term relation has been programmed as non-zero. Cells 1, 3, 7, and 9 more obviously involve a 3-term relation because, in each of the four cases, you have a particular 3-term relation, one which is not explicitly programmed (in our imaginery examples) but which follows automatically from the specification of both 2-term relations.

The concurrent 2-term correlations illustrated by cells 1, 3, 7, and 9 represent situations that cannot be realistically programmed. (If correlations of less than 1

---

[3]Like the term *relation*, the term *correlation* is also being used rather vaguely here, as any index of the relationship between two variables between $+1$ and -1, with $+1$ implying a 1:1 relationship, 0.0 implying no relationship, and -1.0 implying a perfectly inverse relationship. There are many different formulae which meet such criteria. When dealing with specific cases we shall use a contingency formula based on differences in reinforcement probabilities. However, as will be explained in the text, we will deal only with the quality of the difference, not with its quantitative value.

TABLE 9.1
The Orthogonal Combination of Two-Term Relations

	Signal Positively Correlated with S*	Signal Uncorrelated with S*	Signal Negatively Correlated with S*
Response positively correlated with S*	(1) S-S* +1.0 R-S* +1.0	(2) S-S* 0.0 R-S* +1.0	(3) S-S* -1.0 R-S* +1.0
Responses uncorrelated with S*	(4) S-S* +1.0 R-S* 0.0	(5) S-S* 0.0 R-S* 0.0	(6) S-S* -1.0 R-S* 0.0
Responses negatively correlated with S*	(7) S-S* +1.0 R-S* -1.0	(8) S-S* 0.0 R-S* -1.0	(9) S-S* -1.0 R-S* -1.0

were used, they could be programmed, but it is infinitely less complicated to describe and use as illustrations these simpler, extreme cases.) First of all, in the free operant situation, reinforcement would be present in every instance of stimulus and response. Second, even if this were accomplished with discrete trials (which increases the number of stimuli), instances of stimulus or no stimulus cannot be guaranteed to contain the response or no response event required by the table. (This is the problem of subject control over responding in contingency manipulation discussed by Gibbon, Berryman, & Thompson, 1974).

Table 9.1 is useful mainly in defining the space of orthogonal conjunctions between 2-term relations. Given this space, let us now discuss some imagined cases where 2-term relations with intermediate positive correlations between them occur together. What I find particularly interesting about such cases is that one can establish particular S-S* and R-S* relations and, while maintaining these correlations, still have considerable (but restricted freedom to manipulate the value of the 3-term relations. This partial independence between 2- and 3-term relations provides an opportunity to examine a contingency interpretation of Skinner's analysis of operant stimulus control (Skinner, 1938), in contrast with the two-process analysis.

The truly constant probability schedule provides an opportunity to better control the events whose combination creates 2- and 3-term relations. With this technique, one can examine the sufficiency of the 2-term relations combined orthogonally to explain behavior that is expected to vary according to changes in the 3-term relation. In the yet-to-be explored example described below, which could evaluate Skinner's theory of discrimination in this new context of examining qualitative contingencies based on unearned as well as earned reinforcement, the 2-term relations will be held constant while the 3-term relation will be varied so that one would expect differential stimulus control of behavior.

In order to make this evaluation, consider first, some different cases of reinforcement probabilities given different relations. A typical set of such probabilities is shown in Table 9.2. The 3-term relation is specified in the upper half of the table, and both of the 2-term relations (one for R and one for S) appear in the lower half of the table. In each relation, the left hand side shows the reinforcement probabilities, and the right hand side shows the non-reinforcement probabilities, which turn out to be the compliments of the reinforcement probabilities because the probability of reinforcement and non-reinforcement, given a particular condition, must sum to 1. (The right hand side of the Table is redundant—once you know about reinforcement probabilities, you also know non-reinforcement probabilities.) There are only two reinforcement probabilities for 2-term relations—*if R (or CS) then S** and *if not-R (or not-CS) then S**. In the 3-term relation, there are four possible antecedent conditions and therefore four different S* probabilities to specify.

It should be emphasized once again that there are many ways in which a 3-term relation can be specified. First of all, the manner in which we are doing this has been designed to treat the R-S*, 2-term relation as nested within the S-S*, 2-term relation. That is, earned and unearned S* are treated here as two single terms by definition. If we treat these as unitary events and put a signal in front of them, then we have a higher-order 2-term relation which is a 3-term relation—

TABLE 9.2[a]
Two-Term Versus Three-Term Reinforcement Probabilities
for a Given Situation

I. Three-Term Relations

$P(S^* \mid R,S) = .3 = x$	$P(\bar{S}^* \mid R,S) = .7$
$P(S^* \mid \bar{R},S) = .1 = y$	$P(\bar{S}^* \mid \bar{R},S) = .9$
$P(S^* \mid R,\bar{S}) = .1 = w$	$P(\bar{S}^* \mid R,\bar{S}) = .9$
$P(S^* \mid \bar{R},\bar{S}) = .1 = z$	$P(\bar{S}^* \mid \bar{R},\bar{S}) = .9$

II. Two-Term Relations

A. S-S*

$P(S^* \mid S) = .2 = (x+y)/2$	$P(\bar{S}^* \mid S) = .8$
$P(S^* \mid \bar{S}) = .1 = (w+z)/2$	$P(\bar{S}^* \mid \bar{S}) = .9$

B. R-S*

$P(S^* \mid R) = .2 = (x+w)/2$	$P(\bar{S}^* \mid R) = .8$
$P(S^* \mid \bar{R}) = .1 = (x+z)/2$	$P(\bar{S}^* \mid \bar{R}) = .9$

[a]Each two-term probability turns out to be the weighted mean of two particular three-term probabilities shown by the formula following each two-term probability.

for example, a signal for unearned S* is S-(not-R-S*), where the S outside the parentheses in one term, and everything inside in another term. (If you think this is a meaningless exercise, try reversing the R's and the S's in such higher-order 2-term relations). We treat the 3-term relations this way because, as will become apparent, that is how we program our experiments.

Second, we are expressing the relations as conditional reinforcement probabilities because we will evaluate these relations in the context of a qualitative version of the probability difference or delta-P contingency theory (Hammond & Paynter, 1983). As mentioned above, by *qualitative* we simply mean that the sign of the larger probability differences (+ or −), along with the rest of the probability differences that will be treated as zero, will be the only aspects of contingency that will be considered predictive.

Now for our hypothetical, but testable example. In both Table 9.2 and its twin, Table 9.3, the same reinforcement probabilities (and thus the same contingency according to our qualitative notion) would be in effect for both the S-S* and the R-S* relation, but the reinforcement probabilities differ for the 3-term relation in Table 9.2 versus Table 9.3. Because both the 2-term and the 3-term sub-tables represent the same molar situation, the probabilities in the 3-term sub-tables are mathematically related to the probabilities in the 2-term sub-tables. Mainly, each probability in the 2-term sub-tables is a weighted mean of two of the probabilities in the 3-term sub-table. For example, the probability of S* given S is a weighted mean of two probabilities, that for S* given both S and R (labelled x in the table) and that for S* given both S and not-R (y). To facilitate understanding of this relationship between the 2- and 3-term relations, the rein-

TABLE 9.3[a]
Two-Term Versus Three-Term Reinforcement Probabilities
for a Given Situation

I.   Three-Term Relations

$P(S^* \mid R,S)$ = .2 = x	$P(\bar{S}^* \mid R,S)$ = .8		
$P(S^* \mid \bar{R},S)$ = .2 = y	$P(\bar{S}^* \mid \bar{R},S)$ = .8		
$P(S^* \mid R,\bar{S})$ = .2 = w	$P(\bar{S}^* \mid R,\bar{S})$ = .8		
$P(S^* \mid \bar{R},\bar{S})$ = .0 = z	$P(\bar{S}^* \mid \bar{R},\bar{S})$ = 1.0		

II.   Two-Term Relations

A.   S-S*

$P(S^* \mid S)$ = .2 = $(x+y)/2$	$P(\bar{S}^* \mid S)$ = .8		
$P(S^* \mid \bar{S})$ = .1 = $(w+y)/2$	$P(\bar{S}^* \mid \bar{S})$ = .9		

B.   R-S*

$P(S^* \mid R)$ = .2 = $(x+w)/2$	$P(\bar{S}^* \mid R)$ = .8		
$P(S^* \mid \bar{R})$ = .1 = $(y+z)/2$	$P(\bar{S}^* \mid \bar{R})$ = .9		

[a]Each two-term probability turns out to be the weighted mean of two particular three-term probabilities shown by the formula following each two-term probability.

forcement probabilities in the 3-term sub-table have been arbitrarily labeled x, y, w, and z. The four probabilities from the 2-term sub-tables have their particular weighted mean formula listed after them.

In the specific cases described in Table 9.2 and Table 9.3, the weighting for these formulae was based on the assumption that S and not-S occur equally often, and R and not-R also occur equally often. The assumption about the stimuli is easily handled by programming decision. The assumption about responses requires a rat which occupies about half of the seconds in the experimental situation by at least one response and makes no responses in the other seconds. We have studied rats in the past whose responding roughly meets these requirements. For rats with different response rates, the weighted mean formulas would have to be changed accordingly. The fact that responses are programmed by the animal rather than the experimenter considerably complicates matters here as elsewhere in operant conditioning, but the hypothetical point we are examining can still be described as a practical experiment.

Turning once again to our specific example in Table 9.2 and 9.3, the same intermediate positive contingency between antecedent and reinforcement has been arbitrarily selected for both S-S* and R-S*; this was a difference between the probabilities of .2 and .1. But the probabilities in the 3-term sub-table are meaningfully different in Tables 9.2 and 9.3. In Table 9.2, the 3-term contingency is such that no contingency exists between response and reinforcement, given no stimulus, but much more reinforcement could be earned by responding in the presence of the stimulus; here, one would expect that a discrimination would be formed based on the 3-term relations (S would become a discriminative stimulus broadly defined). But in Table 9.3, the 3-term contingency programmed would be expected to make the absence of S a discriminative stimulus for responding. Thus, in the two cases represented by Table 9.2 and 9.3, the 2-term relations remain the same overall, but, because of differences in the 3-term relation, one would expect rats to respond mostly in the presence of the signal in the case shown by Table 9.2 and respond mostly in the absence of the signal in the case shown by Table 9.3. (Note that the 3-term relation probabilities in both Table 9.2 and 9.3 mathematically combine according to the same formula in each case to produce the same 2-term relation probabilities.) We have yet to conduct this experiment, but, like most readers, we anticipate that the 3-term relation will prove more important than the 2-term relations in this instance.

In the example above, we described the contingencies for a rat who was responding in half of the seconds of the session. For rats with different response rates, the formulas for going from the programmed 3-term reinforcement probabilities to the 2-term probabilities will be different as the weighting will differ. The higher the response rate, the more the weighted 2-term probability will approximate the 3-term earned S* probabilities. For response rates in the range of those for most of the rats which we have studied, the qualitative predictions which are shown for particular quantitative values in Table 9.2 and 9.3, would be the same as we described above.

We have done some experiments that are germane to this analysis, but the experiments led to the analysis rather than the other way around. For one, Michael Weinberg and I placed rats on a zero contingency schedule (0.5-0.5) after initial positive contingency training (0.5-.00), and the response rate declined dramatically, as would be expected, with equal unearned to earned reinforcement. But then we placed a 5-second, light signal before each such programmed unearned reinforcement. Everything else remained the same. Gradually, the overall lever-pressing rate for most rats returned to its positive contingency level, while no responding occurred in the presence of the light. The sequence of procedures was then repeated on these same rats, and the results for the entire experiment for 3 rats is shown in Figure 9.2 (from Hammond & Weinberg, in press). Note that phases 6 and 10 had the zero contingency, while phases 7 and 11 received the added signal. Our initial reasons for doing this experiment shall remain obscure, but now, after the fact, the 2-term and 3-term relations for phases 7 and 11 in this experiment can be described by the same type of table as in our hypothetical example above. Such a description of the relations during the signal period appears in Table 9.4, where it can be seen that the 3-term contingencies are radically different, with respect to the value of responding, from the 2-term contingency for R-S*, which is zero.

Finally, Michael Weinberg, Joshua Blustein, and I have conducted an unpublished experiment highly similar to the signal experiment above, except that

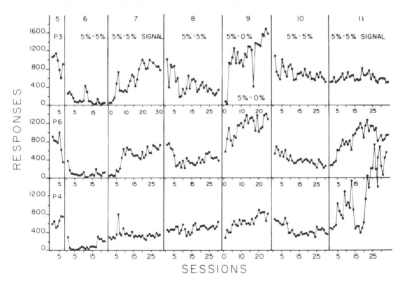

FIG. 9.2.   Response totals for each 30 min session during the relevant phases (5 through 11, indicated at the top of the figure) for rats P3, P4, and P6 from Hammond and Weinberg (in press). Reinforcement outcomes given a response and given no response are expressed in percentages (i.e., 5% means .05 probability of reinforcement per second). In phase 5 the schedule was 5%-0%—a strong positive contingency.

TABLE 9.4[a]

Two-Term Versus Three-Term Reinforcement Probabilities for A
Given Situation

I. Three-Term Relation

$P(S* \mid R,S) = .05 = x$	$P(\bar{S}* \mid R,S) = .95$
$P(S* \mid \bar{R},S) = .20 = y$	$P(\bar{S}* \mid \bar{R},S) = .80$
$P(S* \mid R,\bar{S}) = .05 = w$	$P(\bar{S}* \mid R,\bar{S}) = .95$
$P(S* \mid \bar{R},\bar{S}) = .00 = z$	$P(\bar{S}* \mid \bar{R},\bar{S}) = 1.00$

II. Two-Term Relations

A. S-S*

| $P(S* \mid S) = .125 = (x+y)/2$ | $P(\bar{S}* \mid S) = .875$ |
| $P(S* \mid \bar{S}) = .025 = (w+z)/2$ | $P(\bar{S}* \mid \bar{S}) = .975$ |

B. R-S*

| $P(S* \mid R) = .05 = (x+w)/2$ | $P(\bar{S}* \mid R) = .95$ |
| $P(S* \mid \bar{R}) = .05 = (y+z)/2$ | $P(\bar{S}* \mid \bar{R}) = .95$ |

---

[a]Each two-term probability turns out to be the weighted mean of
two particular three-term probabilities shown by the formula
following each two-term probability.

here are three groups which, in the Solomon tradition of the mid-sixties, consisted of an S+ group, where the light signaled all unearned reinforcements as in the
experiment above, a random control group where the light was presented randomly in relation to the unearned reinforcement and an S− group, where the
light was never paired with the unearned reinforcement (a negative correlation or
contingency, with respect to unearned reinforcement). The results indicate
marked suppression to S+ (positive conditioned suppression), slight suppression
by the random stimulus, and a very large facilitation effect to S− that developed
very slowly. The effects of these stimuli upon operant behavior have nothing to
do with the S-dee/S-delta manipulations of conventional operant stimulus control
procedures, for earned reinforcement was equally likely both in the presence and
absence of these signals in all three groups; thus, there could be no molecular R-
extinction and no conventional differential conditioning in the presence and
absence of these stimuli. Yet this experiment shows clearly that the 3-term
contingency and not the 2-term contingency modulates operant responding in a
manner analogous to earlier findings about Pavlovian conditioning that stress
Pavlovian inhibition (e.g., Bull & Overmier, 1968; Hammond, 1967; Rescorla
& LoLordo, 1965). This is not to argue for inhibitory processes in the production
of 3-term effects but only to argue about an empirical parallel.

In this paper, we have explored one legacy of two-process learning theory—
the empirical investigation of S-S* and R-S* relations considered separately and
then considered together in appetitive operant conditioning. The robustness and
general applicabililty of our preliminary findings attest to the heuristic value of

this approach. Empirical notions that emerged in Solomon's laboratory almost two decades ago (such as the idea that a stimulus which is negatively correlated with a reinforcing event, broadly defined, will have an effect upon operant behavior, which is the opposite to that produced by a stimulus positively correlated with that reinforcing event) are still proving useful today.

ACKNOWLEDGMENTS

The research discussed in this article was supported in part by a grant-in-aid to Temple University. The author thanks Walter Paynter and Michael Weinberg whose ideas and empirical contributions run throughout this paper.

REFERENCES

Bolles, R. C. (1972). Reinforcement, expectancy and learning. *Psychological Review, 79,* 394–409.

Bull, J. A., III, & Overmier, J. B. (1968). Additive and subtractive properties of excitation and inhibition. *Journal of Comparative and Physiological Psychology, 66,* 511–514.

Catania, A. C. (1971. Elicitation, reinforcement, and stimulus control. In R. Glaser (Ed.), *The nature of reinforcement* (pp. 196–220). New York: Academic Press.

Gibbon, J., & Balsam P. (1981). Spreading association in time. In C. M. Locurto, H. S. Terrace, & Gibbon (Eds.), *Autoshaping and conditioning theory* (pp. 219–253). New York: Academic Press.

Gibbon, J., Berryman, R., & Thompson, R. L. (1974). Contingency spaces and measures in classical and instrumental conditioning. *Journal of the Experimental Analysis of Behavior, 21,* 585–605.

Hammond, L. J. (1967). A traditional demonstration of the active properties of Pavlovian inhibition using differential CER. *Psychonomic Science, 9,* 65–66.

Hammond, L. J. (1980). The effect of contingency upon the appetitive conditioning of free-operant behavior. *Journal of the Experimental Analysis of Behavior, 34,* 297–304.

Hammond, L. J., & Paynter, W. E., Jr. (1983). Probabilistic contingency theories of animal conditioning: A critical analysis. *Learning and Motivation, 14,* 527–550.

Hammond, L. J., & Weinberg, M. (in press). Signaling unearned reinforcers removes the suppression produced by a zero correlation in a operant paradigm. *Animal Learning and Behavior.*

Herrnstein, R. J., & Hineline, P. N. (1966). Negative reinforcement as shock frequency reduction. *Journal of the Experimental Analysis of Behavior, 13,* 243–266.

Jenkins, H. M. (1977). Sensitivity of different response systems to stimulus-reinforcer and response-reinforcer relations. In H. Davis & H. M. B. Hurwitz (Eds.), *Operant-Pavlovian interactions* (pp. 47–62). Hillsdale, NJ: Lawrence Erlbaum Associates.

Mackintosh, N. J. (1973). Stimulus selection: Learning to ignore stimuli that predict no change in reinforcement. In R. A. Hinde & J. Steveson-Hinde (Eds.), *Constraints on learning* (pp. 75–100). New York: Academic Press.

Mackintosh, N. J. (1974). *The psychology of animal learning.* New York: Academic Press.

Maier, S. F., Seligman, M. E. P., & Solomon, R. L. (1969). Pavlovian fear conditioning and learned helplessness. In B. A. Campbell & R. M. Church (Eds.), *Punishment and aversive behavior* (pp. 299–343). New York: Appleton-Century Crofts.

Rescorla, R. A. (1967). Pavlovian conditioning and its proper control procedures. *Psychological Review, 74,* 71–79.

Rescorla, R. A., & LoLordo, V. M. (1965). Inhibition of avoidance behavior. *Journal of Comparative and Physiological Psychology, 59,* 406–412.

Rescorla, R. A., & Solomon, R. L. (1957). Two-processes learning theory: Relationships between Pavlovian conditioning and instrumental learning. *Psychological Review, 74,* 151–182.

Schwartz, B., & Gamzu, E. (1977). Pavlovian control of operant behavior. In W. K. Honig & J. E. R. Staddon (Eds.), *Handbook of operant behavior* (pp. 53–97). Engelwood Cliffs, NJ: Prentice-Hall.

Schoenfeld, W. N., Cummings, W. W., & Hearst, E. (1956). On the classification of reinforcement schedules. *Procedings of the National Academy of Science, 42,* 563–570.

Sidley, N. A., & Schoenfeld, W. N. (1964). Behavior stability and response rate as functions of reinforcement probability on "random ratio" schedules. *Journal of the Experimental Analysis of Behavior, 7,* 281–283.

Sidman, M. (1953). Avoidance conditioning with brief shock and no exteroceptive warning signal. *Science, 188,* 157–158.

Sidman, M. (1955). Some properties of the warning stimulus in avoidance behavior. *Journal of Comparative and Physiological Psychology, 48,* 444–450.

Skinner, B. F. (1938). *The behavior of organisms.* New York: Appleton-Century-Crofts.

Weinberg, M. (1982). *The effect of concurrent random-interval schedules of reinforcement on choice behavior in the rat.* Unpublished master's thesis, Temple University, Philadelphia, PA.

Williams, D. R. (1981). Biconditional behavior: Conditioning without constraint. In C. M. Locurto, H. S. Terrace & J. Gibbon (Eds.), *Autoshaping and conditioning theory* (pp. 55–99). New York: Academic Press.

10 Approaches to the Study of Behavior: Examples from Behavioral Pharmacology

Russell M. Church
Brown University

By definition, behavioral pharmacology is the study of the effect of drugs on behavior. Investigators in this field differ in their goals and types of explanation. The purpose of this chapter is to describe the major goals and types of explanation and, with examples of research from our laboratory, to claim that the approaches can be mutually complementary.

A. GOALS OF BEHAVIORAL PHARMACOLOGY

1. Applied

Those who study the effect of drugs on behavior do so for many different reasons, some applied and some basic. Much of the applied effort has been devoted to the development and assessment of drugs with therapeutic potential for physical disabilities, such as those characteristic of Parkinson's disease, and for mental disabilities, such as those characteristic of depression. These drugs often produce side effects—serious physical and mental disabilities. The attempt to prevent, minimize or reverse such side effects is another important motivation for applied research. Some of the applied effort has been devoted to the development and assessment of drugs with potential for improvement of the functioning of normal individuals. For example, vasopressin appears to facilitate memory of normal individuals in word recognition tasks (Weingartner, Gold, Ballenger, Smallberg, Summers, Rubinow, Post, & Goodwin, 1981). The increased use of drugs has made drug abuse a major social and medical problem, and applied research has been devoted to the study of the causes and treatment of addiction. Research in behavioral pharmacology with applied goals normally would be conducted with human subjects in clinical settings or with animal models of psychiatric disabilities (Kuman, 1977). The primary consideration is to select a behavior that has the essential characteristics of the disability under study. The textbook by Barchas, Berger, Ciaranello, & Elliott (1977) provides a good review of the connections between pharmacological agents, neuroregulations, and psychiatric disorders.

2. Basic

Basic research activities have also been conducted for many different reasons. An understanding of an investigator's goal is necessary for an understanding of the investigator's choice of research problem and attitude toward various research activities. Some wish to understand the body (anatomy, physiology, neurochemistry, etc.); some wish to understand the mind (attention, memory, learning, etc.); some wish to understand behavior (response rate, choice, movement patterns, etc.). The goal of the researcher—biological, psychological or behavioral—influences the choice of pharmacological interventions, behavioral dependent variables, and the type of explanation of the observed input-output regularities.

   A. Biological.   Neuroscientists, and some psychologists, are interested in how the nervous system works. They use many different methods to find out: They stimulate electrically with surface electrodes, implanted macroelectrodes and microelectrodes with tips small enough to penetrate a single cell; they stimulate chemically, injecting drugs systemically or applying them topically to selected locations on the brain; they lesion large structures in the brain, transect major pathways, or make small localized lesions; they make chemical lesions by injecting neurotoxins systemically or applying them topically to selected locations on the brain; they record from surface electrodes, implanted macroelectrodes, or microelectrodes; they conduct neuroanatomical studies. As the degree of understanding of a system increases, the stimuli can be administered to more localized areas, and the responses can be measured from more localized areas. Those interested in understanding the body emphasize anatomical, physiological, and neurochemical measurements, and behavioral measures that are correlated with biological measures. The textbook by Kandel and Schwartz (1981) provides a good example of a neuroscience perspective on the relationship between brain and behavior.

   From this perspective, behavior is only one of the functions of the brain, and the observation of behavior is only one of many tools used to find out how the nervous system works. For those interested in the nervous system, it is desirable to use a variety of methods that produce comparable results. An exclusive reliance on behavioral observations would be a serious limitation: Those who attempt to understand neurochemical mechanisms solely on the basis of behavioral measures are less likely to make progress than those who utilize multiple techniques.

For the purpose of understanding the nervous system, behavior is considered to be an assay, much like a chemical assay. Behavioral observations are used to infer biological events, but they are not unique in this respect. Many biological events are not directly observed but inferred from nonbehavioral assays. Although it is an indirect measure, behavior can have advantages over more direct measures. Since the behavioral measure is less invasive, it may be less likely to disrupt the phenomenon under study, and it may be made repeatedly. An ideal assay would permit a precise specification of the stimulus and it would provide a quantitative behavioral index that is closely correlated with a physiological event. To minimize the cost per measurement, relatively untrained personnel should be able to make such an assay quickly.

Because of the complexity of the intact mammalian nervous system, some researchers believe that more fundamental progress will be made from the analysis of simpler systems such as the headless roach or Aplysia (Cooper, Bloom, & Roth, 1978; Thompson, Patterson, & Teyler, 1972). These methods may not be applicable to reseach on the relationship between the brain and behavior of mammals.

From the biological point of view, the only satisfying explanation is a description of a chain of events from stimulus input through various neural events to muscle contractions. The explanatory goal is to develop a biological process model, as described in a section that follows. Such an explanation would supersede any other explanation.

B. Psychological. Some investigators are interested in how the mind works. The focus of their study is on such mental processes as attention, memory, and learning. Unlike biological concepts, psychological concepts cannot be directly observed. They must be inferred from behavior. Thus, it is necessary for these investigators to relate specific behavioral observations to specific psychological processes. Then it is possible to study how drugs affect particular mental processes. Those interested in understanding the mind emphasize pharmacological manipulations and behavioral measures that are assumed to be related to mental events. From this perspective, pharmacological manipulations are just one of many methods to affect specific, separable, mental processes.

For example, the latency of a tail flick to heat stimulation has been used as a measure of the magnitude of analgesia, especially in the testing of substances (like morphine) that are known to affect subjective reports of pain by human subjects. As another example, resistance to extinction of an avoidance response has been used as a measure of the strength of original avoidance-learning or memory for the learned avoidance. Thus, the fact that vasopressin increases resistance to extinction leads to the conclusion that vasopressin improves learning and memory (deWied & Bohus, 1966). For the purpose of understanding psychological concepts, the behavioral measure must reflect some specific psychological process. Many of the behavioral measures commonly used may either be a complex measure that can be affected by multiple psychological processes (e.g., memory and decision) or a simple measure (e.g., a reflex) that does not reflect any psychological process under study.

The term *animal cognition* has been used to refer to several different concepts. It has been used to refer to reactions to stimuli that are no longer physically present, such as symbolic processing (Hunter, 1913); to behavior that is complex and would be considered to be intelligent if done by a person (Griffin, 1976); to behavior that provides a measure of consciousness (Griffin, 1976); and to behavior that is similar to human behavior (Premack, 1983). The study of human cognition has made extensive use of psychological process models; this may also be the most successful approach for the study of animal cognition.

From the psychological point of view, the only satisfying explanation is a description of a chain of events from stimulus input through various mental processes (iconic storage, working memory, reference memory, etc.) to a response. The explanatory goal is to develop a psychological process model, as described in a section that follows. Such an explanation would supersede any other explanation. Since any particular psychological process model might be implemented with different biological mechanisms by different species, a biological explanation would only be a particular hardware implementation of the psychological process models.

C. Behavior. Many psychologists are primarily interested in behavior and its explanation. Their main method is to observe and record behavior under controlled conditions. The focus on behavior comes from two traditions: ethology and behaviorism. One of the major contributions of ethology is the detailed specification of motor response patterns under well-specified stimulus conditions (Mackintosh, Chance, & Silverman, 1977); one of the major contributions of behaviorism is the detailed specification of the time of occurrence of a repetitive response sequence under well-specified stimulus conditions (Dews, 1971). Both types of behavior are sensitive to pharmacological manipulation.

From the behavioral point of view, explanations can consist of input-output rules, general principles, or formal models that describe the transformations on the stimulus input necessary to achieve the response output. Biological or psychological concepts would be employed only to the extent that they contributed to the prediction of the response output on the basis of the input from the current stimulus and previous experience.

B. TYPES OF EXPLANATIONS

Since our goal is to explain animal behavior, it is useful to consider the meaning of "explanation." Hempel's (1965) treatment of the term fits the activities of practicing scientists. He writes that an explanation is an answer to a particular type of *why question*—one in which the matter to be explained is an empirical statement. He considers an explanation to be a deductive exercise in which various facts and laws are used to deduce the empirical statement to be explained.

The organization of articles in psychological journals corresponds to these three activities. A Methods section contains a series of true propositions about what was done; these correspond to the facts of an explanation. A Discussion section that attempts to explain the results must contain one or more laws; these laws of the explanation are *if . . . then propositions*. At least one law must have an antecedent that corresponds to a fact in the Methods section, and at least one law must have a consequence that corresponds to a statement in the Results section. From the facts in the Methods section and the laws in the Discussion section, the explained results can be generated by standard inference rules. All other results are unexplained.

The facts and laws should be precisely specified so that two readers of a specific model are able to generate exactly the same output predictions from all legitimate input conditions. To make this an objective and feasible task, it is necessary either to state the theory in the form of a mathematical equation or a computer program, or to state the theory so accurately and completely that it is possible for multiple readers to write equations or computer programs that have identical input-output characteristics. Multiple, independent analysts have been proposed to provide a check on whether the procedure described was the procedure administered, and to check on whether the analysis described was the analysis conducted (Roberts, 1980). Based only on the written description of the procedure or analysis to be published, several analysts write implementation programs in very different languages (e.g., APL and Pascal). Each of the programs is tested with a range of input conditions. If the output is identical when the input is identical, a check, but not a proof, has been performed. This method can also be used to check whether the predictions made are the predictions required by the theory.

1. Input-Output

Any explanation must include input variables (e.g., the conditions of drug administration) and output variables (e.g., measurable behavior changes). In a pure input-output model there would be no additional concepts. At the early stages of investigation, such descriptive research is necessary. The aim is to discover phenomena, specify the necessary and sufficient conditions to obtain a particular result, and identify ways in which different treatments produce similar results. The textbook by Thompson and Schuster (1968) provides good examples of this approach.

If the purpose is to understand behavior on the basis of environmental events, biological and psychological concepts are not required. The output can be explained in terms of the input, without the use of any biological or psychological concepts. These input-output rules can be expressed by equations, and curve-fitting procedures may be employed to compare theory and data. Before the input-output relationships are established, it may be premature to speculate about biological and psychological intervening variables; after the input-output relationsisp are established, it may be unnecessary to do so (Skinner, 1950).

In this tradition, behavioral pharmacology involves only the description of the effects of drugs on behavior. The approach appeals to common sense. For example, all behavioral pharmacologists can agree that response rate is affected in some dose-dependent manner by a particular drug, but they may not be able to agree that anxiety is affected in some dose-dependent manner by a particular drug.

In the absence of theoretical guidance, either from advances in biological or psychological knowledge, behavioral pharmacology was a pedestrain field. Drugs were often chosen without clear rationale: A drug might be studied because it was clinically useful or currently abused. The testing procedures were also chosen without clear rationale: One might be used simply because it was conventional or currently in vogue. There was plenty to do, since there were many drugs, many doses, and many procedures. Unfortunately, the data were often unclear and, when a replicable result was obtained, it was an answer to a question that nobody knew how to formulate. For example, a low dose of amphetamine increases response rate under some conditions. That is the answer, but what is the question?

In a later stage of descriptive behaviorism, regularities were identified. One descriptive regularity is called *rate dependency*. The effect of a drug often depends upon the baseline behavior of the animal (Dews & Wenger, 1977). This rule has considerable generality, but its interpretation is not clear. In some cases, it may reflect the fact that drugs can reduce the control of behavior by other stimuli.

2. Principles and Their Extension by Analogy

The effects of drugs on behavior may be special cases of behavioral principles. The principles are production rules (*if . . . then propositions*) that are combined into well-organized sets. These sets of principles can then be applied to a new domain. If they fit in the new domain, the analogy constitutes the explanation. The research approach is to establish the principles in the general case, and then determine whether or not the results with drugs follow the same general rules. This approach to explanation extends the range of phenomena to which the general rules apply, but it does not provide essentially new information. Three explanations by analogy follow:

1. A drug is like a discriminative stimulus. This idea was familiar to Pavlov (1927), and it has been used to explain the effectiveness of drug discrimination experiments (Heise & Milar, 1984) and the state dependency result (Overton, 1984). The drug discrimination experiment has been used mostly to provide a

behavioral method for classifying drugs that can be related to their chemical compositions and physiological effects. One conclusion from this research is that the animals appear to discriminate central as well as peripheral effects.

2. A drug is like an unconditioned stimulus. It now appears that the general rules of classical conditioning, as developed for salivary conditioning, also apply to the conditioned emotional response, autoshaping, and drug tolerance. This idea was developed by Siegel in his research on morphine tolerance, addiction, and withdrawal (e.g., Siegel, 1977). His analysis of the role of conditioning of context cues in the development of tolerance seldom receives favorable attention from those who seek biological explanations of behavior. This may be because it is viewed as a competitor with certain biological explanations of tolerance, although it must be consistent with any biological explanation of classical conditioning.

3. A drug is like a reinforcer. Some drugs can serve as positive, negative, or conditioned reinforcers of instrumental responding. For example, animals will perform an instrumental response that is followed by administration of various stimulants, barbiturates, opioids, and other drugs. Seiden and Dykstra (1977) provide a good review of the evidence.

3. Process Models

In a process model of behavior, in addition to the input variables (e.g., the conditions of drug administration) and output variables (e.g., measurable behavioral changes), there are interrelated intervening concepts. Some of the intervening concepts are closely connected to input variables, some are closely connected to output variables, and some are central concepts more closely connected to other intervening concepts than either input or output variables. The concepts may be psychological, biological, or formal.

A psychological process model refers to mental mechanisms. It may include sensory registers, attentional mechanisms, short-term storage, long-term storage, motivational mechanisms, decision processes, and the relationships among the parts. A major value of a psychological process model is that it is particularly easy to create plausible alternative hypotheses for empirical test. It provides the best heuristic for planning further research.

A biological process model refers to physiological processes, such as chemical and electrical events in various parts of the nervous system and elsewhere in the body. A major value of a biological process model is that it is a palpable reality, while psychological and formal models are human inventions that may be ephemeral. New relationships between apparently unrelated behaviors may be identified if it is found that they involve the same neuronal or biochemical substrate.

A formal model is one in which the terms are sufficiently abstract that they do not necessarily refer either to mental or physiological events. It is often expressed in mathematical terms, but other symbolic notation may be used. If the model provides quantitative predictions, and not merely ordinal predictions, then the constraints on alternative explanations will be greater. Formal models keep theoreticians honest; they cannot be used to explain contradictory results; any missing assumptions can be found; and changes in the model are obvious.

These three types of processes—psychological, biological, and formal—are not unique to behavioral pharmacology. For example, opponent process theory (Solomon & Corbit, 1974) can also be described in psychological terms (such as hedonic states), biological terms (such as autonomic nervous system activity), or formal terms (such as feedback control theory). These three types of terms were also used extensively in the explanation of traumatic avoidance learning of dogs. The acquisition of avoidance was associated with psychological terms, such as learned fear (Solomon & Wynne, 1953), biological terms, such as sympathetic nervous system activity (Solomon & Wynne, 1954), and formal terms, such as stochastic learning theory (Bush & Mosteller, 1955).

A process model should consistently use mental, physiological, or formal terms. It should not require that a physiological stage cause a mental one, or that a mental stage cause a physiological one: This leads to conceptual confusion. A psychological process model is not unnecessary or wrong because a biological one is known or discoverable, nor is a biological model unnecessary or wrong because a psychological one is known or discoverable.

A process model consists of input, intervening, and output variables, and interrelationships among the variables. It can be described either by propositions, a flow diagram, or by a list of modules. Written descriptions of a process model are seldom unambiguous, although many theorists prefer them so that they are not forced to make a precise statement when knowledge is unavailable. In a flow diagram, boxes represent intervening concepts, and arrows show the direction of influence. The transformation rules can be written on the lines or in the boxes. For precise specification of a complicated process model, a list of modules provides the best description. Each module should clearly describe input conditions and output results. Interrelations among modules occur when output of one module provides an input to another module.

The double dissociation test is the primary strategy for separating parts of a process model. The application of this strategy in the simplest case of two parts is as follows: Find two independent variables such that one affects only the first part, and the other affects only the second part. Find two dependent variables such that only the first is affected by one part, and only the second by the other part. If such variables can be found, then the parts are separate. In research on timing, Seth Roberts was the first to use this strategy to separate memory factors from decision factors (Roberts, 1981). In the peak procedure, he found that peak time was affected by the time of reinforcement but not the probability of reinforcement, and that peak rate was affected by the probability of reinforcement but not the time of reinforcement. Meck (1983) used the strategy to separate clock speed from memory storage speed as described in the next section.

C. EXAMPLES

The varied approaches to the study of behavioral pharmacology that have been described are pure types that are seldom, if ever, achieved in practice. Most investigators, even those whose names are closely associated with one of the approaches described, find it useful on occasion to refer to some of the concepts or methods of an alternative approach. Such eclecticism of approach is seldom well-represented in the secondary sources. In this section, I will describe the approaches used in experiments from my laboratory that have employed pharmacological manipulations. The experiments have been reported in the six articles cited below. A general discussion of the methods employed (Church, 1983), the results obtained (Church, 1984), and the application of scalar timing theory (Gibbon, 1977; Gibbon & Church, 1984; Gibbon, Church, & Meck, 1984) are available. This chapter focuses on the alternative explanations that were given for the observed input-output regularities.

If it were necessary to classify this research, it probably would be most appropriate to regard the approach as a psychological process model. Such an information-processing model was developed formally in one of the chapters (Gibbon & Church, 1984) and used in a review article (Church, 1983) and an empirical article (Meck & Church, 1983a). However, the descriptions that follow will make it clear that five different approaches are being used in this research program. It involves input-output analysis in which the behavior is related to the conditions of training; principles are applied such as Weber's law; there is a psychological approach with terms like memory storage and clockspeed; there is a biological approach with consideration of neurotransmitters such as acetylcholine and dopamine; and there is a formal approach through the quantitative application of scalar timing theory. The approach will have an influence on the selection of the experimental manipulation, the behavior to be observed and, especially, on the interpretation of results.

1. Methamphetamine and Time Estimation (Maricq, Roberts & Church, 1981).

Although Maricq, Roberts, and I concluded that the "results suggest that methamphetamine increases the speed of an internal clock used by rats in time discrimination tasks," the three experiments described in this report could have been interpreted with a behavioristic input-output analysis. We selected two very different timing tasks (a peak procedure and a bisection procedure), administered a drug (methamphetamine) to rats, and reported a systematic change in behavior.

In the peak procedure, after an intertrial interval, a signal began, and a single lever was inserted into the box. On some trials, the first lever response after 40 seconds was followed by food and the termination of the signal; on other trials, there was no food, and the signal remained on for a long random duration. The response rate typically increased as a function of time to a maximum near the time that food was sometimes available (40 seconds), and then it decreased. The maximum was called the "peak time", and methamphetamine decreased the time of the peak.

In the bisection procedure, after an intertrial interval, a signal was presented for some period of time, for example, 2 or 8 seconds. Then two levers were presented to the rat. A response on one of the levers following a 2-second signal or a response on the other lever following an 8-second signal resulted in food reward. Any response terminated the trial. After the animals learned the simple short-long temporal discrimination, signals of intermediate durations were added, and neither response resulted in food. As a consequence of this training, the percentage of long responses increased as a function of signal duration, and the latency to make a response was an inverted U-shaped function of signal duration with a maximum near the geometric mean of the two reinforced extreme durations. Methamphetamine shifted both of these functions to the left an equivalent amount.

Three features of this experiment are worthy of attention: the selection of the behavioral paradigm, the use of multiple measures, and the proportionality result. Previous investigations on the effect of methamphetamine and related drugs on timing tasks, such as differential reinforcement of low rates (DRL) and fixed interval schedules (FI), had found that these drugs produced leftward shifts in the response functions. At the doses used, however, methamphetamine also was found in our experiments and many others to increase response rate. Even if the only effect of the drug were to increase the tendency of the rat to respond, leftward shifts would have occurred in DRL and FI response functions. In contrast, the two procedures used in the present experiment would not lead to a leftward shift if only response tendency were increased. Also, the use of two different procedures (peak and bisection) and two different measures in bisection (choice and latency) reduced the number of alternative explanations of the results.

Although the major result of the study was that methamphetamine shifted the functions relating response to time to the left, there was one quantitative manipulation of importance. The question was whether the magnitude of the shift was a constant number of seconds or a constant proportion of the interval to be timed. (More complex alternatives were not considered at this initial stage.) Although in one of the experiments the sensitivity of our experiment with the peak procedure (20 vs 40-sec peak with five subjects per group) was inadequate to distinguish these alternatives, the experiment with the bisection procedure clearly demonstrated that the magnitude of the shift was proportional to the durations to be discriminated (1 vs 4 sec, 2 vs 8 sec, and 4 vs 16 sec). This was consistent with some psychological processes, such as a change in clock speed, and inconsistent with others, such as a change in latency to begin timing.

The goal of this research was to understand a psychological concept, clock speed. We considered the magnitude of a leftward shift in the observed response functions to be a measure of the magnitude of the increase in clock speed. The only other psychological concept involved in the interpretation was *attention*. We assumed that on some trials the animals were not attending to time and responded *long* on half such trials (Heinemann, Avin, Sullivan, & Chase, 1969).

The explanation of the result did not make reference to any biological concepts. In the report, it appeared that methamphetamine was selected solely on the basis of previous empirical work that showed that it affected performance of rats on timing tasks. In fact, there may also have been some influence from reports of the influence of methamphetamine on perceived time. There was also no reference to any formal model, such as scalar timing theory, to fit the data.

2. The Differential Effects of Haloperidol and Methamphetamine on Time Estimation in the Rat (Maricq & Church, 1983).

Maricq and I began to think in terms of biological mechanisms when we planned this experiment. The purpose was to narrow the range of candidate neurotransmitter systems that might be responsible for the increase in clock speed produced by methamphetamine. The predominant effects of methamphetamine are to enhance the release of neuronal catecholamines, primarily dopamine and norepinephrine, and to inhibit their reuptake. One method to attempt to isolate the relevant neurotransmitter system is to employ a selective blocker of dopamine receptors (such as haloperidol) or a selective blocker of norepinephrine receptors (such as phenoxybenzamine as an α-adenergic blocker and propranolol as a β-adrenergic blocker). Another method is to employ a drug that stimulates dopamine receptors (such as apomorphine). In pilot studies we tried several of these methods and decided on the basis of limited evidence that methamphetamine and haloperidol would be the most promising drugs with which to get effects. One advantage of methamphetamine over d-amphetamine, which we also tried, was that we could replicate our previous results.

The results in the bisection task were that methamphetamine produced a leftward shift in the point of indifference, haloperidol produced a rightward shift in the point of indifference, and a combination of the two drugs led to a point of indifference that was indistinguishable from the saline control group. (The point of indifference is the signal duration to which the rat would have made a long response on half the trials.) Methamphetamine and haloperidol, when administered alone, reduced the slope of the psychophysical function. When administered together, however, the slope of the psychophysical function was normalized. This led to the tentative biological conclusion that the observed horizontal shifts in the psychophysical response-time functions were due to the effective level of dopamine, and that the slope was reduced by a change in the effective level of dopamine.

Although we concluded that the drugs probably affected the speed of the internal clock, our main emphasis was on a neurotransmitter account. There was no quantitative analysis in terms of scalar timing theory.

3. A Mode Control Model of Counting and Timing (Meck & Church, 1983a)

The purpose of this experiment was to demonstrate the similarity of animal counting and timing processes. It used a psychological process model and a formal scalar timing model, but not a biological process model.

The psychological notion was that a pacemaker fed pulses into an accumulator for either counting or timing. In the case of timing, the switch was closed for the duration of a signal; for counting, the switch was closed briefly at the onset of each signal. The main behavioral evidence for this was that rats were equally sensitive to a 4:1 ratio of times (with number controlled) as to a 4:1 ratio of counts (with duration controlled) and that the magnitude of cross-modal transfer was equivalent for number and duration. The psychophysical functions for number and duration were fit equally well with a scalar expectancy model with the same parameter values for each attribute.

The drug manipulation in this experiment was used only to test the psychological model. If methamphetamine increases clock speed by a particular amount, and if the same clock is used both for counting and timing, then the magnitude of the leftward shift in the function relating probability of a right response to number of signals should be equal to the magnitude of the leftward shift in the function relating probability of a right response to the duration of the signal. Since this was the case, it provided additional support for the conclusion that the same internal mechanism was used for timing and counting.

4. Selective Adjustment of the Speed of Internal Clock and Memory Processes (Meck, 1983)

Meck, in his Ph.D. thesis, was the first in our laboratory to use all three process models on the same data. His main contribution was to distinguish between two types of effects: In a psychological process model, they were considered to be clock speed and a memory storage effect; in a biological model, they were considered to be the effective level of dopamine and the effective level of acetylcholine; in the formal scalar timing model, they were the mean value of two different random variables.

The data came from psychophysical bisection functions of rats during the initial sessions with the drug, after extended treatment with the drug, and on the initial sessions after the drug had been terminated. With these three measures, a clear distinction could be made between an effect of a drug on clock speed and a memory storage constant.

If a drug affected clock speed we can define t as the subjective clock time of reinforcement when the animal is not drugged, and Λt as the subjective clock time of reinforcement when the animal is drugged. The following pattern of results would occur: (a) There will be an initial effect when the drug is first introduced, since the animal will expect reinforcement when the clock reaches $t;$ (b) there would be no effect after extended treatment with the drug, since the animal will learn to expect reinforcement when the clock reaches $\Lambda t;$ and (c) there would be an effect, equal in magnitude and opposite in direction, when the drug is first terminated, since the animal will continue to expect reinforcement when the clock reaches Λt. This pattern of results were obtained with drugs that increased or decreased the effective level of dopamine (methamphetamine and haloperidol, respectively), and it corroborated the conclusions of the first two experiments, which were based upon the initial effects of the drug only.

On the basis of previous reports that physostigmine had effects on learning and memory, Meck investigated the effects of this drug on a bisection task. The major effect of physostigmine, an anticholinesterase which readily crosses the blood-brain barrier, is to increase the effective level of the neurotransmitter acetylcholine in the brain. Thus, the same logic that led to the choice of a selective blocker of dopamine receptors (haloperidol) led to a selective blocker of acetylcholine receptors (atropine). If a drug affected the translation of the subjective time of reinforcement into reference memory, we can define t as the remembered time of reinforcement when the animal is not drugged, and $K*t$ as the remembered time of reinforcement when the animal is drugged. The following pattern of results would occur: (a) There would be no initial effect when the drug is first introduced since the animal will continue to expect food when the clock reaches $t;$ (b) there would be a constant error as long as the drug is used, since the animal will learn to expect reinforcement when the clock reaches $K*t;$ and (c) there would be no immediate effect when the drug is withheld since the animal will continue to expect reinforcement when the clock reaches $K*t$. This pattern of results was obtained with drugs that increased or decreased the effective level of actylcholine (physostigmine and atropine, respectively). Two neuropeptides, vasopressin and oxytocin, had effects similar to those of physostigmine. Meck speculated that the memory storage constant may be proportional to the time required to move the contents of an accumulator into reference memory, and he referred to the inverse of the memory storage constant as memory storage speed.

The speed of acquisition of the temporal discrimination was facilitated by some drugs (physostigmine, vasopressin, and oxytocin) and retarded by others (atropine, methamphetamine, and haloperidol); Drugs that facilitated acquisition improved the asymptotic temporal discrimination; those that retarded acquisition reduced the asymptotic temporal discrimination. We have not yet attempted to develop a process model of acquisition so these results are unexplained.

5. The Cholinergic Nervous System and Temporal
Memory in Rats (Meck & Church, 1983c, in press a)

The effects of drugs on memory storage reported by Meck were based on the bisection procedure. For generality, it would be useful to replicate them with a very different procedure, the peak procedure. Although the emphasis of this experiment was on a biological account of the memory effects, all three process models were again employed.

The experiment demonstrated that physostigmine decreased the variability of the temporal discrimination and shifted peak times permanently leftward on the scale in a dose dependent manner; atropine, a cholinergic receptor blocker that readily crosses the blood-brain barrier, increased the variability of the temporal discrimination and shifted peak times permanently rightward on the time scale in a dose-dependent manner. Neostigmine, an anticholinesterase that does not readily cross the blood-brain barrier, and methyl-atropine, a cholinergic receptor blocker that does not readily cross the blood-brain barrier, did not produce these effects.

The results extended the memory effects reported in the previous experiment using a bisection procedure to the peak procedure. The conclusion was that the effective level of brain acetylcholine sets memory storage speed for sound durations in the rat. Thus, physostigmine increased memory storage speed, and rats remembered clock readings as shorter than they actually were; atropine decreased memory storage speed, and rats remembered clock readings as longer than they actually were.

6. Nutrients That Modify Internal-Clock and
Memory-Storage Speeds (Meck & Church, 1983b, in
press b)

We had previously reported that some drugs affect behavior in a manner that can best be explained as due to a change in the speed of an internal clock; and that other drugs affect behavior in a manner that can best be explained as a change in a remembered time. In this experiment, we reported that clock and memory effects are not restricted to drugs; they may also be produced by selected foods. In the interpretation of results, we presented a psychological, biological, and formal model and attempted to give them equal emphasis.

Rats were maintained on a normal balanced diet and trained on a 20-sec peak procedure, and then, 20 minutes prior to testing sessions, independent groups were given snacks of (a) saccharine, (b) protein (casein), (c) carbohydrate (sucrose), or (d) choline (lecithin). The pattern of results was as follows: Saccharine was a control condition, and it had no effect; protein led to an immediate, temporary, leftward shift in the peak function, a pattern associated with an increase in clock speed. Carbohydrate led to an immediate, temporary, rightward shift in the peak function, a pattern associated with a decrease in clock speed. Choline led to a gradual, permanent, leftward shift in the peak function, a pattern associated with an increase in memory speed.

The psychological process model and the formal scalar timing model were the same ones used previously. The psychological model provided an explanation for the pattern of results in terms of an increase in clock speed for protein, a decrease in clock speed for carbohydrate, and an increase in memory speed for choline. The scalar timing model accounted for over 98% of the variance in the response functions that consisted of the response rate as a function of time in 1-sec intervals.

The biological process model was somewhat more complicated for a nutrient than for the drugs we had previously used. The argument for lecithin was straightforward (Zeisel, 1982). Lecithin is 60 percent choline; choline crosses the blood-brain barrier by a carrier mechanism that is not normally saturated with choline molecules; when there is more choline in the blood, proportionally more will reach the brain; choline is essential for the synthesis of acetylcholine, and the enzyme involved in this reaction is unsaturated with respect to the precursor, choline. Thus, the consumption of lecithin leads to an increase in brain acetylcholine. An increase in the effective level of acetylcholine produces a gradual, permanent, leftward pattern of results (Meck, 1983; Meck & Church, 1983).

The argument for protein and carbohydrate is more complicated and controversial; it is based primarily on the research of Richard Wurtman and his colleagues (Zeisel, 1982). Dietary protein is a source of amino acids, and it increases the ratio of tyrosine to other amino acids in the plasma. Tyrosine competes with other amino acids for carrier molecules to move across the blood-brain barrier, and it is a precursor for dopamine synthesis. We have already assumed that the effective level of dopamine is related to clockspeed (Maricq & Church, 1983; Meck, 1983). An increase in the effective level of dopamine produced an immediate, leftward pattern of results. Both protein and carbohydrate are a source of amino acids including tryptophan. Carbohydrate, however, leads to increased insulin that increases the uptake of several amino acids other than tryptophan by muscle. Thus, the ratio of tryptophan to other amino acids in the plasma is higher after carbohydrate than protein. Tryptophan competes with other amino acids for carrier molecules to move across the blood-brain barrier. Thus a carbohydrate meal increases the amount of tryptophan that reaches the brain. Tryptophan is a precursor for serotonin. On the basis of some pilot drug studies, but mostly on conclusions reached by others on the basis of non-behavioral studies, there is reason to speculate that the effect of serotonin would be opposite the effect of dopamine. Thus, it is reasonable to assume an increase in the effective level of serotonin is related to a decrease in clock speed. An increase in the effective level of serotonin produced an immediate, temporary, rightward pattern of results.

D. CONCLUSION

In summary, our explanation of the results of these experiments, which employed pharmacological manipulations, began with descriptive research and attempted to establish some general principles, but these were developed with a goal in mind—namely, to develop process models to explain the results.

A psychological process model was used to explain some observations; a biological process model was used for some observations; and a formal scalar timing model was applied to some of the same observations. Finally, we were able to apply all three process models to the same data sets. If the effects of a particular drug on behavior can be interpreted either in psychological, biological, or formal terms, presumably there is an important relationship between psychological processes, neurotransmitters, and parameters of the model.

Although this chapter was written in terms of approaches to behavioral pharmacology, the approaches are generally available for the analysis of any behavior. An input-output analysis can be conducted without any intervening concepts; principles developed in one domain can be applied in others; and process models can be developed with one or more psychological, biological, or formal intervening variables. Perhaps the greatest progress will be made when several process models are used to explain the same experimental data. In that way, we can establish connections between psychological and biological concepts.

ACKNOWLEDGMENT

Research described in this chapter was supported by a grant from the National Institute of Mental Health (MH 37049). Many of the ideas expressed in this chapter were developed in collaboration with John Gibbon, Warren H. Meck and Seth Roberts.

REFERENCES

Barchas, J. D., Berger, P. A., Ciaranello, R. D., & Elliott, G. R. (1977). *Psychopharmacology: From theory to practice.* New York: Oxford.

Bush, R. R., & Mosteller, F. (1955). *Stochastic models for learning.* New York: Wiley.

Church, R. M. (1983). The influence of computers on psychological research: A case study. *Behavior Research Methods & Instrumentation, 15,* 117–126.

Church, R. M. (1984). Properties of the internal clock. In J. Gibbon, L. G. Allan (Eds.), *Annals of The New York Academy of Sciences: Timing and Time Perception* (566–582). New York: New York Academy of Sciences.

Cooper, J. R., Bloom, F. E., & Roth, R. H. (1978). *The Biochemical basis of neuropharmacology* (3rd Ed., pp. 307–322). New York: Oxford.

de Wied, D., & Bohus, B. (1966). Long and short term effects on retention of a conditioned avoidance response in rats by treatment with long acting pitressin and α-MSH. *Nature, 212,* 1484–1486.

Dews, P. B. (1971). Drug-behavior interactions. In J. A. Harvey (Ed.), *Behavioral analysis of drug action* (pp. 9–43). Glenview, Illinois: Scott, Foresman.

Dews, P. B., & Wenger, G. R. (1977). The rate dependency hypothesis. In P. B. Dews & T. Thompson (Eds.), *Advances in Behavioral Pharmacology* (Vol. 1, pp. 167–227). New York: Academic Press.

Gibbon, J. (1977). Scalar expectancy theory and Weber's law in animal timing. *Psychological Review, 84,* 279–325.

Gibbon, J., & Church, R. M. (1984). Sources of variance in information processing theories of timing. In H. L. Roitblat, T. G. Bever, & H. S. Terrace (Eds.), *Animal cognition* (pp. 465–488). Hillsdale, NJ: Lawrence Erlbaum Associates.

Gibbon, J., Church, R. M., & Meck, W. H. (1984). Scalar timing in memory. In J. Gibbon & L. G. Allan (Eds.), *Annals of The New York Academy of Sciences: Timing and Time Perception* (pp. 52–77). New York: New York Academy of Sciences.

Griffin, D. R. (1976). *The question of animal awareness.* New York: Rockefeller University Press.

Heinemann, E. G., Avin, E., Sullivan, M. A., & Chase, S. (1969). Analysis of stimulus generalization with a psychophysical method. *Journal of Experimental Psychology, 80,* 215–224.

Heise, G. A., & Milar, K. S. (1984). Drugs and stimulus control. In L. L. Iversen, S. D. Iversen, & S. H. Snyder (Eds.), *Handbook of Psychopharmacology: Drugs, neurotransmitters, and behavior* (Vol. 18, pp. 129–190). New York: Plenum.

Hempel, C. G. (1965). *Aspects of scientific explanation and other essays in the philosophy of science.* New York: Free Press.

Hunter, W. S. (1913). The delayed reaction in animals and children. *Behavior Monographs, 2*(1) Serial No. 6.

Iversen, L. L., Iversen, S. D., & Snyder, S. H. (Eds.) (1984). *Handbook of Psychopharmacology: Drugs, neurotransmitters, and behavior.* (Vol. 18). New York: Plenum.

Kandel, E. R., & Schwartz, J. H. (1981). *Principles of neural science.* New York: Elsevier/North-Holland.

Kuman, R. (1977). Animal behavioral models of relevance to psychiatry. In L. L. Iversen, S. D. Iversen, & S. H. Snyder (Eds.), *Handbook of psychopharmacology: Principles of behavioral pharmacology* (Vol. 7, pp. 231–261). New York: Plenum.

Mackintosh, J. H., Chance, M. R. A., & Silverman, A. P. (1977). The contribution of ethological techniques to the study of drug effects. In L. L. Iversen, S. D. Snyder (Eds.), *Handbook of pharmacology: Principles of behavioral pharmacology* (Vol. 7, pp. 3–35). New York: Plenum.

Maricq, A. V., Roberts, S., & Church, R. M. (1981). Methamphetamine and time estimation. *Journal of Experimental Psychology: Animal Behavior Processes, 7,* 18–30.

Maricq, A. V., & Church, R. M. (1983). The differential effects of haloperidol and methamphetamine on time estimation in the rat. *Psychopharmacology, 79,* 10–15.

Meck, W. H. (1983). Selective adjustment of the speed of internal clock and memory processes. *Journal of Experimental Psychology: Animal Behavior Processes, 9,* 171–201.

Meck, W. H., & Church, R. M. (1983a). A mode control model of counting and timing processes. *Journal of Experimental Psychology: Animal Behavior Processes, 9,* 320–334.

Meck, W. H., & Church, R. M. (1983b, November). *Nutrients that modify internal-clock and memory-storage speeds.* Paper read at meeting of the psychonomics Society, San Diego, CA.

Meck, W. H., & Church, R. M. (1983c). The cholinergic nervous system and temporal memory in rats. *Society for Neuroscience, 9,* 478 (Abstract 142.3).

Meck, W. H. & Church, R. M. (in press a). Cholinergic modulation of the content of temporal memory. *Behavioral Neuroscience.*

Meck, W. H., & Church, R. M. (in press b). Nutrients that modify the speed of internal clock and memory processes. *Behavioral Neuroscience.*

Overton, D. A. (1984). State dependent learning and drug discriminations. In L. L. Iversen, S. D.

Iversen, & S. H. Snyder (Eds.), *Handbook of psychopharmacology: Drugs, neurotransmitters, and behavior* (Vol. 18). New York: Plenum.

Pavlov, I. P. (1972). *Conditioned reflexes* (Tv., G. V. Anrep). London: Oxford University Press (Reprinted, New York: Dover, 1960).

Premack, D. (1983). Animal cognition. In M. R. Rosenzweig & L. W. Porter (Eds.), *Annual Review of Psychology*. Palo Alto, CA: Annual Reviews.

Roberts, S. (1980). How to check a computer program. *Behavior Research Methods and Instrumentation, 12,* 155–156.

Roberts, S. (1981). Isolation of an internal clock. *Journal of Experimental Psychology: Animal Behavior Processes, 7,* 242–268.

Seiden, L. S., & Dykstra, L. A. (1977). *Psychopharmacology: A biochemical and behavioral approach.* New York: Van Nostrand.

Siegel, S. (1977). Morphine tolerance acquisition as an associative process. *Journal of Experimental Psychology: Animal Behavior Processes, 3,* 1–13.

Skinner, B. F. (1950). Are theories of learning necessary? *Psychological Review, 57,* 193–216.

Solomon, R. L., & Corbit, J. D. (1974). An opponent-process theory of motivation: I. Temporal dynamics of affect. *Psychological Review, 81,* 119–145.

Solomon, R. L., & Wynne, L. C. (1953). Traumatic avoidance learning: Acquisition in normal dogs. *Psychological Monographs, 67,* (Whole No. 354).

Solomon, R. L., & Wynne, L. C. (1954). Traumatic avoidance learning: The principles of anxiety conservation and partial irreversibility. *Psychological Review, 61,* 353–385.

Thompson, R. F., Patterson, M. M., & Teyler, T. I. (1972). The neurophysiology of learning. In P. H. Mussen & M. R. Rosenzweig (Eds.), *Annual Review of Psychology* (Vol. 23, pp. 73–104). Palo Alto, CA: Annual Reviews.

Thompson, T., Schuster, C. R. (1968). *Behavioral pharmacology.* Englewood Cliffs, NJ: Prentice-Hall.

Weingartner, H., Gold, P., Ballenger, J. C., Smallberg, S. A., Summers, R., Rubinow, D. R., Post, R. M., & Goodwin, F. K. (1981). Effects of vasopressin on human memory functions. *Science, 211,* 601–603.

Zeisel, S. H. (1982). The effects of dietary components on brain function. In J. J. Vitale & S. A. Broitman (Eds.), *Advances in human clinical nutrition* (pp. 205–214). Boston: John Wright.

IV

LEARNED HELPLESSNESS

11 Stressor Controllability, Immune Function, and Endogenous Opiates

Steven F. Maier
Mark L. Laudenslager
Susan M. Ryan
University of Colorado and University of Denver

It has long been recognized that there is a relationship between stressful life events and disease (see Hurst, Jenkins, & Rose, 1976; Plaut & Friedman, 1981; Rogers, Dubey, & Reich, 1979, for reviews). For example, grief and bereavement appear to be associated with increased morbidity and mortality among the survivors (Henock, Batson, & Baum, 1978; Jacobs & Ostfeld, 1977; Morillo & Gardner, 1979). Depression, which often follows a loss or separation (Brown, Harris, & Copeland, 1977; Roy, 1981), is associated with a twofold increase in risk of cancer over a 17-year followup period (Shekelle, Raynor, Ostfeld, Garron, Bieliavskas, Liv, Maliza, & Paul, 1981), Similarly, significant correlations, although retrospective, exist between stressful life events and the incidence or onset of major medical disorders (Rabkin & Struening, 1976).

It has been suggested that alteration in immune functioning is a mechanism whereby stressful events could affect disease processes (Jacobs & Charles, 1980; Laudenslager, Reite, & Harbeck, 1982). Indeed, a number of studies have reported direct measures of immune functioning following stressful life experiences. For example, lymphocyte proliferation following mitogenic stimulation is depressed after the death of a spouse (Bartrop, Lazarus, Luckhurst, Kiloh, & Penney, 1977; Schleifer, Keller, Camarino, Thornton, & Stein, 1983). With regard to a less severe stressor, Dorian, Garfinkel, Brown, Shore, Gladman, and Keystone (1982), reported depressed lymphocyte proliferation shortly before psychiatric trainees were to take their final oral examination.

In animals, a variety of simple physical stressors have been shown to alter the development of disease (Riley, 1981; Sklar & Anisman, 1979; Solomon & Amkraut, 1981). Moreover, a variety of investigators have reported direct measures of immune function, with stress often leading to immunosuppression. For example, mitogen-induced proliferation of lymphocytes has been found to be suppressed after exposure to loud noise in mice (Monjan & Collector, 1977), electric shock in rats (Keller, Weiss, Schliefer, Miller, & Stein, 1983), infant-mother separation in bonnet monkeys (Laudenslager, Reite, & Harbeck, 1982), and peer separation in pigtail monkeys (Reite, Harbeck, & Hoffman, 1981). Similarly, acceleration, restraint, and overcrowding in mice have been found to reduce the number of plaque-forming cells (Gisler, 1974).

These stressors are quite diverse, and it is not known which aspect(s) is critical for producing impairment of immune functioning. It has become increasingly clear that stress, or the deleterious consequences of exposure to a stressor, is not the simple result of exposure to a given physical event or psychological condition. Rather, the outcomes of such exposure are modulated by a number of complex psychological and psychosocial conditions, such as prior experience, expectations, availability of a support network, among others (Ursin, Baade, & Levine, 1978). Stress itself is the result of a complex interaction of psychological factors with the actual physical event, and coping processes have come to be viewed as central in this regard (Levine & Ursin, 1979). The term *coping* is not easy to define in a noncircular way (Levine, Weinberg, & Ursin, 1978), but it generally refers to problem solving efforts to adapt to important environmental demands. Coping has often come to be part of the definition of stress itself, such that stress is said to result from exposure to an aversive event only if the individual cannot cope or anticipates that it cannot cope with the event (Lazarus, Averill, & Opton, 1974). Importantly, the ability to cope with stress has been seen as a critical mediator between aversive events and disease (Miller, 1979; 1983).

There are many ways to cope with an event, but one that has been studied intensively is *behavioral control*. Control refers to the organism's ability to alter the onset, termination, duration, intensity, or temporal pattern of the event, and a variety of investigations have explored the consequences of variations of this dimension. Thus, exposure to inescapable and unavoidable (i.e., uncontrollable) electric shocks can result in (a) interference with subsequent learning in active escape (Overmier & Seligman, 1967), passive avoidance (Baker, 1976; Jackson, Maier, & Rapaport, 1978), and choice escape tasks (Jackson, Alexander, & Maier, 1980); (b) decreased unconditioned activity in the presence of shock (Drugan & Maier, 1982); (c) reduced agonistic behavior in shock elicited aggression (Maier, Anderson, & Lieberman, 1972), social dominance (Rapaport & Maier, 1978), and colony intruder attack situations (Williams, 1982); (d) opioid forms of short-term and long-term analgesia (Hyson, Ashcraft, Drugan, Grau, & Maier, 1982; Jackson, Coon & Maier, 1979); (e) enhanced reactivity to opiate (Grau, Hyson, Maier, Madden, & Barchas, 1981) and stimulant drugs (MacLennan & Maier, 1983); (f) severe stress symptomology (Weiss, 1968); and (g) alterations in a variety of neurochemical and hormonal systems (e.g., Anisman & Sklar, 1979; Sherman & Petty, 1982; Swenson & Vogel, 1983; Weiss, Goodman, Nosito, Corrigan, Charry, & Bailey, 1981). This is by no means a complete list, but it should serve to provide the flavor of the changes which are produced by exposure to uncontrollable aversive events. These changes do not typically follow experience with controllable (escapable or avoidable) aversive events (see Anderson, Crowell, Cunningham, & Lupo, 1979, for an exception). Thus, the dimension of control, or some factor involved in the process of control, participates in modulating the impact of exposure to aversive events. It should be emphasized that these widespread effects occur even though the parameters of inescapable shock used are typically not very severe. Most of the deficits just described have been observed following a single session of only 80 shocks of moderate intensity (1.0 mA), if the shocks are inescapable. It should also be noted that effects of uncontrollability are not limited to electric shock and shock-motivated behavior. Inescapably shocked subjects later fail to learn to escape not only shock, but also other aversive events, such as exposure to water (Altenor, Kay, & Richter, 1977). They are even poor at learning to perform responses to obtain positive events, such as food (Rosellini, 1978). Moreover, the uncontrollable aversive event need not be shock. For example, exposure to water that cannot be escaped interferes with the acquisition of both water and shock escape (Altenor et al., 1977). Indeed, the provision of food availability not under the subject's control can interfere with learning to escape shock (Goodkin, 1976).

The seeming importance of controllability suggests that this dimension might also play a role in mediating the effect of exposure to stressors on immune functioning and the disease process. Indeed, a number of experiments have manipulated control over shock and examined tumor growth and tumor rejection. Sklar and Anisman (1979) injected mice with syngeneic P815 tumor cells. They were then given a single session of either escapable or yoked inescapable shocks. The inescapable shock enhanced tumor growth, while the escapable shock had no effect. Visintainer, Volpicelli, and Seligman (1982) reported similar results for the rejection of Walker 256 Sarcoma in rats.

However, tumor growth or rejection does not necessarily reflect immune system functioning, since they can be *directly* affected by factors such as vascular flow, steroids, and prolactin, all of which are increased by stress. Thus, we set out to directly determine if the controllability of shock is important in modulating the activity of the imune system, and the purpose of this chapter is to describe this work.

OVERVIEW OF THE IMMUNE SYSTEM

An understanding of the measures chosen for study and of the implications of the resulting data will be difficult without some knowledge about the immune system. We thus provide a brief description for those unfamiliar with the immune system.

The immune system has two primary tasks—recognition of foreign materials (antigens) and inactivation and removal of these materials. These functions are accomplished by different, but not independent, cell populations. First, recognition of "foreigness" or "not self" is accomplished primarily by a group of cells called lymphocytes (20–45% of the total white blood cell population) of which there are three main types: B-cells (bone marrow-derived precursors of immunoglobulin or antibody secreting plasma cells), T-cells (thymus-derived lymphocytes having many regulatory influences on the B-cells), and null cells. Null cells are active in antibody dependent cell mediated cytotoxicity, and included in this group are a group of important cells called natural killer cells. Both B- and T-cells have cell surface receptors which recognize antigens. For the B-cell, this receptor is simply an immunoglobulin molecule; T-cell receptors have not been clearly identified at present. It is important to realize that there is a great deal of specificity in this receptor recognition process. A given lymphocyte will recognize only one of a small number of antigens. Thus, there are lymphocytes with many different receptors and, therefore, only a small number at any given time that will recognize a particular antigen. After B-cells have undergone antigenic stimulation (a process requiring the cooperation of T-cells and another group of cells, the macrophages), B-cells proliferate via clonal expansion. This clonal expansion results in the formation of many lymphocytes with receptors capable of recognizing the antigen. The cells next differentiate into plasma cells or the antibody secreting cells. Antibody is the soluble copy of the receptor molecule. Antigens are often inactivated by simply binding to the antibody and forming an antigen-antibody complex without further processing. In other instances, additional processing occurs (described later). T-cells, which have undergone antigen stimulation, first proliferate and then differentiate into several functional subpopulations: helper cells, which cooperate with B-cells during antibody formation; suppressor cells, which down-regulate antibody formation; cytotoxic or killer cells, which are cytotoxic to cells expressing the specific antigen; and cells responsible for the delayed hypersensitivity response, such as that observed in a positive tuberculin skin test.

Phagocytic cells, which are involved in the removal of microorganisms, other cells, and foreign materials, include the macrophages and neutrophils. The macrophages, mononuclear cells comprising 5–10% of the total white cell population, are also critical in the initial processing of antigens by the lymphocytes. At this early stage, the macrophage does not recognize the antigen as foreign, but it nonspecifically processes it in some unknown manner for recognition by the lymphocytes. At later stages in the immune response, antigen-activated T-cells or lymphoblasts release lymphokines, which attract the macrophages, which in turn ingest the antigen. The other class of phagocytic cells are the neutrophils, a polymorphonuclear cell. These cells are quite numerous and may account for up to 70% of the total white blood cell count. Like the macrophages, they contain enzymatic systems for digesting engulfed materials. Neutrophils are attracted to antibody-antigen complexes and components of the complement system, which is activated in the presence of antibody-antigen complexes. The complement system is a complex chain of chemical events occurring at the site of antigen-antibody interaction, which produces protein complement components. These proteins are chemoattractive for neutrophils. As the neutrophils move into sites of antigen-antibody interactions, they engulf and digest these antigen-antibody complexes and, frequently, normal tissue in the process. In sum, T- and B-cells are involved in a number of different methods for removing invaders. Some activated T-cells are directly cytotoxic and can lyse (damage the cell membrane) target cells, while other activated T-cells can attract macrophages. Activated B-cells produce antibody, and antigen-antibody complexes can attract neutrophils.

A unique feature of the immune response is a phenomenon called immunologic memory. After primary sensitization to an antigen, cells may differentiate into either plasma cells, which produce antibody, or lymphocytes, which react specifically with the antigen. Through proliferation by clonal expansion, the numbers of these cells specifically reacting with the antigen increases dramatically. Numbers of these cells may decline after the initial contact with the antigen. However, on second contact with the same antigen or closely related antigen, a more rapid and greater response occurs. This greater response has been attributed to *memory* expressed by specific T- and B-cells for the antigen. Antibody formed by B-cells in response to the second immunization differs from that following the first challenge, First, it has a greater strength of binding to the antigen, and second, it is of a different immunoglobulin class. Antibody formed after primary immunization is primarily of the IgM class and, after secondary immunization, is primarily of the IgG class. In general, the immunological response to a second challenge by the same antigen is greatly enhanced.

A class of lymphoid cells called natural killer (NK) cells may be of particular importance for tumor development (see Herberman & Ortaldo, 1981, for a review). These cells are nonphagocytic large granular lymphocytes (Timonen, Ranki, Saksela, & Hayry, 1979) which do not have surface markers characteristic of either T-cells or B-cells. They function differently from T- and B-cells in many ways. For present purposes, two are most important. First, NK cells are spontaneously cytotoxic and can rapidly lyse (within hours) tumor and other cells without prior activation. As noted above, T-cells have no detectable spontaneous cytotoxic activity but, rather, must be first activated by exposure to specific antigens or by interaction with accessory cells, such as macrophages which "present" the antigen. This process of activation is usually quite lengthy, requiring 7 to 10 days or more before T-cells develop their maximal primary reactivity. Second, target cell recognition by NK cells is intermediate in specificity between the extreme specificity of T-cells and the nonspecificity of macrophages and polymorphonuclear cells. NK cells appear to be able to recognize a number of widely distributed antigenic specificities. These characteristics have led Herberman and Ortaldo (1981) to propose that NK cells may be part of a primary broad-range defense system that responds quickly to invaders to partially control them, until the more potent and specific arms of the immune system can respond.

Until recently, T-cells were thought to play a central role in immune surveillance against tumors. However, a number of obvious exceptions (e.g., Genetically athymic mice do not have a high incidence of tumors) have led some to reject the general notion of immune surveillance for tumors, and others to retain the concept of immune surveillance but focus on other effector cells such as NK cells. Indeed, a variety of evidence indicates that NK cells function against tumors in vivo. For example, NK activity varies with mouse strain and age, and there is a correlation between level of NK activity and the ability of mice to destory intravenously inoculated tumors (Riccardi, Santoni, Barlozzori, & Herberman, 1980). Moreover, NK deficient homozygous bg/bg mice are more susceptible to the growth and metastasis of transplantable syngeneic tumors than their normal +/bg littermates (Karre, Klein, Kiessling, Klein, & Roder, 1980). Importantly, beige mice, which are deficient in NK activity, have an enhanced incidence of spontaneous lymphomas late in life. In humans, patients with NK deficiencies have an increased incidence of malignancy (Sullivan, Byron, Brewster, & Purtdo, 1980). Finally, some carcinogenic agents have been shown to depress NK activity, thus interfering with host defense and impairing the host's ability to reject transformed cells (see Herberman & Ortaldo, 1981).

Immunocompetence, reflecting the degree to which these events proceed efficiently and protect the organism, has been measured by a variety of in vivo and in vitro techniques. For simplicity, the immune system has often been divided into two primary parts: (a) *humoral immunity* consisting of antibodies and the complement system, and (b) *cellular immunity* consisting of other immunocompetent cells such as T-cells. This division is arbitrary, since both parts interact to a great extent.

Assessment of the humoral component might include procedures which determine total serum immunoglobulin levels, immunoglobulin classes (IgA, IgE, IgG, and IgM), specific antigen-antibody reactions, quantitative levels of specific antibodies, B-cell quantification, quantitative levels of individual components of the complement system, and functional serum complement activity. Competence of the cellular component can be measured by delayed hypersensitivity skin tests, in vitro lymphocyte mitogenic stimulation, in vitro lymphocyte antigenic stimulation, mixed lymphocyte response, enumeration of T- and B-cells, neutrophil quantification, chemotaxis assays which test motility, and oxygen uptake by neurophils during phagocytosis of foreign material. This list of tests is in no way comprehensive but is intended to give the reader a general indication of their relevance.

CONTROLLABILITY AND MITOGEN INDUCED LYMPHOCYTE PROLIFERATION

The purpose of our initial study (Laudenslager, Ryan, Drugan, Hyson, & Maier, 1983) was to directly determine whether the controllability of a stressor is important in modulating the activity of the immune system. We chose to compare the effects of escapable shocks and equal amounts and distributions of inescapable shocks on mitogen-induced proliferation of T-lymphocytes in vitro. This measure was chosen for initial study for several reasons. First, the immune response is quite complex, and it thus seemed desirable to begin by assessing an early aspect of the immune system. Activation of T- and B-cells by an antigen is one of the initial steps and is critical to the entire process. As opposed to antigens, mitogens nonspecifically stimulate lymphocytes and can lead to polyclonal activation. As with antigenic stimulation, this activation is followed by proliferation of the activated cells. This in vitro proliferative response probably does mirror the in vivo response which occurs after antigenic stimulation. Second, mitogen-induced lymphocyte stimulation is used to assess cellular immunity in patients, and the results typically correlate with abnormalities in patients with immune deficiency diseases. Third, lymphocytes may be stimulated to proliferate in vitro by a variety of agents including phytohemagglutinin (PHA), Concanavelin A (ConA), and bacterial lipopolysaccharides (LPS). Proliferation in response to PHA and ConA is a property of the T-cells (Daguillard, 1972). LPS stimulates predominantly B-cells, but cooperation of T-cells may be required (Schreck, Lamberson, & Davey, 1982). There does not seem to be a lymphocyte activator which stimulates only B-cells without also affecting T-cell populations. Thus for clarity, the T-cell specific mitogens PHA and ConA, were chosen for study.

The experimental procedures were those typically used in our laboratory. One group of rats (N = 12) received a single session of 80 escapable shocks in a wheel-turn box. Shocks were delivered to the rat's tail via fixed electrodes, and occurred on the average of once a minute. Shock intensity began at 0.8 mA and was increased by .2 mA every 20 trials. The final shock intensity was thus 1.6 mA. Each shock terminated when the subject turned a wheel located in the front of the chamber, provided that a minimum of 0.8 sec of shock had elapsed. Shock automatically terminated if a response had not occurred after 30 sec. A second yoked group received matched inescapable shocks. Each subject in this group was paired with an escapable shock subject: Shocks began at the same time as for the escapable shock subject and terminated if and when the latter responded. A third group was restrained in the apparatus but was not shocked.

Twenty-four hours later, all three groups were given five 5-sec 0.6 mA footshocks in a shuttlebox. Blood was then collected in heparinized vacutainer tubes by heart puncture under light ether anesthesia. A home cage control group received no experimental treatment prior to heart puncture.

Blood was collected 24 hours after initial shock treatment and shock reexposure, rather than immediately after the initial shock treatment, for several reasons. The immediate effects of the lengthy initial shock treatment could easily mask any differences between escapable and inescapable shocks soon after the session by suppression simply being maximal. Indeed, many of the behavioral effects that depend on whether shock is escapable or inescapable are typically measured 24 hours after the shocks rather than soon after exposure. Finally, endogenous opioids may be involved in modulating immune system functioning, and the evidence for endogenous opiate involvement in inescapable shock effects is best for the 24 hour interval followed by shock reexposure condition.

Lymphocytes were removed from blood by standard Ficoll-Hypaque sedimentation methods described in Laudenslager et al. (1983). Cell cultures were added in triplicate to the wells of a microtiter plate for each of the mitogens to be tested and for control cultures to which media but no mitogens was added. The cultures were then incubated for 72 hours, then pulsed with 3H-thymidine, and finally harvested onto glass-fiber filter paper. The incorporation of 3H-thymidine into newly synthesized DNA in stimulated and unstimulated cultures was determined with a liquid scintillation counter. Thymidine incorporation is a measure of how much new DNA has been formed and reflects the amount of cellular proliferation.

Figure 11.1 shows the lymphocyte proliferation results for various concentrations of the mitogen PHA, expressed as counts/min of triplicate measures of experimental mitogen stimulated cultures (E) minus counts per minute of unstimulated control cultures (C). Neither escapable shock on Day 1 followed by 5 footshocks on Day 2, nor restraint on Day 1 followed by the footshocks altered lymphocyte proliferation. In contrast, inescapable shock led to a suppression of lymphocyte proliferation.

The results for the ConA stimulated cultures are slightly different and are shown in Figure 11.2. Escapable shocks somewhat facilitated lymphocyte proliferation relative to the restrained controls. However, inescapable shocks again led to a suppression of proliferation. The fact that PHA and ConA produced slightly different results was not unexpected, because they may affect different T-cell subpopulations (Nakayama, Dippold, Shiko, Oettgen, & Old, 1980).

In summary, a single session of 80 relatively brief shocks can substantially inhibit lymphocyte proliferation in vitro, if the subject has no control over the shocks. However, identical shocks are without effect, if the subject can escape them. Thus, the ability to control shocks prevented immunosuppression that otherwise would follow exposure to uncontrollable shocks, as reflected by this in vitro measure.

CONTROLLABILITY AND NATURAL KILLER CELL ACTIVITY

As noted previously, NK cells are a class of immune cells that may be particularly important in tumor development. NK cells are spontaneously cytotoxic and lyse tumor cells in vitro. In collaboration with Y. Shavit, J. W. Lewis, G. W. Terman, R. P. Gale, and J. C. Liebeskind, we set out to determine if shock controllability would be an important factor in modulating the ability of NK cells

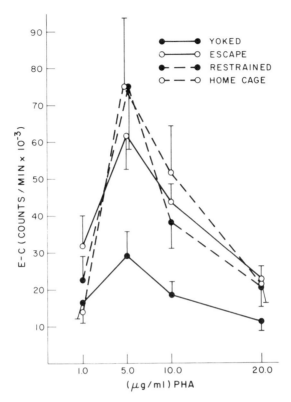

FIG. 11.1. Stimulation of lymphocytes by PHA. Results (mean ± standard errors) are counts per triplicate measures of mitogen stimulated cultures (E) per minute minus counts per triplicate measures of unstimulated cultures (C) per minute.

to kill tumor cells. The experimental design was as before: Rats received a single session of escapable, yoked-inescapable, or no shock (home cage controls), followed by 5 brief shocks 24 hours later. However, instead of blood being drawn, spleens were removed and single cell suspensions prepared.

A short-term chromium (51Cr) release assay was employed. Cr readily enters most cells and binds to intracellular proteins. Cr is released into the medium upon cell lysis or when the cell membrane sustains major damage. Thus, the amount of Cr in the medium provides an indication of the number of cells lysed. Here, YAC-1 tumor cells, a tissue culture cell line derived from a transplantable lymphoma, were labeled with 51Cr. The labeled tumor cells were then incubated with the splenic NK cells from the rat subjects, and the ability of these NK cells to kill the YAC-1 tumor cells was assessed. The amount of 51Cr in the medium was measured by a gamma counter, and this is a reflection of the number of YAC-1 cells lysed.

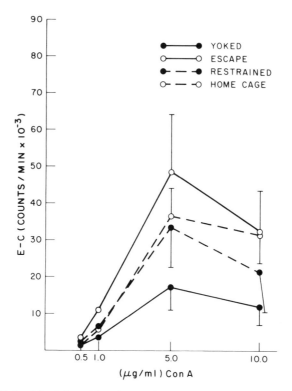

FIG. 11.2.   Stimulation of lymphocytes by conA. Results are expressed as in Figure 11.1.

Figure 11.3 shows the results of this experiment expressed as percent of cytotoxicity of the no shock control subjects. The mean cytotoxicity of NK cells taken from the no shock controls was calculated, and each subject's data was expressed as a percentage of this value. As can be seen, escapable shock did reduce cytotoxicity, but inescapable shock did so even more strongly. In fact, only the inescapable shock group differed reliably from controls, collapsed across the different ratios. Clearly, these results are preliminary and require replication.

MECHANISM OF ACTION

We do not know why inescapable shock inhibits T-lymphocyte proliferation and NK cell cytotoxicity. There are many possibilities, and here we will only describe a small number that are of particular interest. Perhaps the most obvious mediators are adrenal corticosteroids. Corticosteroids are released by stressors

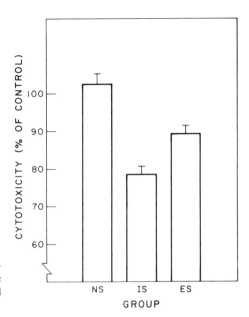

FIG. 11.3. Specific cytotoxic activity of splenic NK cells. Results are expressed as percent of untreated controls.

such as inescapable shock and are known to alter a variety of aspects of immune functioning (Claman, 1972, 1975; Riley, 1981; Solomon & Amkraut, 1981). The nature of the interaction between corticosteroids and the immune system is extremely complex. However, corticosterone has been reported to suppress both lymphocyte proliferation (Monjan, 1981) and natural killer (NK) cell activity.

Thus, it is possible that inescapable, but not escapable, shock, suppresses lymphocyte proliferation and NK cell activity because it produces higher levels of corticosterone. However, several lines of evidence mitigate against this possibility. Greenberg, Dyck, and Sandler (1983) found no correlation between corticosterone levels and the suppression of NK cell activity produced by a variety of conditions. Even stronger evidence is provided by Keller et al. (1983) who found that adrenalectomy did not prevent shock from reducing lymphocyte proliferation. In a preliminary study, we have examined corticosterone levels immediately after initial shock treatment and 24 hour reinstatement using parameters identical to those used in the previous lymphocyte proliferation and NK studies. Rats received either escapable shock (ES), yoked inescapable shock (IS), restraint with no shock (NS), and 5 footshocks 24 hours later. Subgroups were decapitated and bled either immediately after the Day 1 treatment, 24 hours later before shock reexposure, or immediately after the reexposure. Serum corticosterone was determined by radioimmunoassay. The results are shown in Table 11.1 and indicate that corticosterone levels after the initial shock treatment were somewhat higher for inescapable than for escapable shock subjects. However, this difference was not reliable, and it is doubtful whether it would be large

TABLE 11.1
Plasma Corticosterone (μg/dl) of Rats Receiving Escapable (ES),
Inescapable (IS), or No Shock (NS) as a Function of Time
Since the Day 1 Treatment

Group	Time of Sampling		
	Immediately After Day 1 Shocks	24 Hours After Day 1 Shocks	Immediately After Day 2 Shocks
ES	54.5 + 3.6[a]	10.8 + 0.5	39.1 + 4.0
IS	60.4 + 3.6	10[b]	39.8 + 2.6
NS	23.0 + 3.8	13.7 + 3.2	50.4 + 2.8

[a] Mean + SEM
[b] This group was below the minimal detectable level of the assay due to excessive dilution of serum at the time the assay was run.

enough to have a differential effect on lymphocyte function. Interestingly, both groups show a smaller rise following the 5 footshocks than do the previously nonshocked controls. Of course, this does not mean that different shock parameters might not yield a different outcome (i.e., Dess, Linwick, Patterson, Overmier, & Levine, 1983). In addition, a recent study by Swenson and Vogel (1983) found a slower decline in corticosterone levels following uncontrollable shock than controllable shock. Unfortunately, Swenson and Vogel used very different shock conditions than in our experiments. The critical question here is whether the shock parameters we used produce differences in corticosterone, and so we will thus have to more thoroughly examine the time course of corticosterone change with our parameters.

Another possible mechanism revolves around the endogenous opiates. Lymphocytes have been reported to contain opiate receptors (Mehrishi & Mills, 1983), although their exact nature and type remains unclear (Hazum, Chang, & Cuatrecasas, 1979). Moreover, B-endorphin has been reported to suppress mitogen induced T-cell proliferation (McCain, Lamister, Bozzone, & Grbic, 1982), but enhancement has also been found (Gilman, Schwartz, Milner, Bloom, & Feldman, 1982). In neither case were the effects reversed by naloxone, suggesting a receptor other than the Mu type. However, Mehrishi and Mills (1983) have recently reported saturatable binding of naloxone to human lymphocytes. They also found morphine to displace bound naloxone at concentrations typical of those effective in brain tissue membrane homogenates, suggesting that at least some of the receptors are of the Mu type. Moreover, potent, naloxone reversible suppressin of T-dependent and T-independent antibody responses by met- and leu-enkephalin, and alpha-, beta-, and gamma-endorphin, has recently been reported (Johnson, Smith, Torres, & Blalock, 1982). Of direct relevance here, Shavit, Lewis, Terman, Gale, and Liebeskind (1983) have found that shock conditions which produce an opioid analgesia also enhance tumor growth, and this effect was blocked by naltrexone. Shock conditions leading to nonopioid analgesia did not enhance tumor growth. Similarly, Greenberg et al. (1983) have found naltrexone to block the suppressive effects of inescapable shock on the elimination of NK sensitive tumors. Finally, in the absence of a stressor, naloxone and naltrexone can inhibit tumor growth and prolong survival in animals implanted with tumors (Aylsworth, Hodson, & Meites, 1979; Zagon & McLaughlin, 1981).

In sum, a number of lines of evidence suggest that an endogenous opiate may be involved in mediating some of the immunosuppressive effects of stress. However, a note of caution is appropriate here. The research relating endogenous opiates and immune functioning is controversial, and some of the data is contradictory with both enhancement and interference with immunocompetence having been reported. It will be some time before all the relevant controlling factors (e.g., acute vs. chronic opiate stimulation) are identified.

CONTROLLABILITY AND ENDOGENOUS OPIATES

The possibility of mediation by endogenous opiates is of particular interest because the controllability dimension may be a factor in determining the activation of such a system(s). To briefly review this evidence, stress appears to activate both anterior pituitary (Rossier, French, Rivier, Ling, Guillemin, & Bloom, 1977) and brain (Madden, Akil, Patrick, & Barchas, 1977) opiate systems. Consistent with these findings, stress also produces a variety of opioid effects, such as decreased pain sensitivity/reactivity (so-called stress-induced analgesia, or SIA). However, exposure to a physically painful event does not always lead to opioid effects. For example, SIA is sometimes reversed by opiate antagonists, such as naloxone and naltrexone, and cross tolerant with morphine, but sometimes is not (Maier, Drugan, Grau, Hyson, MacLennan, Moye, Madden, & Barchas, 1983; Watkins & Mayer, 1982), and both conditions are necessary conditions for the implication of opiate involvement in a phenomenon (Sawynok, Pinsky, & LaBella, 1979). These sorts of data have led to the conclusion that there exist multiple analgesia systems, some being opioid and some nonopioid in nature.

We have studied the role of the controllability/uncontrollability of the stressor in determining opiate system involvement and whether SIA will be opioid or nonopioid. It appears that the organism's learning that it has no control over an uncontrollable stressor is one factor in leading to opiate system activation. The major supporting findings are that inescapable, but not equal escapable, shock produces an analgesia that can be reinstated by brief shock 24 hours later (Jackson, Coon, & Maier, 1979), and this analgesia is completely reversed by opiate antagonists (Maier, Davies, Grau, Jackson, Morrison, Moye, Madden, & Barchas, 1980) and cross tolerant with morphine (Drugan, Grau, Maier, Madden, & Barches, 1981). Both controllable and uncontrollable shock produce an analgesia immediately after the shock session, but only the analgesia produced by uncontrollable shock is reversed by opiate antagonists (Hyson et al., 1982).

This conclusion about uncontrollability and opioid analgesia might seem inconsistent with the fact that the stressor has been nominally inescapable in many SIA studies which obtained nonopioid SIA. However, if the learning that stress is uncontrollable is critical, then learning variables ought to be important. For example, this form of learning is quite complex and ought to require many trials or exposures. Indeed, many of the studies finding SIA employed a brief exposure to the stressor. This argument suggests that as the organism experiences a long sequence of inescapable shocks, nonopioid analgesia should occur first and then be replaced by opioid SIA, as the subject learns about the uncontrollability of the stressor. To examine this idea, Grau et al. (1981) repeatedly measured pain sensitivity/reactivity during a session of 80 inescapable shocks. Analgesia occurred after 3 to 5 shocks, was maintained until 20 shocks, dissipated by 40 shocks, and reappeared after 60–80 shocks. Thus, there were early and late analgesic peaks, and only the late peak was sensitive to naltrexone. That is, the SIA after 60 to 80 shocks was reversed by naltrexone, while the SIA following 5 and 20 shocks was not. In addition, we have tested some of the shock conditions used in other laboratories, and those that produce opioid SIA lead to a learned helplessness effect, while procedures that produce nonopioid SIA do not (Maier, Sherman, Lewis, Terman, & Liebeskind, 1983). Supporting the role of the learning of uncontrollability as critical, the opioid analgesia (the reinstated analgesia and the late analgesia peak) can be blocked by prior or subsequent experience with escapable shock (Moye, Grau, Coon, & Maier, 1981).

Reversal by opiate antagonists and cross tolerance with morphine are necessary but not sufficient conditions to implicate endogenous opiate systems. Grau et al. (1981) have employed an additional strategy. If inescapable shock leads to analgesia 24 hours later upon shock reexposure, because it activates an opiate system (thereby facilitating later release of opiates or altering receptor sensitivity), then this analgesia ought to be produced by activating opiate processes directly without even administering inescapable shock. Thus, Grau et al. (1981) repeated the usual experiment but administered a small dose of morphine (4 mg/kg) on the first day rather than inescapable shock. Morphine could be substituted for inescapable shock. That is, the brief shock exposure on Day 2 produces SIA in rats that had received morphine 24 hours earlier. Obviously, SIA did not occur in subjects that had received only saline on Day 1, nor did morphine on Day 1 by itself produce SIA on Day 2. Similarly, inescapable, but not escapable shock, was found to exaggerate the organism's responsivity to morphine 24 hours later. Thus, morphine and inescapable shock do appear to involve a degree of mutual subsitutability, and this is consistent with the argument that uncontrollability is involved in the activation of endogenous opiate systems. Perhaps this is partly or wholly responsible for the resulting immunosuppression. Obviously, direct plasma assay data would be desirable here. Radioimmunoassay for regional CNS B-endorphin, met-enkephalin, and leu-enkephalin, has been conducted, but differences have not yet emerged.

CAVEATS

The results reported in this chapter are preliminary and should not be over-generalized. Lymphocyte proliferation and NK activity were measured under only one set of conditions—immediately after shock reexposure occurring 24 hours following 80 1.0-mA shocks. Thus, it is not known whether any or all of these parameters are critical in producing the observed effects. Indeed, Greenberg et al. (1983) have clearly shown that the particular shock parameters can be quite critical. In their experiments, natural resistance in mice against NK sensitive tumors was both enhanced and suppressed under different shock conditions.

It should also be carefully noted that our data do not indicate the manner in which T-cells and NK cells were altered. For example, T-cells could have undergone actual cellular alteration, or, instead, recirculation patterns could have been changed so that a different subpopulation was represented in the circulation. Different functional subpopulations could result in a different proliferative response. Alternatively, effects on other cell populations involved in activation of T-cells such as macrophages, could have been responsible.

Similarly, we have focused on corticosteroids and endogenous opioids as mediators, but there are many other possibilities. For example, lymphocytes possess many other receptor types, including beta-adrenergic and cholinergic receptors (Hall & Goldstein, 1981), and a role for prostaglandins has also been proposed (Goodwin & Webb, 1980).

Finally, it is not even clear whether immune suppression represents a breakdown of functioning or whether it is an adaptive response. It seems difficult to envisage how immunosuppression could be adaptive, but there are many possibilities (see Cohen & Crnic, 1983, for a discussion). For example, lymphocyte proliferation could have been reduced because specific subpopulations were sequestered in the bone marrow, thus facilitating blood cell formation. Alternatively, the immune system sometimes attacks injured tissue as if it were a foreign invader, and suppression of such autoimmune responses might be useful under some circumstances. Clearly, much more will have to be known about the relationship between controllability and immune functioning, before we can even speculate about the answers to such questions.

ACKNOWLEDGMENT

This research was supported by NSF Grants BNS 82-00944, RSDA MH 00314, and BRSG RR07013 to S. F. Maier and by MH 37373 and MH 39216 to Mark L. Laudenslager.

REFERENCES

Altenor, A., Kay, E., & Richter, M. (1977). The generality of learned helplessness in the rat. *Learning and Motivation, 8,* 54–61.

Anderson, D. C., Crowell, C. R., Cunningham, C. L., & Lupo, J. V. (1979). Behavior during shock exposure as a determinant of subsequent interference with shuttlebox escape-avoidance learning in the rat. *Journal of Experimental Psychology: Animal Behavior Processes, 5,* 143–157.

Anisman, H., & Sklar, L. S. (1979). Catecholamine depletion in mice upon reexposure to stress: Mediation of the escape deficits produced by inescapable shock. *Journal of Comparative and Physiological Psychology, 93,* 610–625.

Aylsworth, C. F., Hodson, C. A., & Meites, J. (1979). Opiate antagonists can inhibit mammary tumor growth in rats. *Proceedings of the Society for Experimental Biology and Medicine, 161,* 18–20.

Baker, A. G. (1976). Learned irrelevance and learned helplessness: Rats learn that stimuli reinforcers and responses are uncorrelated. *Journal of Experimental Psychology: Animal Behavior Processes, 2,* 130–142.

Bartrop, R. W., Lazarus, L., Luckhurst, E., Kiloh, L. G., & Penney, R. (1977). Depressed lymphocyte functions after bereavement. *Lancet, 1,* (B016), 834–836.

Brown, G. W., Harris, T., & Copeland, J. R. (1977). Depression and loss. *British Journal of Psychiatry, 1130,* 1–8.

Claman, H. N. (1972). Corticosteroids and lymphoid cells. *New England Journal of Medicine, 287,* 388–397.

Claman, H. N. (1975). How corticosteroids work. *Journal of Allergy and Clinical Immunology, 55,* 145–151.

Cohen, J. J., & Crnic, K. S. (1983). Glucocorticoids, stress and the immune response. In D. R. Webb, Jr. (Ed.), *Immunopharmacology* (pp. 61–91). New York: Marcel Dekker.

Daguillard, F. (1972). Immunologic significance of *in vitro* lymphocyte responses. *Medical Clinics of North America, 56,* 293–303.

Dess, N. K., Linwick, D., Patterson, J., Overmier, J. B., & Levine, S. (1983). Immediate and proactive effects of controllability and predictability on plasma cortisol responses to shocks in dogs. *Behavioral Neuroscience, 97,* 1005–1017.

Dorian, B., Garfinkel, P., Brown, G., Shore, A., Gladman, D., & Keystone, E. (1982). - Aberrations in lymphocyte subpopulations and function during psychological stress. *Clinical and Experimental Immunology, 50,* 132–138.

Drugan, R. C., Grau, J. W., Maier, S. F., Madden, J., & Barchas, J. D. (1981). Stress tolerance between morphine and the long-term analgesic reactions to inescapable shock. *Pharmacology, Biochemistry and Behavior, 14,* 677–682.

Drugan, R. C., & Maier, S. F. (1982). The nature of the activity deficit produced by inescapable shock. *Animal Learning and Behavior, 10,* 401–406.

Gilman, S. C., Schwartz, J. M. Milner, R. J., Bloom, F. E., & Feldman, J. D. (1982). Beta-endorphin enhances lymphocyte proliferative responses. *Proceedings of the National Academy of Sciences USA, 79,* 4226–4230.

Gisler, R. G. (1974). Stress and the hormonal regulation of the immune response in mice. *Psychotherapy and Psychosomatics, 23,* 197–208.

Goodkin, F. (1976). Rats learn the relationship between responding and environmental events: An expansion of the learned helplessness hypothesis. *Learning and Motivation, 7,* 382–393.

Goodwin, J. S., & Webb, D. R. (1980). Regulation of the immune response by prostaglandins. *Clinical Immunology and Immunopathology, 15,* 106–122.

Grau, J. W., Hyson, R. L., Maier, S. F., Madden, J., & Barchas, J. D. (1981). Long-term induced analgesia and activation of an opiate system. *Science, 203,* 1409–1412.

Greenberg, A. H., Dyck, D. G., & Sandler, L. S. (1983). Opponent processes, neuro-hormones, and natural resistance. In B. H. Fox & B. H. Newberry (Eds.), *Impace of psychoendocrine systems in cancer and immunity* (pp. 112–141). Toronto: Hogrefe Press.

Hall, N. R., & Goldstein, A. L. (1981). Neurotransmitters and the immune system. In R. Ader (Ed.), *Psychoneuroimmunology* (pp. 521–543). New York: Academic Press.

Hazum, E., Chang, K-J, & Cuatrecasas, P. (1979). Specific nonopiate receptors for Beta-endorphin. *Science, 205,* 1033–1035.

Henock, J. J., Batson, J. W., & Baum, J. (1978). Psychosocial factors in juvenile rheumatoid arthritis. *Arthritis Rheumatism, 21,* 229–233.

Herberman, R. B., & Ortaldo, J. R. (1981). Natural killer cells: Their role in defenses against disease. *Science, 214,* 24–30.

Hurst, M. J., Jenkins, D., & Rose, R. M. (1976). The relation of psychological stress to the onset of medical illness. *Annual Review of Medicine, 72,* 302–312.

Hyson, R. L., Ashcraft, L. J., Drugan, R. C., Grau, J. W., & Maier, S. F. (1982). Extent and control of shock affects naltrexone sensitivity of stress-induced analgesia and reactivity to morphine. *Pharmacology, Biochemistry and Behavior, 17,* 1019–1025.

Jackson, R. L., Alexander, J. H., & Maier, S. F. (1980). Learned helplessness, inactivity, and associative deficits: The effects of inescapable shock on response choice escape learning. *Journal of Experimental Psychology: Animal Behavior Processes, 6,* 1–20.

Jackson, R. L., Coon, D. J., & Maier, S. F. (1979). Long-term analgesic effects of inescapable shock and learned helplessness. *Science, 206,* 91–94.

Jackson, R. L., Maier, S. F., & Rapaport, P. M. (1978). Exposure to inescapable shock produces both activity and associative deficits in rats. *Learning and Motivation, 9,* 69–98.

Jacobs, T. J., & Charles, E. (1980). Life events and the occurrence of cancer in children. *Psychosomatic Medicine, 42,* 11–24.

Jacobs, S., & Ostfeld, A. (1977). An epidemiological review of the mortality of bereavement. *Psychosomatic Medicine, 39,* 344–357.

Johnson, H. M., Smith, E. M., Torres, B. A., & Blalock, J. E. (1982). Regulation of the *in vitro* antibody response by neuroendocrine hormones. *Proceedings of the National Academy of Sciences USA, 79,* 4171–4174.

Karre, K., Klein, G. O., Kiessling, R., Klein, G., & Roder, J. C. (1980). Low natural *in vivo* resistance to syngeneic leukemias in natural killer deficient mice. *Nature, 284,* 624–626.

Keller, S. E., Weiss, J. M., Schliefer, S. J., Miller, N. E., & Stein, M. (1981). Suppression of immunity by stress: Effect of a graded series of stressors on lymphocyte stimulation in the rat. *Science, 213,* 1397–1400.

Keller, S. E., Weiss, J. M., Schliefer, S. J., Miller, N. E., & Stein, M. (1983). Suppression of lymphocyte stimulation by stress in the rat: Effect of adrenalectomy. *Psychosomatic Medicine, 45,* 75.

Laudenslager, M. L., Reite, M. L., & Harbeck, R. J. (1982). Suppressed immune response in infant monkeys associated with maternal separation. *Behavioral and Neural Biology, 36,* 40–48.

Laudenslager, M. L., Ryan, S. M., Drugan, R. C., Hyson, R. L. & Maier, S. F. (1983). Coping and immunosuppression: Inescapable but not escapable shock suppresses lymphocyte proliferation. *Science, 221,* 568–570.

Lazarus, R. S., Averill, J. R., & Opton, E. M. The psychology of coping: Issues of research and assessment. (1974). G. V. Coelho, D. A. Hamburg, & J. E. Adams (Eds.), *Coping and Adaptation* (pp. 192–219). New York: Basic Books.

Levine, S., & Ursin, H. (1979). *.Coping and Health.* New York: Plenum Press.

Levine, S., Weinberg, J., & Ursin, H. (1978). Definition of the coping process and statement of the problems. In H. Ursin, E. Baade, & S. Levine (Eds.), *Psychobiology of stress* (pp. 3–23). New York: Academic Press.

MacLennan, A. J., & Maier, S. F. (1983). Coping and the stress-induced potentiation of stimulus stereotypy in the rat. *Science, 219,* 1091–1093.

Madden, J., Akil, H., Patrick, R. L., & Barchas, J. D. (1977). Stressed-induced parallel changes in central opioid levels and pain responsiveness in the rat. *Nature, 265,* 358–360.

Maier, S. F., Anderson, C., & Lieberman, D. (1972). The influence of control of shock on subsequent shock-elicited aggression. *Journal of Comparative and Physiological Psychology, 81,* 94–101.

Maier, S. F., Davies, S., Grau, J. W., Jackson, R. L., Morrison, D., Moye, T., Madden, J., & Barchas, J. D. (1980). Opiate antagonists and the long-term analgesic reaction induced by inescapable shock. *Journal of Comparative and Physiological Psychology, 94,* 1172–1184.

Maier, S. F., Drugan, R., Grau, J. W., Hyson, R., MacLennan, A. J., Moye, T., Madden, J., & Barchas, J. D. (1983). Learned helplessness, pain inhibition, and the endogenous opiates. In Zeiler, M. D., & Harzem, P., (Eds.), *Advances in the analysis of behavior, Vol. 3* (pp. 275–325). New York: Wiley.

Maier, S. F., Sherman, J. E., Lewis, J. W., Terman, G. W., & Liebeskind, J. C. (1983). The opioid/nonopioid nature of stress-induced analgesia and learned helplessness. *Journal of Experimental Psychology: Animal Behavior Processes, 9,* 80–91.

McCain, H. W., Lamister, I. B., Bozzone, J. M., & Grbic, J. T. (1982). Beta-endorphine modulates human immune activity via non-opiate receptors. *Life Sciences, 31,* 1619–1624.

Mehrishi, J. N., & Mills, I. H. (1983). Opiate receptors on lymphocytes and platelets in man. *Clinical Immunology and Immunopathology, 27,* 240–249.

Miller, N. E. (1979/1983). A perspective on the effects of stress and coping on disease and health. In S. Levine & H. Ursin (Eds.), *Coping and health* (pp. 323–355). New York: Plenum Press. i-5

Miller, N. E. (1983) Behavioral medicine: Symbosis between laboratory and clinic.j *Annual Reviews of Psychology, 34,* 1–31.

Monjan, A. A. (1983). Effects of acute and chronic stress upon lymphocyte blastogenesis in mice and humans: "Of mice and men". In E. L. Cooper (Ed.), *Stress, immunity, and cancer* (pp. 81–108). New York: Marcell Dekker.

Monjan, A. A., & Collector, M. I. (1977). Stress-induced modulation of the immune response. *Science, 196,* 307–308.

Morillo, E., & Gardner, L. II. (1979). Bereavement as an antecedent factor in thyrotoxicosis of childhood: Four case studies with survey of possible metabolic pathways. *Psychosomatic Medicine, 41,* 545–554.

Moye, T. B., Grau, J. W., Coon, D. J., & Maier, S. F. (1981). Therapy and immunization of long-term analgesia in the rat. *Learning and Motivation, 12,* 133–149.

Nakayama, F., Dippold, W., Shiko, H., Oettgen, H. F., & Old, L. J. (1980). Alloantigen-induced T-cell proliferation: Lyt phenotype of responding cells and blocking of proliferation by Lyt antisera. *Proceedings of the National Academy of Sciences USA, 77,* 2890–2894.

Overmier, J. B., & Seligman, M. E. P. (1967). Effects of inescapable shock upon subsequent escape and avoidance learning. *Journal of Comparative and Physiological Psychology, 63,* 23–33.

Plaut, S. M., & Friedman, S. B. (1981). Psychosocial factors in infectious disease. In R. Ader (Ed.), *Psychoneuroimmunology* (pp. 3–30). New York: Academic Press.

Rabkin, J. G., & Struening, E. L. (1976). Life events, stress, and illness. *Science, 194,* 1013–1020.

Rapaport, P. M., & Maier, S. F. (1978). The effects of inescapable shock on food competition dominance in rats. *Animal Learning and Behavior, 6,* 160–168.

Reite, M., Harbeck, R., & Hoffman, A. (1981). Altered cellular immune response following peer separation. *Life Sciences, 29,* 1133–1136.

Riccardi, C., Santoni, A., Barlozzori, T., & Herberman, R. B. (1980). Role of NK cells in rapid *in vivo* clearance of radiolabeled tumor cells. In R. B. Herberman (ed.), *Natural cell mediated immunity against tumors.* New York: Academic Press.

Riley, V. (1981). Psychoneuroendocrine influences on immunocompetence and neoplasia. *Science, 212,* 1100–1109.

Rogers, M. P., Dubey, D., & Reich, P. (1979). The influence of the psyche and the brain on immunity and disease susceptibility: A critical review. *Psychosomatic Medicine, 41*, 147–164.

Rosellini, R. A. (1978). Inescapable shock interferes with the acquisition of a free appetitive operant. *Animal Learning and Behavior, 6*, 155–519.

Rossier, J., French, E. D., Rivier, C., Ling, N., Guillemin, R., & Bloom, F. E. (1977). Footshock induced stress increases beta-endorphin levels in blood but not brain. *Nature, 270*, 618–620.

Roy, A. (1981). Specificity of risk factors for depression. *American Journal of Psychiatry, 138*, 959–961.

Sawynok, J., Pinsky, C., & LaBella, F. S. (1979). On the specificity of naloxone as an opiate antagonist. *Life Science, 25*, 1621–1632.

Schliefer, S. J., Keller, S. E., Camarino, M., Thornton, J. C., & Stein, M. (1983). Suppression of lymphocyte stimulation following bereavement. *Journal of the American Medical Association, 250*, 374–377.

Schreck, C., Lamberson, H., & Davey, F. (1982). Characterization of the lymphocyte response to pokeweek mitogen. *Annals of Clinical and Laboratory Science, 12*, 455–462.

Shavit, Y., Lewis, J. W., Terman, G. W., Gale, R. P., & Liebeskind, J. C. (1983). Endogenous opioids may mediate the effects of stress on tumor growth and immune function. *Proceedings of the Western Pharmacological Society, 26*, 53–56.

Shekelle, R. B., Raynor, W. J., Ostfeld, A. M., Garron, D. C., Bieliavskas, La A., Liv, S. C., Maliza, C., & Paul, O. (1981). Psychological depression and the 17-year risk of cancer. *Psychosomatic Medicine, 43*, 117–125.

Sherman, A. D., & Petty, F. (1982). Additivity of neurochemical changes in learned helplessness and imipramine. *Behavioral and Neural Biology, 35*, 344–353.

Sklar, L. S., & Anisman, H. (1979). Stress and coping factors influence tumor growth. *Science, 205*, 513–515.

Solomon, G. F., & Amkraut, A. A. (1981). Psychoneuroendocrinological effects on the immune response. *Annual Review of Microbiology, 35*, 155–184.

Sullivan, J. L., Byron, K. S., Brewster, F. F., & Purtdo, D. (1980). Deficient natural killer cell activity in X-linked lympho-proliferative syndrome. *Science, 210*, 543–555.

Swenson, R. M., & Vogel, W. H. (1983). Plasma catecholamine and corticosterone as well as brain catecholamine changes during coping in rats exposed to stressful footshock. *Pharmacology, Biochemistry and Behavior, 18*, 689–693.

Timonen, T., Ranki, A., Saksela, E., & Hayry, P. (1979). Fractionation, morphological and functional classification of effector cells responsible for human killer cell activity against cell-line targets. *Clinical Immunology, 48*, 121–132.

Ursin, H., Baade, E., & Levine, S. (1978). *Psychobiology of stress.* New York: Academic Press.

Visintainer, M. A., Volpicelli, J. R., & Seligman, M. E. P. (1982). Tumor rejection in rats after inescapable or escapable shock. *Science, 216*, 437–439.

Watkins, L. R., & Mayer, D. J. (1982). Organization of endogenous opioid and nonopioid pain control systems. *Science, 216*, 1185–1192.

Weiss, J. M. (1968). Effects of coping responses on stress. *Journal of Comparative and Physiological Psychology, 65*, 251–260.

Weiss, J. M., Goodman, P. A., Nosito, B. G., Corrigan, S., Charry, J. M., & Bailey, W. H. (1981). Behavioral depression produced by an uncontrollable stressor: Relationship to norepinephrine, dopamine and serotonin levels in various regions of rat brain. *Brain Research Reviews, 3*, 167–175.

Williams, J. L. (1982). Influence of shock controllability by dominant rats on subsequent attacks and defense behaviors towards colony intruders. *Animal Learning and Behavior, 10*, 305–314.

Zagon, I. S., & McLaughlin, P. J. (1981). Naloxone prolongs the survival time of mice treated with neuroblastoma. *Life Sciences, 28*, 1095–1102.

12 Tumor Rejection and Early Experience of Uncontrollable Shock in the Rat

Martin E. P. Seligman
University of Pennsylvania

Madelon A. Visintainer
Yale University

How does early experience with helplessness or mastery change an adult's ability to cope with challenge? Dick Solomon has long had an interest in this problem. Early in the career of the first author, he and Steve Maier and Solomon explored this question using escape behavior and its failure as one index of coping (Maier, Seligman, & Solomon, 1969; Seligman, Maier, & Solomon, 1971). We found that animals could be "immunized" against helplessness by first learning that their responses controlled shock (Seligman & Maier, 1967; Hannum, Rosellini, & Seligman, 1976). In this paper, we ask the same question except that our target is not immunization against helplessness, but immunization in its original sense—against disease. Are rats who experience mastery as weanlings less vulnerable to death from cancer? Are rats who experience helplessness as weanlings more vunerable to death from cancer?

We approached this question by first asking if uncontrollable shock produced heightened vulnerability to cancer. We were led to this by a variety of anecdotes relating the experience of helplessness to the onset or worsening of disease. Here is one cited in Visintainer & Seligman, 1983:

> Jeff was nine years old when the doctors found that he had Burkitt's lymphoma, a rare cancer of the liver. A year of surgery, radiation and chemotherapy followed. The cancer still spread. Jeff's doctors feared they were losing the battle.
>
> Only one person remained optimistic through the months of hospitalization in Salt Lake City: Jeff. He had plans. He was going to be a research scientist and find a cure for cancer so other kids would be safe. Even as the illness worsened, his determination to get well never wavered.
>
> The specialist who had been consulting long distance with Jeff's doctor was flying out to attend a pediatrics conference on the west coast. He had become so

interested and involved that he made arrangements to stop off and see the boy on this way.

Jeff was elated. There was so much he wanted to tell the doctor. He had kept a diary since getting sick and felt that maybe the specialist would be able to discover something.

The day he was coming, Jeff awoke early. Though confined to bed, he directed preparations, asking his doctors if they had charts and X-rays ready to show the specialist.

In the late morning, a fog blanketed Salt Lake City. By noon the airport was closed; the control tower diverted the specialist's plane to another city, and he decided to go directly to San Francisco.

When Jeff heard the news, he cried quietly. His parents encouraged him to rest and promised they would reach the doctor. Jeff could talk to him by phone. But by the next morning, Jeff had developed a dangerous fever and pneumonia. He was listless. By evening, he was in a coma. He died the next afternoon. (p. 58–61)

This is but one of many anecdotes about short-term effects of helplessness on disease, in particular, on cancer. It has been documented correlationally: Individuals who experience loss seem to be more susceptible to cancer. Schmale and Iker (1966) interviewed a number of women who had come in for a pap smear. All of these women had shown in their previous pap smear type two cells, which are indicative of possible uterine cancer. When they came in for their second test, they were interviewed concerning recent helplessness and hopelessness experiences. The women were then divided into two groups, one that had recently experienced helplessness and hopelessness, and one that had not. Significantly more of the group that had experienced helplessness and hopelessness showed type three cells, diagnostic of cancer. Similarly, men with diseased lungs, who had suffered recent loss, such as unemployment and divorce, were more likely to have lung cancer than men who had not suffered a recent loss. In fact, amount of loss was as strong a risk factor for lung cancer as number of cigarettes smoked per day (Horne & Picard, 1979). Both these correlational studies suggest loss and helplessness co-occur with tumor development. A second set of anecdotes implicates long-term psychological processes. It has been alleged that there is a cancer-prone personality, with individuals who are dependent, clinging, and helpless being more vulnerable (LeShan, 1966), and that such vulnerability might be acquired by traumatic experience in childhood (Doszynski, Shaffer, & Thomas, 1981).

So we set out to find out experimentally if the experience of helplessness caused increased risk for cancer, both in the short- and the long-term. We used rats because their life span is manageably short, and because quite a bit is known about tumor induction in this species.

Short-Term Effects of Helplessness on Cancer

The subjects in our first experiment were 193 adult male rats. On day one, each rat was injected with 6,000 live cells of the Walker-256 strain of sarcoma. This is the dose that approximately 50% of rats would reject. On the other hand, if not rejected, a tumor would form. Rats who grow this tumor invariably die within 60 days. Then, 24 hours after sarcoma injection, the rats were divided into the three basic groups of any learned helplessness experiment. One group learned to escape shocks by pressing a bar. A second group received exactly the same pattern of shocks, but were yoked to the first group, so that shock was inescapable, and a third group received no shocks. It is essential to realize that the amounts of physical stressor to which both the escapable and inescapable groups were exposed are identical. The only difference between these two groups must be some psychological result of having control versus not having control over the stressor, since the duration, pattern, and intensity of the shocks are identical.

We then merely waited to see who got the tumor (a *Take*) and who did not (a *Rejection*). Rats that received inescapable shocks were significantly more likely to get the tumor and therefore more likely to die than rats that received escapable shocks or no shocks. Here are the incidences of tumor rejection across the three conditions: In the inescapable shock condition, only 27% of the rats rejected the tumor (12 Rejects vs. 32 Takes) compared to 52% of the rats in the escapable condition (23 Rejects vs. 21 Takes) and 51% in the no shock condition (24 Rejects vs. 23 Takes) (Visintainer, Volpicelli, & Seligman, 1982). These results demonstrate that the experience of inescapable shock in adult rats can decrease the likelihood that they will be able to fight off a tumor challenge encountered at about the same time.

By what biological process does helplessness weaken an organism's ability to reject a tumor? One hint comes from the fact that these are short-term effects. The interval between having the sarcoma implanted and the experience of helplessness was 24 hours in this experiment. We found that when we increased the tumor-shock interval to four days or ten days, uncontrollable shock did not differ from controllable shock in its effect on tumor rejection. So whatever process is responsible must act shortly after the tumor challenge is first encountered.

The immune system is a good candidate for such a mechanism, since Monjan and Collector (1977) found acute noise stress produced T and B cell immune suppression in mice. In addition, Bartrop, Lazarus, Luckhurst, Kiloh, and Penney (1977) reported that, during bereavement, human beings showed suppression of T-lymphocyte proliferation, stimulated by PHA challenge. We therefore asked how inescapable as opposed to escapable shock affected immune suppression.

To that end, we took 23 triads of rats, with one third receiving escapable shocks, one third receiving the same shocks inescapably, and one third receiving no shocks. We then sacrificed these animals and, with the collaboration of Andrew Monjan, looked at immune suppression as measured by T-cell activity in the spleen, when stimulated by PHA challenge. Of the 23 triads, 21 ordered themselves in the following way: The most T-cell activity took place in the group that received no shock, the second most activity in the group that received escapable shock, and the least activity in the group that received inescapable shock. These results were highly significant statistically. We concluded that experience with inescapable negative events may suppress T-cell activity in the immune system, which in turn reduces the probability of rejecting a tumor challenge.

Steven Maier's studies (see chapter 11) present more elegant and extensive confirmation of this hypothesis.

Long-Term Effects of Helplessness on Cancer

We are now in a position to ask the long-term question: How does childhood experience with helplessness affect the ability to meet a tumor challenge as an adult? To test this, we gave a large number of young rats experience with either escapable shock, inescapable shock, or no shock. When these rats reached adulthood, we injected them with the 50% lethal does of sarcoma and then challenged them once again with either escapable shock, inescapable shock, or nothing.

Here is how we carried out the experiment: At 27 days of age, when they were weanlings, 273 rats were randomly assigned to one of three shock conditions: escapable shock ($n = 69$), inescapable shock ($n = 69$), or no shock ($n = 135$). The rats in the escapable shock group received four sessions of escapable shocks, one session every third day until they were 36 days of age. The rats in the inescapable shock group received exactly the same shocks but each was yoked to a partner in the escapable group. The only difference was that responses made by the rat in the yoked inescapable group did not affect the shock. Sixty 0.7 mA shock trials of maximum 60 sec duration were given per session. In the first session, shock stopped when the master rat made one bar press. In the second through fourth session, a fixed ratio of 3 responses was required. Nothing further happened to these rats experimentally until they were adults, 90 days of age.

At 90 days of age, all rats received the injection of the Walker-256 sarcoma preparation. One day after tumor implantation, the rats were randomly reassigned to an escapable, inescapable, or the no shock treatment condition and given additional shock experience as an adult. This procedure generated nine groups: three groups, which had escapable shocks as weanlings and then either escapable ($n = 23$), inescapable ($n = 23$), and no shock ($n = 23$) as adults; three groups which had inescapable shock as weanlings and then either escapable shock ($n = 23$), inescapable shock ($n = 23$), or no shock ($n = 23$) as adults; and three groups which had no shock as weanlings and then either escapable ($n = 44$), inescapable ($n = 44$), or no shock ($n = 47$) as adults. In other words, all permutations of escapable, inescapable or no shock as weanlings, and escapable, inescapable, and no shock as adults were generated. As adults, the rats received two sessions of shocks according to their assigned group. We then watched the animals for 30 days, and tumor rejection was defined by the absence of tumor as confirmed by dissection.

What a rat learned about helplessness as a weanling markedly affected adult tumor rejection, but the effect was indirect. First let us look at the direct effects of weanling experience on adult tumor rejection when there is no adult shock challenge. These three groups (EO, IO, and OO; the first letter refers to the weanling experience, the second letter to the adult experience) did not differ reliably from each other in tumor rejection as adults: 48% (11 out of 23), 57% (13 out of 23), and 51% (24 out of 47) rejected the tumor respectively. We concluded, if there is no further shock challenge as an adult, early experience with helplessness does not change the ability of the adult rat to reject tumor challenges.

In contrast, the rejection of the tumor changed when the rat was further challenged by shock as an adult. Rats given inescapable shock as weanlings and then challenged again with either escapable or inescapable shock as adults fared very badly. Conversely, rats given escapable shock as weanlings and then challenged as adults with *either* inescapable or escapable shock fared very well. Here are the results:

Only 30% of the rats (7 out of 23) that had inescapable shock as weanlings and then escapable shock as adults rejected the tumor, and only 26% (6 out of 23) of the rats that had inescapable shock as weanlings and inescapable shock once again as adults rejected the tumor. Both these groups had significantly higher tumor take than rats that received escapable shock as weanlings and then were shocked again as adults. They also had significantly more tumors than rats that had no shock as weanlings and no shock as adults and than rats that received no shock as weanlings and escapable shock as adults.

In contrast, rats given escapable shock as weanlings and then either escapable or inescapable shock as adults rejected the tumor 65 and 70% of the time respectively (15 out of 23, 16 out of 23). These rats rejected the tumor at least as well as rats that had no shock as weanlings and again no shock as adults (51%) or no shock as weanlings and escapable shock as adults (52%)—perhaps even better, but not significantly so. If this latter finding were reliable, it would mean that childhood experience with mastery made the rats better able to cope with tumors than no early experience at all. Table 12.1 shows these findings.

It can be seen that four basic findings emerge:

(1) inescapable shock as a weanling significantly increases tumor susceptibility if inescapable shock was also experienced as an adult (II vs. OO $p<.01$).

(2) Inescapable shock as a weanling significantly increases tumor susceptibility even if escapable shock is experienced as an adult (IE vs. OO $p<.05$).

(3) Inescapable shock as a weanling does not increase tumor susceptibility if no shock is experienced as an adult (IO vs. OO $p>.10$).

(4) Inescapable shock as an adult does not increase tumor susceptibility if the rat had first learned to escape shock as a weanling (immunization) (EI vs. OO $p>.10$).

We can make sense of this pattern with just two assumptions: (a) the short-term assumption: trauma directly undermines tumor rejection only in the short run, and only if trauma is responded to passively, as if it were inescapable; (b) the immunization assumption: early experience with escapable trauma (mastery)

TABLE 12.1
Tumor Rejection and Take Rate as a Function
of Weanling and Adult Experience

Group Name[a]	Weanling Shock Experience	Adult Shock Experience	Tumor Rejections	Tumor Takes	% Tumor Rejection
EE_A	Escapable	Escapable	15	8	65%
EI_A	Escapable	Inescapable	16	7	70%
EO_A	Escapable	No Shock	11	12	48%
IE_B	Inescapable	Escapable	7	16	30%
II_B	Inescapable	Inescapable	6	17	26%
IO_A	Inescapable	No Shock	13	10	57%
OE_A	No Shock	Escapable	23	21	52%
OI_B	No Shock	Inescapable	12	32	27%
OO_A	No Shock	No Shock	24	23	51%

[a]Groups which share a common subscript do not differ significantly on rate of tumor rejection.

causes later trauma to be responded to actively, as if it were escapable, even if it is actually inescapable. In contrast, early experience with inescapable trauma (helplessness) causes later shock to be responded to passively, as if it were inescapable, even if it is actually escapable.

The short-term assumption seems quite plausible. We found, as did Sklar and Anisman (1979), that inescapable shock undermines tumor rejection only if both the tumor challenge and the shock occur within a short time of each other. And, the temporal characteristics of the immune system also suggest that if immune suppression is the mechanism by which a psychological event like helplessness undermines tumor rejection, short term effects are more probable than long term effects.

The immunization assumption states that the type of early experience with trauma determines how later trauma will be perceived and responded to. Specifically, if early trauma is escaped or mastered, then later trauma will tend to be perceived as escapable and responded to actively, even if it is actually inescapable. This is the process of immunization. Conversely, it claims that if early experience is with helplessness, later trauma will be seen as uncontrollable, and passivity will result, even if the later trauma is actually controllable. A substantial body of learned helplessness literature supports the immunization assumption. In brief, rats, dogs, and people who first control trauma do not give up and become helpless when later challenged with inescapable trauma. Conversely, rats, dogs, and people who have early experience with uncontrollable trauma give up later, even when trauma actually is controllable (e.g., Hannum et al., 1976; Maier & Seligman, 1976; Jones, Nation, & Massad, 1977).

The *immunization assumption* also received direct support in our study of the influences of weaning shock on adult response to cancer. Let us look at the behavior of the rats in our study when they faced the adult shock challenge. There are a number of ways of determining how actively or passively a rat responds to a shock. The running, climbing, and the fast stepping of rats during shock all reflect amount of activity. And so, at the beginning of shock, during shock, and just after shock an overall activity score was computed. Rats receiving inescapable shock as weanlings showed the lowest amounts of activity during adult shock, whether the shock was escapable or inescapable (p<.01). In contrast, rats that had learned to escape shock as weanlings showed the highest level of activity, whether the adult shock was escapable or inescapable (p<.01). Expressed another way: rats that received escapable shock as weanlings were immunized behaviorally against the effects of inescapable shock as adults and responded actively during inescapable shock. In contrast, rats that received inescapable shock as weanlings responded passively as adults, even when shock was actually escapable.

So we infer that rats that responded to adult shock as if it were uncontrollable, that is with passivity, tended to get the tumor. Rats that responded to adult shock as if it were controllable, that is with active coping attempts, tended to reject the tumor. One main determinant of how actively they responded to adult shock was whether their weanling experience was with mastery or with helplessness.

It is often speculated that childhood experience can change the susceptibility to cancer in adulthood (e.g., Doszynski et al., 1981; LeShan, 1966). Our data suggest this may be so, but only in the presence of additional adult stressors. If adult stressors do not occur at the same time as adult tumor challenge, childhood experience has no effect. So let us close by venturing a general principle about how childhood experience can influence coping with disease in adulthood. We are sure this principle will turn out to be much too simple, or even wrong, and we state it only as a testable heuristic.

Only adult life events which occur at about the same time as a physical disease challenge will undermine the ability to fight off the disease. If the response to the adult event is one of helplessness and passivity, the immune system will be suppressed, and the disease will be defended against more poorly. If the response to the adult event is one of mastery attempts and activity, the immune system will not be suppressed (it may even be slightly enhanced), and the disease will be better defended against.

Childhood trauma modifies how adult trauma will be responded to, and this is the only effect of childhood experience on adult coping with disease. Childhood experience with helplessness causes adult trauma to be perceived as uncontrollable and to be responded to passively. Conversely, childhood experience with mastery causes adult trauma to be perceived as controllable and to be responded to actively. The result is that childhood experience with mastery immunizes against the increased susceptibility to disease that adult loss produces.

REFERENCES

Bartrop, R. W., Lazarus, L., Luckhurst, C., Kiloh, L. G., Penney, R. (1977). *Lancet, 1,* 834.

Doszynski, K. R., Shaffer, J. W., & Thomas, C. T. (1981). Neoplasm and traumatic events in childhood. *Archives of General Psychiatry, 38,* 327–331.

Hannum, R. D., Rosellini, R. A., & Seligman, M. E. P. (1976). Retention of learned helplessness and immunization in the rat from weaning to adulthood. *Developmental Psychology, 12*(5), 449–454.

Horne, R. L., & Picard, R. S. (1979). Psychosocial risk factors in lung cancer. *Psychosomatic Medicine, 41,* 503–514.

Jones, S. L., Nation, J. R., & Massad, P. (1977). Immunization against learned helplessness in man. *Journal of Abnormal Psychology, 86,* 75–83.

LeShan, L. (1966). An emotional life-history pattern associated with neoplastic disease. *Annals of the New York Academy of Sciences, 125,* 780–793.

Maier, S. F., & Seligman, M. E. P. (1976). Learned helplessness: Theory and evidence. *Journal of Experimental Psychology: General, 105,* 3–46.

Maier, S. F., Seligman, M. E. P., & Solomon, R. L. (1969). Pavlovian fear conditioning and learned helplessness. In B. A. Campbell & R. M. Church (Eds.), *Punishment* (pp. 299–343). Appleton-Century-Crofts.

Monjan, A. A., & Collector, M. I. (1977). Stress-induced modulation of the immune response. *Science, 196,* 307–308.

Schmale, A., & Iker, H. (1966). The psychological setting of uterine cervical cancer. *Annals of the New York Academy of Sciences, 125,* 807–813.

Seligman, M. E. P., & Maier, S. F. (1967). Failure to escape traumatic shock. *Journal of Experimental Psychology, 74,* 1–9.

Seligman, M. E. P., Maier, S. F., & Solomon, R. L. (1971). Consequences of unpredictable and uncontrollable trauma. In F. R. Brush (Ed.), *Aversive conditioning and learning* (pp. 347–400). New York: Academic Press.

Sklar, L. S., & Anisman, H. (1979). Stress and coping factors influence tumor growth. *Science, 205,* 513–515.

Visintainer, M. A., & Seligman, M. E. P. (1983). Fighting cancer: The hope factor. *American Health, 2,* 58–61.

Visintainer, M. A., Volpicelli, J. R., & Seligman, M. E. P. (1982). Tumor rejection in rats after inescapable or escapable shock. *Science, 216,* 437–439.

13 Toward a Reanalysis of the Causal Structure of the Learned Helplessness Syndrome

J. Bruce Overmier
University of Minnesota

In 1964, several of us were collaborating with R. L. Solomon and R. M. Church on a study of the cardiac responses to shock by curarized dogs (viz., Church, LoLordo, Overmier, Solomon, & Turner, 1966). The results of this experiment later became part of the database for the development of Solomon's "opponent-process" theory of affective dynamics (Solomon & Corbit, 1974). In addition, however, the experiment by Church et al. also indirectly led to the discovery of a "new"—at least to us—phenomenon.

In Church et al.'s second experiment, dogs were placed in a Pavlov harness and simply exposed to 64 shocks of a fixed 5-sec duration presented at 90 sec intershock intervals with heart rates recorded throughout. This constituted the full experimental treatment, and, thus, at the completion of the session, the dogs were scheduled for sacrifice. However, we wished to make maximum use of this precious resource and to follow up on prior observations (e.g., Overmier & Leaf, 1965) that classical conditioning had proactive effects upon subsequent learning of initial avoidance responses. Therefore, some of the dogs from Church et al.'s experiment II were subjected to avoidance training in a shuttlebox a day or so after the exposure to the series of fixed shocks in the harness.

The result was that those dogs pre-exposed to shocks in the hammock 24 hours earlier, but not 48 or more (but see Overmier, Patterson & Wielkiewicz, 1980, Figure 2), simply failed to learn to escape the electric shocks in the shuttlebox. This was a surprising and dramatic observation which Seligman and I explored and came to call "learned helplessness" (Overmier & Seligman, 1967). Learned helplessness was characterized as a *syndrome* with three characteristic facets: (a) a motivational deficit inferred from the failure of the animals to initiate response; (b) an associative deficit inferred from the failure to show

211

increased probabilities of responding following a successful escape or avoidance (i.e., a reinforced response); and (c) an emotional deficit inferred from the reduced vocalizations and general passivity.

The learned helplessness *theory* of Seligman, Maier, & Solomon (1971) emphasizes a single operational factor as the cause of the three deficits comprising the proactive interference syndrome. That factor is the uncontrollable nature of the shocks to which the dogs had been previously exposed, and this emphasis continues (viz., Maier & Seligman, 1976). This attribution was natural enough because the most salient thing about the shocks that Church et al. administered (and those in our follow up experiments) was that they were uncontrollable. Indeed, Seligman and Maier (1967) used a special triadic design involving contrast between preexposures to inescapable shocks versus escapable shocks to provide an evidential basis for the assertion that the uncontrollability of the shocks caused the deficit in response initiations seen in the learned helplessness syndrome. The inference drawn, however, was that all three features of this syndrome arose as a result of sufficient prior experience with uncontrollable shocks.

Because the three features were hypothesized to have a common cause, they should always co-occur (issues of relative thresholds being held in abeyance for the moment). Now it is known that co-occurrence is not always the case. For example, Jackson, Alexander, and Maier (1980) have found evidence for an associative deficit in the absence of a cooccurring response initiation deficit.

There are at least two approaches to reconciling such findings. One is to hypothesize additional *sequential* intervening variables—a tack taken by Abramson, Seligman, and Teasdale (1978). A second is to hypothesize that the syndrome is not a unitary phenomenon but is multidimensional with different facets (symptoms) being the product of different causal factors. This latter is the approach we have been exploring. But to what additional factor(s) might we look?

Review of the series of demonstration experiments reveals that the preshocks in the helplessness induction phase were typically not only uncontrollable but were also *unpredictable*—presented without warning, as well. Thus, uncontrollability and unpredictability have been conflated. Although the triadic design of Seligman and Maier (1967) makes clear that shocks which are only unpredictable (i.e., but controllable) are not sufficient to induce the deficit in response initiation or *motivational* deficit, the contributory role of unpredictability to the other facets (i.e., associative and emotional) is uncertain. On this view, it is important to note that Alloy and Seligman (1979) and Klosterhalfen and Klosterhalfen (1983) have argued that much of the purported evidence for an associative deficit following exposure to uncontrollable and unpredicted shocks may be accounted for by the response initiation deficit, one exception, however, being that of Jackson et al. (1980).

There is considerable controversy surrounding the intrinsic relationships between controllability and predictability of noxious events (e.g., Averill, 1973;

Geer & Maisel, 1972; Lykken, 1962; Miller, 1979). However, they are at least *operationally* independent, and our data suggest they are functionally independent as well (Dess, Linwick, Patterson, Overmier, & Levine, 1983). If this is correct, then an alternative conceptualization of the learned helplessness syndrome is suggested—a conceptualization that invokes both uncontrollability and unpredictability as contributing causal factors of the facets of the syndrome rather than only the former alone.

What seems to be called for here with respect to the associative and emotional deficits are experiments that test whether or not variations in the predictability of shocks influence these facets of the syndrome. We have begun such a series of experiments. While our work is far from complete, the initial experiments suggest new insights. Let me illustrate this by describing three experiments.

EXPERIMENTS ON ASSOCIATIVE PROCESSES

In the triadic designs, to demonstrate that uncontrollability of prior shocks causes the deficit in response initiation, groups previously exposed to uncontrollable, controllable, or no shocks have been compared on their ability to escape shocks in a shuttlebox, the escape response typically being quite effortful. In parallel fashion, for our test of whether unpredictability could be a causal factor in the associative deficit, groups previously exposed to unpredictable, predictable, or no shocks were compared on their ability to learn.

The purpose of the present research was to amplify current knowledge of the consequences of prior exposure to predictable versus unpredictable shocks that are also uncontrollable. Our question was whether degree of predictability of the uncontrollable shocks would influence the degree of proactive interference relative to a control group that received exposure only to the signal stimulus.

Experiment 1

Our first experiment on the effects of unpredictability as a source of associative interference used a discriminative conditional two-choice escape/avoidance task. The selection of test task is an important feature of the present experiment: A conditional choice task is especially sensitive to associative influences and relatively insensitive to motivational influences (Hillman, Hunter, & Kimble, 1953; Miles, 1959; Trapold & Overmier, 1972) in contrast to the unitary shuttlebox escape task, which has just the opposite pattern of sensitivities (Alloy & Seligman, 1979).

We used 15 adult mongrel dogs (32 to 60 cm tall at the shoulder) maintained in individual cages with free access to food and water. These dogs were randomly assigned to one of three groups of equal size. The experiment had three phases: (a) adaptation, (b) induction, which consisted of pre-exposure to shocks and/or signals, and (c) testing for learning of the discriminative choice escape/avoidance task.

During adaptation, the dog was simply suspended in a rubberized cloth hammock which hung from a metal frame.

In the induction pre-exposure phase, all subjects were placed in the hammock with four legs secured and a pair of electrodes attached to each rear leg. Each session began with the onset of the houselight. Subjects in the Predictable-shocks group and Unpredictable-shocks group were exposed to a series of 240 4.5 MA electric shocks of 4-sec duration presented at varying intervals averaging 2 minutes. A random half of the shocks were delivered to the left rear leg and the remaining shocks were delivered to the right rear leg.

For five dogs in the Predictable-shocks group, each shock was preceded by a 5-sec auditory signal, which then continued until shock termination. For two subjects in this group, shocks to the left rear leg were preceded by the high tone and shocks to the right rear leg were preceded by the low tone. For three subjects, high tones preceded shocks to the right rear leg and low tones preceded the shocks to the other leg.

Each of the five dogs in the Unpredictable-shocks group was matched to a subject in the Predictable-shocks group and, thus, experienced the same number of shocks in the same temporal order and with the same temporal spacing as the partner subject in the Predictable-shocks group. However, for all dogs in the Unpredictable-shocks group, the high and low frequency tones were presented on a random schedule, independent of the schedule for shocks. That is, tones and shocks were uncorrelated in this group, and the shocks were unpredictable both as to the time of occurrence and place of delivery.

Each of the five dogs in the CS-only group was exposed to the same series of high and low tones experienced by a partner subject in the Predictable-shocks group. However, subjects in the CS-only group did not experience any electric shocks in this induction phase.

The day following the last pre-exposure session was the first of three daily test sessions of discriminative conditional choice escape/avoidance training. In this testing phase, the subjects were presented with the following problem: Each trial began with the onset of 10 Hz flashing light (equal on-off cycle) located directly under the left front paw (S^D_1) or right front paw (S^D_2). When an S^D was presented, the animal was required to lift the paw that rested on it to avoid shocks to the opposite side rear leg. If, during the 5 sec S^D interval the *initial* response of the animal was correct, then the trial was immediately terminated, and an intertrial interval was initiated. If the initial response was wrong, a correction procedure allowed the animal to switch responses. If the dog did not perform an initial correct avoidance response within 5 sec of the start of the trial, shock was scheduled for the final 10 sec of the trial, except any period during which the correct response was being performed. In the first 5 sec of each trial, the flashing light was turned off for as long as the dog held the correct response; for the remaining 10 sec of each trial, both the flashing light and shock were off while a correct response was performed. (Correct responses did not include those occasions when the dog lifted both front paws.) The interval between trials averaged 2 min and ranged from 1 to 3 min. Each test session was composed of 10 S^D_1 and 10 S^D_2 trials. Thus, in this test task of learning a discriminative choice escape/avoidance, if subject's initial anticipatory response was correct, shock was avoided; if the initial response was not correct, a correction procedure allowed the subject to find the correct response, but now it had to maintain the response so as to prevent delivery of scheduled aversive stimuli.

Statistical analyses of the data were carried out using Rodger's (1975) procedures. All statistical tests were conducted at the .05 level of significance, two-tailed tests.

The main dependent variable was the amount of time per 15-sec trial during which the subject was *not* performing the correct response (wrong time). This amount was averaged across the five subjects in each group for each test day. Learning the task, then, was reflected by a decline in mean wrong time. The data are presented in Figure 13.1, which shows mean wrong time for the CS-only, Predictable-shocks, and Unpredictable-shocks groups as a function of daily blocks of 20 trials.

It appears that the Unpredictable-shocks group was impaired in learning the task relative to the other two groups. The Groups X Session Blocks analysis of

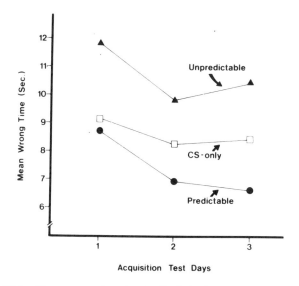

FIG. 13.1. Mean wrong times in the discriminative conditional choice escape/avoidance task achieved by groups which previously had experienced unpredictable shocks, predictable shocks, or no shocks. Each point is based upon a total of 100 trials.

variance for the mean wrong times showed a significant group effect and a significant effect of Trial Blocks. The Groups X Trial Blocks interaction was not significant. Two orthogonal contrasts were performed upon the three group means. The first contrast was performed on the difference between the Predictable-shocks and CS-only groups; this difference was not significant. The second contrast was performed upon the difference between the Unpredictable-shocks group versus the Predictable-shocks and CS-only groups taken together; this difference was significant. Thus, the Unpredictable-shocks group was significantly impaired relative to the Predictable-shocks and CS-only groups, which did not differ from each other.

The pattern of empirical effects in the present experiment is simple and straightforward: Prior exposure to tones and shocks presented on random and independent schedules interferes with subsequent learning to make correct escape/avoidance choice responses to visual S^Ds. This associative interference is ameliorated by having the tones predict the shocks. Indeed, if anything, relative to experiencing only tones, the Predictable-shocks group tended to even be somewhat—but not significantly—better. Thus, prior exposure to unpredictable uncontrollable shocks caused more proactive associative interference than prior exposure to predictable uncontrollable shocks. Indeed, there was no evidence that predictable uncontrollable shocks produced any associative interference.

That prior exposure to predictable, uncontrollable shocks had no interfering effect is at first glance surprising from the traditional ''learned helplessness'' perspective. But recall that the primary deficit observed in the traditional shuttlebox task is one of reduced initiations of the effortful response of jumping over a barrier. Here, we purposefully chose a less effortful task and a measure based upon discriminative choice behavior with the intent of detecting a deficit in associative learning rather than a deficit in response initiation. Indeed, all our animals responded on nearly every test trial, and the latencies of initial choice responses did not differ among groups. Thus, our data primarily reflect the facility with which the dogs learned the $S^D_1 - R_1/S^D_2 - R_2$ discriminative choice problem. Our data suggest that unpredictability is a causal factor in producing the associative deficit and that uncontrollability is not sufficient in itself to produce associative deficit.

Suggestive as these data from our first experiment are, they are not definitive. This is because our test task did involve de novo response initiation, and the effect of the unpredictability manipulation may have exerted its effect by acting as an amplifier of the effect of uncontrollability (cf. Weinberg & Levine, 1980). That is, the data reveal a clear effect of unpredictability but not necessarily an independent effect upon associative processes. Therefore, we carried out a second experiment in which we more directly assessed whether the locus of the effect was one of associative deficit.

Experiment 2

Pavlovian conditioning has long served as a prototype of associative learning. Thus, we chose, as our more direct assessment, to ask whether previous experience of unpredictability of shocks with one stimulus interfered with later learning of a predictive relationship between some new stimulus and shock in some new place. Again, we used our analog-triadic design, in which groups previously exposed to unpredictable, predictable, or no shocks were compared on their ability to condition under Pavlovian procedures.

Fifteen adult mongrel dogs were randomly assigned to one of three equal sized groups. The experiment had four phases: establishment of the baseline index response; induction, which consisted of preexposure to shocks and/or signals; Pavlovian conditioning; and transfer testing to index the degree of conditioning.

In the initial phase, the dogs were trained in a shuttlebox to jump the barrier on a temporally-paced avoidance schedule (viz., Sidman, 1953) to avoid brief footshocks. In the absence of responding, shocks would occur regularly at short intervals. However, each response prevented scheduled shocks for 30 sec. Dogs quickly learned to jump the barrier at regular short intervals so as to prevent all shocks.

In the induction phase, all subjects were placed in a hammock for dogs in a sound-proofed chamber. Subjects in the Predictable-shocks group and the Unpredictable-shocks group were exposed to four daily series of brief electric foot shocks presented at varying intervals averaging about 1½ min.

In the Predictable-shocks group, each shock was preceded by an 8-sec signal. For the first three days, the signal was onset of a pair of lamps and termination of white noise. For the fourth day, the signal was onset of a tone. (This shift was an explicit effort to establish a kind of learning set.) In the Unpredictable-shocks group, a subject experienced the same number of shocks on the same temporal schedule and also the same number of signals on the same schedule, but, for this group, the signal and shocks were uncorrelated with each other. In the No-shocks group, dogs did not experience any shocks in this induction phase.

On the next day, the dogs were in a novel, vertically-striped chamber where they received Pavlovian conditioning. The CS here was an 8-sec, 10 Hz clicker, which was followed by a brief footshock. There were eight spaced trials per day for three days.

To test for the degree of Pavlovian conditioning, each dog was moved to the two-way shuttlebox immediately upon termination of the Pavlovian conditioning treatment. After a brief warm-up period of avoidance responding, transfer-of-control test trials were administered. In these, the 8-sec clicker CS (alone) was presented while the animal was responding on the avoidance baseline. Changes in rate of avoidance responding are known to be an index of excitatory and inhibitory Pavlovian conditioning (Bull & Overmier, 1968), with amount of increase in rate of responding reflecting the degree of association between clicker and shock. The results of the 30 trials of this phase are shown in Figure 13.2.

It appears that the Unpredictable-shocks group was impaired, relative to the other two groups, in learning to associate the new clicker stimulus with the footshocks in a new environment. Statistical analysis confirmed that the Unpre-dictable-shocks group was significantly impaired relative to both the Predictable-shocks and No-shocks groups, which in turn did not quite differ significantly from each other.

The pattern of empirical effects is again straightforward: Prior exposure to visual signals, tone signals and shocks presented on random and independent schedules interferes with subsequent learning to associate a clicker with shock under Pavlovian procedures. This associative interference is ameliorated by hav-ing had the visual and tone signals predict the uncontrollable shocks in the Induction phase. Indeed, if anything, relative to not having experienced any prior uncontrollable shocks, the Predictable-shocks group tended to condition some-what—but not significantly—better. There was no evidence that predictable uncontrollable shocks produced any associative interference, whereas unpredict-able uncontrollable shocks yielded clear associative interference. The pattern of results in our second experiment duplicates exactly that from our first experiment demonstrating the robustness and generality of our finding.

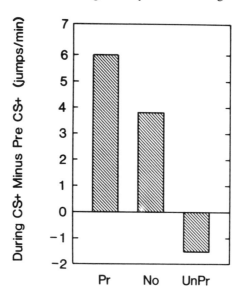

FIG. 13.2.   Mean change of responding scores to presentations of the Pavlovian CS+ for three groups as a function of their prior histories: Pr = prior shocks predicted by stimuli other than the CS+; No = no prior shocks; UnPr = prior unpredictable shocks random with respect to stimuli other than the CS+.

Although the present results are unique within the learned helplessness literature, they may be related to other phenomena documented in the Pavlovian conditioning literature. Mackintosh (1973) has published demonstrations of a phenomenon that has been called *learned irrelevance*. In contrast to Mackintosh's (1973) experiments, in which exposure to uncorrelated presentations of a stimulus and shock interfered with later acquisition of an association between the same stimulus and the same shock, the present finding is that uncorrelated presentations of a CS and shock interfered with acquisition of shock-motivated responding to a distinctly different stimulus. Thus, the present finding might be considered a *generalized* learned irrelevance effect which transcends the CS stimulus conditions of the original exposure to shock.

These first two experiments provide evidence suggesting that the associative deficit of the learned helplessness syndrome may be caused, at least in part, by the unpredictable nature of the uncontrolled shocks. This finding is consistent with our earlier suggestion that the syndrome is not a unitary phenomenon but multidimensional, with each facet (symptom) the product of a different causal factor. Previous demonstrations have shown a clear role for uncontrollability in contributing to the motivational deficit in response initiations. The present data suggest a clear role for unpredictability contributing to the associative deficit. One simple possibility (unrealistically simple, no doubt) is that these two operational factors are independent. A graphic model suggesting this relationship is shown in Figure 13.3. We take the graphic representation not as a serious model but as a heuristic.

This heuristic suggests that although we have shown uncontrollability is not sufficient (i.e., that unpredictability is critical) to cause the associative deficit, we have not yet determined whether uncontrollability is unnecessary for the associative deficit. And, although others have shown that unpredictability is not sufficient (i.e., that uncontrollability is critical) to cause the motivational deficit seen in reduced response initiations, it has not yet been determined whether unpredictability is unnecessary for the motivational deficit. Minimally called for is an experiment fully crossing these two factors, plus the appropriate controls of course, with testing in tasks selectively sensitive to each of the potential deficits.

EXPERIMENT ON EMOTIONAL PROCESSES

Let us now turn to the putative emotional deficit of the learned helplessness syndrome. Before we seek new factors as causal here, it seems appropriate to first assess the emotional reactivity of dogs to the two causal factors we have already identified—uncontrollability and unpredictability. Not only do we wish to assess the direct effects of these factors, but we also wish to assess the proactive effects of these factors upon *emotional reactivity*. Indeed, insofar as the learned helplessness syndrome is one's concern, it is these proactive effects that are of most interest.

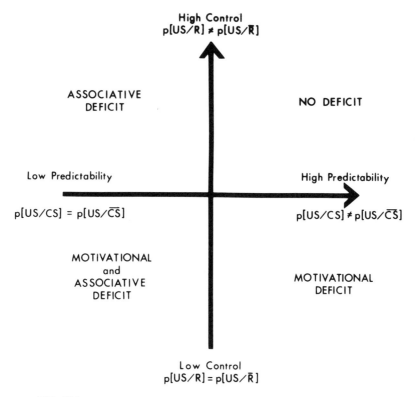

FIG. 13.3. A representation of the heuristic model that Controllability and Predictability could be independent factors causal of separate deficits (motivational
and associative, respectively). The left and bottom quadrants represent the three
different patterns of deficits that might obtain from various combinations of prior
experience. (From Overmier et al., 1980.)

As a first step, we carried out an experiment which independently manipulated both factors in a 2 × 2 design. Thus, there were four key groups exposed to
shocks in an induction session. For one group, the shocks were unpredictable and
uncontrollable (UP/UC), the typical learned helplessness induction treatment.
For the second group, the shocks were unpredictable but controllable (UP/C).
For a third, the shocks were predictable but uncontrollable (P/UC). And for the
fourth, the shocks were both predictable and controllable (P/C).

Establishing the experimental treatments is simpler than measuring the ab-
straction of emotional reactivity. However, there is general agreement that the
pituitary-adrenal system is activated in defensive emotional states (e.g., Mason,
1968). Therefore, we selected serum cortisol level as our indicator response. We
do not claim cortisol is the sole or even the best such possible indicator, but it has
some established validity (Hennessey & Levine, 1979) and is experimentally
tractable.

Twenty-four adult male dogs served as subjects and were housed individually in a kennel with food and water continuously available. Sixteen dogs were randomly assigned in pairs to either Predictable (P) or Unpredictable (UP) shock conditions. Each pair was then randomly divided into a master dog (Controllable, C, condition) and a yoked dog (Uncontrollable, UC, condition). Thus, four experimental groups (P/C, P/UC, UP/C, and UP/UC) of four dogs each were formed from this 2×2 factorial combination of Predictability and Controllability. Two additional dogs were assigned to the UP/UC condition as a result of experimental error. Finally, six dogs served as controls and received no shocks during the induction sessions. The whole experiment was run in two equal-sized replications.

The dogs received a series of four sessions, each separated by 24 hours. In each session of the experiment, two blood samples were drawn, one immediately before the treatments and one immediately after. Plasma cortisol was assayed by radioimmunoassay to assess the relative impact on adrenocortical functioning of each experimental treatment.

The treatment procedures in each daily session were as follows: Day 1 was one of habituation to the apparatus and handling procedures; dogs were simply placed in the hammocks and restrained there for 1.5 hr with electrodes in place. Days 2 and 3 were Induction sessions. Pairs of dogs in the experimental groups were placed in the hammocks with electrodes fixed. On each day a series of 50 (replication 1) or 40 (replication 2) footshocks were presented once a minute on average. For four pairs of dogs, these shocks were predicted by a 200 Hz tone (P pairs), and for four pairs the shocks were unsignalled (UP pairs). The master animal (C) in each pair could control the shocks for itself and its yoked partner by pressing a response panel with its head. Similar responses by the yoked dog (UC) had no effect on shock delivery. If no panel press response was made by the master, the shocks ended after a fixed amount of time. Because the dogs in a pair were mechanically yoked to each other, the type, duration, and distribution of all stimuli were identical within a pair. All four experimental groups were equated on the number and temporal distribution of shocks within each session. The control animals were simply restrained in the hammock for these two daily sessions, and no shocks were delivered.

Finally, on Day 4, all dogs were individually administered a test treatment in the shuttlebox. This test treatment was to allow assessment of the proactive effects of the initial induction sessions upon adrenocortical responses to later shocks. In the test, shock trials signalled by a 10 Hz flashing light occurred once a minute on average. This signal was *different* from the tone CS that the P animals had experienced during induction. Although a shuttling response during the signal could terminate the signal and prevent shock delivery, such responses did not occur. In the absence of an avoidance response, a fixed duration shock followed the automatic signal termination.

A change measure of cortisol reactivity was computed to index the response of each animal to a treatment session. Post-session cortisol values were divided by pre-session cortisol values (microgram percents) and multiplied by 100 to yield a percent-of-baseline cortisol score for each dog on each day of treatment. These scores were analyzed using Edgington's randomizations procedure (1969) using $\alpha = 0.05$ and two-tailed tests. The results of the statistical analysis of these cortisol scores as a function of Controllability and Predictability in the Stress Induction and Test phases are reported next.

Induction

Acquisition of shock-controlling responses proceeded somewhat more slowly for UP/C than for P/C in both replications. However, both exercised control, and UP/C did not incur significantly more seconds of shock than P/C. It follows, of course, that UP/UC and P/UC dogs also did not receive different amounts of shock.

Differences in cortisol scores were analyzed as a function of Induction Day, Replication, Controllability, and Predictability: There were no significant main effects of Induction Day or Replication, and first or second order interactions involving these two factors. Therefore, the data were collapsed across Replication and Induction Day in subsequent analyses of cortisol scores. Mean cortisol scores as a function of the Induction treatments of Predictability and Controllability are presented in Table 13.1. Both factors appear to modulate the cortisol score.

Dogs with control over shocks had significantly lower cortisol scores than dogs without control (C = 260% vs. UC = 394%). However, the effect of Predictability (P = 296% vs. UP = 358%) was not significant. Furthermore, the effect of Controllability did not differ as a function of level of Predictability (i.e., no Controllability × Predictability interaction).

TABLE 13.1
Effects of Current Shock Treatments Upon Induction Session Cortisol Levels as a Percentage of Pre-Induction Baseline[a]

	Predictable	Unpredictable	
Controllable	241	279	260
Uncontrollable	352	437	394
	296	358	

No Shocks Control	279

[a] The marginal values shown are means.

Test

Cortisol scores in the new shock conditions of the Test were analyzed for the proactive influence of the Induction treatment factors of Predictability and Controllability. Again, in the absence of a main effect of, or any first or second order interactions involving Replications, cortisol scores within Induction treatment groups were collapsed across replications. Group mean cortisol scores for Test are reported in Table 13.2 as a function of Induction treatments.

Predictability of induction shock significantly modulated the effect of Test shocks on cortisol scores. Groups that experienced unpredictable shocks during Induction had significantly higher cortisol scores during Test than those previously exposed to predictable shocks (P = 254% vs. UP = 474%). Although Controllability had been a significant factor influencing Induction-phase cortisol scores, there was no effect of prior Controllability upon Test-phase cortisol scores. There was no significant interaction between Controllability and Predictability with respect to Test cortisol scores. Because the groups did not differ in the number or amount of shock experienced in Test, the pattern of cortisol scores obtained in Test reflects subjects' different responses to shocks in a novel situation unconfounded by variations in behavior or physical stimulation in the Test phase itself.

On the surface, the results of our second experiment are clear: both factors were important determinants of the dogs' adrenocortical responses to shocks. Absence of control over shocks resulted in augmented responsivity to the initial shock experience, as compared to dogs that received exactly the same shocks but with control. This result confirms and extends the effects of controllability on other physiological indices reported in other species (e.g., Weiss, 1968). In

TABLE 13.2

Effects of Prior Shock Treatments Upon Test Session Cortisol
Levels as a Percentage of Pretest Baseline[a]

	Predictable	Unpredictable	
Controllable	270	442	356
Uncontrollable	238	505	372
	254	474	

No Shocks Control	490

[a]The marginal values shown are means.

contrast to the significant influence Controllability had in Induction, this factor was not important in determining cortisol responses to novel Test shocks.

Predictability, on the other hand, did not significantly modulate the cortisol response to induction shocks. This result was unexpected but may reflect more the relative insensitivity of our experiment rather than absence of an effect.[1] Unpredictability of shocks did, however, have powerful proactive effects. Dogs that experienced unsignalled shocks in Induction were much more reactive to shocks in the new Test situation than were dogs previously given signalled shocks. A proactive alteration in adrenocortical responses to shocks as a function of prior unpredictability of shock is implied by these results. Whether these between-phase interactions are general or unique to our Test procedures remains to be determined.

This reversal in the relative importance of Controllability and Predictability factors between Induction and Test is of special interest. Thus, the present and previous results (e.g., MacLennan, Drugan, Hyson & Maier, 1982) suggest that immediate responses are but a subset of a stressor's total effects; proactive effects may occur that (a) are dependent on psychological factors orthogonal to those important initially and (b) are independent of the immediate physiological impact of the original experience on central and effector systems.

Both Controllability and Predictability factors modulated the physiological impact of shocks. However, the two factors appeared to have quite different loci of effects. This conclusion, too, is consistent with the conceptualization of predictability and controllability as operationalized in the present study and our heuristic model of separable and independent factors (Overmier et al., 1980; see also Miller, 1979), and inconsistent with those views that they are "functionally equivalent" (e.g., Burger & Arkin, 1980).

But what are the implications of these results for understanding the purported emotional deficit of the learned helplessness syndrome? First of all, they suggest that the Predictability factor is more important in causing the proactive effects upon emotional reactivity than the Controllability factor. Beyond this, however, the story must be much more complicated. This is because we have taken increased cortisol scores as an indicator of increased emotional reaction, and the group with the highest cortisol score in Test was the UP/UC group—the traditional learned helplessness treatment. Yet, it is this very group for which reduced emotional reactivity has been inferred! This inference has been based upon reduced vocalizations and other behaviors that usually occur when an animal is experiencing painful and emotion-arousing events.

Is it possible that the reduced vocalizations and other behaviors do not reflect reduced emotional reactivity per se but rather functionally reduced painfulness of

---

[1]Although a Predictability effect might have emerged in our study with continued exposure to the Induction conditions, it would still be the case that the effects of Controllability on cortisol reactivity recruited more rapidly than those of Predictability.

the presented shocks? This suggestion follows directly from MacLennan et al.'s observation that corticoids mediate a form of "stress-induced" analgesia. However, our suggestion then applies to those pain elicited responses, like vocalizations, that are reduced in tests following exposure to uncontrollable and unpredictable shocks and were taken as a basis for inferring an emotional deficit. Do not take this suggestion to imply that I believe the deficit in response initiation is to be accounted for by reference to this same stress-induced analgesia; I do not believe this, because MacLennan, Drugan, Hyson, Maier, Madden, and Barchas (1982) have demonstrated that the deficit in response initiation occurs even in the absence of this stress-induced analgesia, and Mah, Suissa, and Anisman (1980) have suggested that the deficit in response initiation and stress-induced analgesia are independent of each other.

If there is merit to these speculations and if cortisol scores do reflect emotional responsivity, then the present results suggest that the original conceptualization of the helplessness syndrome as including a *reduced* emotional reactivity was wrong. Rather, it would appear, based upon the current physiological measures, that the learned helplessness induction treatment actually may engender *greater* emotional reactivity.[2]

SUMMARY

A reanalysis of the learned helplessness experiments led to the hypothesis that the features of the proactive interference syndrome might have separable causal factors beyond the uncontrollability already known to be responsible for the deficit in response initiation (motivation). Behavioral experiments confirmed that unpredictability of shocks contributes to an associative deficit over and above the contribution, if any, of controllability. A psychobiological experiment sought to assess the role of these two factors upon the emotional reactivity of the organism as indexed by cortisol levels. Again, prior unpredictability was shown to be a pre-eminent proactive factor. But beyond this, the pattern of psychobiological results suggested that the proactive effect is one of relatively increased emotional reactivity rather than the previously described decrease! In sum, the experiments imply that our conception of learned helplessness as a unitary phenomenon is wrong and that the specific components, as well as their causal factors, may have been misidentified. Extensive reevaluation—both empirical and conceptual—is called for.

---

[2]If, as suggested here, prior unpredictability of shocks results in greater emotionality ("anxiety"?) in subsequent shock-motivated tasks, then the possibility is raised that the effect of unpredictable shocks on later learning in the conditional choice task—but not the Pavlovian task—is a byproduct of this greater emotionality (Taylor & Spence, 1952, but see Miles, 1959).

ACKNOWLEDGMENT

This research was supported by grants from N.I.C.H.H.D. (HD-01136 and 5T32-HD-07151) and N.S.F. (BNS-77-22075) to the Center for Research in Human Learning, J. B. Overmier, Co-PI, and, in part, from N.I.C.H.H.D. (HD-02881) to S. Levine. Thanks are due to my student colleagues, Nancy Dess, Daniel Linwick, Jeff Patterson, and Richard Wielkiewicz who contributed their expertise to the experiments discussed here.

REFERENCES

Abramson, L. Y., Seligman, M. E. P., & Teasdale, J. (1978). Learned helplessness in humans: Critique and reformulation. *Journal of Abnormal Psychology, 87,* 49–74.

Alloy, L. B., & Seligman, M. E. P. (1979). On the cognitive component of learned helplessness and depression. *The Psychology of Learning and Motivation, 13,* 219–276.

Averill, J. R. (1973). Personal control over aversive stimuli and its relationship to stress. *Psychological Bulletin, 80,* 286–310.

Bull, J. A., & Overmier, J. B. (1968). The additive and subtractive properties of excitation and inhibition. *Journal of Comparative and Physiological Psychology, 66,* 511–514.

Burger, J. M., & Arkin, R. M. (1980). Prediction, control, and learned helplessness. *Journal of Personality and Social Psychology, 38,* 482–491.

Church, R. M., LoLordo, V. M., Overmier, J. B., Solomon, R. L., & Turner, L. H. (1966). Cardiac response to shock in curarized dogs. *Journal of Comparative and Physiological Psychology, 62,* 1–7.

Dess, N. K., Linwick, D., Patterson, J., Overmier, J. B., & Levine, S. (1983). Immediate and proactive effects of controllability and predictability on plasma cortisol responses to shocks in dogs. *Behavioral Neurosciences, 97,* 1005–1016.

Edgington, E. S. (1969). *Statistical inference: The distribution free approach.* New York: McGraw-Hill.

Geer, J. H., & Maisel, E. (1972). Evaluating the effects of the prediction-control confound. *Journal of Personality and Social Psychology, 23,* 314–319.

Hennessey, J. W., & Levine, S. (1979). Stress, arousal and the pituitary-adrenal system: A psychoendocrine hypothesis. In J. M. Sprague & A. N. Epstein (Eds.), *Progress in psychobiology and physiological psychology* (pp. 134–179). New York: Academic Press.

Hillman, B., Hunter, W. S., & Kimble, G. A. (1953). The effect of drive level on the maze performance of the white rat. *Journal of Comparative and Physiological Psychology, 46,* 87–89.

Jackson, R. L., Alexander, J. H., & Maier, S. F. (1980). Learned helplessness, inactivity, and associative deficits: Effects of inescapable shock on response choice escape learning. *Journal of Experimental Psychology: Animal Behavior Processes, 6,* 1–20.

Klosterhalfen, W., & Klosterhalfen, S. (1983). A critical analysis of the animal experiments cited in support of learned helplessness. *Psychologische Beiträge, 25,* 436–458.

Lykken, D. T. (1962). Perception in the rat: Autonomic responses to shock as a function of length of warning interval. *Science, 137,* 665–666.

Mackintosh, N. J. (1973). Stimulus selection: Learning to ignore stimuli that predict no change in reinforcement. In R. A. Hinde & J. Stevenson-Hinde (Eds.), *Constraints on learning* (pp. 75–100). London: Academic Press.

MacLennan, A. J., Drugan, R. C., Hyson, R. L., & Maier, S. F. (1982). Corticosterone: A critical factor in an opioid form of stres-induced analgesia. *Science, 215,* 1530–1532.

MacLennan, A. J., Drugan, R. C., Hyson, R. L., Maier, S. F., Madden, J., IV, & Barchas, J. D. (1982). Dissociation of long-term analgesia and the shuttle box escape deficit caused by inescapable shock. *Journal of Comparative and Physiological Psychology, 96,* 904–912.

Mah, C., Suissa, A., & Anisman, H. (1980). Dissociation of antinocioception and escape deficits induced by stress in mice. *Journal of Comparative and Physiological Psychology, 94,* 1160–1171.

Maier, S. F., & Seligman, M. E. P. (1976). Learned helplessness: Theory and evidence. *Journal of Experimental Psychology: General, 105,* 3–46.

Mason, J. W. (1968). A review of psychoendocrine research on the pituitary-adrenocortical system. *Psychosomatic Medicine, 30,* 576–607.

Miles, R. C. (1959). Discrimination in the squirrel monkey as a function of deprivation and problem difficulty. *Journal of Experimental Psychology, 57,* 15–19.

Miller, S. M. (1979). Controllability and human stress: Methods, evidence, and theory. *Behavior Research and Therapy, 17,* 287–304.

Overmier, J. B., & Leaf, R. C. (1965). Effects of discriminative Pavlovian fear conditioning upon previously or subsequently acquired avoidance responding. *Journal of Comparative and Physiological Psychology, 60,* 213–217.

Overmier, J. B., Patterson, J., & Wielkiewicz, R. M. (1980). Environmental contingencies as sources of stress in animals. In S. Levine & H. Ursin (Eds.), *Coping and Health* (pp. 1–38). New York: Plenum.

Overmier, J. B., & Seligman, M. E. P. (1967). Effects of unescapable shocks upon subsequent escape and avoidance responding (pp. 28–33). *Journal of Comparative and Physiological Psychology, 63.*

Pubols, B. H., Jr. (1960). Incentive magnitude, learning, and performance in animals. *Psychological Bulletin, 57,* 89–115.

Rodger, R. A. (1975). The number of non-zero, post-hoc contrasts from ANOVA and error rate. *British Journal of Mathematical and Statistical Psychology, 28,* 71–78.

Seligman, M. E. P., & Maier, S. F. (1967). Failure to escape traumatic shock. *Journal of Experimental Psychology, 74,* 1–9.

Seligman, M. E. P., Maier, S. F., & Solomon, R. L. (1971). Unpredictable and Unctonrollable Aversive Events. In F. R. Brush (Ed.), *Aversive Conditioning and Learning* (pp. 347–400). New York: Academic Press.

Sidman, M. (1953). Avoidance conditioning with brief shock and no exteroceptive warning signal. *Science, 118,* 157–158.

Solomon, R. L., & Corbit, J. D. (1974). An opponent-process theory of motivation: I. Temporal dynamics of affect. *Psychological Review, 81,* 119–145.

Taylor, J. A., & Spence, K. W. (1952). The relationship of anxiety level to performance in serial learning. *Journal of Experimental Psychology, 44,* 61–64.

Trapold, M. A., & Overmier, J. B. (1972). The second learning process in instrumental learning. In A. H. Black & W. F. Prodasy (Eds.), *Classical Conditioning II: Current theory and research* (pp. 427–452). New York: Appleton, Century Crofts.

Weinberg, J., & Levine, S. (1980). Psychobiology of coping in animals: The effects of predictability. In S. Levine & H. Ursin (Eds.), *Coping and Health.* New York: Plenum.

Weiss, J. M. (1968). Effects of coping responses on stress. *Journal of Comparative and Physiological Psychology, 65,* 251–260.

14 The Judgment of Predictability in Depressed and Nondepressed College Students

Lauren B. Alloy
Northwestern University

Lyn Y. Abramson
University of Wisconsin-Madison

Debra A. Kossman
University of Pennsylvania

Learning about relationships between events is an important part of people's knowledge of the world. Information about the degree to which one event predicts another or one response controls an outcome would seem to be crucial for adaptive behavior.

Along with other theorists (e.g., Jenkins & Ward, 1965; Maier & Seligman, 1976; Rescorla, 1967; Seligman, 1975), we use the term *contingency* to refer to the degree of relationship between any two events. When the two events of interest are both stimuli in the environment, external to an individual, the relationship between them is best construed as one of *predictability*. The first stimulus event provides either some or no information relevant to forecasting the occurrence of the second. Alternatively, when the two events of interest consist of an individual's responses and some outcome, the relationship between them may be described as one of *controllability*. The individual's responses exert either some or no control over the outcome. An example highlights the distinction between prediction and control. From the standpoint of a child, the event of his mother being berated by her boss may predict the event of his parents having a fight, whereas the child's response of showing admiration for his mother may exert some control over the outcome of whether or not his parents have a fight.

SUBJECTIVE ASSESSMENTS OF CONTINGENCY

An important question emerges in an analysis of people's experience with environmental contingencies: Do people form subjective representations (e.g., beliefs, expectations, cognitive representations, etc.) of contingencies that mirror objective, real world contingencies (Alloy & Abramson, 1979)? To provide an empirical answer to this question, investigators representing diverse perspectives in psychology have conducted studies to examine people's judgments of controllability and predictability (see Alloy & Tabachnik, 1984 for a review of work on perceptions of contingency by humans and animals and a theoretical model for understanding these perceptions).

With respect to judgments of controllability, during the 1960s, a number of investigators in the operant learning tradition became interested in *superstitious* responding in humans (e.g., Bruner & Revusky, 1961; Catania & Cutts, 1963; Jenkins & Ward, 1965; Wright, 1962). Abramson and Alloy (1980) reviewed these studies of human learning and concluded that a general theme runs through them: People often act as if their responses control outcomes when, objectively speaking, they do not.

Social psychologists also have been intrigued by people's erroneous beliefs about their control over outcomes. Within this social psychological tradition, Langer (Langer, 1975; Langer & Roth, 1975) and Wortman (1975) identified some of the conditions in which people are most likely to exhibit an illusion of control (Geer, Davison, & Gatchel, 1970; Langer, 1975) and judge that they exert some control over an outcome when, in fact, they do not. Taken together, the results of the studies in social psychology parallel those of the studies in human learning: Although people sometimes accurately assess the degree of relationship between their responses and outcomes, they often show systematic errors in judging how much control their responses exert over outcomes (Abramson & Alloy, 1980; Alloy & Abramson, 1979; Alloy & Tabachnik, 1984).

Empirical work also has examined people's judgments about the degree to which the occurrence of one event predicts the occurrence of another event. In the human learning tradition, Hake and Hyman (1953) reported that their subjects did not respond as though a random series actually were random. Instead, Hake and Hyman's subjects acted as if they believed that future behavior of the random series could be predicted from past or present subsequences in the series. Also, from a human learning perspective, Ward and Jenkins (1965) reported that subjects were more accurate in discerning whether or not cloud seeding predicted rainfall when the information relevant to assessing the contingency between these two stimulus events was presented in summary form than when it was presented in a serial fashion over time.

Studies of clinical diagnosis also have documented that people sometimes succumb to an illusion of prediction and judge that one event predicts another event when it does not. For example, a number of clinical researchers (e.g.,

Chapman & Chapman, 1967; Meehl, 1960) have commented on the puzzling tendency of practicing clinical psychologists to agree in their clinical observations that various symptoms or behavioral characteristics of psychiatric patients are correlated with scores on conventional psychodiagnostic tests, despite research suggesting that these symptoms do not, in fact, predict the relevant test scores. In a study of the sources of such illusory correlation, Chapman and Chapman (1967) reported that naive college undergraduates "rediscovered" the same correlations (erroneous) between patients' symptoms and scores on a conventional psychodiagnostic test typically reported by clinicians (see also Starr & Katkin, 1969).

The work of Smedslund (1963) shows that illusory correlations about diagnosis are not confined to the psychiatric setting. Smedslund presented student nurses with information about the frequency of various symptoms and medical diagnoses. The results indicated that the judgments of student nurses showed no relation to the actual contingency between symptom and diagnosis. Thus, with respect to psychiatric and medical diagnosis, naive observers and experienced clinicians exhibit illusions of prediction and claim to see relationships between events that are unrelated in reality (see Alloy & Kayne (1985) for a review of work on contingency assessment in psychodiagnostic and psychotherapy outcome judgments).

DEPRESSION AND THE JUDGMENT OF CONTROLLABILITY

The work we have reviewed thus far shows that normal individuals sometimes show systematic errors in judging the degree of contingency between events in the world and between their responses and outcomes. One might think that such erroneous beliefs about contingencies would be exaggerated in individuals suffering from various types of psychopathology. In fact, a number of clinicians have classified individuals exhibiting psychopathology on the basis of the type of alleged cognitive distortions about reality. For example, Beck (1967, 1976) has characterized the manic individual as suffering from unrealistic beliefs about their personal control over environmental events. Drawing on these clinical intuitions, Langer (1975) has speculated that manic or hypomanic individuals may be especially susceptible to the illusion of control.

The greater part of theorizing and experimentation on psychopathological individuals' beliefs about the relationships between events has been in the area of depression. Both practicing clinicians and academic psychologists have proposed theories of depression that embody the core concept of helplessness or hopelessness (e.g., Arieti, 1970; Beck, 1967, 1976; Bibring, 1953; Halberstadt, Andrews, Metalsky, & Abramson, in press; Lichtenberg, 1957; Melges & Bowlby, 1969; Seligman, 1975). In these theories, the depressive is characterized as one who believes that he or she is ineffective and powerless to control personally important outcomes.

The learned helplessness model of depression (Seligman, 1975; Seligman, Klein, & Miller, 1976) and its more recent reformulation (Abramson, Seligman, & Teasdale, 1978) are the most explicit statements of the relationship among helplessness, hopelessness, and depression. According to the original and reformulated models of depression and learned helplessness, a subset of depressed people (i.e., those who exhibit the subtype of helplessness or hopelessness depression) are hypothesized to exhibit generalized expectancies of independence between their responses and outcomes that cause the motivational and cognitive symptoms of their depression. The motivational symptom consists of retarded initiation of voluntary responses and is reflected in the passivity of the individual suffering from helplessness depression. The cognitive symptom has been referred to as a negative cognitive set (Beck, 1967) that makes it difficult for the depressed individual to see that personal responses do control environmental outcomes when such a relationship between responses and outcomes actually exists.

We (Alloy & Abramson, 1979) and other investigators (e.g., Alloy & Seligman, 1979) derived from the original and reformulated models of helplessness and depression the prediction that compared to nondepressives, depressed individuals will be biased toward seeing noncontingency between responses and outcomes when contingency actually exists. In other words, we predicted that compared to nondepressives, depressives should tend to underestimate the degree of control their responses exert over outcomes. With the advantage of hindsight, we now realize that it probably was inappropriate to draw predictions from the original and reformulated models of helplessness and depression about depressed individuals as a group versus nondepressed individuals as a group. The problem is that depression may be a very heterogeneous disorder composed of a number of functional or etiologic subtypes (e.g., Craighead, 1980; Depue & Monroe, 1978; Fowles & Gersh, 1979; Hamilton & Abramson, 1983). In essence, the original and reformulated models of helplessness and depression postulate the existence of an, as yet unidentified in nature, subtype of depression— helplessness or hopelessness depression (Halberstadt et al., in press; Seligman, 1978). Strictly speaking, predictions drawn from the original and reformulated models of helplessness and depression about depressives' biases in judging their personal control over outcomes would apply only to helplessness or hopelessness depressives and not to individuals suffering from other forms of depression characterized by processes other than those featured in the original and reformulated helplessness theory. However, because we only are beginning to specify the kind of research program that would allow for identification of individuals suffering from helplessness or hopelessness depression as opposed to some other form of depression (e.g., Abramson, Metalsky, & Alloy, 1985), we have focused our research efforts on depressives in general, as opposed to helplessness or hopelessness depressives in particular.

To date, we have conducted a number of studies examining depressed and nondepressed individuals' judgments of their personal control over outcomes (Abramson, Alloy, & Rosoff, 1981; Alloy & Abramson, 1979, 1982; Alloy, Abramson, & Viscusi, 1981; Martin, Abramson, & Alloy, 1984). In our first set of experiments about depression and the judgment of personal control, we brought depressed and nondepressed college students into the laboratory and presented them with one of a series of contingency problems varying in the actual degree of control their responses exerted over outcomes. In each problem, students estimated the degree of contingency between their responses (pressing or not pressing a button) and an environmental outcome (onset of a green light) (Alloy & Abramson, 1979).

From the perspective of the original and reformulated models of helplessness and depression as well as our everyday intuitions about depression, we were quite surprised by the results of this first set of experiments. Unexpectedly, depressed college students were quite accurate in judging how much control they actually exerted over the experimental outcome in all conditions of all experiments, whereas nondepressed college students succumbed to some intriguing illusions about their control over the experimental outcome. Specifically, nondepressives overestimated their personal control over objectively uncontrollable outcomes that were frequent or associated with success (i.e., winning money), and they underestimated their personal control over objectively controllable outcomes that were associated with failure (i.e., losing money). We have speculated that these biases in nondepressives' judgments of their personal control over outcomes may enable them to see themselves and their world in an optimistic light (e.g., Abramson & Alloy, 1981). In addition to the above biases, nondepressed students also underestimated their degree of personal control over the experimental outcome when the passive response of not pressing the button was associated with the higher percentage of reward (i.e., winning money) in a hedonically charged situation.

Although we originally designed our studies examining depression and the judgment of control in order to obtain a more complete description of depressive cognition, our findings of nondepressive cognitive illusions suggested that it was important to provide a more comprehensive description of nondepressive cognition as well. Consequently, we embarked on a program of research in which we attempted to identify factors that influenced whether or not nondepressed subjects would exhibit an illusion of personal control in our experimental situation. In this regard, we found that previous experience with controllable noises (Alloy & Abramson, 1982) and instatement of a depressive mood (Alloy et al., 1981) decreased the likelihood that nondepressed college students would exhibit an illusion of control in the situation in which they were most likely to exhibit such an illusion in our original study—when an outcome was objectively uncontrollable but associated with success (i.e., winning money).

What generality is there to our intriguing finding that nondepressed students exhibit an illusion of control in some situations whereas depressed students do not? Using the experimental paradigm developed by Langer (1975), Golin and his colleagues (Golin, Terrell, & Johnson, 1977; Golin, Terrell, Weitz, & Drost, 1979) similarly reported that nondepressed normal and psychiatric control subjects exhibited an illusion of control in a chance situation into which elements typically associated with skill tasks had been introduced (e.g., active involvement). In contrast, neither mildly nor severely depressed subjects succumbed to this illusion of control. The finding that depressed individuals are relatively invulnerable to an illusion of control is consistent with a growing body of work suggesting that depressed people are less susceptible than nondepressed people to a number of cognitive biases that would allow them to perceive themselves and their interactions with the environment in an optimistic manner (Abramson & Alloy, 1981; Alloy, 1982; Alloy, Ahrens, & Kayne, 1985; Lewinsohn, Mischel, Chaplain, & Barton, 1980; Nelson & Craighead, 1977; Rozensky, Rehm, Pry, & Roth, 1977; Tabachnik, Crocker, & Alloy, 1983).

DEPRESSION AND THE JUDGMENT OF PREDICTABILITY

To date, work on depression, nondepression, and the judgment of contingency has focused on people's judgments of their control over outcomes. What is the relationship among depression, nondepression, and the judgment of predictability? Are depressives as accurate in judging the degree to which one event predicts another event as they are in judging their personal control over outcomes? Do nondepressives succumb to an illusion of prediction as well as an illusion of control? According to the original and reformulated models of helplessness and depression, there is no reason to expect differential accuracy between depressives and nondepressives in judging the degree to which one event predicts another. However, insofar as previous studies of behavior in event prediction situations have demonstrated that people often believe that noncontingently related stimulus events are correlated (e.g., Chapman & Chapman, 1967; Hake & Hyman, 1953; Starr & Katkin, 1969), it is tempting to speculate that perhaps nondepressives' overestimation of the control their responses exert over outcomes simply may be one manifestation of a general tendency to overestimate the degree of relationship between events.

We now present three studies that begin to examine whether or not depressed individuals' relative accuracy in judging the degree of control that their responses exert over outcomes is matched by similar accuracy in judging the degree of contingency between two stimulus events in a prediction situation. In these three studies, college students were presented with contingency problems identical to those used by Alloy and Abramson (1979), except that subjects had to learn the relationship between an external stimulus event (the occurrence of a red light—Experiments 1 and 2; the occurrence of a tone—Experiment 3), rather than their own responses, and the occurrence of an environmental outcome (onset of a green light). That is, the occurrence or nonoccurrence of a stimulus event (red light or tone) was substituted for subjects' pressing and not pressing of a button as the antecedent event in the contingency judgment problems. By employing the Alloy and Abramson procedure, we could compare the relative accuracy of subjects' contingency judgments for stimulus-outcome versus response-outcome relations. In Experiment 1, the red light did forecast the onset of the green light to some degree; whereas, in Experiments 2 and 3, the first stimulus event did not predict the onset of the green light.

Experiment 1: Contingent Events[1]

Experiment 1 examined depressed[2] and nondepressed college students' abilities to detect the degree of contingency between a stimulus event and an environmental outcome in a situation in which there was some degree of covariation between the two events, and the outcome was neutral. Alloy and Abramson (1979, Experiment 1) previously reported that under similar conditions, both depressed and nondepressed students gave accurate judgments of the degree of contingency between their responses (pressing and not pressing a button) and an experimental outcome (green light onset). In particular, students were presented with one of two contingency problems used by Alloy and Abramson (1979, Experiment 1) that differed in the actual degree of contingency[3] between the stimulus events. In Problem 1, the red light provided 25% predictability of the green light; whereas, in Problem 2, it provided 75% predictability of the green light. Each contingency problem consisted of a series of forty trials on which the subject observed one of two stimuli (a red light or no red light), followed by one of two possible outcomes (a green light or no green light). At the end of the forty trials, the

---

[1]The three predictability experiments are described briefly in this chapter. All details of the methods, procedures, and results may be obtained from Lauren Alloy.

[2]For convenience of exposition, we refer to subjects as depressed or nondepressed in our experiments. However, it is important to emphasize that subjects were classified as depressed or nondepressed on the basis of the severity of self-reported depressive symptoms and mood, rather than on the basis of meeting diagnostic criteria for the clinical syndrome of depression. Subjects with Beck Depression Inventory (BDI; Beck, 1967) scores of 9 or greater *and* Multiple Affect Adjective Check List (MAACL; Zuckerman & Lubin, 1965) depression scale scores of 14 or greater were classified as depressed, whereas subjects with BDI scores of 8 or less *and* MAACL depression scale scores of 13 or less were classified as nondepressed. Subjects who did not meet both criteria were not included in the experiments. In each of the three experiments, approximately one-third of the depressed subjects scored in the moderate to severe range on the BDI, according to the cutpoints for severity of depression established by Kovacs and Beck (1977).

[3]In all three experiments, the delta coefficient was used as the index of the objective degree of contingency between the stimulus events because it allowed for comparison of the current studies with our prior work on judgments of control. The delta coefficient is the difference between the conditional probabilities of green light onset, given the occurrence versus nonoccurrence of the red light.

subject was asked to judge the degree of contingency or predictability (on a 0 to 100 scale) that existed between red light onset and green light onset. In addition, as in Alloy and Abramson (1979, Experiment 1), the present study was designed so that the frequency of green light onset was negatively correlated with the actual level of contingency. This insured that a strategy of judging contingency relying on outcome frequency would yield incorrect judgments of predictability.

The left panel of Figure 14.1 presents subjects' judgments of predictability for the two contingency problems. For comparison purposes, the right panel of Figure 14.1 displays judgments of control for the parallel problems in Alloy and Abramson (1979, Experiment 1). As can be seen in the left panel of the figure, both depressed and nondepressed subjects gave quite accurate judgments of the degree of predictability the red light provided for the green light. Subjects believed that the red light provided greater prediction of the green light in the 75% contingency problem (64.12) than in the 25% contingency problem (45.29). In addition, similar to Alloy and Abramson's (1979; Experiment 1) findings for response-outcome contingencies (right panel of Figure 14.1), subjects' judgments clearly were correlated more highly with the actual stimulus contingency ($r = .493$; dashed line in Figure 14.1) than with the overall frequency of reinforcement ($r = -.340$; dotted line in Figure 14.1). Moreover, subjective judgments were as accurate when the absence of the red light was associated with the

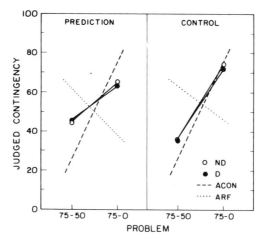

FIG. 14.1.   Judged contingency for depressed (D) and nondepressed (ND) students as a function of problem type in Experiment 1. The 75-50 problem represents a 25% contingency, and the 75-0 problem represents a 75% contingency. The left panel of the figure displays judgments of predictability for Experiment 1. For comparison, the right panel of the figure displays judgments of control for the same problems given by subjects in Alloy and Abramson's (1979) Experiment 1. Actual degree of contingency (ACON) and actual frequency of reinforcement (ARF) are also shown as a function of problem type.

higher percentage of green light onset as when the presence of the red light was associated with this higher percentage of reinforcement.

While judgments of predictability were relatively accurate in this experiment; they were somewhat conservative, as compared to the actual degree of contingency represented in the two problems and as compared to subjective judgments of control (right side of Figure 14.1). That is, subjects tended to overestimate the red light's predictive power in the 25% contingency problem and to slightly underestimate its predictability in the 75% contingency problem. In sum, though, depressed and nondepressed subjects' judgments did not differ from each other, and both groups' judgments were significantly related to the actual contingencies with neither group exhibiting major errors in judging predictability.

Experiment 2: Noncontingent Events

Experiment 2 examined depressed and nondepressed subjects' abilities to detect a noncontingent stimulus-outcome relationship in circumstances in which the outcome was positively or negatively valenced. Under these conditions, Alloy and Abramson (1979; Experiment 3) had found that whereas depressed subjects accurately judged that their responses exerted little control over the outcome, whether positive or negative, nondepressed subjects succumbed to an illusion of control and overestimated their impact on the outcome when it was positively valenced. We wondered whether nondepressed individuals would exhibit a similar illusion of predictability for a positive outcome in the present experiment. Thus, depressed and nondepressed subjects were assigned to one of two problems identical to those used by Alloy and Abramson (1979; Experiment 3), except that a red light, rather than subjects' responses, was randomly related to green light onset. In one problem, green light onset occurred on 50% of the trials and was associated with the gain of money, whereas in the other problem, it occurred on 50% of the trials but was associated with the loss of money.

Figure 14.2 displays subjects' judgments of predictability for the present experiment (left panel) as well as judgments of control for the parallel problems given by subjects in Alloy and Abramson's (1979) Experiment 3 (right panel). Again as in Experiment 1, there were no differences between depressed and nondepressed subjects' judgments of predictability, and both groups judged relatively accurately that the red light provided little prediction of the green light. Thus, nondepressed subjects did not succumb to an illusion of predictability when the green light occurred noncontingently but was associated with success (winning money), as they had succumbed to an illusion of control in Alloy and Abramson's control experiment (Experiment 3). These findings suggest that depressives' greater accuracy than nondepressives' in judging control in Alloy and Abramson's experiments is not due to superior problem solving skills or ability to assess contingencies in general. When the events in the contingency

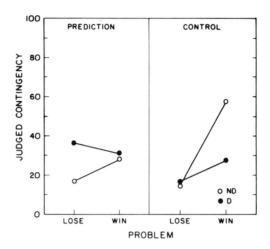

FIG. 14.2. Judged contingency for depressed (D) and nondepressed (ND) students as a function of problem type in Experiment 2. The left panel of the figure displays judgments of predictability for Experiment 2. For comparison, the right panel of the figure displays judgments of control for the same problems given by subjects in Alloy and Abramson's (1979) Experiment 3.

problem do not involve subjects' own responses, nondepressives are as accurate as depressives and do not exhibit systematic errors. Thus, nondepressive illusions of contingency may be specific to response-outcome relationships.

Experiment 3: Predictability versus Controllability

Taken together, Experiments 1 and 2 suggest that while nondepressed individuals are equally proficient at detecting a positive contingency between stimulus events and outcomes and between their own responses and outcomes (Experiment 1), they are better at detecting a noncontingent stimulus-outcome than a response-outcome relationship (Experiment 2). Depressed individuals, on the other hand, appear to be equally proficient at assessing stimulus-outcome and response-outcome contingencies, whether of positive or zero value. A shortcoming of our first two experiments with respect to comparing individuals' covariation assessment abilities in predictability versus control situations is that we did not actually include stimulus-outcome and response-outcome contingency problems within a single experiment. Experiment 3 remedies this situation by specifically comparing depressed and nondepressed subjects' susceptibility to an illusion of contingency for noncontingent stimulus-outcome versus response-outcome relationships.

In this third experiment, we examined subjects' judgments of contingency for an event contingency in which the outcome was noncontingent but occurred with high probability. In particular, we utilized the 75-75 noncontingency problem used by Alloy and Abramson (1979) in their Experiment 2. Half of the subjects judged the contingency between their own responses (pressing and not pressing a button) and green light onset (control condition), and half judged the contingency between stimulus events (presence and absence of a tone) and green light onset (prediction condition). Alloy and Abramson had found that whereas depressed subjects (especially depressed females) accurately judged they exerted little control in this high-frequency noncontingency problem, nondepressed subjects (especially nondepressed females) exhibited an illusion of control. Given the results of our first two predictability studies suggesting that nondepressives do not make systematic errors in assessing stimulus-outcome covariations, we would predict a mood by type of contingency interaction for the present experiment. Specifically, nondepressed subjects should overestimate their control over the noncontingent but frequent outcome relative to depressed subjects; whereas, the two groups should not differ and both should give relatively accurate low judgments of predictability.

As predicted, nondepressed subjects exhibited a larger illusion of contingency for a noncontingent but frequent outcome when judging the control their responses exerted over the outcome than when judging the predictability a tone provided for the outcome. Depressed subjects, on the other hand, gave equally low judgments of contingency in both the prediction and control conditions (see the left panel of Figure 14.3). However, an examination of the middle and right panels of Figure 14.3 shows that this Mood X Condition interaction was produced almost entirely by females rather than males. It is interesting that nondepressed females were more likely to overestimate contingency, especially response-outcome contingency, than nondepressed males, when judging a noncontingent relationship in which the outcome occurred frequently. Alloy and Abramson (1979) similarly found in their Experiment 2 that nondepressed females were more likely to overestimate their control over a noncontingent but frequent outcome than were nondepressed males, whereas depressed males and females gave equally accurate low judgments of control as in the present experiment. Thus, nondepressed females appear to be more susceptible to an illusion of contingency than nondepressed males regardless of whether they are assessing stimulus-outcome or response-outcome relationships. However, nondepressives as a group are more susceptible to an illusion of control than an illusion of predictability (Experiments 2 and 3) and more susceptible to an illusion of control than are depressed subjects.

IMPLICATIONS AND SPECULATIONS

To summarize the experimental findings, in Experiment 1, both depressed and nondepressed students were relatively accurate in judging the degree to which the occurrence of one stimulus event (onset of a red light) predicted the occurrence

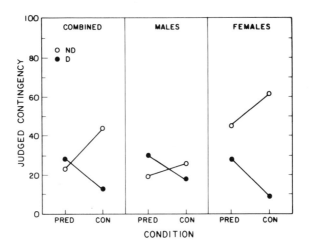

FIG. 14.3.   Judged contingency for depressed (D) and nondepressed (ND) students as a function of condition (prediction vs. control) in Experiment 3. The left panel of the figure displays judgments for both sexes combined. The middle and right panels display judgments for males and females, respectively.

of another stimulus event (onset of a green light), when a contingency, in fact, existed between these two stimulus events. These results parallel those of Alloy and Abramson (1979, Experiment 1), who reported that in a situation not involving hedonically charged outcomes, depressed and nondepressed students were equally accurate in judging the degree of contingency between their responses and outcomes. Similar to Experiment 1, but in contrast to prior work on the judgment of personal control, in Experiment 2, nondepressed students were no more likely than depressed students to succumb to an illusion of prediction in a situation in which, objectively speaking, no contingency existed between a predictor event and an apparently desirable predicted outcome. Finally, in Experiment 3, whereas nondepressed subjects as a group were more likely than depressed subjects as a group to exhibit an illusion of personal control when the experimental outcome was noncontingent but frequent, nondepressives were no more likely than depressives to exhibit an illusion of prediction about this same outcome.

Taken together, then, the results of Experiments 1 through 3 provided no evidence that nondepressed students are more likely to succumb to illusions of prediction than are depressed students. Moreover, at least on our experimental tasks, neither depressed nor nondepressed students appeared to exhibit any systematic biases in judging the degree to which one stimulus event predicts another stimulus event. These results are usefully contrasted to prior work (e.g., Alloy & Abramson, 1979; Golin et al., 1977) as well as the results of Experiment 3 showing that nondepressed individuals are more likely than depressed individuals to exhibit a number of intriguing biases in judging their personal control over events. Apparently, then, differences between depressed and nondepressed individuals' judgments of personal control are not a manifestation of widespread differences between these two groups, in the judgment of relationships between events in general. We do caution, however, that it would be inappropriate to infer from the absence of differences between depressed and nondepressed students' judgments of predictability in the present experiments that these two groups never will differ in their judgments of predictability. It is quite possible that in some situations (to be discussed), depressed and nondepressed individuals will differ in their judgments of the degree to which the occurrence of one event forecasts the occurrence of another event (cf. Alloy et al., 1985).

Before discussing the specific implications of our findings for work on depressive and nondepressive cognition, it is useful to examine the results from the perspective of general work on the judgment of predictability. From the standpoint of work on illusory correlation (e.g., Chapman & Chapman, 1967), our results, on first inspection, seem surprising. Whereas previous investigators have reported results suggesting that humans succumb to persistent illusions of prediction, neither our nondepressed group nor our depressed group showed a strong tendency to succumb to illusory correlation in our prediction task.

How can our failure to obtain evidence of illusory correlation be reconciled with previous demonstrations of this phenomenon (e.g., Chapman & Chapman, 1967; Ward & Jenkins, 1965)? In attempting to account for this apparent discrepancy, we suggest that an important difference may exist between our prediction task and the prediction tasks used by investigators demonstrating illusory correlation (cf. Alloy & Tabachnik, 1984). Specifically, we suspect that subjects probably came to our study with no prior beliefs or expectations about the degree of relationship between the two stimulus events in our prediction problems. In contrast, it is likely that subjects did have prior beliefs or expectations about the degree of relationship between the stimulus events used in studies demonstrating illusory correlation. Indeed, Chapman and Chapman (1967) showed that their subjects were likely to exhibit illusory correlation when the event to be predicted was a strong associate of the predictor event. Similarly, the subjects of Ward & Jenkins (1965) probably had prior beliefs about the degree of relationship between cloud seeding and rain. It is noteworthy that a number of theorists (Abramson & Alloy, 1980; Alloy & Tabachnik, 1984; Crocker, 1981; Jennings, Amabile, & Ross, 1982; Metalsky & Abramson, 1981; Nisbett & Ross, 1980; Kayne & Alloy, in press) have presented theory and evidence suggesting that people's prior beliefs or expectations about a contingency between events often may override situational information about the objective contingency between events. That is, people's judgments about the degree of contingency between events may conform more to their prior beliefs or expectations about what the contingency should be than to the actual degree of contingency itself. Given this line of reasoning, it no longer is surprising that other investigators have obtained evidence of illusory correlation; whereas, we did not. An implication of this discussion is that there may be some situations in which depressed individuals differ from nondepressed individuals in their prior beliefs or expectations about a contingency between two stimulus events. In these situations, we would predict that depressed and nondepressed individuals would differ in their judgments of predictability.

At this point, it is useful to discuss the implications of our results for work on depressive and nondepressive cognition. One implication of our findings is that depressives' relative accuracy in judging personal control is not due to superior ability in assessing contingencies in general. If depressives simply were superior to nondepressives in general ability to assess contingencies, we would have expected these two groups to differ in the judgment of predictability in this set of experiments.

In comparing the present results with work on the judgment of personal control (e.g., Alloy & Abramson, 1979), one might be tempted to infer that perhaps it is the control versus prediction distinction that is relevant to explaining when nondepressives will be more likely than depressives to succumb to illusory contingency. That is, one might believe that nondepressives will exhibit illusions of contingency in situations involving judgment of control but not in situations involving judgment of predictability; whereas, depressives would not exhibit illusions of contingency in either of these situations. This interpretation, however, is ruled out by our finding that when judging other people's control over events, depressives sometimes exhibit an illusion of control (Martin et al., 1984). Given the work conducted to date, it appears that the condition in which nondepressives exhibit an illusion of contingency, whereas depressives do not, is when judging *personal control*—the degree of relationship between outcomes and the self's responses.

Describing the boundary conditions of the situations in which nondepressives are more likely than depressives to succumb to illusory contingency may suggest mechanisms to explain differences in susceptibility to illusory contingency between depressed and nondepressed people. We suggest two noncompeting mechanisms to explain these differences. First, differences in susceptibility to the illusion of personal control between depressed and nondepressed people may result from the two groups having different prior beliefs or expectations about their personal control. Nondepressives may have the prior belief that they control positive outcomes. This hypothesized expectation may bias the way in which the nondepressive interprets information that is relevant to assessing personal control. In contrast, the depressive may have weaker preconceptions about personal control and therefore be more sensitive to incoming situational information in judging personal control (cf. Alloy & Tabachnik, 1984; Kayne & Alloy, in press). A second explanation of nondepressives' greater susceptibility to the illusion of personal control relative to depressives is that nondepressives may be more motivated than depressives to preserve or increase their self-esteem (Alloy

& Abramson, 1979, 1982). Consequently, nondepressives may interpret incoming information about personal control in a way that is pleasing or satisfying; whereas, depressives will not show such a bias. According to this motivational account, nondepressives exhibited an illusion of contingency in the judgment of personal control task but not in the present judgment of predictability tasks because the former was relevant to their self-esteem concerns; whereas, the latter was not. We currently are conducting research to test these two hypotheses about the processes giving rise to differences between depressed and nondepressed people in susceptibility to the illusion of personal control.

ACKNOWLEDGMENT

Preparation of this chapter was supported by a grant from the John D. and Catherine T. MacArthur Foundation to Lauren Alloy and Lyn Abramson. The order of the authors' names is random. Requests for experiment details should be sent to Lauren B. Alloy, Department of Psychology, Northwestern University, 1859 Sheridan Road, Evanston, Illinois, 60201. We would like to thank Linda Kanefield and Jeff Sturza for serving as experimenters in Experiments 1 and 2, respectively.

REFERENCES

Abramson, L. Y., & Alloy, L. B. (1980). Judgment of contingency: Errors and their implications. In A. Baum & J. Singer (Eds.), *Advances in environmental psychology* (Volume 2) (pp. 111–130). Hillsdale, NJ: Lawrence Erlbaum Associates.

Abramson, L. Y., & Alloy, L. B. (1981). Depression, nondepression, and cognitive illusions: A reply to Schwartz. *Journal of Experimental Psychology: General, 110,* 436–447.

Abramson, L. Y., Alloy, L. B., & Rosoff, R. (1981). Depression and the generation of complex hypotheses in the judgment of contingency. *Behaviour Research and Therapy, 19,* 35–45.

Abramson, L. Y., Metalsky, G. I., & Alloy, L. B. (1985). *The reformulated helplessness theory of depression: Does the research test the theory?* Unpublished manuscript.

Abramson, L. Y., Seligman, M. E. P., & Teasdale, J. (1978). Learned helplessness in humans: Critique and reformulation. *Journal of Abnormal Psychology, 87,* 49–74.

Alloy, L. B. (1982, August). *Depression: On the absence of self-serving cognitive biases.* Paper presented at the Ninetieth Annual Meeting of the American Psychological Association, Washington, D.C.

Alloy, L. B., & Abramson, L. Y. (1979). Judgment of contingency in depressed and nondepressed college students: Sadder but wiser? *Journal of Experimental Psychology: General, 108,* 441–485.

Alloy, L. B., & Abramson, L. Y. (1982). Learned helplessness, depression, and the illusion of control. *Journal of Personality and Social Psychology, 42,* 1114–1126.

Alloy, L. B., Abramson, L. Y., & Viscusi, D. (1981). Induced mood and the illusion of control. *Journal of Personality and Social Psychology, 41,* 1129–1140.

Alloy, L. B., Ahrens, A., & Kayne, N. T. (1985). *Depression, predictions, and causal schemata I: Biased use of statistically relevant information in predictions for self and others.* Unpublished manuscript.

Alloy, L. B., & Kayne, N. T. (1985). *Clinical inference in psychodiagnostic and psychotherapy outcome judgments: An application of an expectation by situational information interactional model of covariation assessment.* Unpublished manuscript.

Alloy, L. B., & Seligman, M. E. P. (1979). On the cognitive component of learned helplessness and depression. In G. H. Bower (Ed.), *The psychology of learning and motivation: Vol. 13* (pp. 219–296). New York: Academic Press.

Alloy, L. B., & Tabachnik, N. (1984). Assessment of covariation by humans and animals: The joint influence of prior expectations and current situational information. *Psychological Review, 91,* 112–149.

Arieti, S. (1970). Cognition and feeling. In M. B. Arnold (Ed.), *Feelings and emotions* (pp. 135–143). New York: Academic Press.

Beck, A. T. (1967). *Depression: Clinical, experimental, and theoretical aspects.* New York: Harper & Row.

Beck, A. T. (1976). *Cognitive therapy and the emotional disorders.* New York: International Universities Press.

Bibring, E. (1953). The mechanism of depression. In P. Greenacre (Ed.), *Affective disorders* (pp. 13–48). New York: International Universities Press.

Bruner, A., & Revusky, S. H. (1961). Collateral behavior in humans. *Journal of the Experimental Analysis of Behavior, 4,* 349–350.

Catania, A. C., & Cutts, D. (1963). Experimental control of superstitious responding in humans. *Journal of the Experimental Analysis of Behavior, 6,* 203–208.

Chapman, L. J., & Chapman, J. P. (1967). Genesis of popular but erroneous psychodiagnostic observations. *Journal of Abnormal Psychology, 72,* 193–204.

Craighead, W. E. (1980). Away from a unitary model of depression. *Behavior Therapy, 11,* 122–128.

Crocker, J. (1981). Judgment of covariation by social perceivers. *Psychological Bulletin, 90,* 272–292.

Depue, R. A., & Monroe, S. M. (1978). Learned helplessness in the perspective of the depressive disorders. *Journal of Abnormal Psychology, 87,* 3–20.

Fowles, D. C., & Gersh, F. (1979). Neurotic depression: The endogenous-neurotic distinction. In R. A. Depue (Ed.), *The psychobiology of the depressive disorders: Implications for the effects of stress* (pp. 55–80). New York: Academic Press.

Geer, J. H., Davison, G. C., & Gatchel, R. I. (1970). Reduction of stress in humans through nonveridical perceived control of aversive stimulation. *Journal of Personality and Social Psychology, 16,* 731–738.

Golin, S., Terrell, F., & Johnson, B. (1977). Depression and the illusion of control. *Journal of Abnormal Psychology, 86,* 440–442.

Golin, S., Terrell, F., Weitz, J., & Drost, P. L. (1979). The illusion of control among depressed patients. *Journal of Abnormal Psychology, 88,* 454–457.

Hake, H. W., & Hyman, R. (1953). Perception of the statistical structure of a random series of binary symbols. *Journal of Experimental Psychology, 45,* 64–74.

Halberstadt, L. J., Andrews, D. J., Metalsky, G. I., & Abramson, L. Y. (in press). Helplessness, hopelessness, and depression: A review of progress and future directions. In N. S. Endler & J. Hunt (Eds.), *Personality and behavior disorders.* New York: Wiley.

Hamilton, E. W., & Abramson, L. Y. (1983). Cognitive patterns and major depressive disorder: A longitudinal study in a hospital setting. *Journal of Abnormal Psychology, 92,* 173–184.

Jenkins, H. M., & Ward, W. C. (1965). Judgment of contingency between responses and outcomes. *Psychological Monographs, 79* (1, Whole No. 594).

Jennings, D. L., Amabile, T., & Ross, L. (1982). Informal covariation assessment: Data-based versus theory-based judgments. In D. Kahneman, P. Slovic, & A. Tversky (Eds.), *Judgment under uncertainty: Heuristics and biases* (pp. 211–230). Cambridge: Cambridge University Press.

Kayne, N. T., & Alloy, L. B. (in press). Clinician and patient as aberrant actuaries: Expectation-based distortions in assessment of covariation. In L. Y. Abramson (Ed.), *Attribution processes and clinical psychology*. New York: Guilford.

Kovacs, M., & Beck, A. T. (1977). Empirical-clinical approach toward a definition of childhood depression. In J. G. Schulterbrandt & A. Raskin (Eds.), *Depression in childhood: Diagnosis, treatment, and conceptual models* (pp. 1–25). New York: Raven Press.

Langer, E. J. (1975). The illusion of control. *Journal of Personality and Social Psychology, 32*, 311–328.

Langer, E. J., & Roth, J. (1975). Heads I win, tails it's chance: The illusion of control as a function of the sequence of outcomes in a purely chance task. *Journal of Personality and Social Psychology, 32*, 951–955.

Lewinsohn, P. M., Mischel, W., Chaplain, W., & Barton, R. (1980). Social competence and depression: The role of illusory self-perceptions? *Journal of Abnormal Psychology, 89*, 203–212.

Lichtenberg, P. (1957). A definition and analysis of depression. *Archives of Neurology and Psychiatry, 77*, 516–527.

Maier, S. F., & Seligman, M. E. P. (1976). Learned helplessness: Theory and evidence. *Journal of Experimental Psychology: General, 105*, 3–46.

Martin, D. J., Abramson, L. Y., & Alloy, L. B. (1984). The illusion of control for self and others in depressed and nondepressed college students. *Journal of Personality and Social Psychology, 46*, 125–136.

Meehl, P. E. (1960). The cognitive activity of the clinician. *American Psychologist, 15*, 19–27.

Melges, F. J., & Bowlby, J. (1969). Types of hopelessness in psychopathological process. *Archives of General Psychiatry, 20*, 690–699.

Metalsky, G. I., & Abramson, L. Y. (1981). Attributional styles: Toward a framework for concep-tualization and assessment. In P. C. Kendall & S. D. Hollon (Eds.), *Assessment strategies for cognitive-behavioral interventions* (pp. 13–57). New York: Academic Press.

Nelson, R. E., & Craighead, W. E. (1977). Selective recall of positive and negative feedback, self-control behaviors, and depression. *Journal of Abnormal Psychology, 86*, 379–388.

Nisbett, R. E., & Ross, L. (1980). *Human inference: Strategies and shortcomings of social judg-ment*. Englewood Cliffs, NJ: Prentice-Hall.

Rescorla, R. A. (1967). Pavlovian conditioning and its proper control procedures. *Psychological Review, 74*, 71–79.

Rozensky, R. H., Rehm, L. P., Pry, G., & Roth, D. (1977). Depression and self-reinforcement behavior in hospitalized patients. *Journal of Behavior Therapy and Experimental Psychiatry, 8*, 35–38.

Seligman, M. E. P. (1975). *Helplessness: On depression, development, and death*. San Francisco: Freeman.

Seligman, M. E. P. (1978). Comment and integration. *Journal of Abnormal Psychology, 87*, 165–179.

Seligman, M. E. P., Klein, D. C., & Miller, W. R. (1976). Depression. In H. Leitenberg (Ed.), *Handbook of behavior modification and behavior therapy* (pp. 168–210). Englewood Cliffs, NJ: Prentice-Hall.

Smedslund, J. (1963). The concept of correlation in adults. *Scandinavian Journal of Psychology, 4*, 165–173.

Starr, J. G., & Katkin, E. (1969). The clinician as aberrant actuary: Illusory correlation and the Incomplete Sentences Blank. *Journal of Abnormal Psychology, 74*, 670–675.

Tabachnik, N., Crocker, J., & Alloy, L. B. (1983). Depression, social comparison, and the false-consensus effect. *Journal of Personality and Social Psychology, 45*, 688–699.

Ward, W. C., & Jenkins, H. M. (1965). The display of information and the judgment of contingen-cy. *Canadian Journal of Psychology, 19,* 231–241.

Wortman, C. B. (1975). Some determinants of perceived control. *Journal of Personality and Social Psychology, 31,* 282–294.

Wright, J. C. (1962). Consistency and complexity of response sequences as a function of schedules of noncontingent reward. *Journal of Experimental Psychology, 63,* 601–609.

Zuckerman, M., & Lubin, B. (1965). *Manual for the Multiple Affect Adjective Check List.* San Diego, CA: Educational and Industrial Testing Service.

V OPPONENT PROCESS THEORY

15

Growth of Morphine Tolerance: The Effect of Dose and Interval Between Doses

Stephen F. Seaman
Fort Atkinson, Wisconsin

A notable aspect of a wide variety of potent pharmacological agents is that of tolerance. Tolerance is defined as the change of effectiveness of a drug "so that an increased amount of drug is required to produce the same specified degree of effect, or less effect is produced by the same dose of drug" (Kalant, LeBlanc & Gibbins, 1971, p. 137). One class of drugs in which tolerance is a very potent phenomenon, and for which there is a long history of research, is the opiates, including morphine.

Claude Bernard (1875) described what he termed "une tolerance relative" in discussing the effects of intravenous (IV) opium in dogs. He noted that dogs which had previously received the drug no longer struggled and cried after an injection (as a drug-naive animal would) even though they had recovered from the acute effects of the previous injection. In short, they appeared resistant to the depressant effects of the opium. Since Bernard there has been a long history of both description of the phenomenon of tolerance and theorizing about the mechanisms involved.

In general, prior research has used two main approaches. The first uses pharmacological methods to identify possible physiological substrates for tolerance. Mechanisms which have been studied include: the operation of immune mechanisms (cf. Cochin & Kornetsky, 1966; Feinberg & Cochin, 1968; Meisheri & Isom, 1978); changes in protein synthesis (cf. Huidobro, Huidobro-Toro & Way, 1976; Loh, Shen & Way, 1968; Smith, Karmin & Gavitt, 1967); changes in adrenal activity (cf. Gebhart & Mitchell, 1972a; Jacquet, 1978; Wei, 1973); and changes in neurotransmitters (cf. Gebhart & Mitchell, 1973; Kaufman, Koski & Peat, 1975; Way, Loh & Shen, 1968).

The second is a "molar" approach to the behavioral phenomena of tolerance, with little attention to possible physiological substrates. Much of the research of this type, particularly more recently, has focused on conditional aspects of tolerance. In its most extreme form, conditional tolerance is seen as the mechanism of all tolerance (Siegel, 1978a). Siegel showed that subjects receiving morphine in the presence of cues associated with morphine showed tolerance, whereas subjects receiving unexpected morphine showed no tolerance (Siegel, 1975). He has further supported this position by demonstrating the partial reinforcement effect, latent inhibition, and extinction, all phenomena of classical conditioning (Siegel, 1977, 1978b).

However, Sherman (1979) found no evidence for conditional tolerance. Indeed, a number of researchers have found evidence of conditional drug effects in responses to cues predictive of injection (Drawbaugh & Lal, 1974; Lal, Miksic, Drawbaugh, Numan & Smith, 1976; Lal, Miksic & Smith, 1976). In fact, Rush and co-workers, using a 10 mg/kg morphine UCS in dogs, found conditional salivation, similar to the drug UCR, while also finding conditional tachycardia, opposite to the drug UCR (Rush, Pearson & Lange, 1970).

A related set of findings has been grouped under the label of *behavioral tolerance*. This line of research arose out of hypotheses relating to physiological substrates of tolerance. It was noted in these studies that prior exposure to the test apparatus, while drugged, resulted in more tolerance than no such prior exposure (Adams, Yeh, Woods, & Mitchell, 1969; Kayan, Ferguson, & Mitchell, 1973; Kayan, Woods, & Mitchell, 1969). This phenomenon differs from conditional tolerance as described by Siegel, because exposure to the environment per se was not sufficient, although exposure even to some elements of the test apparatus was sufficient for the phenomenon (Gebhart & Mitchell, 1971, 1972b). Further, these studies clearly demonstrated that the phenomenon is an adjunct to what was considered "real" or unconditional tolerance.

Relatively little work has been done to describe the rate of development of unconditional tolerance, that is, the effect of different dosage schedules upon tolerance. It has long been known for instance, that large doses result in more profound tolerance than small doses. Schmidt and Livingston (1933), for example, demonstrated less tolerance in dogs treated with lower doses of morphine. The degree of tolerance was not quantified, however, and the dosage was confounded by a different original pretreatment dosage. As such, it is difficult to infer any orderly relationship between size of dose and magnitude of tolerance from these data. More recently, Miller and Cochin (1968) showed that mice, infused daily with either 8 mg/kg or 6 mg/kg of morphine developed different degrees of tolerance. In fact, by the fourth injection, the animals given the higher dosage showed less analgesia than the animals which received the lower dose. However, it is difficult to compare quantitatively the relative tolerance in each group, since the animals were tested with different dosages. In addition, the repeated exposure to testing with each injection also allowed for the development of behavioral tolerance as well.

Kayan, Ferguson, and Mitchell (1973) showed less tolerance in animals that received 11 daily 5 mg/kg doses of morphine than in animals receiving 11 daily

10 mg/kg doses. Again, however, animals were tested at their pretreatment dosage levels. In contrast, Huidobro, Huidobro-Toro and Way (1976) found single dose tolerance for mice which received more than 10 mg/kg, *none* for doses less than this. They also found no relationship between dose size and amount of tolerance for the higher dose. To date, there has been no clear parametric variation of dose size for repeated injections with a test at a standard dose to quantify the relationship between dose size and tolerance to morphine.

The effect of interdose interval (IDI) for repeated doses of morphine on tolerance development has been the subject of even less study. Virtually all of the work in this area has been done by Mitchell and co-workers and was mentioned only in passing in their work on behavioral tolerance. For instance, Kayan, Woods and Mitchell (1969) noted that animals tested on the Hot Plate only after their last injection showed tolerance if previous injections had been either daily or every three days, but not if injections were weekly. However, the three groups of animals received different total numbers of injections, making it impossible to make any direct comparisons. In a related study, Kayan and Mitchell (1972a, 1972b) found no tolerance in animals receiving five weekly doses and a great deal of tolerance in animals that received five daily doses. As in the literature on the relation between dose size and tolerance, the relation between IDI and tolerance is far from clear.

Not only is there a sparseness of data exploring the effects of dose size and IDI on morphine tolerance, there is also a near absence of theorizing in this area. In fact, the only comprehensive theory of the development of unconditional tolerance is the opponent-process theory of Solomon and Corbit (1974).

The opponent-process theory of motivation is a generalized formulation which is meant to describe the way in which affectively potent stimuli become less powerful in their effect with repeated exposures. This model suggests that any affective deviation (*a*-process) in an organism gives rise to an hedonically opposite and subtractive process (*b*-process), which tends to return it to affective neutrality. The *b*-process is postulated to grow unconditionally with repeated exercise of the *a*-process. The rate at which the opponent-process grows is thought to be a function of the relative potency of the stimulus (the magnitude of the *a*-process) and the time interval between exposures.

This model has been used in an analysis of the phenomena of drug tolerance and dependence (Solomon, 1977). Specifically, without postulating a particular underlying mechanism, Solomon proposes an orderly relationship between dose size (hedonic potency), IDI (frequency of exposure), and tolerance (*b*-process). These factors are proposed to affect both the rate of tolerance development and its asymptotic level.

The model has received good support in a number of different hedonic systems. Starr (1978) has demonstrated the utility of the model in the realm of imprinting in ducklings. Consistent with predictions by the model, the amount of distress calling by the ducklings (which is assumed to be an index of the *b*-process) is found to be a function of the frequency of presentations of the imprinting stimulus (the affectively potent stimulus). In particular, presentations spaced in time resulted in slower growth of the amount and a lower final level of distress calling when compared to more frequent presentations. In fact, if the presentations were infrequent enough, there was no growth of distress calling at all.

In a different motivational system, Rosellini and Burdette (1980) found similar results. Their study examined the utility of the model in a polydipsia paradigm (one in which regularly presented food pellets give rise to copious drinking of water). They took drinking to be an index of the b-process. As did Starr, they varied the interstimulus interval, and, in addition, they also varied the affective power of the stimulus by varying pellet size. As suggested by opponent-process theory, more frequent pellets resulted in greater and more quickly acquired polydipsia than less frequent pellets; similar effects were found for large, relative to small, pellets of food.

The model, however, has never been directly assessed in the realm of opiate tolerance. As noted, there are some suggestions in the literature that larger doses of morphine tend to result in more tolerance than do smaller doses, but this has not been explored parametrically. Likewise, the literature suggests that longer interdose intervals tend to result in less tolerance than shorter IDI, but, again, this has not been systematically explored.

PRESENT STUDY

As noted, the area of research that has received the most attention recently and generated the most controversy is that centered around conditional tolerance. A related area of slightly longer history is the body of research on behavioral tolerance. What must be noted is that, despite much research, we still have little understanding of these phenomena. We know empirically that certain manipulations result in behavioral tolerance, but there is no strong theoretical notion which has successfully identified new manipulations that might give rise to the phenomenon. Likewise, in the area of conditional tolerance, in certain situations, we see CRs which appear to be opposite to the drug UCRs; whereas, in other situations, we see CRs which resemble their respective UCRs. Again, we have no clear understanding of which situations should give rise to which type CR.

Rather than add further to the confusion in these areas, the present study proposes to take a more basic approach. Until we have a good knowledge of the nonassociative factors which affect tolerance, we stand little chance of fully understanding any associative overlays. Therefore, we take a parametric approach and examine effects of the dose size and interdose interval on tolerance, while attempting to minimize the impact of associative factors. In the process, we test some of the basic tenets of opponent-process theory.

As suggested above, opponent-process theory suggests there should be a clear and orderly effect of dose size on tolerance development. That is, larger doses should result in more tolerance than smaller doses. This theory also proposes an orderly relationship between IDI and tolerance, with shorter IDIs leading to more tolerance than larger IDIs.

The present study was designed to determine the degree of tolerance development at four dosage levels and four interdose intervals. All animals were tested at the same dose of morphine after six pretreatment dosages to allow for quantitative comparisons of the groups. They were retested one week later to determine the residual effects of the pretreatment. Morphine was delivered through a chronic indwelling jugular catheter which allowed for assessment of the immediate effect of morphine. It further served to eliminate any variance due to different rates of absorption of morphine from the subcutaneous tissue. The animals were maintained in a constant light environment to eliminate the effects of diurnal variation in the effects of morphine (Lutsch and Morris, 1972). The response to test doses of morphine was determined, using the Hot Plate Analgesiometer (Eddy and Leimbach, 1953). This design allowed for the testing of Solomon's model in the realm of morphine tolerance, and further allowed for quantification of the particular relationships.

Rather than the usual latency measure, the present study utilized a computed *analgesic index*. This measure essentially computes the change from the pre-drug baseline as a ratio of the maximum possible change (cf. Cox, Ginsburg, & Willis, 1975). A second computed measure also utilized was the area under the curve generated by plotting analgesic indices as a function of the time since drug administration (cf. Winter & Flataker, 1950). This measure includes both *peak* and *duration*.

SUBJECTS

The subjects were 175 male Charles River Wistar strain rats between 55 and 70 days old. Fourty-four subjects were dropped from the study prior to the first test day and an additional 20 were dropped from the study prior to the second test day. After an initial acclimation and implantation of the jugular catheter, the animals were maintained in constant light conditions with ad-lib food.

The subjects were divided into 18 groups, 16 experimental groups and 2 control groups. The 16 experimental groups received 6 pre-test infusions of morphine at one of four dosage levels (5 mg/kg., 10 mg/kg., 20 mg/kg., or 40 mg/kg.) and one of four IDIs (8 hr., 24 hr., 48 hr., 120 hr.). All subjects in the experimental groups were tested on each of two test days after an infusion of 20 mg/kg. of morphine. The drug naive control group (*Naive*) received no pre-test morphine but was tested following a 20 mg/kg. infusion of morphine. The no drug control group (*Saline*) received no pre-test morphine and was tested after an iso-volume saline infusion. The animals were run through the procedure in squads of 11 to 26 rats over the course of 14 months with members of the various groups in each squad. Table 15.1 provides details of the group sizes. After recovery from the catheter implantation, subjects received daily infusions of antibiotics. In addition, experimental subjects received infusions of morphine at the dosage level and schedule for their group. This continued for 6 morphine infusions for experimental subjects and 5 to 15 days for control subjects.

Tolerance was assessed on the first test day by measuring the analgesic effect of a test dose of morphine (except for the Saline group). A pre-drug baseline response latency on the Hot Plate was determined for each animal one half hour prior to the test infusion. Post-drug response latencies were determined 2 minutes, 20 minutes, 40 minutes and 60 minutes after infusion. A maximum latency of 60 seconds was allowed. The test procedure was repeated seven days later to establish residual tolerance differences.

Analgesic Indices were computed for each of the four post-drug response latencies as follows: Index = [(Test Latency − Baseline) / (60 − Baseline)]. This yielded four Indices (Index 1 through Index 4) for each subject on each test day. In addition, the area under the curve determined by plotting Analgesic Index as a function of time was computed: Area = (Index 1 + 2 × Index 2 + 2 × Index 3 + Index 4) × 10. This is essentially a time average of the Index which takes into account both peak and duration of analgesia.

ANOVAS OF FIRST TEST DAY DATA

A two-way (IDI × DOSE) ANOVA of each of the four post-drug Indices (Index 1 through Index 4) on the first test day revealed highly significant main effects for both DOSE and IDI ($p < .01$). As can be seen in Figure 15.1, higher pretreat-

TABLE 15.1
Group Sizes for Each of the Eighteen Groups
for Both First and Second Test Days
(Second Test Day Number in Parentheses)

		Dose Size (Mg/Kg)			
		5	10	20	40
I	8	8(7)	7(7)	7(4)	7(7)
D	24	9(6)	6(3)	8(8)	9(7)
I	48	8(6)	9(7)	7(7)	7(7)
	120	9(6)	6(4)	6(3)	3(3)

	Naive	Saline
	10(7)	5(5)

ment doses tend to result in smaller Indices (less analgesia). In addition, we can see that each successive Index tends to be smaller than the previous one. As Figure 15.2 demonstrates, IDI has an inverse effect, that is, the greater the IDI, the larger the Index tends to be (more analgesia). Again, each successive Index is smaller than the previous. In other words, higher pretreatment doses result in less analgesia, or more tolerance; larger pretreatment IDIs result in more analgesia, or less tolerance, and analgesia fades with the passage of time. The results of the ANOVAs of the Area data are in direct accordinace with previously presented forms of the data. That is, there is a significant main effect of DOSE on the area under the analgesic index curve ($p<.001$). There is also significant main effect for the IDI Index ($p<.001$).

As can be seen in Figure 15.3, dose size has an inverse effect upon Analgesic Index Area. Contrarily, pretreatment IDI has a direct effect upon Analgesic Index Area (Figure 15.4).

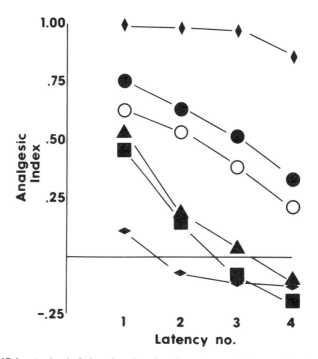

FIG. 15.1.   Analgesic Index plotted against time since receiving morphine by pre-treatment dosage level. Filled circles represent a mean for all animals pre-treated with 5 mg/kg; open circles, 10 mg/kg; triangles, 20 mg/kg; squares, 40 mg/kg. Vertical diamonds represent the naive control group, horizontal diamonds represent the saline control group.

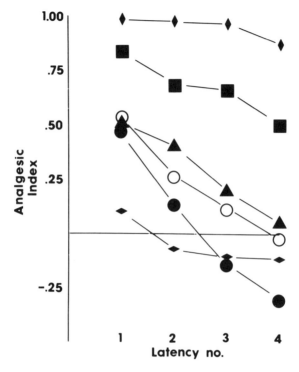

FIG. 15.2.   Analgesic Index plotted against time since receiving morphine by
pre-treatment IDI. Squares represent a mean for all animals that received their pre-
treatment dose on a 120 hr. IDI; triangles, 48 hr.; open circles, 24 hr.; filled
circles, 8 hr. Vertical Diamonds represent the naive control group, horizontal
diamonds represent the saline control group.

ANOVAS OF SECOND TEST DAY DATA

As with the data from the first test day, the second test day data were subjected to
a two-way random effects analysis of variance. There were no significant effects
for pretreatment Dose or IDI on any of the post injection tests, or on the overall
weighted average (Area).

INDIVIDUAL GROUP COMPARISONS

Comparisons between Experimental groups and Control groups of data from the
first test day reveal significant tolerance ($p < .05$) for all groups (compared to
Naive group animals), except for the groups which received either 5 mg/kg. or
10 mg/kg. at 120 hr. IDIs. Animals which received relatively higher pretest

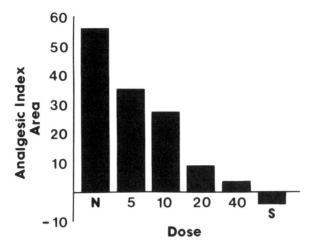

FIG. 15.3.   Analgesic Index as a function of pre-treatment dosage level, for each
of the four dosage levels: 5 mg/kg (5), 10 mg/kg (10), 20 mg/kg (20), 40 mg/kg
(40); and the two control groups: naive (N) and saline (S).

dosage levels at short IDIs (8 hr. IDI, all dosage levels; 24 hr. IDI, 20 or 40
mg/kg.) did not show any appreciable overall analgesic effect for the test infusion when compared to the Saline group which received no morphine $(p > .1)$.
When comparing data for only the first post drug test, however, all groups
showed significant analgesia, $(p < .05)$ when compared to Saline animals, except
those which had received 40 mg/kg. at either 8 or 24 hour intervals. There also
was significant hyperalgesia 40 and 60 minutes after infusion for subjects in the 8
hr. IDI 40 mg/kg. group, when compared to the Saline group.

REGRESSIONS

In light of the highly significant effects of pretreatment dose and IDI on the first
test day morphine effect, further investigation of the nature of this relationship
was conducted. Multiple linear regressions were performed to determine to what
extent these two independent variables and a variety of their transforms could
account for test day analgesia.

   Previous pilot work suggested that the most likely independent variables for
these analyses included IDI, inverse IDI, IDI^2, DOSE and log DOSE. Thus,
multiple linear regressions, with each of the four Analgesic Indices and the
weighted average, were performed, using combinations of these independent
variables and their transforms. Regressions utilizing log DOSE did consistently
better than corresponding analyses using DOSE. Analyses using IDI^2 did slightly
better than analyses using IDI for Index 1 data. However, for subsequent Indices

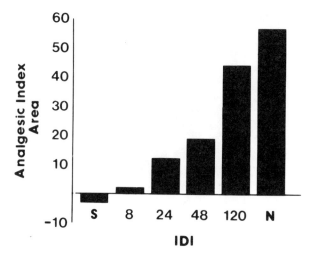

FIG. 15.4. Analgesic Index as a function of pre-treatment dosage schedule, for each of the four IDIs: 8 hr. (8), 24 hr. (24), 48 hr. (48), 120 hr. (120); and the two control groups: naive (N) and saline (S).

and Area data, IDI did somewhat better than IDI^2. All regressions were significant at the .001 level. Table 15.2 presents the individual standardized partial coefficients for the analyses. Note that for earlier Analgesic Indices (Index 1 and 2), DOSE makes a greater contribution, whereas for later indices (Index 4), IDI makes a greater contribution.

TABLE 15.2
Standardized Partial Coefficients

	Log Dose-IDI	Log Dose-IDI^2
Index 1		
Dose	-.309	-.306
IDI	.271	.282
Index 2		
Dose	-.372	-.373
IDI	.310	.289
Index 3		
Dose	-.414	-.415
IDI	.406	.385
Index 4		
Dose	-.349	-.351
IDI	.434	.408
Area		
Dose	-.416	-.416
IDI	.401	.381

DISCUSSION

The first point which is clear from the data in this study is that larger pretest doses of morphine result in shorter latencies following a standard test dose, and shorter pretest interdose intervals also result in shorter latencies. Since all animals had the same pretest Hot Plate experience, we can assume that latencies, which are directly related to analgesia, are inversely related to tolerance. In other words, the data suggest that larger doses of morphine result in more tolerance, and shorter IDIs result in more tolerance. This conclusion is suggested, whether we look at individual analgesic indices (which correct for both initial latency and maximum latency) or area measures, which include both amount and duration of analgesia.

The data also demonstrate that subjects that had previously received relatively high doses with relatively short intervals between doses showed virtually complete tolerance. That is, they showed no analgesic benefit from the test infusion of morphine. Furthermore, subjects that received the highest pretreatment dose were significantly more responsive to pain 40 minutes after the test infusion than animals receiving no morphine, suggesting that perhaps they might have been "better off" not receiving the morphine on the test day. Finally, the individual comparisons show that there is virtually no tolerance development when small doses are spaced far apart.

The conclusions are consistent with assumptions which have been present in the literature for some time. However, the clear and orderly relationship between morphine tolerance on the one hand, and drug dose size and interdose interval on the other has not previously been parametrically demonstrated. These findings are quite congenial to Solomon and Corbit's opponent-process model. According to the model, more frequent or more vigorous exercising of the morphine hedonic system (a-process) should result in a more powerful opponent (b-process) to that system (Solomon and Corbit, 1974). This is in contrast to what might be expected from a conditional tolerance model, which would suggest (consistent with the principles of Pavlovian conditioning) that larger time spans between drug administration should result in better learning and, thus, more tolerance (cf. Schull, 1979).

Also consistent with the opponent-process model is the fact that frequent dosing with a 40 mg/kg. dose can lead to hyperalgesia when tested with a 20 mg/kg. dose. That is, the b-process developed in response to a previous 40 mg/kg. dose will be larger than the a-process of the 20 mg/kg. test dose. Thus, when the "affective algebra" postulated by the model is performed, the result is a relative B-State (hyperalgesia).

The present study also goes some way in specifying the particular relationship between size and frequency of a-process stimulation and the resultant b-process in the realm of morphine tolerance. In particular, it would appear that there is a log-linear relationship between dose and tolerance. This corresponds to the finding that tolerance can be represented as a linear (parallel) shift in the log-dose-response curve (Fernandes, Kluwe, & Coper, 1977a, 1977b). On the other hand, the relationship between IDI and tolerance is essentially inverse linear, at least for most of the present range of values. However, this cannot be a full representation of the relationship as, even with the present values, there is virtually no tolerance at the largest IDI, suggesting that further increase in the IDI would have a minimal effect upon tolerance. Indeed, this would be consistent with the notion of *critical decay duration* developed by Starr (1978) to denote a critical inter-stimulus-interval, beyond which the *b*-process will not develop. The present data suggest that the critical decay duration will be a function of the size of the *a*-process (dose size). This is consistent with the findings of Starr (1978) and Rosellini and Burdette (1980).

In examining the relative contributions of DOSE and IDI to tolerance (Standardized Partial Coefficients, Table 15.2) it can be seen that whereas DOSE accounts for more of the Index 1 through Index 3 variance, IDI accounts for more of the variance for Index 4. This might suggest two different mechanisms involved in the growth of tolerance. One relatively quick to recruit, seems to peak at about 40 minutes (Index 3) and is more affected by pretreatment dose size. The other, slower to recruit, seems to grow throughout the course of the full hour examined in the present study, and is more affected by interdose interval than by the dose size.

This represents a divergence from opponent-process theory, which generally sees both intensity and frequency of stimulation as important factors in the development of the *b*-process. It is generally (if silently) assumed that size of the *b*-process is a *unitary* concept, encompassing both *peak* and *duration* of the *b*-process. The present data suggest that different mechanisms may underly these two aspects of the *b*-process. In particular, a tentative conclusion would be that the frequency of stimulation has a greater impact on duration of the *b*-process, whereas the intensity of the stimulation has its greatest effect on the peak of the *b*-process. Further investigation will be important to further delineate this issue.

ACKNOWLEDGMENT

The present study is based upon the doctoral dissertation of the author. The research was conducted at the University of Pennsylvania and was supported by Grant #MH 29187 from NIMH to Richard L. Solomon.

REFERENCES

Adams, W. J., Yeh, S. Y., Woods, L. A., & Mitchell, C. L. (1969). Drug test interaction as a factor in the development of tolerance to the analgesic effect of morphine. *Journal of Pharmacology and Experimental Therapeutics, 168,* 251–257.

Bernard, C. (1933). *Lecons sur les anesthesiques* et sur l'asphixie. (p. 201–204.) (Cited by: Schmidt, C. F., & Livingston, A. E.) Paris: Baillière, (Original work published 1875)

Cochin, J., & Kornetsky, C. (1966). Factors in the blood of morphine-tolerant animals that attenuate or enhance effects of morphine in non-tolerant animals. *Research Publications of the Association of Nervous and Mental Disease, XLVI,* 268–279.

Cox, B. M., Ginsburg, M., & Willis, J. (1975). The offset of morphine tolerance in rats and mice. *British Journal of Pharmacology, 53,* 383–391.

Drawbaugh, R., & Lal, H. (1974). Reversal by narcotic antagonist of a narcotic action elicited by a conditional stimulus. *Nature, 247,* 65–67.

Eddy, N. B., & Leimbach, D. (1953). Synthetic analgesics. II. Dithienylbutenyl- and dithienylbutylamides. *Journal of Pharmacology, 107,* 385–393.

Feinberg, M. P., & Cochin, J. (1968). Effect of cyclophosphamide (Cytoxan) on tolerance to morphine. *Pharmacologist, 10,* 188. (Abstract #191)

Fernandes, M., Kluwe, S., & Coper, H. (1977a). The development of tolerance to morphine in the rat. *Psychopharmacology, 54,* 197–201.

Fernandes, M., Kluwe, S., & Coper, H. (1977b). Quantitative assessment of tolerance and dependence on morphine in mice. *Naunyn Schmiederbergs Archives Pharmacology, 297,* 53–60.

Gebhart, G. F., & Mitchell, C. L. (1971). Further studies on the development of tolerance to the analgesic effect of morphine: The role played by the cylinder in the hot plate testing procedure. *Archives Internationales de Pharmacodynamie et de Therapie, 191,* 96–103.

Gebhart, G. F., & Mitchell, C. L. (1972a). The effect of adrenalectomy on morphine analgesia and tolerance development in rats. *European Journal of Pharmacology, 18,* 37–42.

Gebhart, G. F., & Mitchell, C. L. (1972b). The relative contributions of the testing cylinder and the heated plate in the hot plate procedures to the development of tolerance to morphine in rats. *European Journal of Pharmacology, 18,* 56–62.

Gebhart, G. F., & Mitchell, C. L. (1973). Strain differences in the analgesic response to morphine as measured on the hot plate. *Archives Internationale de Pharmacodynamie et de Therapie, 201,* 128–140.

Huidobro, F., Huidobro-Toro, J. P., & Way, L. E. (1976). Studies on toilerance development to single doses of morphine. *Journal of Pharmacology and Experimental Therapeutics, 198,* 318–329.

Jacquet, Y. F. (1978). Opiate effects after adrenocorticotropin and beta-endorphin injection in the periaqueductal gray matter of rats. *Science, 201,* 1032–1034.

Kalant, H., LeBlanc, A. E., & Gibbins, R. J. (1971). Tolerance to and dependence on some non-opiate psychotropic drugs. *Pharmacology Review, 23,* 135–191.

Kaufman, J. J., Koski, W. S., & Peat, K. (1975). A systems and control theory approach to dynamic neurotransmitter balance in narcotic addiction and narcotic antagonism. *Life Sciences, 17,* 83–84.

Kayan, S., Ferguson, R. K., & Mitchell, C. L. (1973). An investigation of pharmacologic and behavioral tolerance to morphine in rats. *Journal of Pharmacology and Experimental Therapeutics, 185,* 300–306.

Kayan, S., & Mitchell, C. L. (1972a). The role of dose-interval on the development of tolerance to morphine. *Archives Internationales de Pharmacodynamie et de Therapie, 198,* 238–241.

Kayan, S., & Mitchell, C. L. (1972b). Studies on tolerance development to morphine: effect of the dose-interval on the development of single dose tolerance. *Archives Internationales de Pharmacodynamie et de Therapie, 199,* 407–414.

Kayan, S., Woods, L. A., & Mitchell, C. L. (1969). Experience as a factor in the development of tolerance to the analgesic effect of morphine. *European Journal of Pharmacology, 6,* 333–339.

Lal, H., Miksic, S., Drawbaugh, R., Numan, R., & Smith, N. (1976). Alleviation of narcotic withdrawal syndrome by conditional stimuli. *Pavlovian Journal of Biological Science, 11,* 251–261.

Lal, H., Miksic, S., & Smith, N. (1976). Naloxone antagonism of conditioned hyperthermia: evidence for release of an endogenous opioid. *Life Sciences, 18,* 971–975.

Loh, H. H., Shen, F., & Way, E. L. (1968). Effects of cycloheximide on the development of morphine tolerance and physical dependence. *Pharmacologist, 10,* 188. (Abstract #192)

Lutsch, E. F., & Morris, R. W. (1972). Effect of constant lighting on the morpine susceptibility rhythm. *Experientia, 28,* 673–674.

Meisheri, K. D., & Isom, G. E. (1978). Influence of immune stimulation and suppression on morphine physical dependence and tolerance. *Research Communications in Chemical Pathology and Pharmacology, 19,* 85–99.

Miller, J. M., & Cochin, J. (1968). Dose-related aspects of tolerance to the analgesic effect of chronically administered morphine sulfate (MS) in mice. *Pharmacologist, 10,* 189. (Abstract #197)

Rosellini, R. A., & Burdette, D. R. (1980). Meal size and intermeal interval both regulate schedule-induced drinking in the rat. *Animal Learning and Behavior, 8,* 647–652.

Rush, M. L., Pearson, L., & Lang, W. J. (1970). Conditional autonomic responses induced in dogs by atropine and morphine. *European Journal of Pharmacology, 11,* 22–28.

Schmidt, C. F., & Livingston, A. E. (1933). The relation of dosage to the development of tolerance to morphine in dogs. *Journal of Pharmacology and Experimental Therapeutics, 47,* 443–471.

Schull, J. (1979). A conditional opponent theory of Pavlovian conditioning and habituation. In J. H. Bower (ed). *The Psychology of Learning and Motivation* (pp. 57–90). New York: Academic Press.

Sherman, J. E. (1979). The effects of conditioning and novelty on the rat's analgesic and pyretic responses to morphine. *Learning and Motivation, 10,* 383–418.

Siegel, S. (1975). Evidence from rats that morphine tolerance is a learned response. *Journal of Comparative and Physiological Psychology, 89,* 498–506.

Siegel, S. (1977). Morphine tolerance acquisition as an associative process. *Journal of Experimental Psychology [Animal Behavior Processes], 3,* 1–13.

Siegel, S. (1978a). Pavlovian conditioning analysis of morphine tolerance. *National Institute of Drug Abuse Research Monograph Series, 18,* 27–53.

Siegel, S. (1978b). Tolerance to the hyperthermic effect of morphine in the rat is a learned response. *Journal of Comparative and Physiological Psychology, 92,* 1137–1149.

Smith, A. M., Karmin, M., & Gavitt, J. (1967). Tolerance to the lenticular effects of opiate. *Journal of Pharmacology and Experimental Therapeutics, 156,* 85–91.

Solomon, R. L. (1977). An opponent-process theory of acquired motivation: IV. The affective dynamics of addiction. In: J. D. Maser and M. E. P. Seligman (eds), *Psychopathology: Experimental Models* (pp. 66–103). San Francisco: Freeman.

Solomon, R. L., & Corbit, J. D. (1974). An opponent-process theory of motivation: I. Temporal dynamics of affect. *Psychological Review, 81,* 119–145.

Starr, M. (1978). An opponent-process theory of motivation: VI. Time and intensity variables in the development of separation induced distress calling in ducklings. *Journal of Experimental Psychology: Animal Behavior Processes, 4,* 338–355.

Way, E. L., Loh, H. H., & Shen, F. (1968). Morphine tolerance, physical dependence, and synthesis of brain 5-hydroxytryptamine. *Science, 162,* 1290–1292.

Wei, E. (1973). Morphine analgesia, tolerance and physical dependence in the adrenalectomized rat. *British Journal of Pharmacology, 47,* 693–699.

Winter, C. A., & Flataker, L. (1950). Studies on Heptazone (6-Morphino-4,4-Diphenyl-3-Heptanone Hydrochloride) in comparison with other analgesic drugs. *Journal of Pharmacology and Experimental Therapeutics, 98,* 305–317.

16 An Application of Opponent-Process Theory to Adjunctive Behavior

Robert A. Rosellini
State University of New York at Albany

Historically, a dominant concern of students of learning and conditioning has been investigation of the effects of hedonically valued stimuli on antecedent behavior or on the response-evoking properties of other stimuli predictive of their occurrence. In contrast to this, Solomon and Corbit (1974) have proposed a general theory of acquired motivation, which, in large part, emphasizes the importance of the aftereffects of exposure to hedonically valued stimuli. Briefly, the theory proposes that such exposure induces an affective reaction that will quickly rise to a peak, stabilize, and subsequently return to baseline at or shortly after termination of the stimulus. The onset of this primary affective process, termed the *A-process,* is held to trigger an opponent reaction of opposite hedonic sign. This aftereffect, or B-process, can be seen in its pure form only following stimulus termination. It is held to have at least five unique properties: (a) a slow rise-time relative to the A-process, (b) a relatively long decay time, (c) a weakening with disuse, (d) strengthening as a function of repeated exposure to the inducing stimulus, and (e) a reinforcement function.

With these relatively few assumptions, the theory appears capable of encompassing a wide variety of behavioral phenomena, ranging from the formation of social attachment in ducks (Hoffman & Solomon, 1974) and monkeys (Mineka & Suomi, 1978) to drug addiction in humans (Solomon, 1980). Impressive empirical support has also been obtained from investigations employing the imprinting paradigm (Starr, 1978), and the defensive Pavlovian conditioning paradigm (Overmier, Payne, Brackbill, Linder, & Lawry, 1979).

In our laboratory, we have attempted to extend the opponent-process theory to the area of adjunctive behavior. A great deal of experimental work has been conducted in this area since Falk's (1961) report of excessive water consumption in animals exposed to periodic schedules of food delivery. A general review of this literature points out a number of variables known to be important in the development and maintenance of this class of behaviors. Generally, these are variables which would be expected to be important if an opponent-process approach is applied to these behaviors. Before reviewing our experimental work on this issue, we will briefly outline four major reasons why we view the theory as relevant to adjunctive behavior.

The first reason is that periodic delivery of food to hungry animals induces a wide variety of behaviors which depend on the species used and the environmental stimuli available in the experimental context. For example, if a hungry rat is exposed to intermittent delivery of small amounts of food, excessive post-pellet drinking will occur if water is available (Falk, 1977)—schedule-induced polydipsia. A variety of other behaviors have also been observed when appropriate environmental supports are made available. In addition to drinking, attack (Cohen & Looney, 1973; Flory, 1969), wheel running (Levitsky & Collier, 1968), and escape (Brown & Flory, 1972) have all been observed. This variety of behaviors strongly suggests that they are expressions of an underlying motivational state. Indeed, motivational accounts of these behaviors have already been proposed (e.g., Killeen, 1975; Staddon, 1977; Thomka & Rosellini, 1976). The well documented post-pellet nature of adjunctive behaviors additionally suggests that any underlying motivational state must be one which is triggered by pellet consumption. This, of course, is the type of motivational system which is the particular focus of opponent-process theory.

The second reason is that schedule-induced behaviors, such as polydipsia and attack, begin shortly after pellet consumption, quickly rise to a maximal level, and gradually decrease during the interpellet interval (Rosellini & Burdette, 1980; Staddon & Ayers, 1975). The interpellet time course of these behaviors bears a striking resemblance to the theoretically prescribed time course of the opponent process, which is presumably triggered by ingestion of the food. It should be noted, however, that the exact temporal distribution of these behaviors, particularly that of wheel running, can vary somewhat when the animal has the opportunity to engage in a variety of other behaviors (e.g., Penney & Schull, 1977; Staddon & Ayers, 1975).

The third reason is that experimental manipulations, which should theoretically affect the intensity of the A-, and consequently the B-process, are known to regulate the strength of adjunctive behaviors. For example, increasing the amount of food the animal receives at each exposure increases the level of polydipsia (Flory, 1971; Rosellini & Burdette, 1980). Similarly, increasing the food deprivation level of the animal also increases the level of polydipsia (Freed & Hymowitz, 1972; Roper & Nieto, 1979).

The fourth reason is that if the interpellet interval is sufficiently long (240–300 sec), polydipsia is not observed (Falk, 1969). Although problematic for most views of adjunctive behavior, this observation is in keeping with the assumption that the B-process is strengthened only by repeated elicitations which occur within some critical time period (Solomon, 1980; Starr, 1978). This has been termed the *critical decay duration*.

These four reasons have led us to consider the possibility that adjunctive behavior is an index of an underlying opponent process triggered by food consumption. While other theories may be capable of accounting for some of the above observations, they usually do so in a piecemeal fashion. Opponent-process theory, however, is unique in its ability to integrate these facts. Although the above facts are consistent with the theory, it accounts for them in a post-hoc manner. However, the theory does specify a number of variables, such as reinforcer quality and quantity, and relationships among these variables, which should be important for the development of the B-process. Thus, if the theory is to provide a viable account of schedule-induced behaviors, manipulation of these variables and their relationships should predictably affect the development and maintenance of these behaviors. The general focus of our research has been to test predictions of the opponent process theory employing the schedule-induced polydipsia paradigm. We will first review these experiments, and then go on to discuss data which appear problematic for an opponent-process approach.

In an early study, Burdette and I investigated the possibility, suggested by the theory (Solomon, 1980), that the intensity of the inducing stimulus interacts with the temporal interval of stimulus presentation in controlling the development of the opponent process. As mentioned above, schedule-induced polydipsia does not develop if the interpellet interval exceeds 240 sec., which is in agreement with the proposal of a critical decay duration. Opponent-process theory suggests that the failure to develop the behavior under these conditions stems from the fact that the interpellet interval exceeds the critical decay duration value, thereby precluding the growth of the B-process. In addition, it suggests that the value of the critical decay duration should be a function of the intensity of the inducing stimulus. Thus, a particular inducing stimulus may fail to promote the development of the B-process at a certain interstimulus interval value, but if its intensity were increased, then the opponent process may grow at this interval value.

To test this prediction, we conducted a study in which we investigated the relationship between the interpellet interval length and pellet magnitude (Rosellini & Burdette, 1980, Experiment 2). This consisted of a 3 × 3 factorial design where separate groups of rats were exposed to one of three pellet magnitudes (Small = 45 mg, Medium = 190 mg, Large = 500 mg) presented on one of three Fixed Time schedule values (4, 8, & 12 min). The study was conducted in 14 sessions with each session consisting of 10 pellet deliveries of the appropriate size and on the appropriate schedule. Figure 16.1 shows the mean amount of water consumed on the final four sessions as a function of pellet magnitude and interpellet interval. As can be seen, there is a general tendency for larger pellets to induce more drinking. In addition, with the exception of the Large magnitude groups, there appears to be a linear effect of interpellet interval on the amount of

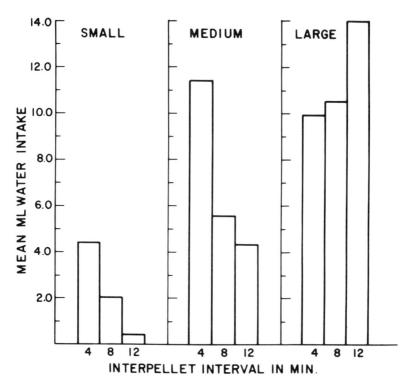

FIG. 16.1. Mean asymptotic water intake (ml) as a function of pellet quantity (Small = 45 mg, Medium = 190 mg, Large = 500 mg) and interpellet interval length (4, 8, and 12 min.). (Rosselini & Burdette, 1980)

water intake. More importantly, the expected relationship between pellet magnitude and interpellet interval is clearly observed. The left hand panel of the figure shows that small pellets (45 mg) support relatively little drinking at any of the intervals used, although there is the tendency even here for lengthening of the interval to have a decremental effect on consumption. The middle panel shows that the medium pellets (190 mg) do support polydipsic levels of intake at the shortest interval with decreases in drinking as the interval is increased. The large pellets (500 mg) supported drinking at each of the intervals employed. These data clearly demonstrate that the development and maintenance of schedule-induced polydipsia is not limited by the absolute value of the schedule employed but is instead controlled by this variable and the magnitude of the pellet employed. This is consistent with the expectation from opponent-process theory that intensity of the inducing stimulus and the critical decay duration should interact.

In the next two studies, we examined the theory's prediction concerning the effect of US quality on the development of polydipsia (Rosellini & Lashley, 1982). Here the theory predicts that if polydipsia can indeed be taken as an index of the underlying B-process, then the amount observed should be a function of the quality of the inducing stimulus, because this should affect the intensity of the primary process and, hence, that of the opponent process.

In the first of these studies, we obtained a preference rating from rats for three different types of pellets (formula A, peanut flavor, and quinine-flavored pellets). This was done by presenting each animal with a choice between two of the three types of pellets on six preference tests, each of which consisted of simultaneous access to the pellets for 10 min and measuring the amount of each type of pellet consumed. In general, animals preferred formula A to the peanut-flavored, and the peanut- to the quinine-flavored pellets. Animals were then assigned to one of three groups which were equated on their percent preference for the different pellets. Subsequently, each group received polydipsia training with either the preferred formula A pellets, the less preferred peanut-flavored pellets, or the least preferred quinine-flavored pellet. Training consisted of 19 sessions during which 30 pellets were delivered on a Fixed Time 120-sec schedule. During subsequent sessions, all animals received Formula A pellets. Figure 16.2 shows the mean amount of water consumed by each of the three groups during

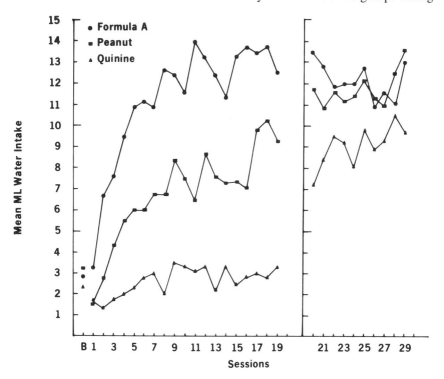

FIG. 16.2. Mean water intake (ml) per session for the Formula A, peanut, and quinine groups. The left hand panel shows the behavior during the acquisition phase of the study. The right hand panel shows the drinking during the second phase when all groups received the most preferred (Formula A) pellet. B represents intakes during a baseline condition. (Rosellini & Lashley, 1982)

the experiment. As can be seen in the left hand panel, animals receiving the most preferred formula A pellets showed the most rapid increment and the highest asymptotic level of drinking. Those receiving the next most preferred pellet (peanut) showed somewhat slower development and a lower asymptotic level of drinking. The group receiving the least preferred quinine pellets showed the slowest development and lowest asymptotic drinking. Indeed, this group failed to show polydipsic levels of intake as indicated by their failure to demonstrate a two-fold increase in drinking over baseline levels, which is the accepted criterion for polydipsia (Flory, 1971). The right hand panel of the figure further demonstrates that the group differences in asymptotic levels are due to the quality of the pellets, because all groups develop polydipsia when they were given the most preferred formula A pellets (Session 21–30).

This relationship between pellet quality and amount of polydipsia was replicated and extended in an additional experiment, in which sucrose pellets were employed in place of the peanut flavored pellets. Preference tests showed that the animals preferred these sucrose pellets to the formula A and, again, preferred the formula A to the quinine-flavored pellets. On the basis of this preference ranking, we would expect the sucrose pellets to generate the highest levels of polydipsia, the formula A pellets the next most, and the quinine-flavored pellets the least. This, indeed, was found to be the case, as demonstrated by water intake levels across sessions for the three groups shown in Figure 16.3.

The results of these three studies are consistent with the predictions of opponent-process theory. The theory states that the intensity of the A- and consequent B-process is a function of the magnitude and quality of the inducing stimulus: in the present case, the food pellet. Thus, if schedule-induced polydipsia is to be considered an index of the underlying opponent process, then it must also be sensitive to manipulations of these variables. In agreement with this, we find that the amount of water consumed in schedule-induced polydipsia is a function of pellet quality, as demonstrated in the preceding two studies, and pellet quantity, as demonstrated in the first experiment.

In addition to specifying these direct relationships, the theory further suggests that the above two variables affect the behavior through the same basic underlying mechanism—modulation of the intensity of the opponent process elicited by pellet consumption. On this basis, it might be expected that these two independent variables may be additive in their control of the intensity of the A- and consequent B-process. Thus, the theory suggests that the amount of water consumed in the schedule-induced polydipsia situation should be simultaneously influenced by both pellet quality and quantity. This possibility was investigated in a simple experiment which factorially manipulated these two variables and measured their effect on level of water consumption (Rosellini & Lashley, 1982, Experiment 2). One group of animals received polydipsia training with large-preferred pellets (190 mg, formula A); a second group with large-nonpreferred pellets (190 mg, quinine-flavored); a third with small-preferred pellets (45 mg,

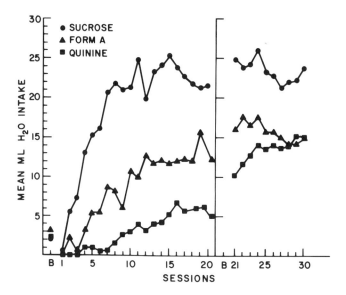

FIG. 16.3.   Mean water intake (ml) per session for the sucrose, Formula A, and quinine groups. The left hand panel shows the behavior during the acquisition phase of the study. The right hand panel shows the drinking during the second phase when all groups received the medium preference (Formula A) pellet. B represents intakes during a baseline condition.

formula A); and a fourth with small-nonpreferred pellets (45 mg, quinine-flavored pellets). Training was conducted for 19 sessions, each of which consisted of 20 pellet presentations on an FT 180-sec schedule.

As can be seen in the top panel of Figure 16.4, the small-preferred pellets were capable of inducing polydipsia, whereas the small-nonpreferred pellets did not. The bottom panel shows that large pellets generally resulted in polydipsic intakes and supported considerably higher levels of drinking than the small pellets. In addition, even with the large pellets, the preferred pellets resulted in more rapid acquisition and higher levels of drinking than the nonpreferred pellets. These results are consistent with opponent-process theory, because the development and maintenance of schedule-induced polydipsia are controlled by both pellet quality and quantity, and these two variables interact in their control of the behavior.

In summary, the outcomes of the above experiments are consistent with the predictions of the theory and are thus supportive of an account of schedule-induced behavior in opponent process terms. As expected by the theory: (a) Both the development and the asymptotic level of schedule-induced polydipsia are controlled by pellet quantity and quality; (b) these two variables appear to interact in their control; and (c) the interpellet interval length and pellet quantity interact to control the development of this behavior.

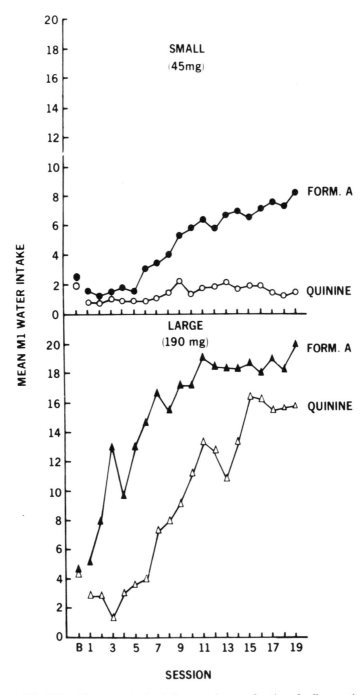

FIG. 16.4. Mean water intake (ml) per session as a function of pellet quantity (Small and Large) and pellet quality (Form A - prefered, Quinine - nonprefered). B represents intakes during a baseline condition. (Rosellini & Lashley, 1982)

Thus far, we have emphasized the congruence of empirical observations and predictions from the theory. This appears quite impressive, particularly in view of the fact that in this case the theory is being transposed to a behavioral realm far removed from that which provided the original data base for the formulation of the theory. Historically, however, it has been the case that as more data are collected to test predictions from a theory, the more data appear which are problematic for the theory. Opponent-process theory is no exception to this. For example, as pointed out above, an opponent-process view of schedule-induced polydipsia demands that the behavior induced by consumption of a pellet be observed to peak shortly after consumption of the pellet. We, like others (e.g., Staddon, 1977), have generally found this to be the case. However, close inspection of the temporal pattern of drinking during the interpellet interval shows that its peak level is shifted away from the time of pellet delivery as a function of increasing interval length (Rosellini & Burdette, 1980, Experiment 1). This observation, although by no means applicable to all adjunctive behaviors (see Cohen et al., this volume), appears problematic for the opponent-process theory as presently formulated. These data suggest that the distribution of drinking within the interpellet interval may serve a timing function. Although this does not contradict the theory, it is not anticipated by it.

Data which may ultimately prove to be of more central difficulty for the theory as applied to adjunctive behavior have recently emerged from another line of experimentation. This research has focused on the theory's assumption that the opponent-process grows simply as a function of repeated exposure to the A-process inducing stimulus (Solomon & Corbit, 1974), provided each exposure occurs within some critical time period (i.e., *critical decay duration*). This growth is held to result solely from nonassociative factors. It should be noted that the experiments reported above are not capable of assessing the validity of this assumption. All of our experiments, and indeed, the majority of others in this general area, have employed procedures in which the inducing stimulus is presented on a temporally regular schedule, typically *Fixed Time*. Such regularity introduces the possibility of temporal conditioning (Pavlov, 1927), thus making it impossible to determine whether the development of adjunctive behavior is due to associative factors arising from temporal conditioning, or to nonassociative factors as suggested by opponent-process theory. Parenthetically, it should be noted that the temporal regularity inherent in Fixed Time schedules is not a necessary condition for the development of polydipsia, since it can be obtained on *Variable Interval* schedules (e.g., King & Schaeffer, 1973). However, these demonstrations do not directly address this issue. Although temporal prediction is degraded on Variable schedules compared to Fixed schedules, it nevertheless exists since these Variable schedules typically employ a minimum interpellet interval often as long as 10 sec. Thus, the occurrence of one pellet can come to signal the unavailability of the next pellet for this minimum interval.

A more direct test of the importance of associative and nonassociative factors in the development of schedule-induced polydipsia can be made by determining whether this behavior will emerge under conditions where the possibility of temporal prediction, particularly in terms of the minimum interpellet interval, is removed. This can be accomplished by delivering pellets on a Random schedule, where delivery of one pellet should not predict the temporal occurrence of subsequent pellets, thereby removing the possibility of temporal conditioning. Thus, if temporal prediction is a necessary component for the development of adjunctive behavior, then these behaviors should not develop under Random schedules. Two experiments available in the literature on this issue (Millenson, Allen, & Pinker, 1977; Keehn & Burton, 1978) show that delivery of food on a *Random Interval* schedule decreases the amount of drinking observed in the schedule-induced polydipsia paradigm. Although these studies indicate that temporal factors are important in polydipsia and thus suggest that temporal conditioning may place a role in this phenomenon, their results cannot be unambiguously interpreted for the present purpose. Both studies employed Random Interval schedules. This leaves open the possibility that the requirement of the instrumental response, inherent in such a schedule, may have competed with the full expression of drinking. Thus, although suggestive of an involvement of associative factors, they cannot be taken as conclusive concerning their necessity (see also, Yoburn, Cohen, & Campagnoni, 1981).

In order to more unambiguously assess the importance of associative factors in this regard, we have examined the development of schedule-induced polydipsia on Random Time schedules. Because pellet deliveries on such a schedule occur solely on the basis of time, without an instrumental response requirement, they should more clearly point out the importance of temporal conditioning on the development of this behavior. In this study (Lashley & Rosellini, 1980), we factorially manipulated the possibility of temporal conditioning by delivering pellets on either a Fixed Time 120-sec or Random Time 120-sec schedule. To further test the importance of associative factors, we also manipulated the presence of a specific external signal for pellet delivery. This consisted of providing one-half the animals in each of the two schedule conditions with a 5-sec absence of a background white noise stimulus as a signal for the delivery of the pellet. For the other half of the animals, the white noise was present throughout the experimental session, and the delivery of the pellet was unsignalled. The design of the study was a 2 × 2 factorial with Schedule (FT or RT) and Signal (Signaled or Unsignalled) as the two factors. Thus, the experiment consisted of four groups (i.e., FT-Signal, FT-No Signal, RT-Signal, and RT-No Signal), each of which received 28 sessions of 30 pellets deliveries. Figure 16.5 shows the amount of water consumed for each animal in each of the groups. As can be seen, the majority of animals in the RT-No Signal condition failed to develop polydipsia, whereas the majority of those in the other three conditions show the typical development and high asymptotic levels of water intake as a function of sessions. Animals for whom pellet delivery was signalled either by an external stimulus—white noise termination—(Group RT-Signal), by the temporal cues arising from the regularity of the schedule (Group FT-No Signal), or by both temporal and

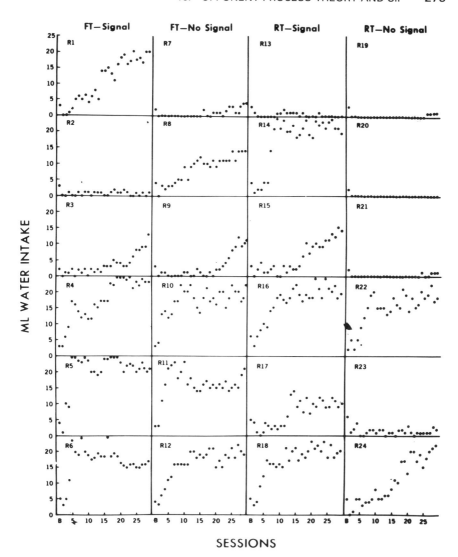

FIG. 16.5.   Water intake (ml) per session for each animal in each condition. The experimental conditions are represented by the four columns (FT = Fixed Time, RT = Random Time). B represents intakes during a baseline condition. (Lashley & Rosellini, 1980)

external cues (Group FT-Signal) did develop polydipsia. However, animals that received identical exposure to pellets but were not signalled by an external cue, where the possibility of temporal conditioning was precluded, in large part failed to develop polydipsia.

In general, these results suggest that associative factors are important in the development of polydipsia, and, thus, they appear inconsistent with the nonassociative opponent-process view. However, when we examine the behavior of the individual animals, the results are somewhat puzzling because there appear to be two distinct populations of animals within the RT-No Signal group, one which does develop polydipsia (R22, & R24) and the other which does not (R19, R20, R21, & R23). The failure to develop polydipsia in the latter animals is favorable to an associative opponent-process account, such as that proposed by Schull (1979). On the other hand, the development of polydipsia in the former animals is favorable to a nonassociative opponent-process account (Solomon, 1980), which led to this line of research. This ambiguity is exacerbated by two recent reports that schedule-induced polydipsia does develop on Random Time schedules (Allen & Weidinger, 1980; Shurtleff, Delamater, & Riley, 1983). Arguments can be advanced from each position to attempt to account for the data embarrassing to it. In the remainder of this chapter, we examine these arguments and the data relevant to them.

An associative position can propose that the animals which do develop polydipsia on Random Time schedules in our study, do so because we were not completely successful in eliminating all signals for pellet delivery in the nominal No Signal conditions. For example, it may be that even though we used procedures to minimize this possibility (i.e., high levels of background white noise, and the pellet dispenser mounted outside the sound-attenuating chamber housing the operant chamber), some of the animals may still have been capable of detecting stimuli that were positively correlated with pellet delivery, such as tactile/vibratory cues emanating from the operation of the pellet dispenser requisite for delivery of the pellet. Such an argument could also account for the development of polydipsia on Random Time schedules reported by Allen et al. (1980) and Shurtleff et al. (1983). This argument is even more tenable for these studies, because the pellet dispensers were mounted on the operant chambers and therefore undoubtedly produce both auditory and tactile/vibratory cues. Finally, this interpretation may resolve the apparent discrepancy between our finding, that the majority of animals fail to develop polydipsia under the RT-No Signal condition, and those reporting the normal development of polydipsia under Random Time schedules. That is, to the extent that cues predictive of pellet delivery are important in the development of polydipsia on Random Time schedules, we would expect its development to be greater in the latter studies, whose procedures leave this possibility open, than in our studies, where this possibility is minimized.

In order to address this issue, we have recently completed several studies aimed at determining the conditions under which polydipsia develops on Random Time schedules. In the Lashley & Rosellini (1980) study, we observed that an external signal was a powerful determinant of this effect. However, the signal used was of considerably longer duration than that typical of stimuli—in the range of 100–150 msec—produced by pellet dispenser operation. Thus, in the first study, we investigated the possibility that such a brief signal could be an effective determinant of the development of polydipsia on Random Time schedules. We simply replicated the Random Time condition of our earlier study with two exceptions: (a) The external signal consisted of a 150-msec absence of background white noise, and (b) an RT 60 schedule of pellet delivery was used to make the schedule conditions similar to those of Shurtleff et al. (1983). The results are presented in Figure 16.6. As can be seen, these results essentially replicate those of the Lashley and Rosellini (1980) study. Three of the six animals in the RT-No Signal condition failed to develop polydipsia and one of the three animals that did develop polydipsia shows severely retarded acquisition, whereas five of the six animals in the RT-Signalled condition developed polydipsia. Thus, a brief external signal was effective in allowing for the development of this behavior on a Random Time schedule. These results suggest that cues arising from pellet dispenser operation may also be capable of serving this function. Furthermore, the bimodality observed in the nominally unsignalled condition replicates our earlier findings, suggesting that some of these animals were capable of detecting an external cue associated with dispenser operation.

As a further demonstration of the importance of these cues, we have recently conducted another experiment where we attempted to further reduce the possibility of stimuli from the pellet dispenser coming to serve as signals for pellet delivery. We again tried to mask these cues by using a high level of background white noise. More importantly, we used a 10% partial reinforcement procedure of potential dispenser cues by operation of an empty (dummy) pellet dispenser during the interpellet interval. This procedure should degrade the signal value of any such cues (Mackintosh, 1974). Therefore, it should result in even more severe retardation of the development of polydipsia on a Random Time schedule than in our earlier studies. The results of this study demonstrated this to be the case. Of nine animals trained using this procedure, only two developed polydipsia.

The outcomes of the above studies demonstrate that signals for pellet delivery are important determinants of the development of schedule-induced polydipsia, suggesting that associative factors are important modulators of this phenomenon and possibly of other adjunctive behaviors (cf. Yoburn et al., 1981). Thus, they are amenable to an associative account, such as that proposed by Schull (1979), which holds that the growth of the B-process is determined, in part, by associative factors.

In view of these results, which highlight the role of associative factors in this behavior, the nonassociative opponent-process position proposed by Solomon & Corbit (1974) need not remain silent. From their position, it can be argued that the failure to observe polydipsia on Random Time unsignalled conditions stems not from the growth of the opponent-process being associative in nature, but from a failure in the expression of the behavior under these conditions because of competing response tendencies. For example, it can be argued that polydipsia develops on a signalled Random Time schedule, not because the presence of the

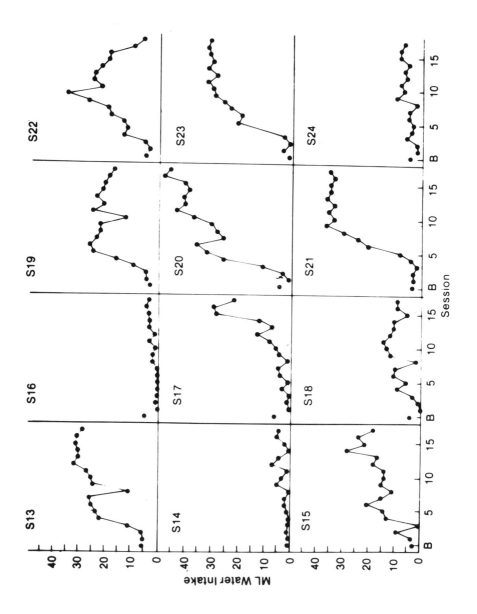

276

signal is necessary for the growth of the B-process, but because it may serve an "enabling" function, which releases the animal from the necessity of engaging in food relevant behaviors throughout the interval and may thus allow drinking to occur. In contrast, animals under RT-Unsignalled conditions may not express the underlying opponent process in drinking behavior because of their tendency to engage in food-relevant behaviors since pellet delivery is unpredictable. This argument is made more plausible by the fact that in our experimental situation, the foodcup and the water source are spatially separated, thus preventing the animal from simultaneously engaging in drinking and monitoring food availability. Although this argument is posthoc, it does suggest that if such competing response tendencies are responsible for the failure to observe polydipsia under these conditions, then they should be evidenced by direct observation of the animals during the experimental session.

To assess this, we have recently observed the behavior of animals under both Signalled and Unsignalled Random Time conditions, using a time sampling technique. We scored the animals for the occurrence of two behaviors: (a) drinking and (b) proximity to and orientation toward the foodcup. The latter behavior is one which seems likely to compete with drinking. In addition, we scored the total number of times each animal examined the foodcup. This measure showed that the animals in the Unsignalled condition examined the foodcup three times more often than those in the Signalled condition. The other behaviors observed also showed dramatic differences between the two conditions, as illustrated in Figure 16.7, which presents the data from one representative animal from each condition. It is clear from these behavioral protocols that under the Unsignalled condition (S16), the animal spends a large proportion of its time in close proximity to the foodcup and that the probability of this behavior is relatively constant throughout the interpellet interval. In contrast to this, the animal in the Signalled condition (S21) shows the typical post-pellet drinking pattern, and a concomitant low probability of foodcup proximity, which increases during the latter portion of the interval. Generally, these findings are in agreement with the proposal that polydipsia may fail to develop under Random Time Unsignalled conditions, due to competing response tendencies. Additional research, however, must be conducted to further investigate this issue. The above results suggest that polydipsia may indeed be observable even under these conditions if the procedures are arranged in a manner that allows the animal to engage in food relevant behaviors, without these behaviors coming into competition with drinking.

FIG. 16.6. Water intake (ml) of each animal for each session of the study. The two left hand columns present the data from the animals in the Random Time-Unsignalled condition whereas the two right hand columns represent the data from the Random Time Signalled condition. B represents intakes during a baseline condition.

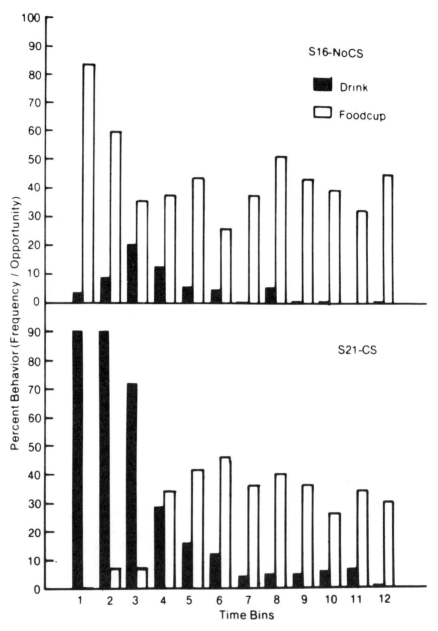

FIG. 16.7. Percent of observations of drinking (dashed bars) and foodcup proximity (open bars) for a typical animal (S16) in the Random Time Unsignalled condition and a typical animal (S21) in the Random Time Signalled condition.

In conclusion, the general outcome of our experiments is in agreement with predictions of the opponent-process theory, because the basic independent variables and relationships among them, specified to be important for the growth of the B-process, are observed to be important in the control of the development and maintenance of schedule-induced polydipsia. However, additional experiments have also raised some potential problems for this approach. In particular, we now know that associative factors do play an important role in this behavioral paradigm. Although this issue does not obviate the importance of the opponent-process approach to adjunctive behavior, it raises the question of whether the growth of the opponent process, in this case, should be considered to result from nonassociative factors, as proposed by Solomon & Corbit (1974), or from associative factors, as proposed by Schull (1979). Additional research must be conducted to address this issue.

ACKNOWLEDGEMENT

A portion of the research presented here was supported by Grant BNS 7820678 from the National Science Foundation. I wish to thank Robin Lashley, Mark Plonsky, Cynthia Driscoll, and Donald Warren for their assistance in the execution of this research. I also want to acknowledge the considerable contribution made by David R. Burdette to the initiation of this research project. Finally, I must express my gratitude to Professor Richard L. Solomon for his unqualified support.

REFERENCES

Allen, J. P., & Weidinger, R. C. (1980, November). *Truly random reinforcement intervals do produce schedule-induced polydipsia.* Paper presented at the Psychonomic Society Meeting, St. Louis, Mo.

Brown, T. G., & Flory, R. K. (1972). Schedule-induced escape from fixed interval reinforcement. *Journal of the Experimental Analysis of Behavior, 17,* 395–403.

Cohen, P. S., & Looney, T. A. (1973). Schedule-induced mirror responding in the pigeon. *Journal of the Experimental Analysis of Behavior, 19,* 395–408.

Falk, J. L. (1961). Production of polydipsia in normal rats by an intermittent food schedule. *Science, 133,* 195–196.

Falk, J. L. (1969). Conditions producing psychogenic polydipsia in animals. *Annals of the New York Academy of Science, 157,* 569–593.

Falk, J. L. (1971). The nature and determinants of adjunctive behavior. *Physiology and Behavior, 6,* 577–588.

Falk, J. L. (1977). The origin and function of adjunctive behavior. *Animal Learning and Behavior, 5,* 325–335.

Flory, R. K. (1969). Attack behavior as a function of minimum interfood interval. *Journal of the Experimental Analysis of Behavior, 12,* 825–828.

Flory, R. K. (1971). The control of schedule-induced polydipsia: Frequency and magnitude of reinforcement. *Learning and Motivation, 2,* 215–227.

Freed, E., & Hymowith, N. (1972). Effects of schedule, percent body weight, and magnitude of reinforcer on acquisition of schedule-induced polydipsia. *Psychological Reports, 31,* 95–101.

Hoffman, H. S., & Solomon, R. L. (1974). An opponent-process theory of motivation: III. Some affective dynamics in imprinting. *Learning and Motivation, 5,* 149–164.

Keehn, J. D., & Burton, M. (1978). Schedule-induced drinking: Entrainment by fixed- and random-interval schedule-controlled feeding. *Life Sciences, 8,* 93–97.

Killeen, P. (1975). On the temporal control of behavior. *Psychological Review, 82,* 89–115.

King, G. D., & Schaeffer, R. W. (1973). Developmental analysis of schedule-induced polydipsia. *Psychological Reports, 32,* 1087–1095.

Lashley, R. L., & Rosellini, R. A. (1980). Modulation of schedule-induced polydipsia by Pavlovian conditioned states. *Physiology and Behavior, 24,* 411–414.

Levitsky, D., & Collier, G. (1968). Schedule-induced wheel running. *Physiology and Behavior, 3,* 571–573.

Mackintosh, N. J. (1974). *The Psychology of Animal Learning.* New York: Academic Press.

Mineka, S., & Suomi, S. J. (1978). Social separation in monkeys. *Psychological Bulletin, 85,* 1376–1400.

Millenson, J. R., Allen, R. B., & Pinker, S. (1977). Adjunctive drinking during variable and random-interval food reinforcement schedules. *Animal Learning and Behavior, 5,* 285–290.

Overmier, J. B., Payne, R. J., Brackbill, R. M., Linder, B., & Lawry, J. A. (1979). On the mechanism of the post-asymptotic decrement phenomenon. *Acta Neurobiologiae Experimentalis, 39,* 603–620.

Pavlov, I. P. (1927). *Conditioned Reflexes.* Oxford: Oxford University Press.

Penney, J., & Schull, J. (1977). Functional differentiation of adjunctive drinking and wheel running in rats. *Animal Learning and Behavior, 5,* 272–280.

Roper, T. J., & Nieto, J. (1979). Schedule-induced drinking and other behavior in the rat as a function of body weight deficit. *Physiology and Behavior, 23,* 673–678.

Rosellini, R. A., & Burdette, D. R. (1980). Meal size and intermeal interval both regulate schedule-induced water intake in rats. *Animal Learning and Behavior, 8,* 647–652.

Rosellini, R. A., & Lashley, R. L. (1982). The opponent-process theory of motivation: VIII. Quantitative and qualitative manipulations of food both modulate adjunctive behavior. *Learning and Motivation, 13,* 222–239.

Schull, J. (1979). A conditioned opponent theory of Pavlovian conditioning and habituation. In G. Bower (Ed.) *The Psychology of Learning and Motivation* (pp. 57–90). New York: Academic Press.

Shurtleff, D., Delamater, A. R., & Riley, A. L. (1983). A reevaluation of the CS- hypothesis for schedule-induced polydipsia under intermittent schedules of pellet delivery. *Animal Learning and Behavior, 11,* 247–254.

Solomon, R. L., (1980). The opponent-process theory of acquired motivation: The cost of pleasure and the benefits of pain. *American Psychologist, 35,* 691–712.

Solomon, R. L., & Corbit, J. D. (1974). An opponent-process theory of motivation: I. Temporal dynamics of affect. *Psychological Review, 81,* 119–145.

Staddon, J. E. R. (1977). Schedule-induced behavior. In W. K. Honig & J. E. R. Staddon (Eds.) *Handbook of Operant Behavior* (pp. 125–152). Englewood Cliffs, NJ: Prentice-Hall.

Staddon, J. E. R., & Ayers, S. L. (1975). Sequential and temporal properties of behavior induced by schedules of periodic food delivery. *Behaviour, 54,* 26–49.

Starr, M. D., (1978). An opponent-process theory of motivation: VI. Time and intensity variables in the development of separation induced distress calling in ducklings. *Journal of Experimental Psychology: Animal Behavior Processes, 4,* 338–355.

Thomka, M. L., & Rosellini, R. A. (1976). Frustration and the production of schedule-induced polydipsia. *Animal Learning and Behavior, 3,* 380–384.

Yoburn, B. C., Cohen, P. S., & Campagnoni, F. R. (1981). The role of intermittent food in the induction of attack in pigeons *Journal of the Experimental Analysis of Behavior, 36,* 101–118.

17 A Two-State Model of Reinforcer-Induced Motivation

Perrin S. Cohen
Northeastern University

Thomas A. Looney
Lynchburg College

Frank R. Campagnoni
Cindy P. Lawler
Northeastern University

When a positive reinforcer is scheduled contingently upon the occurrence of a behavior, that behavior is likely to increase in frequency (e.g., Skinner, 1938). Most theoretical and practical interest in positive reinforcers and in reinforcer schedules has focused on this aspect of the reinforcement process. In contrast, less attention has been addressed to the fact that a reinforcer can also engender behaviors such as general activity (Killeen, 1975), distress calling (Starr, 1978), and drinking (Falk, 1961): activities that can be established and maintained without a contingent relationship between that behavior and the scheduled reinforcer. This chapter is concerned with this latter aspect of positive reinforcement and, in particular, with the possibility that such behaviors are induced by one of two types of motivational states that persist following reinforcer termination. We describe the results of recent experiments suggesting that a positive reinforcer induces one type of state that potentiates stereotyped patterns of species-typical behavior and a second type of state that enhances exploratory-like behaviors that operate on and modify the organism's environment.

Although there are several lines of research that have focused on the motivation-inducing aspects of reinforcement (e.g., Bindra, 1969; Daly, 1974), one of the most extensive and varied sources of experimental evidence is found in the literature on schedule-induced behavior (Falk, 1971; Staddon, 1977). Schedule-induced behaviors are ones that are enhanced in frequency (Cohen & Looney, 1984) by reinforcer schedules but that do not develop through association with the scheduled reinforcer. This group of behaviors is quite broad, including activities such as drinking water, attacking inanimate and—in some cases—animate objects, and increased levels of general activity or ambulation, all of which tend to occur following termination of a reinforcer. These behaviors have been observed in rats, pigeons, monkeys, humans, and other species, and the levels of such activities are known to be sensitive to changes in properties of the reinforcer and to its rate of occurrence (Cohen & Looney, 1984).

Schedule-induced behaviors are thought to reflect a reinforcer-induced change of state of the organism because the opportunity to engage in schedule-induced drinking (Falk, 1966) and schedule-induced attack (Cherek, Thompson & Heistad, 1973) has been shown to be positively reinforcing. In other words, when exposed to reinforcer schedule conditions that are known to induce those behaviors, a subject will engage in operant responding that is reinforced by the opportunity to participate in that activity. Theorists have conceptualized these and other schedule-induced behaviors as being the consequence of a single, reinforcer-induced motivational state. The most prevalent view has been that the presentation (e.g., Solomon & Corbit, 1974) or termination (Azrin, Hutchinson & Hake, 1966) of a positive reinforcer induces an aversive state in the organism that either directly (e.g., Azrin et al., 1966; Solomon & Corbit, 1974) or indirectly (Falk, 1977) increases the level of a behavior. Alternatively, others (Killeen, 1975; Wayner, 1970) have suggested that induced behaviors are potentiated by a nonspecific excitatory aftereffect of the reinforcer that enhances the subject's reactivity to normally occurring stimuli.

These motivational models of schedule-induced behavior assume that the reinforcer induces a single change in state of the organism following reinforcer termination, which in conjunction with the availability of certain stimuli (e.g., water), potentiates the induced behavior. In this chapter, we examine this premise in the light of recent evidence that there are two classes of schedule-induced behaviors. We propose that reinforcers induce two independent types of motivational states following reinforcer termination, and we outline what we suspect are some of the structural and functional properties of those states.

INDUCED STATE I

This type of induced state potentiates stereotyped patterns of species-typical behavior such as drinking water in rats (Falk, 1961), intraspecific attack in pigeons (Azrin et al., 1966), and distress calling in ducklings (Starr, 1978). Induced State I begins at approximately the same time following reinforcer termination over a wide range of inter-reinforcer interval values. The invariant and absolute temporal relation of Induced State I to reinforcer termination is

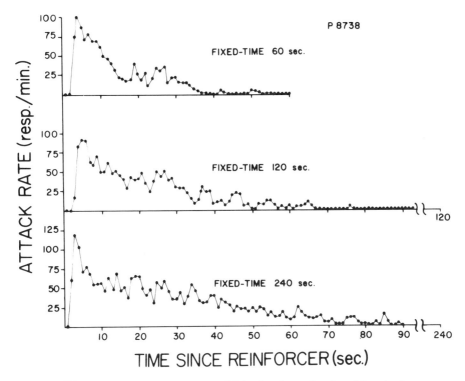

FIG. 17.1.   Attack rate (responses/min) is plotted as a function of time (sec) since reinforcer termination for three interreinforcer interval values (sec). The data are for one representative pigeon (P8738).

illustrated in recent experiments that examine the temporal pattern of activities associated with that state. In a study of schedule-induced attack, for example, Campagnoni and Cohen (1983a) exposed hungry pigeons to periodic presentations of food with a conspecific target continuously available. They measured rate of attack within each of three interreinforcer intervals—1, 2 and 4 min. The results for one representative pigeon are shown in Figure 17.1, which plots attack rate (responses/min) as a function of time (sec) since reinforcer termination. Regardless of the interreinforcer interval, attack rate was highest immediately after reinforcer termination (in this case within 3 to 5 sec), and then gradually declined as time to the next reinforcer approached. The same type of temporal pattern of behavior has been observed in studies of schedule-induced drinking in rats (e.g., J. D. Allen, personal communication, July, 1983; Roper, 1978) and in monkeys (Allen & Kenshalo, 1978). With water continuously available to a subject, schedule-induced drinking typically occurs at a maximum level within 15 or 20 sec after reinforcer termination, regardless of the interreinforcer interval.

From these results, it is evident that Induced State I occurs with maximum intensity during the same time period following reinforcer termination over a wide range of interreinforcer intervals. This temporal feature is important for two reasons. First, as we discuss later, it serves as a major basis for differentiating this first type of induced motivational state from a second type that potentiates exploratory activities. Secondly, this temporal feature is consistent with Solomon's (1980) speculation that the temporal distribution of schedule-induced behaviors following reinforcer termination reflects the initiation of an acquired opponent process during the postreinforcer period. Specifically, opponent process theory (Solomon & Corbit, 1974) postulates that the presentation of a positive reinforcer engenders a primary affective process (A process) which terminates abruptly following reinforcer termination. With repeated presentation of a positive reinforcer, the A process strengthens an aversive opponent process (B process) which, unlike the A process, decays gradually following reinforcer termination. Regardless of the interval between reinforcers, the B process is thought to achieve maximum strength immediately after reinforcer termination. The fact that behaviors associated with Induced State I (e.g., drinking and attack) occur with maximum strength within the same time period following reinforcer termination at different interreinforcer interval values is consistent with opponent process theory. Recently, Starr (1978) and Rosellini and Lashley (1982) have identified other ways in which properties of reinforcer-induced drinking and distress calling are consistent with the laws of opponent process theory. Rosellini further discusses the relation of opponent process theory to reinforcer-induced behavior in another chapter of this volume.

INDUCED STATE II

Unlike the first type of reinforcer-induced state, which potentiates highly organized patterns of species-typical behavior, the second type enhances locomotor and other skeletal activities, including conditioned operant responses, that operate on and change the subject's environment. These induced activities have traditionally been thought to reflect a heightened level of arousal (e.g., Wayner, 1970) or the aversive properties of terminating a positive reinforcer (e.g., Azrin, 1961; Azrin et al., 1966). We conceptualize these reinforcer-induced activities in a different way. We view them as exploratory behaviors (Berlyne, 1960; Woodworth, 1958) that under natural conditions serve to keep the subject in contact with its current environment and thus prepared for action (e.g., ingesting new food items as they become available, avoiding a predator). In the studies to be discussed, activities of this type include a tendency for subjects to turn away (Staddon & Simmelhag, 1971) or spend time away from the place where the reinforcer is dispensed (Anderson & Shettleworth, 1977; Campagnoni & Cohen, 1984; Muller, Crow & Cheney, 1979), to engage in operant responding to change the intensity of stimuli (e.g., Brown & Flory, 1972), and to exhibit increased levels of general behavioral activity (Killeen, 1975) and wheel running (King, 1974; Levitsky & Collier, 1968; cf. Staddon & Ayers, 1975).

Like Induced State I, Induced State II occurs with maximum intensity soon after the termination of a reinforcer. Induced State II, however, occurs after Induced State I and unlike Induced State I, its peak intensity following reinforcer termination is affected by the duration of the interval between reinforcers. Following reinforcer termination, Induced State II reaches its maximum value after an approximately constant proportion of the interreinforcer interval has elapsed. This peak is typically followed by a gradual decline as time to the next reinforcer approaches. If the interreinforcer interval is gradually increased, this peak level of Induced State II gradually shifts to longer and longer delays following reinforcer termination. This proportional aspect of Induced State II and of the exploratory behaviors associated with it is illustrated in a recent study by Campagnoni and Cohen (1983b). In their experiment, hungry pigeons were exposed to a fixed-time periodic feeding schedule ranging in value from .5 to 8 min. Three different measures of exploratory behavior were recorded.

In one condition, the amount of time that the pigeons spent in the rear of the test chamber away from the reinforcer dispenser was recorded. This was done by recording the amount of time the bird interrupted a photobeam in the rear of the chamber. In a second condition, time in the rear of the chamber was again measured, but, in this case, interruption of the rear photobeam produced a stimulus change—a gross increase in the level of chamber illumination. The stimulus change persisted for the duration of time that the bird interrupted the rear photobeam. As expected (Brown & Flory, 1972), birds in this second condition spent more time in the rear than in the condition in which no explicit stimulus change was programmed. In the third condition, the situation was arranged so that a bird could produce the same stimulus change possible in the previous condition but could do so only by pecking a response key mounted in the front of the chamber. One peck initiated the stimulus change, and a second peck terminated it. Again, as expected, stimulus change during exposure to intermittent reinforcement was positively reinforcing, and the birds readily learned to peck the stimulus change key.

Figure 17.2 shows, for one representative bird, how each of these three measures of exploratory behavior changed within the interval between reinforcers. Relative time in the rear or in stimulus change is plotted as a function of relative time since a reinforcer, for a range of inter-reinforcer interval values. In general, maximum levels of all three behaviors (time in rear, with and without stimulus change, and keypeck stimulus change) tended to occur at approximately the same relative time within the interreinforcer interval. This proportional aspect of the distribution is robust but still only approximate, since the distributions do not exactly superimpose on one another. With a decrease in the interreinforcer interval, there is a slight, but systematic, tendency for exploratory

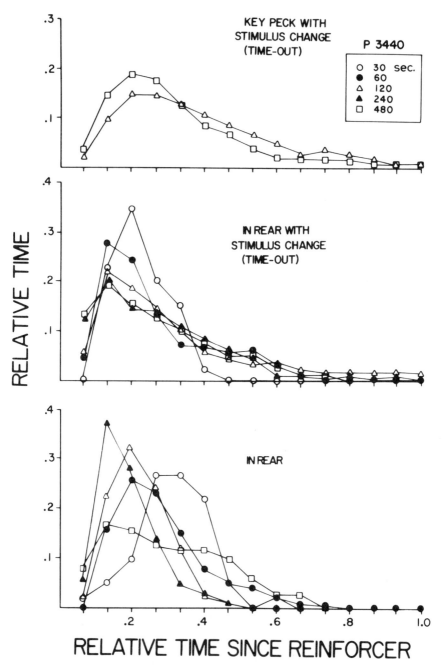

FIG. 17.2.   Relative time in the rear or in stimulus change is plotted as a function of the proportion of the interreinforcer interval for a range of interreinforcer interval values (sec). The data are for one representative pigeon (P3440).

behaviors to occur proportionally later in the interval. This shift may reflect, in part, the relative effect of postreinforcer behaviors (e.g., head in food magazine) on the probability function (Gibbon, 1977). The relative time engaged in such aftereffects of a reinforcer would be expected to constitute a greater proportion of the interreinforcer interval at shorter interval values than at longer ones. In a relative sense, this should constrain the onset of exploratory behaviors more at shorter interval values than at longer ones.

Proportional distributions of the type described above have also been reported by Killeen (1975), who measured changes in the level of schedule-induced activity, a behavioral measure that we suspect corresponds, in part, to the behaviors recorded in the Campagnoni and Cohen (1983b) experiment. Killeen exposed hungry pigeons to a fixed-time periodic feeding schedule and measured general activity in terms of the rate of floor panel activation. Figure 17.3 is Gibbon's (1977) replot of Killeen's activity data obtained at three different fixed-time intervals. Relative amount of activity is plotted as a function of relative time since reinforcer termination. Like the various behavioral measures of exploratory behavior in the Campagnoni and Cohen (1983b) study, general activity is distributed in an approximately proportional manner within the interreinforcer interval, with maximum levels occurring during the initial quarter of the interval. The similarity of these distributions to those obtained in the Campagnoni and Cohen (1983b) study leads us to conclude that the same class of behavior was recorded in both. We suggest that the increased levels of activity in Killeen's experiment reflect, at least in part, the increased reinforcing properties of stimulus feedback associated with such behavior. In more general terms, we suggest that intermittent reinforcement enhances the positively reinforcing properties of stimulus change associated with various activities we have characterized as exploratory in nature. We suggest that all forms of reinforcer-induced exploratory behavior (including general activity or ambulation) are potentiated by Induced State II.

The proportional distributions of exploratory behavior within the interval between reinforcers suggest that the underlying motivational state is modulated by temporal conditioning processes associated with periodic reinforcement. This idea is similar to Killeen's (1975) notion that temporal conditioning processes modulate reinforcer-enhanced levels of arousal. The present approach, however, differs from Killeen's in two ways. First, unlike Killeen's emphasis on arousal, we conceptualize the reinforcer-induced motivational state as enhancing the reinforcing properties of stimulus change associated with locomotor behaviors and, in so doing, facilitating the rate of those behaviors. Secondly, unlike Killeen, we propose that this particular type of induced motivational state (Induced State II) potentiates one class of induced activities (ambulation and other loosely constrained activities that operate on the environment) and not stereotyped patterns of species-typical behavior associated with Induced State I. The relation of Killeen's (1975) experimental results to Induced States I and II is discussed in a subsequent section. The manner in which we think temporal conditioning pro-

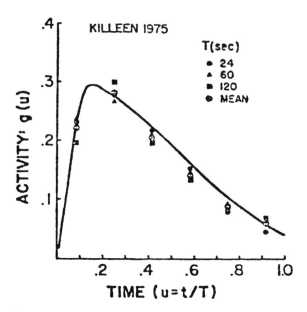

FIG. 17.3. Normalized activity distributions g(U) are plotted as a function of proportion of the interreinforcer interval for three interreinforcer interval values (sec). The data are the averages obtained from three pigeons. See Gibbon (1977) for explanation of theoretical function fit to data. (©1977 by the American Psychological Association. Reprinted by permission.)

cesses modulate Induced State II is graphically illustrated by Killeen's (1975) model in Figure 17.4.

From our perspective, this figure depicts the hypothetical distribution of a tendency for a subject to work to produce stimulus change within the interval between reinforcers. The upper solid line corresponds to the relatively constant level of the underlying induced motivational state when it is not suppressed by the conditioned inhibitory and excitatory effects of periodic reinforcement (Staddon, 1974, 1977). When only the conditioned inhibitory effects of reinforcer termination suppress the induced motivational state, the level of the state is lowest following reinforcer termination and gradually rises as time to the next reinforcer approaches (rising dashed line). Likewise, with only the conditioned excitatory effects of reinforcement suppressing the induced motivational state, that state is highest at the beginning of the interval and decreases as time to the next reinforcer approaches (decreasing dashed line). With both of these temporal conditioning processes modulating the induced motivational state, that state initially increases and then decreases within the interval (lower solid line). This model can account for the proportional nature of the distributions of exploratory behavior already described. For example, in the case of conditioned inhibition following reinforcer termination, the longer the interval, the longer the absolute period of post-reinforcer conditioned inhibition and, thus, the greater the delay in onset, in absolute time, of exploratory behavior.

CONCURRENT MEASUREMENT OF INDUCED STATES
I AND II

We have proposed that intermittent positive reinforcement induces not one but two types of motivational states following reinforcer termination. One state is an aversive afterreaction to a reinforcer that potentiates drinking, attack, distress calling and other species-typical activities. The second type is quite different in that it potentiates the positively reinforcing properties of stimulus change and in so doing enhances the level of skeletal movement (e.g., bar pressing, locomo-

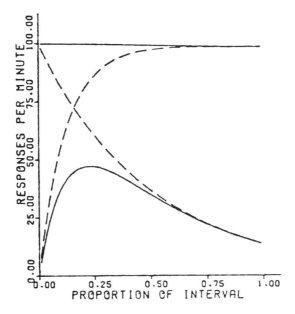

FIG. 17.4. Hypothetical distributions of the tendency for a subject to produce (responses/min) stimulus change as a function of proportion of the interreinforcer interval. The upper solid line corresponds to the relatively constant level of the underlying motivational state when it is not affected by conditioning processes. The rising dashed line corresponds to the motivational state when it is only suppressed by conditioned inhibitory effects of reinforcer termination. The decreasing dashed line corresponds to the level of the motivational state when it is suppressed by conditioned excitatory effects that precede reinforcement. The lower solid line corresponds to the underlying motivational state when it is modulated by both types of conditioning processes. (After Killeen, 1975, © 1975 by the American Psychological Association. Reprinted by permission.)

tion) that keeps the subject's behavior and, consequently, its perceptual environment in flux. This idea of two reinforcer-induced states is consistent with two recent studies that concurrently measured each of the two types of induced behaviors within the same testing situation (Ator, 1980; Brantley, 1977). Ator (1980), for example, exposed hungry pigeons to fixed-ratio (FR) schedules of food reinforcement (Multiple FRFR) and measured both schedule-induced attack (Induced State I) and the tendency to make a conditioned operant response that produced a change in the level of illumination (Induced State II). The results are consistent with our two-state model. When only the opportunity to attack was possible, it occurred early in the post-reinforcer period, immediately following reinforcer termination. When only the opportunity to produce a stimulus change was possible, it occurred later in the post-reinforcer period. When both the opportunity to attack and to produce a stimulus change were available, attack continued to occur immediately following reinforcer termination, and working-for-stimulus-change continued to occur later in the post-reinforcer period. In short, the two induced activities did not appreciably compete with one another, but, rather, each had their own temporal locus within the interval as our model would predict.

Additional support for the two state model is found in a related experiment (Brantley, 1977) in which hungry rats were exposed to a fixed-interval (FI) schedule of food reinforcement and had opportunities to both drink from a water bottle (Induced State I) and to press a lever to produce stimulus change (Induced State II). As in the Ator (1980) experiment, each of the two types of schedule-induced activities had its own temporal locus within the interreinforcer interval. Drinking occurred immediately following reinforcer termination and working-for-stimulus change occurred later in the interval. In addition, there was no evidence that the activities competed for expression with one another, because each maintained the same temporal position within the interval when the other one was either eliminated or reduced in frequency. Although Ator (1980) and Brantley (1977) did not increase the duration of the interreinforcer interval in their studies, we would predict that, if this were done, the differences in temporal distributions of the two types of schedule-induced activities would become even more noticeable.

FUNCTIONS OF BEHAVIORS ASSOCIATED WITH INDUCED STATES I AND II

Up to this point, we have distinguished between two reinforcer-induced motivational states following reinforcer termination and have made this distinction on the basis of the temporal properties and the topographies of the behaviors associated with them. It appears that the functions of the behaviors associated with the two states are different as well. Activities associated with Induced State I (e.g., licking, pecking, vocalizing) are repetitive and stereotyped; they often occur in discrete bouts and have species-typical characteristics. Recently, it has been shown that the opportunity to engage in this type of organized behavioral pattern can reduce physiological stress associated with physical trauma (e.g., Weiss, Pohorecky, Salman, & Gruenthal, 1976). We propose that schedule-induced activities and conditioned stimuli associated with Induced State I serve the same stress-reducing function during the period of time that Induced State I is in effect. In other words, we suggest that behaviors such as drinking and attack serve the homeostatic function of reducing physiological stress engendered by Induced State I. Rather than being inappropriate, behaviors of this type might be quite efficient coping responses that provide physiological benefit to the organism. From this perspective, physiological stress associated with intermittent reinforcement (Hennessey & Levine, 1979) should be reduced when there is an opportunity to engage in schedule-induced behavior of this type, relative to a condition in which there is not such an opportunity.

Brett and Levine (1979) have found experimental evidence for this type of coping mechanism in a study of schedule-induced drinking in rats. They compared the level of pituitary-adrenal activity, as indicated by plasma levels of corticosterone in rats exposed to an intermittent reinforcement schedule either with or without an opportunity to engage in drinking. They found that the opportunity to engage in schedule-induced drinking suppressed pituitary-adrenal activity. Looney and Cohen (1982) have suggested, on the basis of a recent study by Weiss et al. (1976), that schedule-induced attack also may serve this type of coping function. Weiss et al. showed that, in rats, the opportunity to attack a target can reduce the incidence of gastric lesions during exposure to uncontrollable, electric shock relative to a condition in which rats receive the same shocks without an opportunity to attack. Perhaps the opportunity to engage in schedule-induced attack would also suppress pituitary-adrenal activity.

In some species, a coping activity associated with Induced State I may have other functions as well. For example, schedule-induced aggression in pigeons may not only serve to reduce physiological stress associated with intermittent reinforcement but, under natural conditions, may also serve as a mechanism for preserving or maximizing access to a scarce commodity. Evidence for this latter function is found in a recent field study (Cohen, Telson, Campagnoni & Lawler, 1983) in which interrupted communal feeding in pigeons was observed to engender intraspecific aggression. This aggression was similar to schedule-induced aggression observed under laboratory conditions (Yoburn & Cohen, 1979), and its development was accompanied by the establishment of a social dominance hierarchy in the vicinity of the feeding site. Thus, a coping activity associated with Induced State I may serve other functions that are only evident in the subject's natural environment.

Activities associated with Induced State II appear to have a quite different function. As discussed previously, this induced state potentiates the positively reinforcing properties of stimulus change and, in so doing, enhances the level of skeletal movement that keeps the subject's perceptual environment in flux. This perceptual flux is achieved either indirectly through ambulation or by explicit physical manipulation of the environment (e.g., conditioned responding to produce a stimulus change). We have conceptualized these activities as exploratory, since, under natural conditions, they most likely serve to keep the subject intimate with its immediate environment by clarifying and intensifying stimulation and thus prepared for action. If these activities serve this purpose, then increasing the intensity, novelty, and complexity of stimulus change associated with them might be expected to increase their frequency. This is the case in experiments in which the intensity of stimulus feedback has been varied (Campagnoni and Cohen, 1983b; Zimmerman & Ferster, 1964), but the effects of novelty and complexity have yet to be examined.

Since exploratory activities associated with Induced State II enhance stimulus change, we would expect them also to enhance the level of physiological stress (Hennessy & Levine, 1979), a prediction opposite that we made for activities associated with Induced State I. If this is correct, then we would expect that during exposure to intermittent reinforcement, pituitary-adrenal activity would be higher in a situation in which skeletal activities produce an increased level of stimulation than when they do not. Increased stress levels of this type also would be consistent with the suggestion that schedule-induced behaviors associated with Induced State II are exploratory activities that help prepare the organism for action.

The notion that activities associated with Induced States I and II have opposite effects on the level of physiological stress leads to additional predictions. It suggests that the level of stress during exposure to intermittent reinforcement should be related to the type of behavioral opportunities that the experimenter provides to the subject. For example, the model predicts that the highest levels of physiological stress should occur when there is an opportunity to engage in an induced exploratory behavior associated with Induced State II (e.g., conditioned responding for stimulus change) and the lowest level when there is an opportunity to engage in an activity associated with Induced State I (e.g., attack). Intermediate levels of stress should occur when there is an opportunity to engage in both types of induced activities. Experiments of this type remain to be done.

BEHAVIORAL TOPOGRAPHIES ASSOCIATED WITH INDUCED STATES I AND II

Unlike previous formulations of reinforcer-induced motivational states (cf. Falk, 1977), the present two-state model emphasizes the differences in behavioral topographies between two classes of induced behaviors. Induced State I is thought to engender stereotyped patterns of species-typical behavior whereas

Induced State II enhances more loosely constrained, locomotor activities that operate on and typically modify the subject's environment. In distinguishing between these two types of behavioral topographies, we have drawn upon experimental results that are representative of the two types of schedule-induced behaviors. In this section, we further examine the relation of behavioral topography to induced motivational state and suggest that this aspect of our model may be useful for accounting for, in a post hoc fashion, anomalous results of previous studies of schedule-induced behavior. Most importantly, however, these considerations raise new questions and lead to new experimental predictions.

The present two-state model suggests that if a particular schedule-induced behavior shares the behavioral characteristics of activities associated with each type of induced state, then such an activity would be likely to accompany both states. Of the various schedule-induced behaviors that have been studied, schedule-induced wheel running in rats best fulfills both behavioral descriptions and would thus be a likely candidate to accompany both induced states. Wheel running is a highly stereotyped, locomotor behavior that has species-typical features and also operates on and effects change in the environment.

Evidence for schedule-induced wheel running in rats (cf. Staddon & Ayers, 1975) is found in several experiments (King, 1974; Levitsky & Collier, 1968). In the Levitsky & Collier study, rats received intermittent reinforcement while confined inside a large running wheel. In that situation, the temporal pattern of wheel running within the interval between successive reinforcers was different from that typically observed for schedule-induced behaviors associated with either Induced State I or II. Wheel running began immediately after reinforcer termination, as would be expected of an activity associated with Induced State I, but, unlike that type of activity, it continued to occur later in the interreinforcer interval as well. We suspect that schedule-induced wheel running that began immediately after reinforcer termination reflects the effects of Induced State I, whereas running that occurred later in the interval may reflect, in part, the effect of Induced State II. In other words, the anomalous pattern of wheel running may correspond to the successive inductions of a common activity by different types of motivational states. If this is accurate, then we would predict that with a sufficiently long interreinforcer interval, a bimodal distribution of induced running should occur. An initial mode, corresponding to the effects of Induced State I should occur soon after reinforcer termination, and a second increase in wheel running should occur after a relatively constant proportion of the interval has elapsed. This type of experiment has yet to be done.

As has been discussed, Induced State I is thought to engender stereotyped patterns of species-typical behavior, such as licking in rats and intraspecific attack in pigeons. If the normal rate and duration of a behavior associated with Induced State I were sufficiently restricted, that activity may no longer be appropriate for that state and thus fail to accompany it. Instead, such an activity may become integrated with locomotor and other activities and thus associated with

Induced State II. This may occur (Killeen, 1975) when a rat is exposed to intermittent food reinforcement with concurrent access to a response lever that produces a small quantity of water on a fixed-ratio 1 schedule. The temporal pattern of obtaining water in that situation is different from that which normally occurs when water is freely available to the subject. Maximum levels of obtaining water within the interval between food reinforcers occur at a point that is approximately proportional to the duration of the interreinforcer interval. In other words, lever pressing for a small quantity of water in that situation does not appear to be associated with Induced State I, as is usually the case when water is freely available. Rather, such lever pressing for water appears to be an exploratory activity that accompanies Induced State II. Our model would predict that if the duration and rate of drinking allowed to occur following a lever press were increased sufficiently, then drinking would accompany Induced State I rather than Induced State II. In other words, with drinking less constrained, it should occur at the same point following reinforcer termination over a wide range of interreinforcer interval values.

There may be other ways of influencing whether a particular type of schedule-induced activity accompanies Induced State I or II. Rosellini & Burdette (1980), for example, found that with water continuously available to a rat, maximum levels of schedule-induced drinking occurred after approximately a constant proportion of the interreinforcer interval had elapsed. This experiment is unusual in that drinking developed at the relatively longer interreinforcer intervals (120, 180, 240 sec) without the subjects having had previous experience with reinforcement at shorter interval values. The delayed onset of drinking at the longer interval values may indicate that, during its development, drinking became integrated with locomotor and other activities and, thus, became associated with Induced State II. If this is the case, then our model predicts that such drinking should not occur in discrete bouts as it does when it accompanies Induced State I but rather be temporally integrated with locomotor and other activities. This prediction also remains to be tested.

SUMMARY AND CONCLUSIONS

We have outlined a model of reinforcer-induced motivation that distinguishes between two independent types of motivational states. Induced State I potentiates stereotyped patterns of species-typical behavior that serve to reduce physiological stress associated with that state. Maximum levels of this state occur at the same absolute time period following reinforcer termination over a wide range of inter-reinforcer interval values. Induced State II, on the other hand, engenders more loosely constrained locomotor activities that serve to keep an organism in contact with its environment and, thus, ready for action. We have characterized activities associated with Induced State II as exploratory. Induced States I and II differ in terms of their temporal pattern following reinforcer termination. Induced State II occurs after Induced State I and, unlike Induced State I, occurs at approximately the same relative time following reinforcer termination, regardless of the interreinforcer interval. The two state model accounts for, in a post-hoc fashion, anomalous results of previous experiments and suggests that future research should pay closer attention to the topography, function and temporal organization of reinforcer-induced activities. In addition, the model raises new questions, leads to new experimental predictions, and emphasizes the need for more comprehensive descriptions and theoretical accounts of Induced States I and II.

ACKNOWLEDGMENT

This chapter was written in part with support of funds from USPHS grant RR07143 to Northeastern University and with travel funds provided by Lynchburg College. The authors thank F. Robert Brush, Iver Iversen, Peter Killeen, Robert A. Rosellini, J. E. R. Staddon, and Ronald Telson for their comments on earlier drafts of the manuscript.

REFERENCES

Allen, J. D., & Kenshalo, D. R. (1978). Schedule-induced drinking as functions of inter-pellet interval and draught size in the Java Macaque. *Journal of the Experimental Analysis of Behavior, 30,* 139–151.

Anderson, M. C., & Shettleworth, S. J. (1977). Behavioral adaptation to fixed-interval and fixed-time food delivery in golden hamsters. *Journal of the Experimental Analysis of Behavior, 27,* 33–49.

Ator, N. A. (1980). Mirror pecking and timeout under a multiple fixed-ratio schedule of food delivery. *Journal of the Experimental Analysis of Behavior, 34,* 319–328.

Azrin, N. H. (1961). Time-out from positive reinforcement. *Science, 133,* 382–383.

Azrin, N. H., Hutchinson, R. R., & Hake, D. F. (1966). Extinction-induced aggression. *Journal of the Experimental Analysis of Behavior, 9,* 191–204.

Berlyne, D. E. (1960). *Conflict, arousal and curiosity.* New York: McGraw-Hill.

Bindra, D. (1969). The interrelated mechanisms of reinforcement and motivation, and the nature of their influence on response. In W. J. Arnold & D. Levine (Eds.), *Nebraska Symposium on Motivation* (Vol. 17, pp. 1–38). Lincoln: University of Nebraska Press.

Brantley, J. B. (1977). *Effects of cues signaling a low probability of reinforcement on schedule-induced polydipsia.* Unpublished master's thesis, University of Georgia.

Brett, L. P., & Levine, S. (1979). Schedule-induced polydipsia suppresses pituitary-adrenal activity in rats. *Journal of Comparative and Physiological Psychology, 93,* 946–956.

Brown, T. G., & Flory, R. K. (1972). Schedule-induced escape from fixed-interval reinforcement. *Journal of the Experimental Analysis of Behavior, 17,* 395–403.

Campagnoni, F. R., & Cohen, P. S. (1983a). [Post-reinforcer distributions of schedule-induced attack in pigeons]. Unpublished raw data.

Campagnoni, F. R., & Cohen, P. S. (1983b). *Spatial organization of behavior of pigeons exposed to periodic reward.* Manuscript in preparation.

Campagnoni, F. R., & Cohen, P. S. (1984). Scalar timing and the spatial organization of behavior between reward presentations. *Annals of the New York Academy of Sciences, 423,* 585–587.

Cohen, P. S., & Looney, T. A. (1984). Induction by reinforcer schedules. *Journal of the Experimental Analysis of Behavior, 41,* 345–353.

Cohen, P. S., Telson, R. U., Campagnoni, F. R., & Lawler, C. P. (1983, April). *A field study of aggression during intermittent social feeding in pigeons.* Paper presented at the meeting of the Eastern Psychological Association, Philadelphia, PA.

Cherek, D. R., Thompson, T., & Heistad, G. T. (1973). Responding maintained by the opportunity to attack during an interval food reinforcement schedule. *Journal of the Experimental Analysis of Behavior, 19,* 113–123.

Daly, H. B. (1974). Reinforcing properties of escape from frustration aroused in various learning situations. In G. H. Bower (Ed.), *The psychology of learning and motivation: Vol. 8.* (pp. 187–231). New York: Academic Press.

Falk, J. L. (1961). Production of polydipsia in normal rats by an intermittent food schedule. *Science, 133,* 195–196.

Falk, J. L. (1966). The motivational properties of schedule-induced polydipsia. *Journal of the Experimental Analysis of Behavior, 9,* 19–25.

Falk, J. L. (1971). The nature and determinants of adjunctive behavior. *Physiology and Behavior, 6,* 577–588.

Falk, J. L. (1977). The origin and functions of adjunctive behavior. *Animal Learning and Behavior, 5,* 325–335.

Gibbon, J. (1977). Scalar expectancy theory and Weber's Law in animal timing. *Psychological Review, 84,* 279–325.

Hennessey, J. W., & Levine, S. (1979). Stress, arousal and the pituitary-adrenal system: A psychoendocrine hypothesis. In J. M. Sprague & A. N. Epstein (Eds.), *Progress in psychobiology and physiological psychology: Vol. 8.* (pp. 133–178). New York: Academic Press.

Killeen, P. (1975). On the temporal control of behavior. *Psychological Review, 82,* 89–115.

King, G. D. (1974). Wheel running in the rat induced by a fixed-time presentation of water. *Animal Learning and Behavior, 2,* 325–328.

Levitsky, D., & Collier, G. (1968). Schedule-induced wheel running. *Physiology and Behavior, 3,* 571–573.

Looney, T. A., & Cohen, P. S. (1982). Aggression induced by intermittent positive reinforcement. *Neuroscience and biobehavioral reviews, 6,* 15–37.

Muller, P. G., Crow, R. E., & Cheney, C. D. (1979). Schedule-induced locomotor activity in humans. *Journal of Experimental Analysis of Behavior, 31,* 83–90.

Roper, T. J. (1978). Diversity and substitutability of adjunctive activities under fixed-interval schedules of food reinforcement. *Journal of the Experimental Analysis of Behavior, 30,* 83–96.

Rosellini, R. A., & Burdette, D. R. (1980). Meal size and intermeal interval both regulate schedule-induced water intake in rats. *Animal Learning and Behavior, 8,* 647–652.

Rosellini, R. A., & Lashley, R. L. (1982). The opponent-process theory of motivation: VII. Quantitative and qualitative manipulations of food both modulate adjunctive behavior. *Learning and Motivation, 13,* 222–239.

Skinner, B. F. (1938). *The behavior of organisms.* New York: Appleton-Century-Crofts.

Solomon, R. L. (1980). Recent experiments testing an opponent-process theory of acquired motivation. *Acta Neurobiologiae Experimentalis, 40,* 271–289.

Solomon, R. L., & Corbit, J. D. (1974). An opponent process theory of motivation: I. Temporal dynamics of affect. *Psychological Review, 81,* 119–145.

Staddon, J. E. R. (1974). Temporal control, attention, and memory. *Psychological Review, 81,* 375–391.

Staddon, J. E. R. (1977). Schedule-induced behavior. In W. K. Honig & J. E. R. Staddon (Eds.), *Handbook of operant behavior* (pp. 125–152). Englewood Cliffs, NJ: Prentice-Hall.

Staddon, J. E. R., & Ayers, S. L. (1975). Sequential and temporal properties of behavior induced by a schedule of periodic food delivery. *Behaviour, 54,* 26–49.

Staddon, J. E. R., & Simmelhag, V. L. (1971). The superstition experiment: A re-examination of its implications for the principles of adaptive behavior. *Psychological Review, 78,* 3–43.

Starr, M. D. (1978). An opponent-process theory of motivation: VI. Time and intensity variables in the development of separation-induced distress calling in ducklings. *Journal of Experimental Psychology: Animal Behavior Processes, 4,* 338–355.

Wayner, M. J. (1970). Motor control functions of the lateral hypothalamus and adjunctive behavior. *Physiology and Behavior, 5,* 1319–1325.

Weiss, J. M., Pohorecky, L. A., Salman, S., & Gruenthal, M. (1976). Attenuation of gastric lesions by psychological aspects of aggression in rats. *Journal of Comparative and Physiological Psychology, 90,* 252–259.

Woodworth, R. S. (1958). *Dynamics of behavior,* New York: Holt.

Yoburn, B. C., & Cohen, P. S. (1979). Schedule-induced attack on a pictoral target in feral pigeons (*Columba livia*). *Bulletin of the Psychonomic Society, 13,* 7–8.

Zimmerman, J., & Ferster, C. B. (1964). Some notes on time out from reinforcement. *Journal of the Experimental Analysis of Behavior, 7,* 13–19.

18 Feeding the Face: New Directions in Adjunctive Behavior Research

Michael B. Cantor
Michael B. Cantor Associates, Atlanta, Georgia

Josephine F. Wilson
Wittenberg University, Springfield, Ohio

The writer sits at his desk, fiddling with the blank paper in his typewriter. Where to start? He gets up and paces about the room. Scratching his face, he is surprised to find cookie crumbs clinging to his chin. The pantry has been visited. Our hero is barely conscious.

Two classes of behavior are represented here. The first is information processing of the highest order: writing words on paper in a coherent way. The second is adjunctive behavior: the long list of "involuntary," stereotyped behaviors that fill the gaps between bouts of information processing. Examples of adjunctive behavior in humans include eating, drinking, nail-biting, smoking, grooming, and hair-twirling. Each results in strong oro-facial stimulation and hence the title of this chapter. Fiddling with objects and pacing about the room also belong to the large family of adjunctive behavior as does laughing, perhaps the most distinctively human adjunctive behavior of all.

Here we review some of the animal research on the adjunctive behaviors with the goal of pinning down the necessary and sufficient conditions for inducing them. Then we review some of the more recent work on human adjunctive behavior. Finally, we put the matter of adjunctive behavior into perspective and show that it is an important class of behavior that deserves careful scrutiny. Indeed, there is no area of behavioral technology—be it clinical, industrial, school, or family application—where an understanding of adjunctive behavior is not important.

ADJUNCTIVE BEHAVIOR IN RATS

Adjunctive behavior has been studied in a variety of species (see reviews by Christian, Schaffer, & King, 1978; Falk, 1971; Staddon, 1977, among others) and is primarily seen as *adjunctive* to behavior controlled by an interval schedule of reinforcement. We prefer to view it in more general terms and as the outcome of many different procedures. We here mention four of those procedures and then suggest, as others have (e.g., Cantor, 1981b; Robbins & Fray, 1980), that adjunctive behavior is mediated by arousal which, in turn, stems from either an unconditioned stimulus or uncertainty (H_T) about such stimulus (Cantor, 1981b; Cantor, Smith, & Bryan, 1982).

Induction by Reinforcement Schedule

Falk (1961) was the first to show that a rat, while pressing a lever for food on a fixed interval schedule, will drink copious drafts of water—half its body weight in a three-hour session. Many subsequent experiments have shown that a variety of reinforcers and schedules induce a wide range of adjunctive behaviors. For example, Cantor (1981b) and Wilson and Cantor (1985) have shown that satiated rats pressing a lever for reinforcing electrical stimulation of the brain available on a fixed interval two-minute schedule will eat as much as 50 gms of wet mash in a three-hour session—more than three times their baseline rate. Extensive testing revealed that eating was not induced by the brain stimulation per se, but by the interval schedule on which the stimulation was presented.

We have argued elsewhere (Cantor, 1981b; Cantor et al., 1982) that schedule-induced behavior may be seen, in general, as behavior that is induced by a degree of quantifiable uncertainty (H_T) about the occurrence of reinforcement (Shannon & Weaver, 1949). Cantor (1981a) and Cantor and Wilson (1981) showed that fixed and variable interval reinforcement schedules are essentially watchkeeping or vigilance tasks wherein the organism presses the lever to check for the presence of food in the same way that a radar operator checks his screen for the presence of blips. When the programmed intervals between pellets are quantified in terms of information theory, the very same relationship as seen in watchkeeping experiments holds true: Response rate is inversely related to temporal uncertainty about the occurrence of reinforcement.[1] Because adjunctive behavior increases as the length of the inducing fixed interval schedule is increased up to 2–

---

[1]Cantor (1981a) and Cantor and Wilson (1981) showed that two important problems can be solved if learning experiments are defined in the terms of information theory and viewed as studies in communication between experimenter and subject. In one case, information theory solves the double language problem of Pavlovian conditioning and instrumental learning, two historically different procedures that are shown to have identical outcomes. In the other, information theory subsumes the notions of contiguity and contingency with a single associative metric that quantifies the occurrence of important events (such as reinforcers) in both space and time.

3 minutes (with a standard pellet; e.g., Falk, 1969), it follows that adjunctive behavior is directly related to uncertainly about the onset of reinforcement.

That the frequency of adjunctive behavior is proportional to uncertainty (H_T) about reinforcement can be stated more colloquially and from the organism's point of view: Adjunctive behavior is more likely when the reinforcement is unlikely or, so to speak, when the occurrence of the reinforcer is more surprising. We return to this notion shortly.

Induction by Tail-Pinch

A mild pinch to a rat's tail with a hemostat or alligator clip also induces eating (e.g., Antelman, Rowland, & Fisher, 1976), as well as other stereotyped behaviors, such as pica, aggression, and copulation. These induced behaviors bear striking resemblance to the schedule-induced behaviors. The tail-pinch procedure, then, defines another sufficient condition for inducing adjunctive behavior.

Cantor (1981b) described an animal model of binge eating with the tail-pinch procedure. While being maintained on ad libitum chow, rats were given wet mash in daily ten-minute sessions. On alternate days, the tail was pinched during the session until the animal reliably ate mash in pinch sessions and not in non-pinch baseline sessions. Then, a simulated diet was imposed during pinch sessions but not during baseline sessions. For three sessions, the tail was pinched, *but wet mash was not available.* Animals groomed, licked the floor, aggressed against the experimenter and were extremely irritable. When the mash was again made available during pinch sessions, a 63% increase in eating resulted on the first day off the diet, compared to the tail-pinch session *before* the diet. This phenomenon occurred reliably in two of three animals, each tested three times for the effect.

We regard these results as an animal model of the binges that humans engage in when they (a) go off a diet (eating); (b) fall off the wagon (drinking alcohol); and (c) break down and buy a pack of cigarettes (smoking). In all cases, when the denied object is reinstated, it is initially consumed in excess. The binge phenomenon may also be viewed as one more instance of behavioral contrast wherein reinforcement is programmed in alternating periods (of a multiple schedule) of availability and non-availability. Response rate (lever pressing or in the present case, eating) increases dramatically at the onset of a period when reinforcement becomes available.

Induction by Noise

Drew (1937) was the first to report that many irrelevant stimuli such as noises in combination with lights or buzzers could induce brief and inconsistent bouts of eating. Kupferman (1964) reported that 80 db white noise produced active eat-

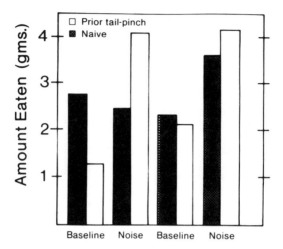

FIG. 18.1.   In satiated naive rats, 90 db noise had no effect on eating behavior compared to baseline. Eating *was* controlled by noise, however, in another group which had been induced to eat in a prior tail-pinch experiment.

ing, although his results are difficult to interpret because his animals were also food-deprived. In addition, Robbins and Fray (1980) were unable to repeat Kupferman's work in pilot studies.

We (Wilson & Cantor, 1983a) also had initial difficulty inducing rats to eat with loud (90 db) noise. After five daily fifteen-min baseline sessions where wet mash was available, eight satiated, naive rats were exposed to the baseline conditions in the presence of 90 db white noise. The sequence was repeated again. As Figure 18.1 shows, no difference in amount eaten was evident between baseline and noise sessions.

The crucial step for producing noise-induced eating turned out to be prior experience with tail pinch. That is, when the noise experiment was carried out with animals that had previously been induced to eat in a tail-pinch experiment, the noise induced eating in an impressive fashion (see Figure 18.1).

The strong conclusion would appear to be that rats can be induced to eat by a relatively mild stimulus such as 90 db noise if they have previously been induced to eat by a more intense stimulus, tail pinch.[2]

More work is needed, but it is clear that noise can reliably induce eating in satiated rats. It may well be that chronic airport and factory noise do the very same thing to people!

---

[2]Alternatively, the eating response, acquired rather slowly and not the moment that a stimulus such as noise or tail pinch is applied, may have simply required the extra number of sessions that the tail-pinch animals had.

Induction by Sexual Frustration

We now know that substantial eating can be induced in food-satiated male rats when attempts to copulate with a receptive female are thwarted (Wilson & Cantor, 1983b). Addressing the second experiment in Figure 18.2 first, 11 rats ate an average of 2.3 gms of mash in five 15-min baseline sessions. In the second phase of the experiment, the animals were placed with a nonreceptive (anestrous) female for ten min; little sexual activity took place. The males were then immediately removed to an adjacent chamber separated from the female by a wire mesh screen and there they were given a dish of wet mash. After another five baseline sessions, the animals were placed with a receptive female until three mounts with intromission occurred (ordinarily, ejaculation and termination of copulation occurs only after 7–15 mounts with intromission). Immediately afterward they were placed in the adjacent chamber for 15 min and allowed to eat mash. Figure 18.2 shows that eating more than doubled compared to prior control sessions. Some rats ate more than eight times their baseline rate!

The first experiment (with 19 animals) was the same as the second, except that the receptive female was presented as the first treatment condition instead of the second. Figure 18.2 shows that thwarted copulation more than quadrupled

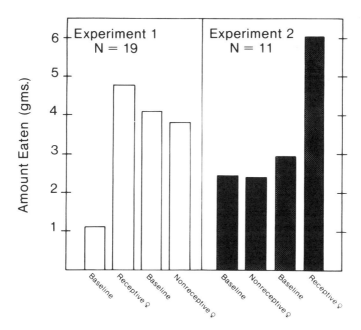

FIG. 18.2.   Interrupted copulation with a receptive female induced eating in satiated male rats compared to a baseline period with the female absent. See text for details.

eating compared to the initial baseline. In subsequent sessions of baseline and exposure to the non-receptive female, the level of eating remained elevated, a generalization to the chamber where the previous action had taken place.

These experiments provide a new way to study induced eating in food-satiated animals. They show not only a direct induction by thwarted copulation but also an effect by conditioned environmental stimuli.

Numerous experiments suggest themselves. How long after intromission does the male continue to eat? How long does the conditioned effect last? Does thwarted copulation induce eating in the female?

A SYNTHESIS OF THE ANIMAL EXPERIMENTS

Although the four procedures described above are quite different, the type and quantity of behaviors that they produce are virtually identical. Cantor (1981b) has reviewed the similarities among tail-pinch and schedule-induction experiments and found striking overlap in four aspects of the phenomena. We now review those similarities and add new findings with noise and sexual frustration.

First, Proximity of the Food is Important.   Adjunctive eating is more likely when food is brought close to the animal. It is best placed under his nose in the case of tail-pinch and for schedule-induction placed across the path of an animal leaving the site of the lever during the post-reinforcement pause.

Location of the food was also important in the noise experiments and particularly important in the sexual frustration studies. In the latter, food dishes were placed at the screen separating the male from the female and at the back wall. In both experiments, there was a greater tendency to eat from the dish on the back wall. Just as in schedule-induction, where rats leave the lever during non-reinforcement (presumably to get the aversive, frustrating stimulus "out of their sight") male rats turned their backs to the inaccessible female. With food placed strategically in their path, they ate plenteously!

Second, the Induced Behavior is Sensitive to Parametric Manipulation.   The amount of eating produced in the tail-pinch procedure is directly related to pinch intensity within narrow limits. Similarly, the amount eaten with schedule induction is directly related to both the time between reinforcers and the magnitude and quality of reinforcement (Falk, 1969).

In pilot studies, we have found that noise-induced eating is directly related to noise intensity; there is little or no effect below 70 db. Sexual-frustration-induced eating, also sensitive to parametric variation, appears to depend upon the number of intromissions allowed, but more data are needed on that point.

Third, the Range of Adjunctive Behaviors is Restricted.   The range of adjunctive behaviors induced by tail-pinch and schedules includes all the familiar oro-facial behaviors of eating, grooming, floor-licking, aggression, and pica.

Induced drinking (polydipsia), however, is common with schedule-induction but has not been shown with tail-pinch.

Sexual frustration and noise also induce the range of oro-facial behaviors, though we have not tested for induced drinking with either procedure. The important point is that there is substantial overlap in both the type and quantity of adjunctive behaviors induced by the four procedures.

We are particularly intrigued by the fact that not all animals eat under a given procedure. The percentage which eat among at least 20 animals tested per procedure is the same—about 70%. In other words, eating is not the way that *all* animals respond to stressors. As we will discuss shortly, the same is true of humans.

Cantor (1981b) reported a negative correlation between amount eaten in a tail-pinch test and the latency with which the animals remove their tails from a standard heat lamp. In other words, the lower their pain threshold, the more they can be induced to eat with a mild tail-pinch. Whether pain threshold also determines the tendency of an animal to eat in the other three procedures—sexual frustration, reinforcement schedule, and noise—we do not know. Indeed, we do not know whether a likelihood of eating in one procedure predicts a likelihood of eating in another. Nor do we know whether animals have a favorite adjunctive behavior that transcends the particular method of induction used.

Fourth, Engaging in Adjunctive Behavior is Reinforcing.   Under both tail-pinch and schedule induction, the opportunity to engage in oro-facial adjunctive behavior is reinforcing. For example, Koob, Fray, and Iversen (1976) have shown that tail-pinched rats will learn the route in a Y-maze where the only reinforcer is a wood block to chew on. Without a pinch, animals did not run the maze. Similar results have been shown with schedule-induced drinking (Falk, 1966). That the opportunity to engage in adjunctive behavior is reinforcing in noise and sexual frustration procedures has not yet been specifically tested.

In summary, no matter which inducing procedure is used—tail-pinch, reinforcement schedule, noise, or sexual frustration—animals emit the same type and quantity of adjunctive behaviors; the arrangement of food in the environment determines eating; and all outcomes are sensitive to parametric manipulation. From a theoretical standpoint, the appropriate way to account for similar adjunctive behaviors from widely dissimilar inducing procedures is to posit a mediating intervening variable.

ADJUNCTIVE BEHAVIOR IS A BY-PRODUCT OF AROUSAL

We prefer to call the intervening variable *arousal* (see also Cantor & Wilson, 1978; Cantor, 1981; Killeen, et al., 1978; Robbins & Fray, 1980), though *stress, motivation,* or *drive* would do just as well. Regardless of what the intervening variable is called, we can state formally that the necessary and sufficient condition for inducing adjunctive behavior is arousal, and that arousal may be produced by at least two basic manipulations: (a) unconditioned stimuli, and (b) uncertainty (H_T) about the occurrence of unconditioned stimuli. Tail-pinch and noise are examples of the first category, whereas schedule induction and separation of the male from the receptive female (a simple extinction procedure) are examples of the second category. Adjunctive behavior, then, is seen as a by-product of stimuli that serve as unconditioned stimuli or reinforcers and uncertainty (H_T) about such stimuli.[3]

This view is quite compatible with an opponent process (Solomon & Corbit, 1974) view of adjunctive behavior. The present emphasis, however, is on the effect of uncertainty about important events as an inducing agent. This notion is expanded in the next section as we discuss procedures that induce adjunctive behavior in humans.

ADJUNCTIVE BEHAVIOR IN PEOPLE

More than 22 years have passed since schedule-induced behavior was first identified in rats (Falk, 1961), yet disappointingly few experiments have addressed this important part of the human behavioral repertoire. Some studies have reported schedule-induced activity (Muller, Crow, & Cheney, 1979) and water drinking (Kachanoff, Leveille, McLelland, & Wayner, 1973), but only two studies have reported induced eating in a systematic way. Cantor (1981b) and Cantor et al. (1982) used a pursuit rotor to induce people to eat, drink soda pop, groom, and fiddle with objects.

Undergraduate volunteers for an "eye-hand coordination experiment" tracked a rotating spot of light for 10-sec periods that alternated with 15-sec time-out periods. During the time-outs, subjects were told that they were "welcome to eat" the food and drink the soda that lay at their right hand and under the beam of a desk lamp whose onset signaled the start of the time-out.

The food, said to be the remains of a "new-Ph.D. party," consisted of Chinese noodles and small bits of scraped carrots. The pieces were purposely kept small and *digital* to facilitate the observation and counting of ingestive responses by the experimenter via closed circuit television.

---

[3]Recently, Mittleman and Valenstein (1984) demonstrated that ingestion induced by central stimulation of the lateral hypothalamus is comparable to schedule induced ingestion. Animals that ate or drank during electrical stimulation tended to be the very same animals that displayed schedule-induced polydipsia. Presumably, then, hypothalamic stimulation produces the same arousal that is produced naturally by the environmental manipulations discussed here.

The major dependent variable, varied within subjects in one experiment (Cantor, 1981b) and between subjects in the other, was information load as defined by the following formula:

$$H_T = f\left(\log_2 \frac{R\omega t}{Aa}\right)$$

where H_T is uncertainty about the location of the light spot; R is the radius of the circle swept by the rotating light spot of the rotor; ω is its angular velocity; A is the area of the spot; a is the area of the tip of the hand-held stylus; and t is the duration of the tracking. In both experiments, all variables were held constant except ω which was tested at two levels, 73 and 5.8 radians per second.

There were five major results and conclusions from this study:

1. High-speed tracking (high uncertainty) induced more adjunctive behavior in its aftermath than did low-speed tracking (low uncertainty). This result provides support for our claim that uncertainty about an important stimulus, in this case the target to be tracked, is a sufficient condition for inducing adjunctive behavior and that food deprivation, explicit reinforcement, and/or interval schedules of reinforcement are not necessary.

2. As in every animal experiment we have ever performed (noise, tail-pinch, and schedule induction), there was more adjunctive behavior (particularly ingestion and grooming) at the start of the session than at the end. We regard this habituation effect as more evidence that informative, nonredundant stimulation is a sufficient condition for inducing adjunctive behavior. In this case, the stimulation is the new environment in which the subject finds himself.

3. The subjects who traced the best (i.e., who had the greatest time on target) tended to eat; whereas, the worst trackers tended to groom. This robust effect fits well with the notion (Rodin, 1977, 1981) that some people are more responsive than others to external stimuli—in this case, small, rotating light spots and bits of food. We wonder whether those people who eat under information load, are the people who, like the tail-pinched rats (Cantor, 1981b), also have a lower pain threshold.

4. A within-subject experiment (Cantor, 1981b) revealed that people are highly consistent from session to session in the type and quantity of adjunctive behavior they emit. Put another way, each person has a distinctive adjunctive *signature,* which identifies that person as surely as does gait or facial features.

5. Among subjects, eating and grooming were the dominant adjunctive behaviors and were followed by drinking and fiddling. Cantor et al. (1982) reported normative data on adjunctive behavior and suggested that it could be useful in characterizing the type and quantity of adjunctive behavior exhibited by a given individual. That information could be used for developing a diet plan or generally making the person aware of the extent of his involuntary, off-task behaviors.

To summarize, adjunctive behaviors in general and eating in particular can be induced in a satiated subject by an information processing task that has no other reinforcement than intrinsic satisfaction of tracking on target. We assume that tracking induces arousal in proportion to the information load (i.e., as a function of tracking speed). When the tracking period is over (and the time-out period begins), the remaining arousal induces mostly oro-facial stimulation, including eating, drinking, grooming, and fiddling.

Why subjects differ in the kind and amount of adjunctive behavior they consistently emit, we do not know. Nor do we know the roles of heredity and environment in determining the mix and quantity emitted. We are convinced, however, that answers to these and other questions would considerably advance our understanding of pathological eating, smoking, nail-biting, temporal-mandibular joint syndrome, dental bruxisms, and, as mentioned elsewhere (Cantor, 1981b), attention deficit disorder with hyperactivity.

CONCLUDING COMMENTS

There are two areas of human endeavor where adjunctive behavior is very well represented—work and play—, and they deserve comments. Let us first consider work situations.

Computer Terminals

If, for some perverse reason, a manager were paid ten cents for every instance of adjunctive behavior he could induce in his workers, he would be well advised to place people in front of computer terminals. Intense periods of data entry, programming, or error correction are punctuated with lulls in the action while the computer processes the data or waits its turn in a time-sharing system. Informal observation reveals that operators fill that time with smoking, eating, grooming, or finger drumming.

There can be little doubt that the work and wait rhythm at the video display terminal is stressful, especially if it is done all day long, as is the case with telephone operators, air traffic controllers, and secretaries. If the adjunctive behavior of choice is smoking or eating, a seemingly innocuous job could be hazardous indeed.

Recently, designers of terminals have concerned themselves with the angle and height of the screen, or the intensity of the display. We believe that an area of at least as much concern is the timing of the lulls in the action and the harmful adjunctive behavior that is induced. Computer operators should be made aware that they work under conditions known to induce often harmful involuntary behavior, and that precautions should be taken.

Telephone Sales

With the increase in prices of energy and transportation, door-to-door sales, an American tradition, have declined, and telephone sales have increased. Recently, one of the authors was involved in a project aimed at improving performance of telephone salespeople. A salesperson would typically make a call and have an intense conversation with the customer. (Surprisingly, only one out of nineteen people called hangs up immediately.) After the conversation was over, many of the 22 salespeople engaged in their personal adjunctive behavior. Nine people smoked cigarettes, three consistently ate snack food, and seven people drank coffee. One of the seven drank more than 20 cups per day! Both the task at hand, telephone sales, and the adjunctive behavior were driven at high rates in this environment, because people were paid on ratio schedules of reinforcement (i.e., on commission).

We believe that work environments such as this would benefit from a redesign that would either reduce the cyclic intensity of the work or at least provide, perhaps through education, innocuous (or even constructive) adjunctive behaviors that could be substituted for those that are harmful.

Assembly Lines

Automobile assembly line workers are particularly prone to induced adjunctive behavior. They typically work intensely to get ahead of the constantly moving conveyor and then fill the time gap by lighting a cigarette or tending to their chew of tobacco. The nature of the work, highly regimented and fast-paced, can be very harmful, not because of what happens *on task,* but because of what occurs *off task* as an adjunctive behavior.

In addition to directly harming the worker, induced smoking and tobacco use indirectly harm the product. Cigarette smoking is directly correlated with absenteeism in industry. Absenteeism, in turn, is a primary cause of low productivity and, because of errors by inexperienced substitute workers, general poor quality.

Again, in designing industrial jobs, it would be valuable to consider not only the details of the job itself, but also the adjunctive behavior it will surely generate. Indeed, the welfare of both the worker and the product may depend upon it.

Comedy

Here and elsewhere (Cantor, 1981b; Cantor et al., 1982), it has been said that adjunctive behavior is a byproduct of exposure to informative stimuli (i.e., to stimuli that are improbable, non-redundant, or from the organism's standpoint, surprising). There is abundant evidence from many different kinds of experiments that organisms attend to such stimuli (e.g., Attneave, 1954; Zusne &

Michels, 1964). Consequently, adjunctive behavior may be seen as a byproduct of attending to informative, surprising stimuli. For example, we would expect that watching an exciting, scary (informative) movie would induce more pop-corn-eating than would a boring movie or the scary one seen for the third time. From the same point of view, a difficult question, that is, one with many possible answers, would induce more adjunctive head scratching than an easy one.

Having made these connections, we can talk about play and the relationship between adjunctive behavior and comedy and magic, that is, carefully prepared stimulus material which is at its best when informative, improbable, non-redundant . . . surprising.

Jokes hold attention by the nature of the story or by virtue of the promise of a surprise punchline at the end. Arousal is built up during the telling of the story (see also Berlyne, 1972). At its peak, the punchline is delivered, the story ends, and the arousal remains. Built-up arousal, then, drives laughter just as surely as it drives eating in the aftermath of tracking on a pursuit rotor. Indeed, informal observation of people listening to jokes suggests that there is a degree of sub-stitutability in the adjunctive behaviors elicited by a joke. A person may pop candy into his mouth, take a drink, or reach for a cigarette when the punchline is told.

For some people, jokes elicit aggression and heckling. Puns often do this, because they are usually so surprising. Does adjunctive aggression occur instead of laughter because the information load of the punchline is too high, or is the type of adjunctive behavior elicited simply a matter of individual differences? There is much to be learned about laughing as an induced behavior, and, for purposes of introspection, we offer the following as stimulus material:

> Mr. Carrot and Mr. Celery were walking down the street. Carrot stepped off the curb and was hit by a car. With siren wailing, an ambulance took him to the hospital. Mr. Celery paced back and forth as he awaited the outcome of emergency surgery. Finally, after a two-hour wait, the tired surgeon enters saying, "I have good news and bad news: The good news is that he will live . . . the bad news is that he'll be a vegetable for the rest of his life."

Magic

Magic holds the attention of an audience according to the same principles that govern comedy. An audience watches the prosaic buildup of a magic trick because of an implicit promise that learned object permanence will be violated. Red cards turn black. Big things come out of small places. Things vanish and appear inexplicably. Objects levitate without visible support. It is this surprise, that is, the information, like the punchline of a joke, that actually does the job of entertaining. Consider this bit of business:

A magician has a member of the audience randomly choose a card from the deck. While the magician's back is turned, the card is shown to the rest of the audience. The spectator returns the card to the deck and shuffles three times. The magician fans the deck artfully and announces triumphantly, "And here is your card." "No," says the audience. He tries again. "Pardon me," he says with a flourish. "Here is the chosen card." "Not a chance," says the audience, delighting in his embarrassment. "Well, I hate to end on a sour note," says the magician, as he at once douses the lights and gestures grandly to a Jack of Spades projected on the front screen. The audience cheers wildly and guffaws loudly.

A magician, like any showman, does a trick many times. If he is a psychologist, a magic trick becomes much like a standardized personality test. That is, in a relatively constant setting, a fixed stimulus is presented to a subject who views it alone or in a small group of two or three people. Though most people enjoy watching magic performed, the adjunctive behavior induced by magical surprise is not always predictable. Some people shriek. Others laugh or clap their hands. But others, as with comedy, get angry and heckle the entertainer. Magicians who perform at close range often encounter spectators who actually grab the hand that fools them.

To conclude, the repertoire of adjunctive behavior induced directly by an important event or, through learning, by uncertainty (H_T) about the event is both fascinating and important. In humans, we believe that an explication of adjunctive behavior is central to an understanding of many maladaptive "bad habits" including excessive eating, drinking, and smoking. Very little is known about the moment-to-moment environmental changes that induce the adjunctive behaviors or about the wide range of individual differences among people. We encourage researchers to fill this gap.

REFERENCES

Antelman, S. M., Rowland, N. E., & Fisher, A. E. (1976). Stimulation bound ingestive behavior: A view from the tail. *Physiology & Behavior, 17,* 743–748.

Attneave, F. (1954). Some informational aspects of visual information. *Psychological Review, 61,* 183–193.

Berlyne, D. E. (1972). Humor and its kin. In J. Goldstein & P. McGhee (Eds.), *The psychology of humor* (pp. 120–129). New York: Academic Press.

Cantor, M. B. (1981a). Information theory: A solution to two big problems in the analysis of behavior. In P. Harzem & M. Zeiler (Eds.), *Advances in the analysis of behavior: vol. 2. Predictability, correlation, and contiguity* (pp. 287–320). Chichester: Wiley.

Cantor, M. B. (1981b). Bad habits: Models of induced ingestion in satiated rats and people. In S. Miller (Ed.), *Behavior and nutrition.* Franklin Institute Press.

Cantor, M. B., Smith, S. E., & Bryan, B. R. (1982). Induced bad habits: Adjunctive ingestion and grooming in human subjects. *Appetite: Journal for Intake Research, 3,* 1–17.

Cantor, M. B., & Wilson, J. F. (1978). Polydipsia induced by a schedule of brain stimulation reinforcement. *Learning and Motivation, 9*, 428–445.

Cantor, M. B., & Wilson, J. F. (1981). Temporal uncertainty as an associative metric: Operant simulations of Pavlovian conditioning. *Journal of Experimental Psychology: General, 110*, 232–268.

Christian, W. P., Schaffer, R. W., & King, G. D. (1978). *Schedule-induced behavior.* Montreal: Eden Press.

Drew, G. C. (1937). The recurrence of eating in rats after apparent satiation. *Proceedings of the Zoological Society of London, 107*, 95–106.

Falk, J. L. (1961). Production of polydipsia in normal rats by an intermittent food schedule. *Science, 133*, 195–196.

Falk, J. L. (1966). The motivational properties of schedule-induced polydipsia. *Journal of the Experimental Analysis of Behavior, 9*, 37–39.

Falk, J. L. (1969). Conditions producing psychogenic polydipsia in animals. *Annals of the New York Academy of Science, 157*, 569–593.

Falk, J. L. (1971). The nature and determinants of adjunctive behavior. *Physiology and Behavior, 6*, 577–588.

Kachanoff, R., Leveille, R., McLelland, J. P., & Wayner, M. J. (1973). Schedule induced behavior in humans. *Physiology and Behavior, 11*, 395–398.

Killeen, P. R., Hanson, S. J., & Osborne, S. R. (1978). Arousal: Its genesis and manifestations as response rate. *Psychological Review, 85*, 571–581.

Koob, G. F., Fray, P. J., & Iversen, S. D. (1976). Tail-pinch stimulation: Sufficient motivation for learning. *Science, 194*, 637–639.

Kupfermann, I. (1964). Eating behavior induced by sounds. *Nature, 201*, 324.

Mittleman, G., & Valenstein, E. S. (1984). Ingestive behavior evoked by hypothalamic stimulation and schedule-induced polydipsia are related. *Science, 224*, 415–417.

Muller, P. G., Crow, R. E., & Cheney, C. D. (1979). Schedule-induced locomotor activity in humans. *Journal of the Experimental Analysis of Behavior, 31*, 83–90.

Robbins, T. W., & Fray, P. J. (1980). Stress-induced eating: Fact, fiction, or misunderstanding? *Appetite: Journal for Intake Research, 1*, 103–133.

Rodin, J. (1977). Bidirectional influences of emotionality, stimulus responsivity, and metabolic events in obesity. In J. D. Maser & M. E. P. Seligman (Eds.), *Psychopathology: Experimental models* (pp. 27–65). San Francisco: Freeman.

Rodin, J. (1981). Current status of the internal-external hypothesis for obesity: What went wrong? *American Psychologist, 36*, 361–372.

Shannon, C. E., & Weaver, W. (1949). *The Mathematical Theory of Communication.* Urbana-University of Illinois Press.

Solomon, R. L., & Corbit, J. D. (1974). An opponent process theory of motivation. *Psychological Review, 81*, 119–145.

Staddon, J. E. R. (1977). Schedule induced behavior. In V. Honig & J. Staddon (Eds.), *Handbook of Operant Behavior*, (pp. 125–152). Englewood Cliffs, NJ: Prentice-Hall.

Wilson, J. F., & Cantor, M. B. (1983a). *Noise-induced eating in rats.* Paper presented at the meeting of the Midwestern Psychological Association.

Wilson, J. F., & Cantor, M. B. (1983b). *Is eating a substitute for sex?* Paper presented at the meeting of the Eastern Psychological Association. Philadelphia.

Wilson, J. F., & Cantor, M. B. (1985). *An animal model of excessive eating: Schedule-induced hyperphagia in food-satiated rats.* Manuscript submitted for publication.

Zusne, L., & Michels, K. M. (1964). Nonrepresentational shapes and eye movements. *Perceptual and Motor Skills, 18*, 11–20.

VI EXTENSIONS TO HUMAN AND CULTURAL ISSUES

19 Organizational Culture: Skill, Defense Mechanism, or Addiction?

Edgar H. Schein
Sloan School of Management, MIT

INTRODUCTION

One of the hopes of the experiment integrating several fields into Harvard's Department of Social Relations in the 1940s and 1950s was to stimulate genuine interdisciplinary approaches to the study of behavioral phenomena. The impact of this experiment on me, Richard Solomon's role, in particular, and a new conceptualization that has now emerged from my education are described in this brief paper.

I did my graduate course work in social psychology in 1949 and 1950. Following a clinical internship at the Walter Reed Army Institute of Research, I did my thesis research under Allport and Solomon. It was an experimental study of human imitation—how it was learned initially and how it then generalized from the learning situation to others of varying degrees of similarity. During the experience, Solomon instilled in me a healthy respect for experimentation and an intellectual excitement about crossing disciplinary boundaries.

At that time, Solomon was excited about whether or not dogs had Freudian consciences, and he was out to design an experiment that would prove or disprove this notion. The idea of applying Freudian theory to dogs and then designing an experiment to try to support or disprove the theory has always stuck in my mind as the hallmark of Dick's enthusiasm and intellectual breadth. As I recall the outcome, by the way, dogs showed no evidence of shame or remorse when they soiled an area in which they had been trained not to relieve themselves, unless they knew they were being observed, which clearly supported the notion that dogs had *shame* but not *guilt,* hence no Freudian conscience. Later, Solomon, Turner, and Lessac (1968) went on to study, in a detailed way, the role of delay of punishment in generating shame as compared with guilt.

315

What does this bit of history have to do with my topic? It turns out that some 30 years later, I find myself asking a similar provocative question in a setting which, unfortunately, is not as resolvable by experimentation. My current interest is corporate or organizational culture which, as you may know, has become a fad recently because of the alleged superiority of some Japanese-style organizations in generating high levels of commitment and productivity through creating what are hypothesized to be stronger organizational cultures (Deal & Kennedy, 1982; Ouchi, 1981; Pascale & Athos, 1981).

In trying to analyze what might be involved in this hypothesis, I have found myself over the past several years drawing on all my intellectual background— anthropology, sociology, and especially clinical psychology. Hence the provocative question: Is organizational culture a *skill*, learned through the mechanisms of positive reinforcement; is it a *defense* learned through avoidance conditioning; or is it even an *addiction*, learned through opponent-process mechanisms of the kind that Solomon postulates?

What is Organizational Culture?

Based on my own experience in organizations and as a consultant to organizations, it is apparent to me that the concept of culture, as developed in anthropology, can be validly transposed to units smaller than societies, specifically, to organizations, if we focus on how culture is learned and unlearned. This dynamic evolutionary perspective has actually given the anthropologists some trouble because of the difficulty of getting historical data from preliterate societies. But, in the case of organizations, we sometimes have complete histories from origins, through critical growth periods, to periods of stability and then stagnation. I have had a number of consulting experiences where it was possible to observe from the inside many of the critical events that were shared by the organizations, and it is these clinical data which have fed the theoretical notions I want to lay before you.

One of the most salient characteristics of organizations that plagues all of us as members, consultants, managers, and citizens is their incredible resistance to change. Even when they are clearly failing in their primary mission, organizations sometimes go cheerfully to their demise while frustrated managers and consultants try to figure out why certain adaptations could not be achieved. For example, organizations that achieve their initial success on the basis of technical invention and development have a remarkably difficult time learning that in highly competitive markets they must become more marketing and customer-oriented to survive. Companies that have succeeded with certain product lines often cannot switch to other product lines when the market is saturated or the competition has a better, cheaper product. Companies whose success has depended on tight financial controls and an elaborate accounting system cannot manage newly-acquired organizations running with less overhead. Companies that have succeeded initially, by developing autocratic/paternalistic structures suitable for the rapid introduction of an invention, cannot learn more participative and delegative styles needed when they must diversify and involve employees more.

From Kurt Lewin on, we have acknowledged this stability by noting that any change process in a human system has to begin with a period of destabilization, what Lewin correctly termed the *unfreezing* of a quasi-stationary equilibrium (Lewin, 1952). I elaborated this notion in my work on coercive persuasion, by noting that unfreezing consists of two basic processes: (a) the presentation of disconfirming information and, simultaneously, (b) the creation of psychological safety (Schein, 1961; Schein, 1964). If individuals did not feel psychologically safe, they would defend themselves against the disconfirming information by denial or by even more basic perceptual defenses.

All of us in those early days of formulating the field of organizational development thought we were changing culture, or at least were trying to change culture (Beckhard, 1969; Bennis, 1969; Schein, 1969). But the full significance of putting together what we know from anthropology about culture and what we learned as change agents about the difficulties of overcoming resistance to change is only now becoming clear.

The key question is, "Why is resistance to change so great?" Or, in dynamic terms, "Why is it necessary to create psychological safety to get someone to correctly perceive disconfirming information, even when it is in one's best interests to do so?" The answer lies in the nature of how culture is learned, what basic functions it serves, and what we know about avoidance conditioning (Schein, 1981; 1983, 1985).

Before I discuss the mechanisms in more detail, let me give a more formal definition of *organizational culture:* It is (a) the pattern of basic assumptions (b) which a given group has invented, discovered, or developed (c) in learning to cope with its problems of external adaptation and internal integration and (d) which have worked well enough to be considered valid, and, therefore, (e) desirable to be taught to new members as (f) the correct way to perceive, think, and feel in relation to those problems.

The important point to recognize in this definition is that the essence of organizational culture is the pattern of basic assumptions, many of which have dropped out of consciousness and have a *taken for granted* quality. Many analyses of culture are stuck at the level of what are thought of as basic values. I am arguing that the essence of culture goes beyond the level of values, to the unquestioned cognitive assumptions on which values are based. Culture, if it is to mean for organizations what anthropologists mean in describing societies, must be defined in these basic cognitive terms.

If culture is a learned solution to problems, what are the problems organizations face? What I mean by *problems of external adaptation* are such matters as figuring out what to do to survive, developing the means and tools to make it happen, developing concepts and tools for measuring progress, and generally learning to cope with a dynamic environment. What I mean by *problems of internal integration* is developing a common language and conceptual categories and a set of social categories and rules which permit the management of basic feelings of aggression and love, and, thus, make it possible for people to live in safety and harmony while they pursue their survival tasks.

As we learn to solve our problems and get along with each other in a given group by developing a language, the necessary conceptual categories for dealing with the environment and each other, and the social rules for managing feelings and relationships, we are learning a skill through reinforcement principles. In this sense, culture can be seen as a set of cognitive, emotional, and behavioral skills for dealing with the environment and each other, which we pass on to successive generations and which will presumably survive as long as they work. Is it not sufficient, then, to argue that culture is basically a set of skills learned by a group?

But our reinforcement learning model also tells us that if particular cultural assumptions cease to work, they should gradually become extinguished. Yet this seems to happen rarely. People cling to cultural assumptions, even when they no longer seem to work. Some additional learning mechanisms must be at work, if we see cultural behavior and cognitions persisting. I believe the basic reason for observed cultural stability is that the learned skills not only produce positive solutions, but, and perhaps more importantly, they also reduce the primary anxiety of uncertainty and instability by stabilizing our environment!

The internal and external problems described above are potential sources of what I will call *primary anxiety,* in the sense that we are ultimately anxious when we do not have stable categories for relating to our physical and social environment. Most of us have not felt such anxiety because "culture" provides a protective cocoon (Hebb, 1954), but we can infer it and extrapolate it from extreme experiences of (a) culture shock, (b) the chaos which follows after natural disasters such as earthquakes, or (c) during wartime when social norms and rules of interaction break down. Bettelheim's (1943) accounts of concentration camps and Lifton's (1956) and my studies (Schein, 1956; 1961) of prisoners of war during the Korean conflict illustrate such extreme disorganization and the primary anxiety that can be aroused in victims when culture becomes ambiguous and/or unstable.

To the extent that the learning of a given cultural element successfully reduces such primary anxiety, it can be appropriately labeled as a *defensive response.* And, to the extent that learning how to defend against primary anxiety occurs through avoidance-conditioning mechanisms, we can see that such cultural learning will be hard to extinguish, even though it no longer produces positive reinforcement, just as Solomon and others have shown us (Solomon, Kamin, & Wynne, 1953; Solomon & Wynne, 1953).

In other words, once we have succeeded in building some common categories of meaning, a status and authority system, and a set of ground rules for the management of our positive and aggressive feelings, we not only have skills for dealing with the environment and each other, but we also have the means to avoid uncertainty, disorder, cognitive overload, and social chaos. Culture, as a learned set of assumptions of what is true in our physical and social environment, helps us avoid the anxiety that would result if we had to learn anew what various physical and social stimuli meant, which ones had to be attended to, and which ones could be ignored. The cognitive structures underlying culture allow us to judge what is true and false, what is physically real and what is not, what one should pay attention to and what one can ignore, and, thus, to attain a sense of reality that permits us to relax to a certain degree, to define our identity and the nature of the world, to manage time and space, and to manage others. The stability of culture rests, then, on the fact that it is learned not only by positive reinforcement mechanisms, but, at a more fundamental level, by avoidance-conditioning mechanisms.

Can one talk of such learning of "culture" at the level of the human group or organization? If culture is the learned solution to problems of external and internal survival, then any group that faces such problems for any significant period of its history will develop a culture of its own. It will develop an organizational culture, because the members of a new organization initially suffer from some of the same cognitive and social anxieties as any new group (Schein & Bennis, 1965; Schein 1969). Whether or not one calls such a culture a *subculture* is a matter of definition. The important point to recognize is that any group can develop a culture of its own: The mechanisms by which learning occurs should be the same, no matter what size the unit.

My own experience with organizations, as well as what historians and ethnographers of our contemporary scene have documented, suggests that such processes of culture formation do indeed replicate themselves in organizations, provided there is some degree of stability of membership and enough shared experience to have made possible the formation of new categories and assumptions. The process is not, of course, as traumatic as is postulated for ultimate cultural origins, because the members of a new organization all come from cultural units that have ready-made solutions available. But the process of reaching genuinely shared meanings and consensus in a new organization can be quite tramatic in its own right, as we have seen often in mini-organizations such as training or therapy groups (Bion, 1959; Schein & Bennis, 1965).

The shape and content of a particular organizational culture will reflect the biases of its founders, its actual history, the kinds of difficulties it has had to overcome, and, ultimately, the complex interaction between the assumptions of all the members and leaders (Schein, 1983, 1985). For example, in one company I worked with, it was very evident that *truth* was judged by whether or not an idea survived a social combat. Ideas were assumed to come from individuals, and they could come from anyone, because individuals were seen as the source of creativity. But individuals, it was further assumed, are not smart enough to know what is true and valid, and, therefore, cannot be trusted to implement their own ideas. Ideas have to be brought into various levels of group process, committees, and task forces, where they are debated and analyzed. Only as consensus emerged in such groups did senior people in the company agree to go ahead with a proposal. At this point, the executives' belief in the individual reasserted itself, because they always allocated responsibility for the implementation of the idea to individuals once again.

The group was the crucible for determining reality. Authority was based on area of responsibility and ability to be "right." Being the boss did not mean anything if one could not convince people. Insubordination was not only tolerated, it was encouraged if the outcome was likely to be a better solution. People felt very challenged but also very frustrated by the need always to negotiate their solution.

How could the group tolerate such high levels of interpersonal conflict? A correlated assumption was that "we all are part of a family," and, therefore, "our membership is secure even if we fight a lot." As this organization has grown and lost some of its communal family feeling, it has had a harder time sustaining its model of truth. Managers in this organization cannot get acceptance of a more efficient authoritarian mechanism of making decisions, even though most members of senior management acknowledge the need for more rapid, disciplined decision-making. For them to lodge power in individuals involves exposing themselves to high levels of anxiety, something they are not willing to do.

In contrast, in another company I worked with, truth was clearly seen to reside in those who had either scientific credentials or who had been promoted to higher levels in the organization, presumably due to their past track record in having made valid decisions. Once a senior person decided what to do, the action was regarded as valid, and the organization fell into line in implementing the idea. It was unthinkable to challenge the idea or to subvert it, even if one had doubts about it. Jobs were seen as belonging to the job occupant, and only higher authority had the right to influence what a person did on his own turf. In this organization, it became evident that to compete, more innovative ideas would be needed from some of the younger technical and managerial people. Yet the old assumptions about where truth comes from (i.e. the "top") and who "owns" jobs kept the organization from paying attention to the young ideas even when they surfaced. Ideas invented lower down in the organization did not rise to the top, and ideas or new programs tried successfully in one part of the organization did not diffuse laterally to other parts of the organization. Simple suggestions to circulate information more widely were met with silence or disbelief, because it was considered a violation of people's turf to send them information that might hint at the possibility they are not completely on top of their jobs. The structure of jobs and roles provides a basic stability to daily life. Any challenge to this structure unleashes strong anxiety and defensive avoidance.

These two organizations have very different patterns of basic assumptions which influence deeply how they go about their business—the way they solve problems, the kind of authority system they have developed, the kinds of rewards and controls they use, the ways they recruit and develop people, and so on. They each cling to their paradigm because it has successfully reduced their primary anxiety in the past. And, according to elaborated principles of learned defensive responses (Brown, 1965; Melvin, 1971), we can anticipate that any threat of organizational failure will be met with more vigorous efforts within the old paradigm.

CULTURE CHANGE

Organizations exist in dynamic environments, and their assumptions about how to deal with their environment can become maladaptive. Furthermore, it has been observed that young organizations that have successfully survived their early growth spurt and are continuing to grow need their culture as a kind of glue during their growth phase. But as they mature, the very culture which served to hold the group together during its growth can become a problem if the mature organization is no longer adapted well to its environment.

At this point, organizations often develop a need to change, even a motivation to change, yet find that resistance to change is overwhelming. Why should this surprise us, if we know anything about avoidance conditioning? When we ask an organization to develop a different strategy built on different assumptions, we are asking that individuals give up the culture and behavior patterns that have historically enabled them to cope with their anxieties. No matter how convincing we may be on the positive survival value of a new strategy, we cannot convince members of the organization that they will be able to survive the crippling anxiety of the transition when they have to live for a time without the defense mechanism they have relied on successfully for a long time. It is in the nature of avoidance-learning that we cannot test whether or not the anticipated source of pain is still there without bearing the anxiety that signals the possibility. And if that anxiety is the primary anxiety that attends cognitive instability, it will be avoided at all costs.

We next may ask why "unfreezing" an organization requires psychological safety for its members. If the individual asked to change cannot perceive that it is safe to let go of a present behavior, value, or assumption (i.e., that no crippling anxiety will follow), that individual simply will ignore the other available information, no matter how much that information demonstrates the disfunctionality of the present behavior, value, or assumption. So, if we are to change culture, we must first figure out how to create the psychological safety that permits the members of an organization to enter a change process, and this is a technology that is woefully lacking (Beckhard & Harris, 1977). We are much better at escalating disconfirmation than at creating psychological safety.

On the other hand, what do we know about spontaneous or natural change? Organizations do get unfrozen by external circumstances, such as loss of market share, the failure of a product, the inability to make enough profit, the loss of key people, or the like. It seems to me that once organizations realize the necessity of some culture change to prevent organizational death, they do have ways of changing. They have ways of containing or suffering through the period of anxiety, which is inevitable when new cultural assumptions are learned.

But is all organizational change motivated only by external threats? Is some of the pressure to change inherent in the stability itself? I propose that cultural change can also be stimulated by some social version of the opponent-processes known to provide biologically based motivations (Solomon & Corbit, 1974).

If the motivation for change of culture is governed by some kind of opponent process motivation, that is, the more the members of a group succeed in stabilizing their environment, the more they will simultaneously be building forces toward destabilization and novelty; then we should see natural and inherent forces toward culture change which, eventually, can be taken advantage of.

If culture is like an addiction, it would explain both why we "need" to travel to foreign lands periodically, leaving the security of our home culture, and why it is so rewarding to come back home each time after we've been away. Each situation perhaps breeds its opposite, and, in a sense, we need both stability and instability. We need both the security of being totally embedded in a group, and the excitement of creativity, rebelliousness, and individuality.

If we become addicted to stability and learn from Solomon's theory that more stability will breed more need for variety, we could learn when and how to take advantage of the opponent process rather than trying to overcome the primary process. This may be what some managers do implicitly when they periodically re-organize. If part of the culture itself is based on an assumption of perpetual change, improvement, progress, and the like, then the opponent-process energy has an organizationally legitimate outlet.

In effect, this is arguing that anxiety in small doses is not only bearable but possibly exciting, and that cultures can change and evolve, in spite of being learned by avoidance mechanisms, if they change frequently in small steps, rather than in large steps all at once. What Quinn (1980) identifies as the change strategy of *logical incrementalism,* by which he means very small changes whenever an opportunity presents itself, would fit this theoretical model very well, because anxiety never mounts to a high pitch.

CONCLUSION

I have tried to develop the theoretical notion that culture in general, and organizational culture in particular, is learned simultaneously by positive reinforcement and by avoidance conditioning. The stability of organizational culture and the strong resistance to change, which is often observed, can be related to the difficulty of extinguishing responses learned by the avoidance mechanism. If opponent-process theory also applies to this kind of learning, it would provide a further line of exploration in that it would open up possibilities for the management of change, by taking advantage of the natural change forces inherent in the opponent process.

REFERENCES

Beckhard, R. (1969). *Organization development*. Reading, MA: Addison-Wesley.

Beckhard, R., & Harris, R. T. (1977). *Organization transitions*. Reading, MA: Addison-Wesley.

Bennis, W. G. (1969). *Organization development*. Reading, MA: Addison-Wesley.

Bettelheim, B. (1943). Individual and mass behavior in extreme situations. *Journal of Abnormal and Social Psychology, 38,* 417–452.

Bion, W. R. (1959). *Experiences in groups*. New York: Basic Books.

Brown, J. S. (1965). A behavioral analysis of masochism. *Journal of Experimental Research in Personality 1,* 65–70.

Deal, T. E., & Kennedy, A. A. (1982). *Corporate cultures*. Reading, MA: Addison-Wesley.

Hebb, D. (1954). The social significance of animal studies, In G. Lindzey (Ed.), *Handbook of social psychology, Vol. 2* Reading, MA: Addison-Welsey.

Lewin, K. (1952). Group decision and social change. In G. E. Swanson, T. N. Newcomb, & E. L. Hartley (Eds.), *Readings in social psychology* (rev. ed.) (pp. 459–473). New York: Holt.

Lifton, R. J. (1956). ''Thought reform'' of Western civilians in Chinese communist prisons. *Psychiatry, 19,* 173–195.

Melvin, K. B. (1971). Vicious circle behavior. In H. D. Kimmel (Ed.), *Experimental psychopathology: Recent research and theory* (pp. 95–118). New York: Academic Press.

Ouchi, W. (1981). *Theory Z*. Reading, MA: Addison-Wesley.

Pascale, R. T., & Athos, A. G. (1981). *The art of Japanese management*. New York: Simon & Schuster.

Quinn, J. B. (1980). *Strategies for change*. Homewood, IL: Irwin.

Schein, E. H. (1956). The Chinese indoctrination program for prisoners of war. *Psychiatry, 19,* 149–172.

Schein, E. H. (1961). *Coercive persuasion*. New York: Norton.

Schein, E. H. (1964). Personal change through interpersonal relations. In W. G. Bennis, E. H. Schein, D. R. Berlew, & F. I. Steele (Eds.), *Interpersonal dynamics* (pp. 357–392). Homewood, IL: Dorsey.

Schein, E. H. (1969). *Process consultation*. Reading, MA: Addison-Wesley.

Schein, E. H. (1981). Does Japanese management style have a message for American managers? *Sloan Management Review, 23,* 55–68.

Schein, E. H. (1983). The role of the founder in creating organizational culture. *Organizational Dynamics,* 13–28.

Schein, E. H. (1985). *Organizational culture and leadership: A dynamic view*. San Francisco: Jossey-Bass.

Schein, E. H., & Bennis, W. G. (1965). *Personal and organizational change through group methods*. New York: Wiley.

Solomon, R. L., & Corbit, J. D. (1974). An opponent-process theory of acquired motivation: I Temporal dynamics of affect. *Psychological Review, 81,* 119–145.

Solomon, R. L., Kamin, L. J., & Wynne, L. C. (1953). Traumatic avoidance learning: the outcomes of several extinction procedures with dogs. *Journal of Abnormal & Social Psychology, 48,* 291–302.

Solomon, R. L., & Wynne, L. C. (1953). Traumatic avoidance learning: acquisition in normal dogs. *Psychological Monographs, 67,* (Serial No. 354).

Solomon, R. L., Turner, L. H., & Lessac, M. S. (1968). Some effects of delay of punishment on resistance to temptation in dogs. *Journal of Personality and Social Psychology, 8,* 233–236.

20 What Happens to Children When They Act Aggressively in Six Cultures

William W. Lambert
Cornell University

I wish to present here some data from the Six Culture Study, which included an extensive, interdisciplinary cross-cultural observational analysis of the socialization of several systems of behavior, including aggression, which will be our main focus.

Socialization is a complex, recurring psycho-social process which bears a relation to learning similar to that of instruction, acculturation, or stereotyping. As with these other complex matters, the search for a reasonable cross-culturally valid and simple theory of socialization (or its related anthropological concept of enculturation) takes one necessarily into interdisciplinary data sets which must be reduced in order to discover just where (in social space) and when (in the life of developing children) the events occur that may contain the learning or lack of learning experimental principles may help explain.

We first focus on the occurrence of representative positive and negative feedback to the aggressive actions of carefully sampled children as they actually occur in six very different cultures. We next discuss the schedule of such feedback in the context of trying to understand why there is no overall change in the rate of occurrence or the overall proportional importance of aggressive actions among our younger children (3 to 6 years old) and our older ones (6 to 9 years), despite pressure to learn controls of such aggression. We're interested, then, in a failure of *desired* learning to occur in the socialization of aggression of children in several cultures. Consequently, we're interested in what happens to children of different ages in different places when they have behaved so as to (usually) hurt another person. Perhaps the feedback received will help explain why the mean rate of aggression (per 5-min observation) is .746 for the young children and .763 for the older ones and why the mean proportion of aggression (divided by all recorded actions) is .209 for younger children and .187 for our older children.

THE SIX CULTURE STUDY

First, let's talk about the study and its design. The extensive data set of the Six Culture Study was collected to serve the theoretical purposes of applying the behavior theory of the late '50s and '60s to socialization. But these data continue to serve a number of other theoretical interests as well. This is because the data corpus approximates an ecologically valid sample of the actions of children in six very different cultures to which we can return for new analyses, as one might use and reuse the resources of an archeological dig. The behavioral observations were done by trained field workers, including (where needed) a bilingual aide, in natural settings outside the home of the children. The children were observed in settings selected to be as representative of daily life as possible, and each child was observed in a number (12 or more) of 5-min segments. The data were recorded verbatim in the field, then coded, classified and prepared for the computer in a central office (see Whiting & Whiting, 1975, for details). The children selected were representative of children their age in the six communities. These communities can be described as rather homogeneous (with respect to cultural and class structure), but varying structurally, from a polygynous community (Nyansongo, the Gusii tribe in Kenya) to a Baptist group in New England (Orchardtown), a rural barrio in Northern Luzon (Tarong), a village (Taira) in Okinawa, a community of Mexican Indians (in Juxtlahuaca) and a high caste group in a rural village (Khalapur) of Northern India. The observational data were supplemented by interviews with the parents (see Minturn and Lambert, 1964) and children, and extensive ethnographies (see Whiting, 1963).

We have reported some aspects of the aggression data (Lambert, 1974a, 1974b; 1981; Lambert and Tan, 1979), and the reports reflect the range of rate and proportion measures of behavior that are available.

Lambert and Tan, for example, emphasized the fact that there is a striking consistency within all six cultures of the proportion of times that, having been hurt by another child, a child retaliates on the spot. This form of retaliation occurs about ⅓ of the time in boys, about ¼ of the time in girls, and everywhere so far studied, despite great variability from child to child within each culture. They also emphasized the finding that those children who are observed most frequently to have picked on another child for ''no apparent reason'' (We originally thought this might approximate a simple Skinnerian base rate for aggression; it may be such a base rate, but it's not simple.) tend to be the children who, on other occasions, are most frequently observed to have been picked on by others. They also relate these and other measures of aggression to Solomon's theory of punishment (Solomon, 1964). Lambert (1984) has organized many of the findings of the study by pointing out the existence in the children's behavior of the *tit-for-tat* strategy in both a general sense and also in the particular meaning given to this form of behavior by Pisano and Taylor (1971) and by Rapaport and Chammah (1965) and elaborately tested by computerized game simulation by Axelrod and Hamilton (1981). That is, children display in their actions a factorial dimension along which they vary from high to low in their use of a tit-for-tat strategy; they don't "start fights"—they retaliate when the other attacks—; they are prepared to forgive in one trial. In short, the *high* children tend to do what the other person does, a highly self-controlled form of matched dependent behavior. We have also begun to analyze the Six Culture data to uncover where and when such forms come to be learned and how such strategies enter the children's interactions and remain there (see Lambert, 1981, for a start on a theory on the matter).

Our present focus, however, as stated above, is on understanding why, despite the fact that children learn a good deal about where and when to express aggression (see Lambert, 1974b, for a preliminary report), there is no change in overall frequency or mean proportion of aggression expression in children's action up to adolescence. Theories of instrumental learning suggest that we look to naturally occurring feedback for aggressive action, and this is the case, regardless of whether such effects are conceptualized as reinforcers or motivators.

NATURALLY OCCURRING FEEDBACK TO AGGRESSION

In order to obtain measures of these naturally occurring *effect acts,* we had to analyze sequences of actions in complex social interchanges. Our data do not permit extensive sequential analysis, but our basic data unit was an *interaction card* on which was coded an instigation (usually by some other person) followed by an act (*central act*) by the sample child being observed, and this was followed by any coded relevant effect act (again, usually done by somebody else) which followed on the central act. Data on coding reliability can be found in Whiting and Whiting (1975), but we can report that it was adequately reliable for our purposes. Table 20.1 lays out these sequences as analyzed for aggressive acts.

Sequential analyses quickly become extremely complicated. Michael Mann, in an unpublished paper (1970), limited consideration to three kinds of aggressive central acts, namely sociable assaults, physical assaults, and verbal (symbolic) aggressions, and then studied how the effect act (following the central act) varied as a function of what instigation had evoked the central act. One of Mann's findings is interesting and can serve as a good illustration of our coding scheme. Given that a child had (as an instigation) his property taken away from him and that he (in his central act) assaulted the taker of the property on the spot, then it empirically followed that in no case (in any culture) did anyone who was

TABLE 20.1

Analysis of the Total Aggressive Acts by a Child to Others and by Others to Him

Instigations by Some Class of Others	Central Act by Sample Children	Effect Act by Some Class of Others
Rate[a] or Proportion of:	Rate or Proportion[b] of Retaliation by:	Percentage (or rate or proportion) of discouragement of aggressive acts Percentage (or rate or proportion) of encouragement of aggressive acts Percentage (or rate or proportion) of ignorals of aggressive acts No effect action
O hits P O insults P O hits P sociably ignores P other instigations	hitting insulting hitting sociably nonaggression	
No apparent instigation	Self-instigated aggression	Percentage (or rate or proportion) of discouragement of aggressive acts Percentage (or rate or proportion) of encouragement of aggressive acts Percentage (or rate or proportion) ignorals of aggressive acts No effect action
Nonaggressive instigations	"Sneaky" aggressions sent	"Sneaky" aggressions received
	Nonaggressive acts	

[a]Definition of rate = Number of aggressive acts / No. of 5 min. observations

Definitions of proportion = Number of aggressive acts / Total social acts

[b]Retaliatory Proportion = Number of aggressively instigated aggressive acts / Total aggressive instigations received

present (as an effect actor) intervene to punish or discourage the retaliating child: in all cases there was either *no effect act* recorded, or the assault was *actively ignored,* or the other child *avoided the attacker,* or was recorded as having *given up his set* (or intention).

This example can also serve to introduce the fact that *instigations,* central acts (always committed by a *P,* that is, one of the sample children during a sample timed period), and effect acts were always recorded for all the social activity involving the sample children, even when *no instigation* or *no central act,* or *no effect act* was sometimes the content so recorded. Instigations, of course, are usually provided by others (but P sometimes provided his own instigations), and the effect acts were almost always provided by someone other than P.

A FOCUS UPON CENTRAL ACT/EFFECT ACT
SEQUENCES

If we rule out for the present even as partial a sequential analysis as Mann's, we can focus on the sequence which leads from central acts to effect acts. Let us begin with an orienting fact: A very high percentage of all naturally occurring aggressive acts are ignored. (This is true of all actions, in fact.) Sixty percent of aggressive acts are ignored. There is another interesting fact: About 28% of all the effect acts which follow P's aggressive central acts are what we classify as *discouragements.* This percentage is nicely symmetrical with the percentage of instigated aggressions (plus ignorals) which are immediately retaliated to by our sample children. On the average, then, it appears that the children have about the same chance of being hurt back (or at least discouraged back) as they provide retaliation to others who pick on them!

This symmetry may suggest one of the sources of the average child's retaliatory proportion: He may absorb through some process of probability learning the fitting probability of retaliation by vicarious learning through observation of the handling of others as well as himself in his neighborhood and his culture. We can, but have not, checked out further implications of this interpretation.

But let us pause and define some terms. It is useful to glance at Table 20.1, which lays out the overall analysis of aggressive acts which we used, and note the placement of effect acts in that table in the far right column. The various measures of occurrences of effect acts are listed there, along with the three-way categorizations of effect acts into discouragement, encouragement and ignoral that we have used. Given the rich experimental and theoretical work that has been done with the idea of feedback, we were surprised to find how little has been done in validating various classifications of these when they occur naturally. We had to work with ordinary usage and with face validity.

The concept underlying the classification into discouragements, encouragements and ignorals was the idea of reward. (We also tried out classifying effects

TABLE 20.2
Code for Effect Acts (Reward Concept)

Encourage	Discourage	Ignore
gives up set	reprimands	no effect
acts hurt	warns	hides
asks help	assaults	avoids
gives approval	insults	observes
shows pleasure	threatens	ignores
is sociable	takes property	breaks interaction
gives emotional support	reports deviations	solitary play
gives help	blocks	practices skill
depreciates self	arrogates self	
teaches	challenges to complete	
joins group	accepts challenge	
encounters difficulty	suggests	
	seeks contact	

for their arousal properties but will not report this here). An effect act which was likely to be rewarding was classified as encouragement and, as shown in Table 20.2, this would include where the other person gives approval or acts hurt when P has hurt or tried to hurt another. An effect act directed at P, which was unlikely to reward P, was classified as a discouragement (e.g., assaults, suggests, blocks; see Table 20.2). This category also included all forms of punishment. Ignoring was defined as effect acts which were active ignorals or were directed at the actor (P). There were, of course, many cases where the coders merely reported that there existed no effect act, following a further central act by P, and these NA's can be considered irrelevant for analysis, or be considered (as we did) additional ignorals. We should report at once that with use of this three-way code, the three kinds of aggressive acts (sociable, physical and verbal aggressions) are treated, overall, in a similar fashion; about 50 to 60% are ignored; about 25–35% are discouraged, and only 10–15% are encouraged.

DO SOME EFFECT ACTORS REWARD OR DISCOURAGE MORE THAN OTHERS DO?

Possibly the most interesting data on what happens after children aggress is displayed in Table 20.3 and in Figure 20.1, both of which show the differential reactions to aggression by different agents of effect. Clearly, the younger agents of effect, such as infants (children under two years of age) and young children(3–6 years of age) tend to give the highest proportion of encouraging feedback, with some help from older children, (age 6–9) as shown in Figure 20.1 and Table 20.3. Overall, 45% of the feedback for aggression provided by infants is encouraging (and is 52% in the Tarong case). Infants are higher than any other agent in all the cultures in this regard, and by considerable margins (We should quickly refer ourselves back to the coding scheme, of course, and point out that a good percentage of what infants *do* which is encouraging is to "act hurt").

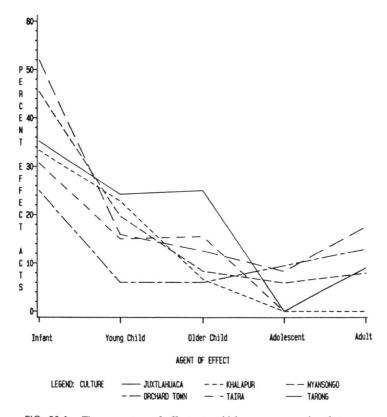

FIG. 20.1. The percentage of effect acts which were encouraging that were given to children of different cultural samples by given agents of effect.

Table 20.3 also displays the clear fact that the feedback given by infants and young children is not the discouraging sort: only 14.9% of infants' effect acts and 35% of those which come from young children are discouragements. Clearly, as the agents of effect become older, their reactions to aggression on the part of our sample children turn increasingly sour. Older children discourage 40.8% of the time, adolescents more than 68%, and adults 64% of the time. Table 20.3 also dramatically points up the fact that older actors appear to have taken on a negative attitude toward aggression, and to share a disposition to act in terms of such values with clear attempts at sanctioning P's behavior. It is interesting that in four of the cultures, the adolescents are equal or more prone to discourage aggression than are adults. Table 20.3 (top) also displays the clear fact that adolescents and/or adults tend to ignore aggression less: They are the more vigilant ones. But in this case, the cultural differences assert themselves more clearly, also. (And that is a long story of another sort.) Statistical tests are not really necessary here, because the general trends in Figure 20.1 (and similar figures giving cultural breakdowns of the data in the top of Table 20.3) tend to be

TABLE 20.3
Percentage of All Effect Acts Provided to Sample Children
by Various Effect Actors Which Were Encouraging,
Discouraging, or Ignoring
(Summed Across All Forms of Sample Child Aggression and All Cultures)

	Infant		Young Child		Older Child		Adolescent		Adult	
	%	freq	%	freq	%	freq	%	freq	%	freq
Encourage	45.1	88	16.2	86	12.9	35	4.3	3	10.9	22
Discourage	14.9	29	35.0	186	40.8	111	68.6	48	64.2	129
Ignore	40.0	78	48.8	260	46.3	126	27.1	19	24.9	50
Total	100%		100%		100%		100%		100%	

Percentage of All Encouragements, Discouragements, and Ignorals
Received by Sample Children from Various Agents of Effect
(Summed Across All Forms of Sample Child Aggression and All Cultures)

	Infant		Young Child		Older Child		Adolescent		Adult		
	%	freq	%	freq	%	freq	%	freq	%	freq	
Encourage	37.6	86	36.8	86	15.0	35	1.3	3	9.4	22	100%
Discourage	5.8	29	37.0	186	22.1	111	9.5	48	25.6	129	100%
Ignore	4.6	78	48.8	260	23.6	126	3.6	19	9.4	50	100%

consistent across all six cultures. Furthermore, the fact that these similarities occur across cultures is more impressive than data from ordinary samples, and six things so clearly alike provide a statistically significant sign test. To summarize: there is a direct gradient of punishment and an inverse gradient of reward and of ignoral as the effect actor gets older.

WHERE DO MOST OF THE ENCOURAGEMENTS AND DISCOURAGEMENTS COME FROM?

It is interesting to turn the matter around and discover where the preponderance of all the discouragements, ignorals, and encouragements for aggression come from in the social space around the child. If most of the effect acts come from older effect agents, then they may, being enculturated, tend to encourage only when the culture would value such feedback. If the feedback generally comes from young, inexperienced, and relatively unvigilant young people who are rarely responsible or effective shapers of behavior, then the matter would be very different, as in empirical fact it is.

It is clear from the bottom section of Table 20.3 that the answer is with the second alternative—the majority of all the feedback for aggression comes from infants, younger, and older children. Specifically, 37% of all the encouragements received by the sample children in our observations came from young children alone, and 15% came from older children; 38%, from infants. Even most of the discouragements came from these groups, also. Despite their high percentage of discouragements, adolescents and adults only give our sample children some 35% of their total discouragements. This is also particularly strongly true for ignorals, with young children providing 49% of these, older children 24%, and infants 15%. Infants tend to cry more easily, and these cries become encouragements and may be at least momentarily rewarding, and, depending on how isolated from adults the setting is, no more may be heard about it.

Another way to state this fact is that (again, according to Table 20.3) over 77% of all the feedback for aggression received by our sample children, in settings which attempted to represent a slice of their lives, came from infants, young children, and older children, and less than 25% of all feedback came from adolescents and adults (over 17 years).

We should remember, of course, that these settings for observation are all outside the household. We have no doubt that adults get into center stage in controlling aggression more in the home. But, outside the house, most of the apparent shaping of aggression (and a great amount of the ignoring of it) is in the hands of neophytes who all display (top of Table 20.3) a very different pattern in reacting to childrens' aggression than adults do: They all ignore more, encourage more, and discourage less. It is this pattern of feedback, with its massive relative frequency, we suggest, which may explain why aggressive tactics and strategies remain in children's repertoires so long and at such relatively high frequencies and percentages of all actions. To summarize: There is a gradient of overall feedback which decreases as the socializing agent gets older. The fate of aggressive habits is in the hands of those least knowledgeable and powerful to control these habits. A decrease in aggression comes, probably, when the people one interacts with are older and more socialized.

OTHER LEARNING THAT OCCURS WITH AGE

We should hasten to make clear that we are not arguing that children's repertoire of aggressive actions doesn't change with age at all. We have a great deal of evidence to the contrary; we have here focussed only on a failure of the overall frequency and proportion of aggression to fall off over the ages in our samples and have pointed to some highly probable ethological facts about human age segregation and propinquity, which may explain the failure of the entire system to decay in importance.

Much learning apparently does take place (see Lambert, 1974b). First, children learn who to take on as a target of aggression—as they get older they stop hurting kin, particularly siblings, and shift the attack to non-kin members of the community.

We recorded for each observation whether or not an intimate of the sample child was present. Young children are most likely to aggress when these intimates are present than when they are not, but older children do not: They appear to have learned otherwise and show their aggression much more when intimates are absent.

An even stronger empirical effect is that younger children show an active preference for aggressing when authority persons (17 yrs. and older) are around; whereas, older children tend to do it when authorities are not present.

There is also a strong tendency for older children to show aggression in play settings 2⅔ times more frequently than in settings of *casual social interaction*. Younger children show almost no sensitivity to this setting difference.

Older children have learned to express aggression away from their own geographical home area or in public places, but, for young children, these settings are not behaviorally discriminated: They agress at home as much as away.

It is very important, we feel, that all children tend to express more aggression when other children are present than when any other people are there. Also, aggression is expressed most frequently (and proportionately) where the others present are peers or slightly older. So, hurting action is more prevalent with other children as coactors, and the presence of adults or adolescents tends to dampen this kind of enthusiasm—the discouraging types may be actively avoided.

The presence of the opposite sex tends to hold down expression of aggression, particularly when one is alone with the other sex. The size of the group present doesn't appear to influence older children, but younger children are more sensitive and show more aggression, the larger the group. Perhaps social facilitation of aggression from the more numerous others works on younger children better.

The presence of the father (alone) has the strong effect of cutting the proportion of aggressive expression in half for older children, whereas which adult is present has no effect on younger children. With older children, the presence of grandmother is correlated with doubled proportions of aggression. Finally, we should also report that the frequency of physical assaults, as a sub-system of aggressive acts, does decrease with age, and we plan to check out carefully the natural history of how this is achieved. Since such physical attacks are a relatively small percentage of all acts, the decrease is easily compensated for to keep the overall measures stable with age.

IS THERE DISPLACEMENT OF AGGRESSION DOWNWARD?

Given the heavy importance of infants and other children in responding rather ineptly to the aggression of our sample children, and given the rather high overall rate and proportion of aggression, there's little doubt that this kind of behavior and the strategies related to it are very important in the lives of the children.

There are three additional sources of information that suggest another kind of *heating up* which makes the early years of our children so filled with aggressive actions of one kind or another. It may well be that young actors and infants tend to bear the brunt of things because they can less well defend themselves from the hurting behavior of older people. This possibility is clear when we consider Table 20.4 (top), where we report, for all children and for each kind of aggressive action, the proportion of times that certain others (e.g., infants, young children, adolescents, or adults) are the objects of the aggression of our child actor, divided by the times that these same others are observed to be the (successful) instigators of such action. The absolute proportions are not as important as the relative ones, of course, which show that infants and other children receive a great deal more aggression than they cause. Infants receive 2 or more times the hurts they cause, whereas adults receive almost as much hurt as they give.

Consider, also, Table 20.4 (bottom), where we display the differential percentages by which our child actor sends aggression toward certain targets, compared to *all* the kinds of behavior those targets receive from our children. Infants, for example, receive 12% more of all the physical assaults our children sent than they receive of the total actions committed by our children. Adults, on the other hand, receive 23% fewer assaults, compared to their percentage of all actions received from our sample children. Our sample children are, then, overshooting in the proportion of all actions they send toward other children while they are relatively undershooting toward adults.

Overall, then, our sample children are emitting more aggression than they receive, and a higher proportion of it is being sent to other children than to adults. When children behave proportionally less aggressively toward adults, they make up for this behavior in the aggressive proportion of all their actions in the child community. Maybe children need even more than protection from one another in the human system, at least from this perspective.

Finally, we should point out in this context the intriguing data of Table 20.5. The first set of rows in the table provide cross-cultural, individual-level correlations between the rates and proportions of aggression directed toward certain targets, such as *YS* (younger siblings); *YNS* (younger non-siblings); *SOS* (same

TABLE 20.4
Proportion of Times that the Following Groups are the OBJECTS of Aggression by Sample Children Divided by the Times These Groups Were Instigators of Such Actions

	Infants	Youngers	Olders	Adolescents	Adults
Assaults:	2.00	1.53	1.60	1.4	1.06
Soc. Assaults:	4.5	3.55	4.13	3.25	1.54
Verbal Aggression:	2.47	1.84	1.94	1.64	1.28

Percentage of times the following groups were objects of aggression minus the percentage of times they were objects of all kinds of behavior by children

	Infants	Youngers	Olders	Adolescents	Adults
Assaults:	+12%	+16%	−1%	0%	−23%
Soc. Assaults:	+6%	+17%	+10%	−1%	−27%
Verbal Aggression:	+4%	+12%	+5%	−9%	−20%

TABLE 20.5
Target Analysis: Correlation of Rates and Proportions of Aggressions
Toward Four Targets with Number of Siblings (Older and Younger)

	Number of Siblings		Number of Younger Siblings		Number of Older Siblings	
	Rates	Props.	Rates	Props.	Rates	Props.
All Cultures Combined						
Aggression toward:						
YS*	.235*	.240*	.006	-.063	.248*	.302*
YNS	-.094	-.077	-.026	-.006	-.-67	-.054
SOS	-.029	-.067	-.206	-.265	.095	.090
SONS	-.063	-.094	.030	-.007	-.075	-.080

[a]See text for details.

age or older siblings); *SONS* (same age or older non-siblings); and the composition of one's family. Interestingly, there is a higher rate and proportion of aggression directed toward one's younger siblings (YS) when one has more siblings, but this correlation is generated not by the number of younger siblings that one has ($r=.006$) but by how many older siblings one has (r's $=.248$ and .302, both significant)!

One interpretation of this result is, of course, the classic picture of displacement of aggression downward (toward YS), when one has many demanding older siblings!

Taken together, but in no sense a final, definitive manner, these data suggest that childhood is fraught with negative affect, because children are often picking on one another in rather unfair ways! And, added to the data of Table 20.4, we begin to see just why early childhood, at least, means dealing with a good deal of interpersonal hurt.

SEX DIFFERENCES IN AGGRESSION BUT NOT IN FEEDBACK

A strong and statistically reliable finding of the Six Culture Study is that boys express more frequent aggression than girls do, as shown by analyses of variance of most of the scores of aggressive action that we have developed. Boys engage in more self-initiated aggression, and they have a higher rate of sociable assaults and of verbal (symbolic) aggression than girls, where the denominator is their own total rate of all actions. Their overall aggression rate, and their overall aggression proportions are very significantly different from the samples of girls. The only exception to this sex difference is very interesting: There is no sex difference in the rate or proportion of physical assaults, though this is the one subsystem of aggression which does decline overall with age, and a sex difference (with boys higher) has been reported between younger boys and younger girls in this regard (see Maccoby, 1966, p. 324) in the six cultures.

We bring the matter up in this context, because our interest in the effect acts to aggression is relevant to a possible explanation of these sex differences; if girls are being discouraged more than boys, for example, then their rates and proportions of aggressions may be being suppressed. This is, however, not the case: The treatment of girls and boys who have acted aggressively is very similar. Girls empirically receive a few more encouragements and discouragements in percentage terms, and they are therefore ignored a bit less than boys, but these results are not statistically reliable. One bit of insight arises when we look at who is the source of these effect acts; boys receive somewhat more of these from younger children, and girls receive somewhat more of them from adults, but these effects appear to be weak, also. So, the sex differences do not arise in any simple and obvious way from the feedback received at the time of our observations.

Another possible origin of the sex differences could lie in a difference in the aggressive instigations received from others; if boys more than girls are instigated by being hurt, then they may aggress more often than girls, particularly (as we have shown above) since boys tend to retaliate on the spot more than girls do. This possibility is fraught with both empirical and logical problems. However, empirically, the rates of sociable assaults, physical assaults, verbal assaults or of ignorals by another (which were the immediate antecedents to about 25% of P's aggressive actions) were the same for boys as for girls. It is fair to say that the rates of all their actions show sex differences on the output side (that is, what P's do) but not on the input side: The higher rate of boys' than girls' aggressions is not relatable to any corresponding, immediately antecedent rate of instigations received. Boys "give it out" more frequently than girls, regardless how frequently they're "picked on."

Scores of proportions of aggression are more complicated on the issue of sex differences. They show a strong sex effect on the output side in all cases (except physical aggression), and these particular proportions are not related to any sex differences in being picked on. So far, the findings are the same as for the rates. But when we aggregate all the instigators into a total instigation score, there is a borderline significant sex effect in that boys manage not only to send a much higher proportion of aggression (relative to all acts) than girls do, they also manage to show that they are being picked on with a barely higher proportion than girls are picked on. When we aggregate all the rates, there continues to be a strong sex difference in the total rates sent, but there are no differences between the sexes in the rate of instigations received.

It is logically surprising, however, that boys do not receive much higher rates and proportions of aggressive instigations, because they tend to play (and have differences) with one another, while girls tend to be among themselves. Perhaps it is the case (as we have suggested elsewhere, Lambert, 1984, in press) that the very existence of a successful tit-for-tat strategy is a game form that keeps boys from being picked on to the extent that might otherwise be, since one of the signs of "success" in the strategy is to be picked on less if you are ready, as many boys are, to retaliate on the spot.

So, generally speaking, neither the aggressive stimulus conditions of their social life nor the immediate feedback they receive from aggressing seem to easily explain the fact that boys are more aggressive. We cannot yet resolve this dilemma with a testable learning hypothesis, but there is another direction we're pursuing.

This direction rests on a very interesting fact about the young children in our samples from the six cultures: The young girls are more active than the boys are. There is an age-sex interaction, too, as well as culture by age interactions and (as usual with most of our scores) large cultural effects on rate of total actions. But there is still the fact that younger girls do more, and have a more lively activity rate than the boys. Given that they receive about the same kind of feedback, then they should (given a higher action rate) be shaped more effectively. But, as we've emphasized throughout, the feedback on aggression at least tends to be in the hands of ill-trained youngsters, despite girls receiving a bit more of their feedbacks from adults.

We're forced to consider an earlier phase in the lives of our children. One correlate of a high action rate, and one which is independent of cultural effects, is the degree to which the mother did the caring for the child when the child was a baby. The more the mother did the baby care, the higher the rate of action in childhood. This result may also relate to a suggestive additional correlate of action rate with mother's use of reward strategies. Young females reared thusly may, then, come into our sample of young children already rather well shaped by a good deal of adult contact, compared to boys.

CONCLUSIONS

We have characterized what happens when children from six cultures act aggressively outside the home. We find that most of the feedback and certainly most of the encouragement (and ignoral) of aggression is provided by peers and infants. As the agent of effect gets older, there is a gradient toward more discouragement, less encouragement, and less ignoral of aggression. This generally aggressively-toned life of children is further enhanced by apparent sources of displacement of aggression toward youngers from olders and from adults. These relationships are suggested as explanations for the fact that the overall aggressive actions, despite opposing cultural values, remain constant over age in samples from six cultures. Much other learning does occur, however. Sex differences do not seem to be easily explained in terms of immediate feedback differences or by differential received levels of instigations, and they may rest on either biological differences or the effect of events earlier in life.

REFERENCES

Axelrod, R., & Hamilton, W. D. (1981). The evolution of cooperation. *Science, 211,* 1390–1396.

Lambert, W. W. (1974a). *A study of children's aggressive actions in six cultures.* (Project No. 9-0664, Grant No. OEG-0-70-2743). Washington, D.C.: U.S. Office of Education.

Lambert, W. W. (1974b). Promise and problems of cross-cultural exploration of children's aggressive strategies. In J. DeWit & W. W. Hartup (Eds.), *Determinants and origins of aggressive behavior* (pp. 437–461). The Hague: Mouton.

Lambert, W. W. (1981). Toward an integrative theory of children's aggression. *Italian Journal of Psychology, 2,* 153–164.

Lambert, W. W. (1985). Some strong strategies in the aggression of children in six cultures. In R. Bolton (Ed.), *The content of culture: Constants and variants. Studies in honor of John M. Roberts.* Human Relations Area Files Press.

Lambert, W. W., & Tan, A. L. (1979). Expressive styles and strategies in the aggressive actions of children of six cultures. *Ethos, 7*(1), 19–36.

Mann, M. (1970). *Analysis of Six Culture Effect Acts.* Unpublished manuscript.

Maccoby, E. (Ed.). (1966). *The development of sex differences.* Palo Alto: Stanford University Press.

Minturn, L., & Lambert, W. W. (1964). *Mothers of six cultures.* New York: Wiley.

Pisano, R., Taylor, S. P. (1971). Reduction of physical aggression: The effects of four strategies. *Journal of Personality and Social Psychology, 19*(2), 237–242.

Rapoport, A., & Chammah, A. M. (1965). *Prisoner's dilemma.* Ann Arbor: University of Michigan Press.

Solomon, R. L. (1964). Punishment. *American Psychologist, 19*(4), 239–253.

Whiting, B. (Ed.). (1963). *Six cultures: Studies of child rearing.* New York: Wiley.

Whiting, B. J., & Whiting, J. W. M. (1975). *Children of six Cultures: A psycho-cultural analysis.* Cambridge, MA: Harvard University Press.

21

Alexis de Tocqueville, John Stuart Mill, and Developmental Psychology

Richard D. Walk
George Washington University

The purpose of this paper is to look at two influential political science thinkers, Tocqueville and Mill, and to investigate the implications of their thinking for developmental psychology, particularly developmental child psychology. The eventual focus will be on the genesis of what might be called the *spirit of liberty*.

My quest began with the change in our concept of the human infant following recent intensive studies of infancy. We now know, for example, that the human infant has form and depth perception soon after birth, that it discriminates its caretaker's voice and face at a very early age, and that it discriminates many dimensions of human speech. (Walk, 1981, is one of several summaries of this research.) This is but a small sample of research's achievements, but it has changed our view of the human infant from that of a rather passive creature to one with an active interest and curiosity about the environment, essentially an active, perceptually rather mature participant from almost the day of its birth.

I wonder about the implications of this new view of infancy for the period after infancy. Surely, such an infant may be said to be "born free" and with infinite potential. One can, of course, concentrate only on postinfancy research, but, in considering this infant and its potential, I thought in broader terms, and one way to approach this task is to look at sources outside the traditional research and theory of developmental psychology. Instead, I have read Alexis de Tocqueville's *Democracy in America,* the first volume of which was published in 1834, and the second in 1840; and John Stuart Mill's essay *On Liberty,* published in 1859, the year of Tocqueville's death. My intention is to describe these works in somewhat general terms, and to point out some of the implications of their thinking for developmental child psychology.

ALEXIS DE TOCQUEVILLE

Tocqueville himself was an aristocrat, a member of the petite noblesse, whose reading made him increasingly liberal. He was a lawyer with a career in the magistry, a judicial officer, who was not in sympathy with the new government of Louis Phillipe. He and his friend Gustave Beaumont petitioned for an 18-month leave of absence to study the prison system of the United States. They had to pay their own way—money raised by their families—but the prison project gave them official introductions and a purpose. Their trip only lasted 9 months, since they were called back, but they did go up and down the eastern United States, south to New Orleans and north into Canada. A secondary purpose, not conveyed to the officials, was to study the implications for Europe of the workings of democracy in America. They were in America from the summer of 1831 to the spring of 1832. Their book on prisons, itself a classic, appeared in 1833, and Tocqueville's first volume on democracy in 1834. Beaumont's observations on America were published separately. Tocqueville was 29 when the first volume on democracy appeared and 35 when the second volume, after much reflection, was published in 1840.

The first volume is mainly descriptive. He describes North America, the origins of the Anglo-Americans, their social condition, local government more than the federal government, the judicial system, political associations, political parties, and liberty of the press. In this volume he also worries about the tyranny of the majority, discusses what keeps the federal government going, and the manners and morals of Americans. (As for the last, they have terrible manners and impeccable morals.)

The second, more interpretative volume discusses the influence of democracy on philosophy, religion, science, language, literature and the arts. There he also discusses the desire for wealth, manners, social and domestic relations, and the general influence of democratic ideas. Throughout, we have Tocqueville grappling with change, with equality, with the implications of the American experiment for a Europe that still had its aristocracy, though he can see that the industrial revolution is changing Europe, and that Europe will face many of America's problems.

Tocqueville praises America, but he also criticizes it, and he does remark that Americans are eager for praise, yet extremely sensitive, so they do not take criticism well, in contrast to the English who, under it all, feel very secure and could not care less what is said about them. His criticisms and praise do have implications for psychology, of course. My aim is to discuss some themes from the book, and, then, when we have some flavor of it, describe the implications for developmental psychology. Obviously, some of his ideas overlap with other thinkers who have discussed political and social issues, and my own familiarity is mainly with Durkheim, Weber, and Fromm, but I am ignoring them to concentrate on Tocqueville. The study of childhood is not far away from some of his themes.

Tocqueville is very cognizant of the role of religion in the liberty of the Americans. The colonists, it will be remembered, fled Europe to practice their own religion, to embrace religious freedom, and to practice a religion for which they felt persecuted in Europe. This religion was often as intolerant of dissent as the society from which they had fled. But there were many groups in the United States, and they had to work together to govern. Tocqueville concludes that the Anglo-American civilization is the result of two elements, of religion and of liberty. Religion had the moral sphere and the political sphere was separate. ''In the moral world everything is classified, systematized . . . in the political world everything is agitated, disputed and uncertain . . . These two tendencies, apparently so discrepant . . advance together and support each other'' (I, 46).[1] Freedom of religion, of religion as separate from the state, was very different from Europe where the two were intertwined. Tocqueville was surprised to find that ministers and priests regarded themselves as more effective outside the state than within it. In the early nineteenth century, when Tocqueville wrote, religion as part of the heritage of liberty was still much alive, an influence that may still be a strong part of our heritage, but it is not as easy to discern.

The legal profession in the United States seemed to constitute an unofficial aristocracy. Lawyers were important for the maintenance of authority, and they were trusted by the people, and the people served on juries to help the law resolve civil as well as criminal issues. Tocqueville, remarks, ''They may be looked upon as the connecting link between the two great classes of society . . . without this admixture of lawyer-like sobriety with the democratic principle, I question whether democratic institutions could long be maintained'' (I, 286). The American lawyer, in the English tradition, may be ''the sole interpreter of an occult science'' (I, 287), but lawyers cement the structure of society; a legal structure mediated by lawyers helps keep the enterprise running in a manner that is trusted, so that disputes are generally resolved judicially rather than through violence.

Tocqueville found an intensely vigorous society, one almost in perpetual motion, one that fostered and concentrated to a fault on commercial activity. Many times he comments on the love of material gratification fostered, he feels, by equality, so that he wonders whether making everyone equal means that the only way you can be different from your neighbor is to make more money than he does. ''The heart of man is of a larger mold,'' he comments. (II, 156). He feels that democracy fosters a certain shallowness, that individuals, despite their freedom, show little independence of mind, that people do not have any interest

---

[1]References to *Democracy in America,* in two volumes, will only refer to the volume number and the page. Thus, ''I, 46'' refers to Volume 1, page 46.

in freedom of discussion, that people get into a habit of inattention, and, so he says, general indifference is a public virtue. "Nothing," he remarks, "is less suited to meditation than the structure of a democratic society." It has, he continues, "a sort of incessant jostling of men, which annoys and disturbs the mind without exciting or elevating it" (II, 43–44).

Individualism somehow proceeds from equality. People have to make it on their own, and they are alone. "They owe nothing to any man, they expect nothing from any man . . . they are apt to imagine that their whole destiny is in their hands" (II, 105). One result is isolated individuals, and he remarks that while the suicide rate is not very high, the American rate of insanity is said to be the highest of all, a result of a "strange melancholy" that afflicts many.

Tocqueville's book has many implications for developmental child psychology. An obvious and far reaching relationship is that of child rearing with its emphasis on individualism. Tocqueville writes that the American is taught from infancy to rely on his (her) own exertions.[2] He refers to the philosophic method of the Americans as that of reasoning things out for oneself, of tending more to the results than to the means, of striking through the form to the substance. An effect on the family, tending toward equality among the children, stems from laws of inheritance that do not favor the eldest son. He feels that this change improves family relationships, that the relations between a father and his sons are closer, and not so threatening, as they are in Europe. But this individualism, in a society where everyone has to make it on one's own, has a dark side. He writes that . . . "democracy . . . throws himself back forever upon himself alone and threatens in the end to confine him entirely within the solitude of his own heart" (II, 106).

A first implication of Tocqueville's observations is to look at child rearing and the way independence, inner as well as outer independence, is brought about, since a rather sturdy independence would seem to be necessary for liberty. Can

---

[2]A note on Tocqueville's treatment of women and minorities in America. He writes very little on women, much of it is very positive, and one might conclude that what he writes applies to both sexes, and, perhaps, if conditions are right, to all races. However, of women he says, "If I were asked to what the singular prosperity and growing strength of that people ought mainly to be attributed, I should reply, 'To the superiority of their women' " (II, 225). He does remark on the intelligence and independence of American women, that those he sees are treated almost similarly to men up to marriage, that they are highly educated. One gets the impression, also, that the freedom and independence of women end when they get married, and, from then on, they are rather restricted.

When Tocqueville wrote (1830), slavery was still practiced in the United States. He wrote a long chapter in Volume 1 on the Indian tribes and on the black population. He was not sympathetic to slavery, and he writes that slavery destroys the character of the master as well as the slave. In his chapter on American honor, he remarks, "I speak here of the Americans inhabiting those states where slavery does not exist . . ." (II, 247). Most of his remarks on democracy might have the same qualifying phrase, since he mainly writes of Americans who are equal to each other. He sees no quick solution to the race issue in the United States, even if slavery is abolished.

we, even in childhood, find a dark side to independence, a dark side to the need to rely on oneself?

A second implication is much broader, and this refers to group influences on the individual. A number of group phenomena will be described: the town meeting, the tendency of Americans to form associations, trial by jury, a broader *group relationship* from associating with individuals who are one's equals in contrast to a ranked society, the social obligations of Americans, and the influence of the generalized other, the tyranny of the majority.

Tocqueville was an admirer of New England, feeling it a bit more judicial and civilized than the rest of the United States. He says the New England town meetings "are to liberty what primary schools are to science; they bring it within the people's reach; they teach men how to use and how to enjoy it" (I, 63). Town meetings are places where people think for themselves, where they show their liberty and independence from possible constrictive local government. Tocqueville also remarks on the citizen of the United States as one who ". . . looks upon the social authority with an eye of mistrust and anxiety . . . this habit (i.e., of independence from authority) may be traced even in the schools where the children in their games are wont to submit to rules which they themselves have established" (I, 198).

Reinforcing town meetings as a social force, we have an American passion for forming associations of all kinds, political, business, cultural. Associations are small special interest groups of all kinds. "Americans of all ages, all conditions, all dispositions, constantly form associations . . . commercial, manufacturing . . . religious, moral, serious, futile, general, or restricted, enormous, or dimunitive. Whenever at the head of some new undertaking you see the government in France, or a man of rank in England, in the United States you will be sure to find an association" (II, 114). The importance of these associations is that an association, even a small one, confers power, or, as he remarks, once a few individuals combine: "from that moment, they are no longer isolated men, but a power seen from afar" (II, 117).

A third group phenomenon is trial by jury. Trial by jury has a positive effect on the national character. It is important for educating people, "places the real direction of society in the hands of the governed," and "imbues all classes with a respect for the thing judged and with the notion of right" (I, 293, 295). He felt that trial by jury was the "soundest possible preparation for free institutions" (I, 295).

A fourth group influence is more difficult to define, and that is the influence of the equality of others on the individual. The general notion that other people are your equals has positive and negative effects. The strong positive effect is that other people are viewed as human beings like oneself. He quotes a letter of 1675 of an aristocratic lady in Brittany who comments on a number of deaths in her region without much feeling (II, 175), and Tocqueville writes that no one of his time would be so indifferent to human suffering, because equality of condition made people have more in common with each other: They identify with each other and treat each other more humanely. Thus, he notes that the United States has virtually abandoned capital punishment, and feels this circumstance can be derived from equality. A negative aspect of equality, of encouraging competition for material goods as a way to stand out from the crowd, has been mentioned before.

A fifth group phenomenon is related to the previous influences, not independent of them, and this is that an American apparently has more social obligations than anyone else. Somehow people work together—we have a paradox of an excess of individuality and an excess of obligations to the larger group. Local affairs in the United States were much more decentralized than Tocqueville had been accustomed to in France. This meant local participation by the citizen in all facets of government and local government lay many obligations on its citizens. The new colonies gave responsibilities to localities to build schools, roads, water systems, levy taxes, take care of police functions, and so forth. The result was many more obligations for the average citizen, and, also, much more participation in the governmental process. Ineffectiveness could be checked by judicial punishment or failure of reelection. Tocqueville was very impressed by the result. The process was a little chaotic, but the results were fine: excellent schools, new churches, and roads kept in good repair. In contrast, he notes the communes of France—"so incorrigible an apathy that they seem to vegetate rather than to live" (I, 95).

A sixth and last group effect, one that Tocqueville comments on several times, is the tyranny of the majority, remarking that Americans have little independence of mind, and there is little freedom of discussion. One of the causes, he feels, is equality: as people become equal to each other, their opinions tend to be more and more alike. Since the majority rules in a democracy, people tend to believe in the omnipotence of the majority. "Nothing is more customary in man than to recognize superior wisdom in the person of the oppressor" (II, 12). He adds, "For myself, when I feel the hand of power lie heavy on my brow, I care but little to know who oppresses me . . ." (II, 13).

A third and last implication from Tocqueville's study, after individualism and the various group effects, concerns the influence of structural factors on liberty. A structural factor interacts with individualism if we consider laws of inheritance relating to the family—the family member relationships are affected by society's rules as to how property is shared after death. A modern structural factor, not discussed by Tocqueville, is the single versus the dual parent household. Structural factors in *Democracy in America* are many, and an important one is the Constitution. Tocqueville considers that the American Constitution can be amended a brilliant stroke against stagnation. Liberty of the press is part of the Constitution, and he remarks on one occasion, "newspapers maintain civilization" (II, 119), and, on another, "the independence of the press . . is the chief and, so to speak, the constitutive element of liberty'' (I, 200). The legal profession, as mentioned before, interprets the legal tradition in America and has the trust of the people. The child starts learning rules from its parents and then from its playmates. These structural factors, depending on how they are applied, may make the child bound to society, a placid nonthinking member, or an active participant who operates flexibly and independently within a tolerant and humane framework. Some structural factors are our own assumptions, picked up in childhood, and these may be difficult to discover.

My brief general summary of the implications of Tocqueville's study of democracy for a developmental study of the genesis of liberty is as follows: somehow the spirit of liberty is forged in an interaction of an early childhood that fosters independence and individuality and the group interactions that follow. This suggests a study of childhood rearing and group relationships that start in infancy and of the explicit and implicit rules that regulate the upbringing.

Two main researchable topics can be derived from Tocqueville's description of democracy in the United States. These, following from the preceding discussion, concern training for individualism and training to act in groups.

Individualism

The American child is trained as an individual, meaning that child rearing stresses the individuality and the independence of the child. How do the principle caretakers transfer this feeling of individuality to the child? How do the interaction patterns in the family help bring about this sense of individualism? How does the sense of individuality relate to notions of equality with other persons, and, associatedly, with notions of liberty? How does it influence children's games? One would presume that one's concepts of rights, of justice, of liberty and of morality are all influenced by the stress on the individual. Then, too, we have the negative side of individualism, the sense of isolation and aloneness? How does that develop?

Group Effects

The child learns to act as a member of a group first in the family and then in an ever widening circle: starting with the nuclear family group, composed of a few members; then to playmates, school and church groups; and then to larger and larger groups; from the beginning we have a wider yet vague identification with unseen members of one's age group and other unseen persons such as one's church members or citizens of one's country. Each group, of course, interacts with individuals, and we have concepts of one's rights, liberty and justice within the group.

As distinct from others, Tocqueville would particularly stress the influence of such groups as associations (meaning small groups having interests similar to ours), town meetings and juries. When do we first understand that a group is more effective than an individual? How do we learn to use our associations to further our own interests within a larger group? How do we learn our proper roles within these larger groups? How do we learn the social obligations of citizenship? And, lastly, how do we feel and respond to the "tyranny of the majority"? Does the American child, because of training for individualism, have trouble here that children in other cultures do not?

These are a few research topics that stem from Tocqueville's book. Obviously, many of the topics noted have been researched by others; my intention has been to look at Tocqueville with an open mind and to try to sketch some of the implications for developmental psychology with no regard for the present state of research evidence in this area.

We do not have *prescriptions* in Tocqueville (though some remarks are close to it), but more a description of American society. Mill, on the other hand, is more prescriptive.

JOHN STUART MILL

John Stuart Mill wrote his essay, *On Liberty,* in 1859, when he was 53 years old. The essay is one of numerous writings of Mill, who also wrote on logic, utilitarianism, political philosophy, and classical economics. It was dedicated to his wife, who died before it was published: "they wrought (it) together, principle by principle, sentence by sentence," according to the 1884 edition of the Encyclopedia Brittanica.

The main thesis of *On Liberty* is as follows (p. 68): "The sole end for which mankind are warranted, individually or collectively, in interfering with the liberty or action of any of their number, is self-protection . . . to prevent harm to others. His own good, either physical or moral, is not sufficient warrant."

The appropriate domain or jurisdiction of liberty is as follows:

> ". . first, inward domain of consciousness . . . liberty of conscience . . . liberty of thought and feeling, absolute freedom of opinion . . . liberty of expressing and publishing opinions. . . . Secondly, the principle requires liberty of tastes and pursuits, of framing the plan of our life to suit our own character . . . without impediment from our fellow creatures. . . . Thirdly, from the liberty of each individual follows the liberty . . . of combinations among individuals. . . . No society in which these liberties are not, on the whole, respected is free." (p. 71)

Mill believed that the vigorous society is one which encourages individuality and not one which suffocates its citizens with the tyranny of the majority. He quotes the German statesman-philosopher-educator Wilhelm von Humboldt that from "freedom and a variety of situations" arise "individual vigor and manifold diversity'' and these lead to original and creative people. "Genius can only breathe freely in an atmosphere of freedom." Eccentricity is to be encouraged since it leads to "genius, mental vigor and moral courage."

But Mill stresses that his doctrine is "not a doctrine of selfish indifference toward others." Everyone who receives the protection of society owes a return to society for its benefit. The general principle is that one can be as foolish as one wants to oneself, through drunkenness or extravagance, for example, but one should not harm others. An example of harming others would be harming one's family, as a father who did not support his children. Harming others is a slippery concept, and Mill is aware religious intolerance can be justified by those who feel they are harmed by someone who does not believe as they do, and, he warns, "to extend the bounds of what may be called moral police until it encroaches most unquestionably legitimate liberty of the individual is one of the most universal of all human propensities" (p. 152).

In a last section, on applications of the principles, Mill spells out some of the implications of his beliefs. He takes a fairly hard line on marriage and the family. He does not believe people should marry who are unable to support a family, and he believes that a man should perform his legal duties to his family: "It is no tyranny to force him to fulfill that obligation by compulsory labor if no other means are available" (p. 168). He is against the "almost despotic power of husbands over wives" and of a man over his children, and he recognizes both sides here, that the other parties cannot exploit this obligation.

Mill believes in compulsory education, not in the sense of State schools, but in the sense that all should have to pass a proficiency examination. This, again, is an obligation of the parent. Mill, who received no formal education himself but was taught by his father, is mistrustful of the State for education and of a formal degree as required for entry into the professions, always believing that a proficiency examination should be a requirement rather than a certificate or degree for teachers or lawyers, for example.

He is suspicious of government, though he does not object to its legitimate functions. Liquor should be taxed not for the moral reason of discouraging drunkenness, but because, since taxation is inevitable, liquor is a commodity that consumers can best spare. The governmental bureaucracy, he feels, discourages initiative and accumulates unnecessary power. The bureaucracy of Imperial Russia, uncontrollable even by the Czar, is a bad example of the abuse of governmental power.

Another reason for restricting governmental power is that the citizens derive benefits from carrying out many of its functions. The jury trial is one example, as is decentralized local and municipal government. The people gain by exercising their own faculties in self government, and it takes them out of the narrow circle of their own familiar affairs, since it forces them to participate in broader responsibilities. Political freedom must rest on a foundation of local liberties; countries where political freedom is brief have an insufficient local base to teach the citizens self-government. "Government operations tend to be everywhere alike. With individuals and voluntary associations . . . there are varied experiments and endless diversity of experience" (p. 181). The Americans and the French are cited positively: ". . let them be left without a government, every body of Americans is able to improvise one . ." (p. 184).

The heritage of *On Liberty* is complex; political scientists have been arguing over it since its publication. Mill himself was more conservative than many of his followers. He was not a "moral relativist" and he took a far harder line on an individual's obligations than many would who profess to follow him. Gertrude Himmelfarb writes in her introduction to the Penguin Books edition: "But it has become, perhaps by a process of cultural assimilation, the gospel of our own time even more than of Mill's day . . . Liberty remains, for good and bad, the only moral principle that commands general assent in the western world" (p. 49).

Mill's book has a number of implications for the developmental psychologist interested in the cultivation of liberty. Mill's prescriptions for liberty are as follows:

1. Children should be reared to encourage their own individuality, not as slavish followers of some right or correct way, but in a variety of ways.

2. All children should be educated up to a required level of proficiency.

3. Originality and creativity should be encouraged, even eccentricity.

4. Freedom of thought and discussion should be encouraged. Children should be taught to question authority in all things, even those we are most sure of (as, he remarks, Newton's principles). Children should also be taught to be tolerant of those who have beliefs that are different from their own.

5. Children should be taught that they have certain unbreakable obligations toward others, towards one's family and one's creditors, for example. They should be taught responsibility, particularly toward those who cannot help themselves.

6. Children should be exposed to self-government. They should gain experience in governing themselves. They should learn not to impose their power on others, but, rather, work out differences in free and open discussion.

DISCUSSION

"Liberty lies in the hearts of men and women; when it dies there, no constitution, no law, no court can save it; no constitution, no law, no court can even do much to help it." This statement by Justice Learned Hand, from his address, *The Spirit of Liberty*, delivered in 1944, and reprinted in Hand, 1953, is the challenge: to investigate the genesis of liberty with all of its difficulties of definition and description. As both Tocqueville and Mill make clear, liberty is complex. In his address, Hand goes on to say that the spirit of liberty is not, "the ruthless, the unbridled will; it is not freedom to do as one likes. That is the denial of liberty, and leads straight to its overthrow" (Hand, 1953, p. 190).

To investigate the spirit of liberty is to start with the passionate and open infant, ready to assimilate the world, and to move on through all of the joys and vicissitudes of childhood, and to hope that our society has imprinted and encouraged enough of that spirit so that it survives into adulthood. Now, obviously, much psychological research is related to the genesis of liberty. Research on attachment behavior, for example, where the caretakers encourage the development of individuality, research on prosocial behavior such as helping, sharing, caring for others, research on creativity, research on fairness and on the sense of justice that is part of moral development. Examples of such research can be found in, among others, Hoffman, 1970, Kohlberg, 1981, Maccoby and Masters, 1970, Mussen and Eisenberg-Berg, 1977, Siegal, 1982. One thinks of Bronfenbrenner's classic study of childhood in the United States as compared to childhood in the U.S.S.R. (Bronfenbrenner, 1970). All of this research is relevant and cannot be ignored, but I am not sure it captures the combination of independence, individuality, and judicious care for others that one gets from Tocqueville's, Mill's and Hand's ideals.

Perhaps the genesis of liberty is too large a canvas for any research to describe. While one can research many topics related to Tocqueville and Mill, I am particularly drawn to two of these. One is the enthusiastic, unbridled and tireless toddler, the emergent imago from the constraints of the cocoon of infancy, the two- to four-year-old. As any caretaker knows, this is a period when the child is most active, most exhausting, almost like a motor without a brake, a foresightless, yet good humored and almost irresistible force.

Another topic, much later, is when children can engage in profitable discussions with each other and even tolerate dissenting points of view. And I suspect, following the classic naturalistic studies of the Opies (Opie and Opie, 1969) this is more open-minded than one might believe from reading too much of the stage research.

Too much of the research on childhood seems to me to be condescending and slightly contemptuous toward this "inferior" being. The child is described as concrete, as egocentric, as perception-bound, as selfish and hedonistic—the concepts are value-laden. From my point of view the two- to four-year-old, the participant setting out on an optimistic journey, convinced that the world is its oyster, can be studied and appreciated just for itself. Perhaps this child does not know calculus or even trigonometry, perhaps it only speaks one language, not three or four, and its knowledge of that one language is far from Shakespeare's. The truth is, I am a little weak on some of that background myself.

At the beginning, I noted my wonder at the achievements of the human infant and thought that an investigation of Tocqueville and Mill might be helpful as a context to help describe the citizen the child might become. The authors have been helpful and have furnished many ideas. The two- to four-year-old starts its journey toward citizenship full of hope. Soon enough it will be soiled by the grime and the guilt of the cities. But, like the school of salmon that starts its journey to its source too numerous to count, where only a few survive, so the child may change, and only a small seed of the original hope remain, yet the seed of liberty will still be there, depending on conditions we do not yet understand. Tocqueville and Mill have shown the way, and they continue to inspire us. An investigation of the genesis of liberty, complex and contradictory as both the concept itself and the research it inspires is likely to be, will surely be fruitful.

In closing, I would like to quote again from Learned Hand's 1944 address:

> "The spirit of liberty is the spirit which is not too sure it is right; the spirit of liberty is the spirit which seeks to understand the minds of other men and women; the spirit of liberty is the spirit which weighs their interests alongside its own without bias; the spirit of liberty remembers that not even a sparrow falls to earth unheeded; the spirit of liberty is the spirit of Him who, nearly two thousand years ago, taught mankind that lesson it has never learned but has never quite forgotten, that there may be a kingdom where the least shall be heard and considered side by side with the greatest. . . . that spirit, that spirit of America which has never been, and which may never be; nay, which never will be except as the conscience and courage of Americans create it; yet . . (it is) . . the spirit of that America which lies hidden in some form in the aspirations of us all . . ." (pp. 190–191)

The spirit of liberty, to reiterate Hand, "is not too sure it is right . . . which seeks to understand . . ." It is a worthy aim.

REFERENCES

Bronfenbrenner, U. (1970). *Two worlds of childhood: U.S. and U.S.S.R.* New York: Russell Sage Foundation.

Hand, L. (1953). *The spirit of liberty.* (2nd ed.) New York: Knopf.

Hoffman, M. L. (1970). Moral development. P. H. Mussen (Ed), *Carmichael's Manual of Child Psychology* (3rd ed., Vol. 2, pp. 261–359). New York: Wiley.

Kohlberg, L. (1981). *Essays on moral development: Vol. 1. The philosophy of moral development.* New York: Harper and Row.

Maccoby, E. E., and Masters, J. C. (1970). Attachment and dependency. In P. H. Mussen (Ed.), *Carmichael's Manual of Child Psychology* (3rd ed., Vol. 2, pp. 73–157). New York: Wiley.

Mill, J. S. (1977). *On liberty.* Middlesex, England: Penguin Books. (Original work published 1859.)

Mussen, P., and Eisenberg-Berg, N. (1977). *Roots of caring, sharing, and helping.* San Francisco: W. H. Freeman.

Opie, I., and Opie, P. (1969). *Children's games in street and playground.* London: Oxford.

Siegal, M. (1982). *Fairness in children.* London: Academic.

Tocqueville, A. de (1945). *Democracy in America* (2 vols.) New York: Vintage Books. (Original work published 1835 and 1840.)

Walk, R. D. (1981). *Perceptual development.* Monterey, CA: Brooks/Cole.

22 Volition is a Nag

Malcolm R. Westcott
York University, Toronto

"If I complain *I* have no will of my own, that people are influencing me in subtle and mysterious ways, you'll accuse me of being paranoid, and direct me to a psychotherapist.

If I put on a white laboratory coat, and assert that *you* have no will of your own, that your action and experience can be manipulated, predicted, and controlled, then I am recognized as a scientific psychologist, and honored.

This is most peculiar." (Jourard, 1968, p. 1)

THE INITIAL PROBLEM

Probably the most troublesome aspect of the notion of volition is the fact that we know, through constant direct experience, that we have the capacity to initiate or terminate behavior unilaterally. We can do this in the absence of compelling stimuli; we can do this in the presence of compelling stimuli to the contrary. We can act or we can forebear from acting when it seems that all the apparent conditions would predict or coerce the opposite. We also experience failures of volition and will—when we are unable to bring ourselves to do, or to forebear from doing—and we can identify and bemoan these states of affairs.

Why should it be—as it certainly has been—that psychologists have focused most of their attention and effort on breaking down the notion of volition—that transparently clear human function—into a set of lower-order mechanisms which necessarily exclude that magnificent human experience of the triumph of the will over adversity, temptation, or indecision?

The question is somewhat rhetorical, of course, but my purpose in this paper is to trace something of the importance of the concepts of volition and will, their appearance, disappearance, underground lives, and reemergence in contemporary psychology. Some of this task has been done before (e.g., Gilbert, 1970; Kimble and Perlmuter, 1970; Rychlak, 1980), but generally from somewhat different perspectives, and of course I will be referring to these other authors.

Most of us have been brought up as psychologists with a fairly mechanistic approach to the analysis and understanding of behavior—both human behavior and infrahuman behavior. We have been schooled in a Humean, more-or-less linear notion of efficient causality and have typically shied away from attributing behavior to higher, more complex functions when they can be attributed to lower, simpler functions. We aspire to treat our experimental subjects—whether human or animal—as if they were relatively inert interchangeable units of a constant substance, as physicists do, whether or not we manipulate that substance by heating, cooling, starving, feeding, or whatever. We try to eliminate or avoid differences among our subjects by randomization, or we may focus on the specific study of individual differences. We try to identify and work with the manipulable external determiners of behavior, and when the behavior in question is random with respect to presumed determinants, we call it error. In all of this procedure, we tend to emulate the physics of the 19th century, the context in which psychology, as an independent experimental science, was conceived and born.

The circumstances of the conception, birth, and early childhood of experimental psychology are known to English speakers mostly through translations of mere fragments of Wundt's massive writings. Recently, there has been a great deal of historical research focused on the clarification and revision of the standard conceptions of Wundt's psychology, and much of the standard conception has been seen as oversimplification and distortion. For all of our delight in the myth of Wundt's liberation of psychology from philosophy and physiology, there is accumulating evidence that Wundt never intended or expected that psychology would be other than a branch of philosophy (Danziger, 1979b). The psychology of structuralism, for which we know Wundt best, is only a snippet of his general and social psychology, which involved a great deal of concern with volition, will, and intention (Blumenthal, 1980; Danziger, 1980). We are rather more aware of these concerns in the work of William James, John Dewey, and the American funtionalists, but they were central for Wundt as well.

Although the problem of volition was absolutely central for both Wundt and James, they took very different stances on it. Wundt was a thoroughgoing determinist, whereas James opted for freedom of the will (cf. Danziger, 1980; Blumenthal, 1980). Wundt believed that all central problems of psychology were problems of volition, and he called his psychology *voluntarism.*

REJECTION OF THE PROBLEM

But almost as soon as Wundt had developed his voluntaristic psychology, a wave of positivism swept over Europe and engulfed even his first generation of students. Volition was seen to be metaphysical and outside the realm of a proper scientific psychology. Although it was some years before Watsonian behaviorism stifled the study of will and consciousness and launched American psychology on the antimentalistic road to almost exclusive concern with overt behavior, there were serious rumblings of this kind in North America before the turn of the century. The terror of anthropomorphism with respect to infrahuman species was extended to an equivalent terror that one might be anthropomorphic with respect to humans as well—the very source of the model. Thus, notions such as volition were to be reduced to the status of secondary or derivative phenomena, explicable in other terms, as dictated by the emerging positivistic scientific psychology, which repudiated both Wundt and James (Danziger, 1979a).

Buchner (1900) expressed great concern about the tyranny involved in the emerging trend that "the elements of conscious experience are to be reduced to those of one kind or quality only" (p. 495). With respect to volition, he said:

"However many might be the detailed propositions that set forth the problem of volition, it must be put upon a par with the specific problems of sensation or of movement, and must be solved . . . with the aid of conceptions appropriate to itself rather than to other forms of consciousness. . . . Through this sweeping negation of certain data, psychology is cast into a form different from that which has prevailed hitherto. Does the ability of psychology to exist as a 'science' depend upon its attitude towards facts of a volitional quality? . . . Can one be justified in lending his efforts to the support of this tendency to eliminate all data which are regarded by some as not readily conforming to the modalities of scientific explanation? Inasmuch as the dominant term in our theme is 'scientific' let us pause a moment to get a proper conception of what science involves . . . To be a scientist is to maintain an assumed attitude towards the content studied . . . the whole of our present thought is concerned with . . . the tendency which would limit the possible number of objects to which the psychologist can legitimately turn his attention . . . How far, might it be dubiously questioned, would a physicist get with his problems should he suddenly propose to push his solutions thereof into the forms of psychological explanation?" (pp. 496–499)

Buchner went on to argue that while action was regarded as a proper topic for a scientific psychology, action is either unintelligible or of no interest unless there is a background of volition included.

While strict behaviorism did effectively preclude a concern with volition with a conscious content worthy of investigation, motivation, as a reducible concept, did persist and, indeed, flourished. But the conscious component—volition—

disappeared, and the scientific effort was to relate experimental manipulations to behavioral outcomes without the intervention of conscious contents, volitional or otherwise. What was left out was the notion of volition as a source of the initiation of behavior—that conscious experience which gives rise to the notion in the first place. Motivation, then, concerned itself with the effect of stimuli of a particular class on responses of a particular class. Reports of conscious experience of choice were eliminated, and even when allowed in, as in psychoanalytic theory, they were suspect.

So the subject of volition, or will, was typically avoided by psychologists for most of the first half of this century. In 1942, Irwin (1942) said,

> "For the general inadequacy of the experimental study of volition, a number of reasons are assignable. Chief of these is the frequently described flight of experimental psychology from 'philosophical' or 'metaphysical' concepts . . . The experimentalist, in his attempt to avoid those aspects of the concept which would hinder him or even be opposed to his program, has gone to such lengths as either to use terms with inadequate analysis of their meaning, or to avoid the problem altogether . . . problems have been determined by methods rather than methods by problems." (p. 115)[1]

Irwin argued that attempts to study the notion of volition in reaction-time experiments and attempts to distinguish voluntary movements from reflex movements in terms of latencies and response curves were not very satisfactory, although he was impressed by Bair's (1901) study of learning to wiggle one's ears. He was concerned about the great investment in simply trying to distinguish between volition and reflex in small muscle groups, and the triviality of the information gained: ". . . and we begin to wonder how we can have departed so far from the spirit of what once was regarded as willed or voluntary that it is now difficult or crucial to distinguish voluntary behavior from the simplest and most mechanical of behaviors" (p. 126).

Supported by Woodworth's (1906) arguments, Irwin argued that the essence of voluntary behavior is not in the movement itself but in the purpose or intention of the movement. He quoted Woodworth: "It would be much truer to speak of our voluntary movement of physical objects than to speak of voluntary bodily movements. If I wish to cut a stick, my intention is not that of making certain back and forth movements of my arm, while simultaneously holding fingers pressed tightly towards each other; my intention is to cut that stick" (Woodworth, 1906, p. 374–375). While noting that teleological concepts were not popular in contemporary psychology, Irwin went on to argue that voluntary

---

[1]For the purposes of this *Festschrift*, it is certainly worth noting that Irwin was Professor of Psychology at the University of Pennsylvania at the time, and that his comments were part of a *Festschrift* for Edgar Singer, Professor of Philosophy at the University of Pennsylvania, who had been assistant to William James, at Harvard in 1895–1896.

behavior is controlled by purpose, and it is in this direction that one should look for its understanding. Subsequently Murphy (1947, p. 291) said, concerning self-initiated reflex behaviors, "The capacity of inner symbols to arouse muscular contractions . . . is perhaps not the full flesh and blood of the volition process." And, indeed, a greater understatement can hardly be imagined. But the unpopularity of teleological notions remained, and little experimental work in this direction was conducted, other than the Miller, Galanter and Pribram (1960) work on plans, and little of that was considered the study of will or volition.

RECONSIDERATION: THE 1960s and 1970s

While the area was rather inactive in psychology during the 1950s and 1960s, philosophical discussions continued unabated. In 1967, Ofstad (1967) provided a bibliography of over 200 philosophical titles on the free will problem, derived from English language sources alone, between 1954 and 1965. But the studied isolation of psychology from philosophy meant that there was almost no cross-fertilization.

However, the late 1960s and the early 1970s turned out to be bumper years. In 1968, at the American Psychological Association meetings in San Francisco, a symposium was held under the title "What ever happened to the will in American Psychology?," and in 1970 several papers from that symposium were published (Gilbert, 1970; Royce, 1970; Strunk, 1970). The papers were primarily historical, and focused on some of the points I have already made, but there was also a focus on the contemporary influences of existentialism and free choice, which were nudging some sectors of psychology in new directions. Almost as if in answer to the question raised by that symposium, Kimble and Perlmuter published "The Problem of Volition" in 1970, and Kahneman published "Attention and Effort" in 1973. The latter is significant because attention and effort were precisely the achievements of will, according to William James: "The essential achievement of will is to attend to a difficult object and hold it fast before the mind" (James, 1890, Vol. II, p. 561). In contrast, Kahneman did not index *will, volition*, or any related terms, and said that the term *attention* merely serves ". . . to provide a label for some of the internal mechanisms that determine the significance of stimuli and thereby make it impossible to predict behavior by stimulus conditions alone" (1973, p. 2). However, he did distinguish between voluntary and involuntary attention. The former is effortful and determined by selection based on current plans and intentions; the latter is determined by stimulus properties such as intensity and the more enduring propensities of the individual.

At about the same time, in the context of studies of decision making, Broadbent (1973, pp. 26, 30) referred unashamedly, if metaphorically, to the ". . . fiat of the will . . ." in describing the shift from deliberation to action in reaction-time studies. He did not index the term, but the fact that he needed to use it indicated a sensitivity to human functions which we need to refer to, however obscure they may be.

Both Kahneman (1973) and Broadbent (1973) did deal with the notions that historically are issues of will and volition, and it seems that these functions of the human being are of abiding interest, even if we are deeply troubled about using them.

But to backtrack a bit: Kimble and Perlmuter (1970) described the ways in which cards had been stacked against the reintroduction of volition to psychology because theories had, for more than 150 years, focused on a special faculty of mind, doomed to ostracism as were other faculties of mind. They traced the history of conceptions of volition, and although Wundt is given rather short shrift, they considered James's view that images of the consequences of acts can serve as stimuli for those acts and give rise to volitional behavior. Although there is evidence that when both kinesthetic and more remote kinds of feedback from behavior are lacking, individuals can still perform the acts, albeit less well, there is also evidence that feedback plays a very large role in the control of voluntary behavior under normal circumstances. In every theoretical case that Kimble and Perlmuter described, the effort was to eliminate something like the will or volition: "The obvious goal of what we have called the classical theory of volition, as it has developed over the years, has been to replace the concept of will with a mechanism that could be subjected to experimental tests and conceivably reduced to neurophysiological status" (p. 368). While James recognized that it was necessary to postulate a complete determinism for scientific purposes, he also recognized that science was situated in a much larger context over which it had no dominion (cf. Fancher, 1979). He remained concerned with the experience of will, and argued in favor of a notion of free will if human life were to make any sense at all. James aspired to reconcile his psychology with his ethics and his experience, something that many psychologists of today can attempt only at their peril. In contrast, Kimble and Perlmuter were concerned primarily with behavior which goes from an initial reflex occurrence to a studiously monitored voluntary state, often guided by considerable attention, effort, and verbal monitoring, to an automatized condition, rolling off quickly, competently, and without attention or obvious direct motivation. They were subsequently concerned with what happens to automatized behavior when it is interrupted or when attention is focused on it.

But automatized behavior is only a limited kind of behavior: behavior which at one time required monitoring and subsequently does not normally require such attention. Other behaviors which involve the operation of volition or will are legion. There are the very difficult decisions requiring great deliberation; there are the rather quicker and trivial choices of a necktie or how much mustard to put on your hotdog. Each of these is usually intentional, and one knows whether a proper choice has been made or not. There are occasions on which one makes a great effort to persist in that which is unpleasant but necessary, or to forebear from doing that which is attractive but destructive or forbidden. These are very human and very important human actions.

Certainly it has been the committment to a particular format of scientific respectability that has hampered the direct investigation of volition and will as elaborate human psychological functions (cf. Irwin, 1942). Kimble and Perlmuter were quite explicit about this: In referring to the classical theories they say that ". . . most classical statements referred voluntary behavior to a faculty of 'willing' or to 'consciousness' or 'intention.' Each of these interpretations suffers from an intransigence towards operational reduction to observables" (p. 381). In effect, they are all seen to be deficient, because they do not conform to the notion that if one cannot reduce human psychology to natural science concepts, one cannot explain human behavior. But more of this later.

Let me add one more windfall from these early years of the last decade. In 1971, a symposium was held at the University of Kent in England, on the philosophy of psychology. It was published in 1974 (Brown, 1974), and one of the sub-sections of the symposium, on determinism, included a paper by Mandler and Kessen (1974) on the appearance of free will. The title was a *double entendre* since they treated the notion of will as a common experience or appearance arising from some identifiable sources, and they also treated this experience from a developmental perspective, discussing the kinds of events which progressively give rise to the appearance of such a belief system and to its maintenance. They argued that there is simply no place in an orderly universe for a concept such as will, which renders events random with respect to evident determining variables. They argued that a great deal of the confusion and concern in this area is due to the intrusion of common language mentalism passing as psychology—which it is not. They noted that physics is not likely to advance very much through attempts to predict the exact course of falling leaves in a wind storm, and "psychologists do not and should not claim explanatory powers for specific human actions *in vivo* . . ." (p. 311). They were clear that the determinist position is not one which is open to logical or empirical test or support: It ". . . is a metatheoretical convention—an axiom for theory and research— pragmatic in intent and often moral in its force" (p. 309).

Although Mandler and Kessen explicitly denied any *truth* for free-will assertions, they argued that such a belief has some probable positive outcomes— principally that individuals believing in free-will are likely to delay decisions, with the consequence that decisions based on maximum information are likely to show an increment in quality over those made more quickly. They were taken to task by several commentators at this symposium for their assertion that belief in a false doctrine should be seen as a virtue. They also may be taken to task for the assertion that the adoption of a free-will position is false, when its purported alternative, determinism, is explicitly presented as an unproved and unprovable metatheoretical axiom. However, their paper serves as a transition from the study of volitional behavior in the laboratory, focusing on reaction times and small muscle groups and reflexes, to something much more focused on the totality of behavior, influenced by beliefs, social situations, and so on.

SOME EMPIRICAL STUDIES: WILL, STRESS, REACTANCE, ATTRIBUTION

In 1977 (Westcott, 1977), I explored in greater detail some of the issues which Mandler and Kessen raised. I violated many of the conventions which had been more or less established for the study of volition, and engaged in an exercise in what Mandler and Kessen decried as common language mentalism. However, to the extent that a belief in free will or the fact of free will has consequences for human behavior, it is not through the psychological analysis of free-will as derivative or epiphenomenal, but through the concrete common language mentalism of the ordinary person. I provided respondents with choice and decision situations and asked them to recount their experiences of will or the lack of it in the course of making the choices or decisions. From these phenomenological data, I identified several forms of choice and decision, some accompanied by experiences of will and others not. Ultimately, I provided a model of experienced will which relied only on well-established psychological principles, none of which are free (in principle) of identifiable determinants.

A little bit earlier, Lefcourt (1973) had also expanded on some of the Mandler and Kessen arguments and attended to the functions of the illusions of control and freedom. In particular, he explored the stress-reducing effects of a belief that one has control of a situation, even if one does not exercise this control. He cited Glass, Singer, and Friedman (1969), who showed that when Ss were given a clerical task coupled with a bothersome auditory input, there was less decrement in performance among those who were told that they could de-activate the noise if they felt they had to than among those who had no such option. This effect was shown, even though the Ss with the option were asked not to use it, and, in fact, did not use it. They did not exercise control, they merely believed they had control.

Another line of research, which spans the entire era from the 60s to the present, and which has been concerned with voluntarism or apparent voluntarism and with threats to freedom and control, is the study of psychological reactance. For nearly 20 years (Brehm, 1966; Brehm and Brehm, 1981; Wicklund, 1974) research has been carried out in which behavioral freedom has been manipulated and the consequences studied. In this extensive literature, behavioral freedom is said to exist when an individual believes he has behavioral options and the requisite skills and resources to carry out any of them. When behavioral freedom is threatened or eliminated, an individual is said to experience psychological reactance, which leads to a motivational state that organizes behavior so as to reinstate the options or to engage in any of several related behaviors. Although this theory is rooted in the very robust common observation of people being stubborn or acting so as to do that which is prohibited, there is, in my view, a considerable catalogue of difficulties in both conceptualization and implementation (cf. Westcott, 1984).

Brehm's theory of psychological reactance illuminates a very interesting paradox which contributes to its widespread application: the fact that in the process of making a choice among behavioral options, one automatically threatens the availability of or eliminates those options one does not favor or has not chosen. Thus, reactance is a consequence of *any* choice, and reactance operates so as to reinstate options, in effect, reversing or opposing the choice process itself. There are several other decision theories which deal with the increase in conflict as the point of decision approaches. None of them has ever made contact with Solomon's opponent process theory of motivation (Solomon, 1980), which might very well subsume them. But theorists are not inclined to seek out ways to classify their theories as special cases of a broader formulation.

Reactance studies are very much in the tradition of experimental social psychology, and the bulk of the stuides are set in laboratories, often with trivial content. Although field studies have also been conducted, research in this tradition almost never makes any direct inquiry into whether Ss actually perceive behavioral options to be present, the extent to which they perceive threat or whether they experience reactance. The experiments rely almost entirely on E's intended consequences for the experimental manipulations. Consequently almost every experimental result—and there are a great many of them—is open to alternative interpretations.

The point here is that the study of human freedom, including volition or the opportunity and capacity to initiate free choice, is consistently under experimental investigation in this paradigm. Note that the theory of psychological reactance bypasses the thorny features of the notion of volition by making the reasonable assumption that ordinary people believe they have a choice when alternatives are present, and they seem to behave in ways to maintain that state of affairs. Whether they actually have choice, in any ultimate sense, is not important. The belief is important. Unfortunately, the belief is rarely assessed in the studies.

There are also studies of human freedom and volition in the tradition of attribution theory (Harvey, 1976; Steiner, 1970). For example, ordinary observers believe that others have more or less freedom in what they do, depending on the surrounding conditions. When observers believe that an actor is free in what he does and acts voluntarily, the observers tend to make dispositional attributions. When behavior appears to be the consequence of external coercion, such attributions are not made. Thus the attribution of freedom to actors is an important mediating variable in the attribution of all other characteristics. In general, it can be said that freedom is attributed to actors by observers when the actors behave in ways that are not predictable from evident external determinants in the situation. This, of course, is one of the notions of volition or will: Behavior which occurs randomly with respect to the usual determinants is self-initiated, willed, or voluntary behavior. But there are limits to this: When an individual behaves in ways which are completely at odds with expectations, we begin to invoke higher (or lower) order determinants—compulsions, demons, madness.

Although absolute behavioral freedom, in the sense of self-initiation of actions, is unacceptable to a fully deterministic view of behavior as part of a fully deterministic universe, such events are part and parcel of ordinary human interaction in the everyday world and are explained in that everyday world by reference to ordinary language mentalism. The social behavior of human beings is controlled by objectively identifiable and manipulable stimuli only to a certain extent, for in the natural world the behaving person's perception or understanding of stimuli and events also governs his actions.

DISSATISFACTIONS AND PROPOSALS

There have been several movements in the past decade that have pressed social psychology in directions quite different from the rather strict laboratory experimental model. There has been a growing dissatisfaction with the representativeness of the laboratory experiment and its generalizability to natural situations; there has been a rise and growing respectability and rigor of the phenomenological psychology movement in North America and development of the ethogenic movement in Britain; there has been a growing interest in the psychology of ordinary language explanation. Finally, there has been a rise of alternative theories of explanation, especially as alternatives to what more and more people see as the failure of positivism. I comment briefly here about each of these.

The literature of disaffection with the psychological experiment as the model of knowledge generation in psychology is perhaps summed up most trenchantly and most recently by Koch (1981). He accuses psychology of *ameaningful thinking*—thinking based on the rigid application of limited rules, and the torturing of phenomena into a format whereby rule-following can yield results, however senseless or trivial the results may be. For my purpose here, one of the principal features of ameaningful thinking is the "tendency to accept any 'finding' conformable to some treasured methodology, in preference to 'traditional' wisdom or *individual experience,* no matter how pellucidly and frequently confirmed the non-scientific knowledge may be" (Koch, 1981, p. 258). This is essentially where I began this paper—with the patent reality of volition and will in our own experience. No wonder it remains a problem. And Koch goes on to argue that the knowledge generating and certainty generating methodologies have also deleted from psychology any means of capturing the antinomies, the ambiguities of human behavior or experience. They have proceeded with what he calls preemptive finalism and, as such, have generated models of human behavior which he considers morally bankrupt.

But Koch is not alone in his criticism, although he has sustained it for some forty years. Other have specifically taken on social psychology (Gergen, 1978; Harré, 1981; Harré and Secord, 1972; Miller, 1972; Silverman, 1977; Smith, 1972) and have argued that the laboratory experiment and the spirit of positivism represent systematic distortions of meaningful conceptions of human behavior.

Human behavior in a humanly meaningful sense is precisely the focus of the rising stars of phenomenological psychology (Giorgi, 1970; Keen, 1975; Kruger, 1981; Thinès, 1977; Valle & King, 1978) and ethnogenic psychology (Harré & Secord, 1972). Both of these approaches aspire to use an explicitly anthropomorphic model of man that accepts and incorporates those features of human psychological functioning which are centrally human, ". . . pellucidly and frequently confirmed . . ." as Koch said. They also include the notion of meaning, and ambiguity of meaning, as central with consciousness and experience at the core of the problems of psychology. This is no mere return to introspectionism, as some ill-informed critics have argued (Greeno, 1982; see also Giorgi, 1982), but the development of rigorous systematic approaches to human behavior based on experience, which attempt to capture not only its regularities but its rich variations as well. Most certainly, these approaches will include the study of volition and will as fundamental human experiences and determiners of behavior, and not as illusory or derivative.

While not obviously affiliated with either of these two above approaches, Rychlak (1975, 1977, 1980) has argued for a more diversified conception of causality in human behavior than the usual material/efficient causality which informs the positivist approach and which excludes a great deal that is peculiarly human in human behavior. In contrast, Rychlak argues that teleological causation is entirely appropriate. Individuals behave for the sake of something (*final causation*) as much as they behave because of something (*efficient causation*). He uses the term *telosponsivity* as a contrast to responsivity. Although it remains true that many varieties of human behavior can be considered in the realm of biology, and models from biological science are appropriate, there are many features of human behavior—some would argue most features—which do not lend themselves to this natural science efficient cause model at all. When one looks to what is special about human functioning, it is precisely this: that people do plan, that people do change their minds, that people have the very compelling experience of initiating their own behavior, often in spite of external circumstances. They behave for the sake of ideas, principles, and plans, which are not encompassed by the most stretched notion of stimuli. Rychlak argues that humans can change ". . . that, for the sake of which . . ." they act; they can and do behave volitionally.

One other point of importance is that these contemporary approaches are not terrorized by the early behavioristic view that verbalizations about oneself are irrelevant, nor by the more recent behavioristic notion that verbal behavior is to be understood only as behavior in its own right and not as reports about some other events, nor by the pervasive Freudian scepticism concerning what people say about themselves. Nor do the recent assertions by Nisbett and Wilson (1977), that people typically misreport their own mental processes, trouble them. Morris (1981) points out, in contrast, that most of the processes and phenomena that Nisbett and Wilson concern themselves with are behaviors which are not typically monitored at all. Therefore, it is not surprising that respondents might well have to fabricate bases for their behavior and, their fabrications might be at odds with the evidence of manipulated variables. Morris argues that when the behavior in question is closely monitored by the actor, the basis of behavior—whether conceived of as cause or as purpose—can be described with reasonable accuracy by the actor.

As we progressively come to believe that ordinary human behavior in the typically complex context of ordinary human interaction is influenced not by events so much as by people's understanding of events, we come to the necessity of understanding the ordinary language mentalisms which are the framework in which these understandings are couched (Antaki, 1981). Whether or not we, as psychologists, credit people's assertions about themselves, the individuals making the assertions do credit them, and they go on to act in accord with them. To consider the notion of volition or will as a concept to be analyzed away is to deny a great deal of human understanding. To argue, as Skinner (1972) does, that talk about freedom and dignity is mischievious and counter-productive, is to commit what Koch calls ". . . ludicrous prescriptionism . . ." (1981, p. 269).

So the notions of volition, will, and freedom haunt us because they are so persistent and functional in human life, while methodological commitments oblige many to deny their very existence.

EXPERIENCED FREEDOM AND BEYOND

In these last few paragraphs, I would like to describe some of my own research. While not rigidly following any of the methodologies which might be prescribed by any of the more radical viewpoints described above, my work is informed by them. Most of what I have to say has been reported in detail elsewhere (Westcott, 1977, 1978, 1981, 1982a, 1982b, 1983, 1984) so I need not go into it extensively. I elected to study volition and freedom as *experiences* because that is the way they present themselves to us. I am satisfied that the ultimate metaphysical or ontological status of freedom or will are not psychological questions, but as experiences they are so fundamental that the nature and conditions of these experiences demand exploration and are well within the realm of psychology. I also adopted the view that human beings can and do provide important and meaningful commentary on their own experience and behavior when approached properly. Indeed, thoughtful civilized social life absolutely depends upon this fact. I incorporated other persons as coinvestigators, and I called them respondents, not subjects.

In one investigation, already mentioned, (Westcott, 1977) I asked them to describe their experiences of will and volition in various choice and decision situations, and obtained evidence that different degrees and varieties of will experiences are related intelligibly to different circumstances. In another study (Westcott, 1981, 1982a), I provided descriptions of various concrete situations which people might easily encounter in everyday life, situations which are criterial conditions for being free—from one point of view or another (e.g., situations where one has no responsibility, where one is explicitly directing one's own activities, or where one is making choices among highly attractive alternatives). Respondents were asked to indicate how free they feel in each of these situations. Repeated samples of university students have given very reliable data showing that different kinds of freedom-inducing situations yield large differences in the extent of "feeling free." Asking comparable samples of university students how free they "are" in exactly the same situations yields responses that are consistently different from the responses to the question of how free they "feel." (Westcott, 1982b, 1983) I also have it on impeccable authority that some of my findings are ". . . consonant with the opponent-process model, and not at all what Skinner might have expected" (Solomon, 1983).

Another method I have adopted (Westcott, 1982a) for exploring the differences in freedom experienced in the different situations is to ask respondents if they feel anything "opposite to free" in the situation described and to supply the best word they can to identify this opposite feeling. The method might be called dialectical, or it can be understood as an attempt to find the bipolar dimensions on which individuals construe the experience of feeling free in the different situations. The "opposite" terms vary widely—I have had more than 200 different words supplied as opposites to "free"—but they can be coded reliably, and different kinds of situations do yield different kinds of constructions of feeling free. These data also show almost perfect replication on successive samples.

I think it has been shown by many that volition, will, and freedom are important features of everyday experience, either by their presence or their absence, and these experiences have important consequences for subsequent experience and behavior. I have argued that the psychological study of volition, grounded in behavioristic and positivistic laboratory methodologies, has robbed the notion of its vitality, of what makes it an important area for study. It is problematical, ambiguous, and very human. I think that until we face up to these problems and confront volition on its own grounds, it will continue to be a nag. When we make our method fit the problem rather than making the problem fit the method, we can move ahead to make volition, will, and freedom real subjects of psychological inquiry.

ACKNOWLEDGEMENT

This chapter was prepared while the author held a Leave Fellowship from the Social Sciences and Humanities Research Council of Canada. The author wishes to thank Michael Cowles, Kurt Danziger, and Ray Fancher for thoughtful comment on earlier drafts.

REFERENCES

Antaki, C. (Ed.) (1981). *The psychology of ordinary explanations of social behaviour.* London: Academic Press.

Bair, J. (1901). Development of voluntary control. *Psychological Review, 8,* 474–510.

Blumenthal, A. (1980). Wundt and early American psychology. In R. Rieber (Ed.), *Wilhelm Wundt and the making of a scientific psychology.* New York: Plenum.

Brehm, J. (1966). *A theory of psychological reactance.* New York: Academic Press.

Brehm, S., & Brehm, J. (1981). *Psychological reactance: a theory of freedom and control.* New York: Academic Press.

Broadbent, D. (1973). *In defense of empirical psychology.* London: Methuen.

Brown, S. (Ed.) (1974). *Philosophy of psychology.* New York: McMillan.

Buchner, E. (1900). Volition as a scientific datum. *Psychological Review, 7,* 494–507.

Danziger, K. (1979a). The positivist repudiation of Wundt. *Journal of the History of the Behavioral Sciences, 15,* 205–230.

Danziger, K. (1979b). The social origins of modern psychology. In A. Buss (Ed.), *Psychology in social context* (pp. 27–45). New York: Irvington Publishers.

Danziger, K. (1980). Wundt's theory of behavior and volition. In R. Rieber (Ed.), *Wilhelm Wundt and the making of a scientific psychology* (pp. 89–115). New York: Plenum.

Fancher, R. (1979). *Pioneers of psychology.* New York: W. W. Norton & Company.

Gergen, K. (1978). Experimentation in social psychology: a reappraisal. *European Journal of Social Psychology, 8,* 507–527.

Gilbert, A. (1970). Whatever happened to the will in American psychology? *Journal of the History of the Behavioral Sciences, 6,* 52–58.

Giorgi, A. (1970). *Psychology as a human science.* New York: Harper & Row.

Giorgi, A. (1982). A disclaimer. *American Psychologist, 37,* 1410.

Glass, D., Singer, J., & Friedman, L. (1969). Psychic cost of adaptation to an environmental stressor. *Journal of Personality and Social Psychology, 12,* 200–210.

Greeno, J. (1982). Response to "The hegemony of natural scientific conceptions of learning." *American Psychologist, 37,* 332–334.

Harré, R. (1981). The positivist-empiricist approach and its alternative. In P. Reason & J. Rowan (Eds.), *Human Inquiry* (pp. 3–17). London: John Wiley & Sons Ltd.

Harré, R., & Secord, P. (1972). *The explanation of social behaviour.* Oxford: Blackwell.

Harvey, J. (1976). Attribution of freedom. In J. Harvey, J. Ickes, & R. Kidd (Eds.), *New directions in attribution research, Vol. I* (pp. 73–96). Hillsdale, NJ: Lawrence Erlbaum Associates.

Irwin, F. W. (1942). The concept of volition in experimental psychology. In F. Clarke & M. Nahm (Eds.), *Philosophical essays in honor of Edgar Arthur Singer, Jr.* (pp. 115–137). Philadelphia: University of Pennsylvania Press.

James, W. (1890). *The principles of psychology.* (Vols. 1–2). New York: Henry Holt.

Jourard, S. (1968). *Disclosing man to himself.* Princeton, NJ: D. Van Nostrand Co. Inc.

Kahneman, D. (1973). *Attention and effort.* Englewood Cliffs, NJ: Prentice Hall.

Keen, E. (1975). *A primer in phenomenological psychology.* New York: Holt, Rinehart & Winston.

Kimble, G., & Perlmuter, L. (1970). The problem of volition. *Psychological Review, 77,* 361–384.

Koch, S. (1981). The nature and limits of psychological knowledge: Lessons of a century qua "science." *American Psychologist, 36,* 257–269.

Kruger, D. (1981). *An introduction to phenomenological psychology.* Pittsburgh: Duquesne University Press.

Lefcourt, H. (1973). The function of the illusions of control and freedom. *American Psychologist, 28,* 41˜–425.

Mandler, G., & Kessen, W. (1974). The appearance of free will. In S. Brown (Ed.), *Philosophy of Psychology* (pp. 305–324). New York: McMillan, 305–324.

Miller, A. (Ed.) (1972). *The social psychology of psychological research.* New York: Free Press.

Miller, G., Galanter, E., & Pribram, K. (1960). *Plans and the structure of behavior.* New York: Wiley.

Morris, P. (1981). The cognitive psychology of self-reports. In C. Antaki (Ed.), *The psychology of ordinary explanations of social behaviour* (pp. 183–203). London: Academic Press.

Murphy, G. (1947). *Personality.* New York: Harper & Brothers.

Nisbett, R., & Wilson, T. (1977). Telling more than we can know: Verbal reports on mental processes. *Psychological Review, 84,* 231–259.

Ofstad, H. (1967). Recent work on the free-will problem. *American Philosophical Quarterly, 4,* 179–207.

Royce, J. (1970). Historical aspects of free choice. *Journal of the History of the Behavioral Sciences, 6,* 48–51.

Rychlak, J. (1975). Psychological science as a humanist views it. In W. Arnold, (Ed.), *Nebraska symposium on motivation* (pp. 205–279). Lincoln: University of Nebraska Press.

Rychlak, J. (1977). *The psychology of rigorous humanism.* New York: Wiley-Interscience.

Rychlak, J. (1980). Concepts of free will in modern psychological science. *The Journal of Mind and Behavior, 1,* 9–32.

Silverman, I. (1977). Why social psychology fails. *Canadian Psychological Review, 18,* 353–358.

Skinner, B. (1972). *Beyond freedom and dignity.* New York: Bantam.

Smith, M. (1972). Is social psychology advancing? *Journal of Experimental Social Psychology, 8,* 86–96.

Solomon, R. L. (1980). The opponent-process theory of motivation. *American Psychologist, 35,* 691–712.

Solomon, R. L. (1983). Personal communication.

Steiner, I. (1970). Perceived freedom. In L. Berkowitz (Ed.), *Advances in Experimental Social Psychology* (pp. 187–248). New York: Academic Press.

Strunk, O. (1970). Values move will: The problem of conceptualization. *Journal of the History of the Behavioral Sciences, 6,* 59–63.

Thinès, G. (1977). *Phenomenology and the science of behaviour.* London: George Allen & Unwin.

Valle, R., & King, M. (Eds.). (1978). *Existential-phenomenological alternatives for psychology.* New York: Oxford University Press.

Westcott, M. (1977). Free will: An exercise in metaphysical truth or psychological consequences. *Canadian Psychological Review, 18,* 249–263.

Westcott, M. (1978). Toward psychological studies of human freedom. *Canadian Psychological Review, 19,* 277–290.

Westcott, M. (1981). Direct and dialectical semantics of human freedom. *Etcetera: A review of general semantics, 38,* 64–75.

Westcott, M. (1982a). Quantitative and qualitative aspects of experienced freedom. *The Journal of Mind and Behavior, 3,* 99–126.

Westcott, M. (1982b, July). *On being free and feeling free.* Presentation at the International Congress of Applied Psychology, Edinburgh.

Westcott, M. (1983, April). *Being free and feeling free.* Poster session, Eastern Psychological Association, Philadelphia.

Westcott, M. (1984). Natural science and human science approaches to the study of human freedom. *The Journal of Mind and Behavior, 5,* 11–28.

Wicklund, R. (1974). *Freedom and reactance.* Potomac, Maryland: Lawrence Erlbaum Associates.

Woodworth, R. (1906). The cause of voluntary movement. In Woodworth, R. *Studies in philosophy and psychology* (pp. 351–392). Boston: Houghton Mifflin.

Author Index

Subject Index